French Politics, Society and Culture Series

General Editor: **Robert Elgie**, Paddy Moriarty Professor of Government and International Studies, Dublin City University

France has always fascinated outside observers. Now, the country is undergoing a period of profound transformation. France is faced with a rapidly changing international and European environment and it is having to rethink some of its most basic social, political and economic orthodoxies. As elsewhere, there is pressure to conform. And yet, while France is responding in ways that are no doubt familiar to people in other European countries, it is also managing to maintain elements of its long-standing distinctiveness. Overall, it remains a place that is not exactly *comme les autres*.

This new series examines all aspects of French politics, society and culture. In so doing it focuses on the changing nature of the French system as well as the established patterns of political, social and cultural life. Contributors to the series are encouraged to present new and innovative arguments so that the informed reader can learn and understand more about one of the most beguiling and compelling of all European countries.

Titles include:

Sylvain Brouard, Andrew Appleton, Amy G. Mazur (*editors*)
THE FRENCH FIFTH REPUBLIC AT FIFTY
Beyond Stereotypes

Jean K. Chalaby
THE DE GAULLE PRESIDENCY AND THE MEDIA
Statism and Public Communications

Pepper D. Culpepper, Bruno Palier and Peter A. Hall (*editors*)
CHANGING FRANCE
The Politics that Markets Make

Gordon D. Cumming
FRENCH NGOs IN THE GLOBAL ERA
A Distinctive Role in International Development

David Drake
FRENCH INTELLECTUALS AND POLITICS FROM THE DREYFUS AFFAIR TO
THE OCCUPATION

David Drake
INTELLECTUALS AND POLITICS IN POST-WAR FRANCE

Graeme Hayes
ENVIRONMENTAL PROTEST AND THE STATE IN FRANCE

David J. Howarth
THE FRENCH ROAD TO EUROPEAN MONETARY UNION

Andrew Knapp
PARTIES AND THE PARTY SYSTEM IN FRANCE
A Disconnected Democracy?

Michael S. Lewis-Beck (*editor*)
THE FRENCH VOTER
Before and After the 2002 Elections

John Loughlin
SUBNATIONAL GOVERNMENT
The French Experience

Mairi Maclean and Joseph Szarka
FRANCE ON THE WORLD STAGE

Mairi Maclean, Charles Harvey and Jon Press
BUSINESS ELITES AND CORPORATE GOVERNANCE IN FRANCE AND THE UK

Susan Milner and Nick Parsons (*editors*)
REINVENTING FRANCE
State and Society in the Twenty-First Century

Gino G. Raymond
THE FRENCH COMMUNIST PARTY DURING THE FIFTH REPUBLIC
A Crisis of Leadership and Ideology

Sarah Waters
SOCIAL MOVEMENTS IN FRANCE
Towards a New Citizenship

Reuben Y. Wong
THE EUROPEANIZATION OF FRENCH FOREIGN POLICY
France and the EU in East Asia

French Politics, Society and Culture
Series Standing Order ISBN 0–333–80440–6 hardcover
Series Standing Order ISBN 0–333–80441–4 paperback
(*outside North America only*)

You can receive future titles in this series as they are published by placing a standing order. Please contact your bookseller or, in case of difficulty, write to us at the address below with your name and address, the title of the series and the ISBN quoted above.

Customer Services Department, Macmillan Distribution Ltd, Houndmills, Basingstoke, Hampshire RG21 6XS, England

French NGOs in the Global Era

A Distinctive Role in International Development

Gordon D. Cumming

palgrave
macmillan

First published 2009 by
PALGRAVE MACMILLAN

Palgrave Macmillan in the UK is an imprint of Macmillan Publishers Limited,
registered in England, company number 785998, of Houndmills, Basingstoke,
Hampshire RG21 6XS.

Palgrave Macmillan in the US is a division of St Martin's Press LLC,
175 Fifth Avenue, New York, NY 10010.

Palgrave Macmillan is the global academic imprint of the above companies
and has companies and representatives throughout the world.

Palgrave® and Macmillan® are registered trademarks in the United States,
the United Kingdom, Europe and other countries.

ISBN-13: 978-1-4039-4524-2 hardback
ISBN-10: 1-4039-4524-1 hardback

This book is printed on paper suitable for recycling and made from fully
managed and sustained forest sources. Logging, pulping and manufacturing
processes are expected to conform to the environmental regulations of the
country of origin.

A catalogue record for this book is available from the British Library.

Library of Congress Cataloging-in-Publication Data

Cumming, Gordon, 1965–
    French NGOs in the global era : A distinctive role in international development /
Gordon D. Cumming
        p. cm.—(French politics, society and culture)
    Includes bibliographical references and index.
    ISBN 978-1-4039-4524-2 (alk. paper)
    1. Non-governmental organizations – France. 2. Economic assistance,
French. I. Title.

HC276.4.C86 2009
338.91'44—dc22   2008034899

10 9 8 7 6 5 4 3 2 1
18 17 16 15 14 13 12 11 10 09

Printed and bound in Great Britain by
CPI Antony Rowe, Chippenham and Eastbourne

To Françoise, Lorna and Leo, with love

Contents

List of Illustrations   ix

List of Abbreviations   x

Acknowledgements   xiv

1 Introduction: French NGOs in a Global Context   1
  Emerging International Trends   3
  Honing in on the French Case   8
  The Literature on French NGOs   10
  Aims and Focus   13
  Methodology   15
  Outline of the Study   16

2 Zooming in on French NGOs   18
  In Search of a Definition   18
  Making Sense of the French NGO Sector   22
  Why Study Developmental NGOs   35

3 The Quest for a Theoretical Framework   41
  Useful Theoretical Perspectives   41
  A Resource Dependence Model   47

4 French NGDOs and their Resource Landscape   54
  The French Central State   55
  Other Official Sources   58
  Private Sources   63

**5 French NGDOs and the State: Paving the Way for a
New Partnership?**   71
  Early French NGO–State Relations   72
  Towards a New Rapport: Overtures by the State   75
  A Measured Response from French NGDOs   81

6 Towards Professionalisation?   89
  Early Militancy and Amateurism   93
  Promoting 'Bureaucratic' Professionalisation   96
  Towards a 'Development Monoculture'?   99

7 Working for or Working on the State?   118
  Early French State Priorities   120
  Early NGDO Priorities   124

The State's New-found Prerogatives   131
A Cautious Welcome from French NGDOs   136

8   **A Resource Dependence Perspective**   **149**
Misreading their Resource Environment?   149
Enacting their Environment   164

9   **Working Together in the Field:**
A Case Study from Cameroon   **177**
Choosing a Case Study   177
Origins and Evolution of the PCPA   179
Overtures by the French State   183
Embracing the State's Advances or Keeping a Safe Distance?   186
Resource Dependence   191

10 **Conclusion: A Distinctive Role in International**
Development   **199**

Annex A   List of Interviews   208

Annex B   List of Main French NGO Federations   210

Annex C   Key French Members of the Altermondialiste *Movement*   212

Notes   213

Bibliography   236

Index   245

Illustrations

Figures

3.1 Resource Dependence Model of NNGOs and
    their Environment   48
7.1 Sectoral Breakdown of French State Aid in 1991–92   122
7.2 Sectoral Breakdown of French State Co-funding of
    NGOs in 1993   123
7.3 Geographic Distribution of French State Aid in 1991   124
7.4 Geographic Breakdown of French NGO
    Expenditure in 1991   127
7.5 Sectoral Breakdown of French State Aid in 2001–02   133
7.6 Sectoral Breakdown of French State Co-Funding
    of NGOs in 2002   134
7.7 Geographic Breakdown of French State's Aid
    Expenditures in 2005–06   135
7.8 Geographic Breakdown of French NGO
    Expenditures in 2003   140
7.9 Sectoral Breakdown of French NGO Spending in 2004   142
9.1 Organigramme of the Key Structures involved
    in the PCPA (as from 2006)   182

Tables

4.1 Overview of Official and Private Resources of
    French NGOs   56
4.2 French Central State Funding of NGOs in
    M€ and in Percentage Terms   59
4.3 French Local Government Funding of NGOs in
    M€ and as Percentage of Total Official Resources   60
4.4 International Funding of French NGOs in
    M€ and as a Percentage of International Resources   62
4.5 NGO Revenue from Private Sources in M€   65
5.1 Aid from European States to NGOs in 1998 in M€ and as a
    Percentage of their Overall and Bilateral Aid Budgets   85
6.1 Percentage of Volunteers Qualified at Various Levels   100
7.1 Most Heavily Subsidised French NGOs in
    Percentage Terms   138
7.2 Most Heavily Subsidised French NGOs in Monetary Terms   139

Abbreviations

ACAT	Action des Chrétiens pour l'Abolition de la Torture
ACF	Action Contre la Faim
AFD	Agence Française de Développement
AFDI	Agriculteurs Français et Développement International
AFM	Association Française contre les Myopathies
AFVP	Association Française des Volontaires du Progrès
ARIADE	Association pour la Recherche et l'Information sur l'Aide au Développement
ATTAC	Association pour la Taxation des Transactions Financières et l'Aide aux Citoyens
BVQI	Bureau Veritas Quality International
BMZ	Bundesministerium für wirtschaftliche Zusammenarbeit und Entwicklung (German Federal Ministry for Economic Cooperation and Development)
C2D	Contrat de Désendettement et de Développement
CARE	Cooperative for Assistance and Relief Everywhere
CCD	Commission Coopération Développement (also abbreviated to COCODEV)
CCFD	Comité Catholique Contre la Faim et pour le Développement
CCS	Cameroonian Civil Society
CFCF	Comité Français Contre la Faim (now CFSI)
CFSI	Comité Français de Solidarité Internationale (formerly CFCF)
CGT	Confédération Générale des Travailleurs
CICDA	Centre International de Coopération pour le Développement Agricole
CICID	Comité Interministériel de la Coopération Internationale et du Développement
CIDR	Centre International de Développement et de Recherche
CIDIC	Comité Interministériel de la Coopération Internationale et du Développement
CIEDEL	Centre International d'Études pour le Développement Local
CIMADE	Comité Inter-Mouvements Auprès Des Evacués
CIVI	Centre d'Information sur le Volontariat International
CLONG-V	Comité de Liaison des ONG de Volontariat
CLONGD-UE	Comité de Liaison des ONG de Développement auprès de l'Union Européenne (now CONCORD)

CLOSI	Comité de Liaison des Organisations de Solidarité Internationale
CNAJEP	Conseil National des Associations de Jeunesse et d'Éducation Populaire
CNCDH	Commission Nationale Consultative des Droits de l'Homme
CONCORD	Confédération Européenne des ONG d'Urgence et de Développement
CRID	Centre de Recherche et d'Information sur le Développement
COSP	Conférence d'Orientation Stratégique et de Programmation
CRS	Catholic Relief Services
DAP	Dotations au Partenariat
DCC	Délégation Catholique pour la Coopération
DFID	Department for International Development
DESC	Droits Économiques, Sociaux et Culturels
DIAL	Développement, Institutions et Analyses de Long terme
DRC	Democratic Republic of Congo
ECHO	European Commission Humanitarian Office
ECOSOC	Economic and Social Council (UN)
EDUCASOL	Plateforme d'Éducation au Développement et à la Solidarité Internationale
F3E	Fonds pour la Promotion des Études préalables, Études transversales et Évaluations
FACILS	Facilité d'Actions Collectives pour les Initiatives Locales de Solidarité
FEE	Fonds pour les Évaluations et les Études transversales
FDH	Frères des Hommes
FEMEC	Fédération des Églises et Missions Évangéliques du Cameroun
FEP	Fonds d'Études Préalables
FIDH	Fédération Internationale (des Ligues) des Droits de l'Homme
FONJEP	Fonds de Coopération de la Jeunesse et de l'Éducation Populaire
FOSCAM	Fédération des Organisations de la Société Civile Camerounaise
FNDVA	Fonds de Développement de la Vie Associative
FORIM	Forum des Organisations de Solidarité Internationale issues des Migrations
FSD	Fonds Social de Développement
GRET	Groupe de Recherche et d'Échanges Technologiques
GRDR	Groupe de Recherche et de Réalisations pour le Développement Rural

GEMDEV	Groupement d'Intérêt Scientifique pour l'Étude de la Mondialisation et du Développement
GTZ	Gesellschaft für Technische Zusammenarbeit (German Development Agency)
HCCI	Haut Conseil de la Coopération Internationale
HIPC	Highly Indebted Poor Countries (initiative)
HRW	Human Rights Watch
IRFED	Institut International de Recherche et de Fédération Education au Développement
ICVA	International Council for Voluntary Agencies
IFOP	Institut Français d'Opinion Publique
IMF	International Monetary Fund
IO	International Organisation
IRAM	Institut de Recherches et d'Applications des Méthodes de Développement
IGAS	Inspection Générale des Affaires Sociales
JSSC	Joint Strategic Steering Committee (PCPA, Cameroon)
LOLF	Loi Organique relative aux Lois de Finances
MAE	Ministère des Affaires Étrangères
MCNG	Mission pour la Coopération Non Gouvernementale
MDM	Médecins du Monde
MSF	Médecins Sans Frontières
NGO	Non-governmental Organisation
NGDO	Developmental NGO (This abbreviation is used in the main body of this text to refer to French *développementalistes* and volunteer agencies)
NGDO	Developmental and emergency NGOs (This acronym is only used in this sense in quotations drawn from the work of Anglo-Saxon writers)
NGLS	Non-governmental Liaison Service
NNGO	Northern NGO
NORAD	Norwegian Agency for Development Cooperation
NOVIB	Nederlandse Organisatie voor Internationale Bijstand
ODI	Overseas Development Institute
OECD	Organisation for Economic Cooperation and Development
OSI	Organisation de Solidarité Internationale
OSIM	Organisations de Solidarité Internationale issues des Migrations
OXFAM	Oxford Committee for Famine Relief
PCPA	Programme Concerté Pluri-Acteurs
PCM	Programme Concerté Maroc
PRSP	Poverty Reduction Strategy Paper
PVO	Private Voluntary Organization
QUANGO	Quasi Non-governmental Organisation

RD	Resource Dependence (theory)
RDVN	Resource Diversification
RITIMO	Réseau d'Information Tiers Monde des Centres de Documentation pour le Développement
SC-CF	Secours Catholique-Caritas France
SCAC	Service de Coopération et d'Action Culturelle
SCF	Save the Children Fund
SCNC	Southern Cameroon's National Council
SNV	Stichting Nederlandse Vrijwilligers
SIDA	Swedish International Development Agency
SNGO	Southern NGO
TDH	Terre des Homme-France
UNDP	United Nations Development Programme
UNHCR	UN High Commission for Refugees
UNICEF	United Nation's Children's Fund
USAID	United States Agency for International Development
VSF	Vétérinaires Sans Frontières
WFP	World Food Programme
WTO	World Trade Organisation

Acknowledgements

I would like to thank a number of people for their help in the preparation of this book. First and foremost, I owe a deep debt of gratitude to Françoise Cumming for her technical and, above all, moral support. I am also particularly grateful to Dr Kenny Meechan, Professor David Hanley and Dr Nick Parsons for their insightful comments, methodological advice and unwavering patience. I would, equally, like to thank Dr Andrew Dowling and Professor Sean Loughlin for their helpful feedback at a later stage in this project. Thanks must also go to the French section of Cardiff University, which allowed me to go on sabbatical; and to the Leverhulme Trust, which funded the primary research for this project. I am, moreover, indebted to Nkiru Onyechi, Katie Mullooly and Anne Cumming, who helped to eliminate typographical errors and stylistic anomalies from the text. Last but not least, I would like to offer my sincere thanks to the dozens of extremely busy NGO practitioners, government officials and academics, who so kindly gave up their valuable time to help with this study. Particular thanks must go to Sylvain Lenaud, as well as to Bruno Angsthelme, Denis Brandt, Michel Brugière, Pierre Castella, Christophe Courtin, Jean-Marie Hatton, François Mabille, Isabelle Müller, Bernard Pinaud, Henri Rouillé d'Orfeuil, Elisabeth Pacquot, Nelly Potevin, Bernard Salamand and Michel Wagner.

1
Introduction: French NGOs in a Global Context

Non-governmental organisations or NGOs have been variously defined as 'independent voluntary associations' (Willetts, 2002: 4), 'private non-profit-making bodies' (Roche, 1999: 251) and organisms which are 'private in their constitution and voluntary in their orientation' (Bettati and Dupuy, 1986: 8).[1] All of these definitions underscore the autonomous character of NGOs, particularly the fact that they are not part of, primarily funded by or in the service of the state. In so doing, they touch upon a central dilemma facing NGOs active in the field of international development and relief, namely whether to collaborate closely with the state or to go it alone.

This burning issue can be traced back to the origins of the NGO movement. Thus, whilst many of today's best-known NGOs were born out of frustration over the failure of states to deal with war-time emergencies, they were also among the very first to enjoy the patronage, 'approval and support of metropolitan governments' (Ruttan, 1996: 221). This was true, for example, of the International Committee of the Red Cross, founded in 1863 to ensure independent medical treatment to soldiers on the battlefield. It was also the case with the Save the Children Fund (SCF), established in 1919 to help refugee children suffering from food shortages in the aftermath of World War I. Equally, it applied to the Oxford Committee for Famine Relief (OXFAM), created in 1942 to channel food relief to the starving population of Nazi-occupied Greece during an Allied blockade.

The quandary over whether to become 'public sector contractors' or to remain 'truly voluntary organizations' (Brown and Korten, 1991: 50) deepened in the post-war era, particularly after Europe's decolonisation of Africa in the 1960s. Northern NGOs (NNGOs), taken here to refer to organisations based in developed countries which are members of the Organisation for Economic Cooperation and Development (OECD), began to turn their attention to developmental alongside emergency work. The pioneers in these fields included mainly British NGOs, such as the SCF and OXFAM, and American organisations, such as Catholic Relief Services (CRS) and

1

the Cooperative for Assistance and Relief Everywhere (CARE).[2] These trailblazers soon came to be joined by a new generation of large NGOs, such as *Misereor* (Germany, 1958), the Catholic Fund for Overseas Development (United Kingdom, 1962), NOVIB and the SNV (Holland, 1956 and 1965), *Terre des Hommes Suisse* (1960) and the *Comité Catholique contre la Faim et pour le Développement* or CCFD (France, 1961).[3] Most of these organisations were formed to help tackle the challenges confronting newly independent countries. They were helped in this task by more systematic forms of support from OECD states, each of which had established its own development assistance programme, aid ministry, co-funding scheme and consultation mechanism for NGOs involved in the delivery of official development and relief projects (Potevin, 2000).[4]

Ultimately, however, the scope for NGO-government collaboration was limited by a number of constraining factors. The first was the fact that, over the Cold War era, Northern NGOs and states adhered rigidly to the norms of a Westphalian state-centric system, which was dominated by the need to respect national sovereignty and only become involved in crises at the behest of the host government. Needless to say, this approach restricted the freedom of NNGOs and states to intervene, individually or jointly, in many situations. It also led directly to the rise of a whole movement of NGOs, the *sans-frontiérestes*, which – taking the lead from *Médecins Sans Frontières* (MSF), formed in the wake of the Nigerian civil war (1967–70) – refused to be constrained by questions of sovereignty and ventured to go anywhere that suffering and injustice were taking place. A second constraint was the relative newness of most NGOs and their limited capacity to work with governments on the kind of macroeconomic scale preferred by states. A third limitation related to divergences in the ideological and policy priorities of NNGOs, which were often inspired by Christian or Marxist thinking, and Northern states, which were usually driven by *realpolitik* ambitions. NNGOs were, for example, at loggerheads with Northern governments over issues, such as decolonisation, sanctions against apartheid in South Africa, and market-led solutions to the challenges of the 'Third World', notably the adoption by the donor community of World Bank-led structural adjustment programmes in the 1980s.

Many of these obstacles to NGO-government cooperation have disappeared or dissipated in the global era, which will be taken here to have begun in the late 1980s, as the Cold War was drawing to a close, the Communist bloc was being integrated into a single global market economy, and satellite communications, transnational corporations, the internet and 'new social movements' were becoming worldwide phenomena. For a start, the concept of sovereignty as an unchallenged given no longer applies, as notions, such as the 'right to interfere' (*le droit d'ingérence*), have been endorsed by the United Nations (UN); and as politicians, such as former UK Prime Minister, Tony Blair (1999), have spelt out the circumstances in which the international community has a duty to intervene in the internal affairs of other states. Against this backdrop, NNGOs and states have had scope to work more closely together during numerous humanitarian crises (e.g. Northern Iraq, 1990; Rwanda, 1994; Kosovo, 1999). They have also had unprecedented opportunities to establish new international bodies (such as the International Criminal Court in 2002), global funding mechanisms (such as the Global Fund to fight AIDS, Malaria and Tuberculosis in 2002), and multilateral agreements (such as the 1997 Ottawa Treaty banning the production and development of all anti-personnel mines). Furthermore, NGOs are no longer 'new' or inexperienced. Instead, they have, in many cases, built up a reputation for effectiveness and for having comparative advantages over the state, the failure of whose aid programmes over the Cold War years has made the search for alternative approaches to overseas development indispensable. The advantages of NNGOs, though unproven in empirical terms (Marcussen, 1996), have been broadly accepted by Northern governments of the Left and Right and include the fact that they are more flexible and cheaper than official agents, as well as being better able to reach the poorest of the poor (Tvedt, 1998: 128–65). Finally, the ideological rift, which separated many NNGOs and states over the early post-colonial era, has narrowed, particularly since the collapse of the communist model in 1989, the end of apartheid in 1990, and the adoption, in the mid-1990s, of poverty reduction as the overarching priority of nearly all donor development programmes (World Bank, 1990, 2000–01). Divisions can, of course, still be discerned in the different stances of NNGOs and states on questions such as globalisation. They are, however, less evident in many other areas, where Northern states have bought into some of the long-standing priorities of NNGOs. These include respect for human rights, the promotion of women's empowerment and the defence of the environment.

Emerging international trends

It follows that the global era has offered unprecedented scope for closer collaboration between NNGOs and their states. In so doing, it has brought the promise of great benefits for non-governmental actors, whether in the form of additional aid, logistical support or fiscal concessions. But it has also involved the danger of an overly close relationship, of unwanted changes to the structure and modus operandi of NNGOs, and, indeed, of instrumentalisation of NGOs by Northern states. Against this background, it is hardly surprising that analysts have looked for evidence of enhanced cooperation between NNGOs and their central governments over the last two decades or so. The literature in this field would appear to point to the emergence of three putative trends across the NNGO sector.

The first relates to a general improvement in the terms of the relationship between NNGOs and their own central states. This rapprochement, with all the compromises it implies, has been particularly remarked upon in the case of Anglo-Saxon countries, many of which have concentrated their funding on a handful of large NGOs and some of which have even set up partnership framework agreements. Honing in on American NGOs or 'Private Voluntary Organizations' (PVOs), Ruttan (1996: 226) has noted how

> The dependence of CARE, Catholic Relief Services, and several other large U.S. PVOs on...food surpluses and other government support has meant that the size and geographic focus of their programs continue to be determined largely by the focus of U.S. strategic interests and the rise and decline of U.S. domestic food surpluses.

Focusing specifically on the United Kingdom, Wallace *et al.* (1997: 81) have observed how NGOs now respond to donor requirements 'in order to access more funding' and how they implicitly see financial dependence on the state 'as an acceptable, or at least inevitable condition.' Zooming in on Germany, Randel and German (1999: 122) have demonstrated that the federal aid ministry BMZ and German NGOs 'are close to each other in their policy positions and approaches to development' and that 'with the formation of VENRO, the common ground has become more marked.'[5] Similar observations can be made in the case of Canada and Australia, where, as Smillie (1999: 15) has shown, levels of NGO dependence on government income were estimated at 47 and 54 per cent, respectively, in 1995–96.[6]

Official and semi-official writings have tended to emphasise the positive side of this trend. Thus, a recent survey by the French Foreign Ministry (2001: 13–14), has welcomed the 'strengthening of the dialogue' between European NGOs and their central states and has demonstrated empirically how all European NGOs now enjoy mechanisms for consultation with the state. The same publication has also noted how, between 1995 and 2000, the governments of Belgium, Britain, Spain, Holland, Greece, Denmark and France improved the terms on which they co-funded NGO programmes and projects (Ibid). Similarly, a major study published by the OECD Development Centre has argued that 'Governments and non-governmental organisations (NGOs) have made remarkable progress since the early 1990s in working together towards common development goals.... Particularly striking is the progress that has been made in creating mutually respectful working partnerships' (Smillie *et al.*, 1999: Preface).[7] The authors of this report have pointed to increases in state funding of NNGOs and to the shift away from matching grants (where states and NGOs co-finance programmes on a broadly equal basis) to more generous funding arrangements, such as longer-term contracts, block grants and the kind of framework agreements offered by aid agencies such as the Department for International Development DFID, United Kingdom, the Norwegian Agency for Development Cooperation (NORAD) and the Swedish International Development Agency (SIDA).

Smillie and his co-writers have also remarked upon the emergence of special and thematic funds, which are sometimes 100 per cent financed by states and created in response to specific challenges, such as the reconstruction of Mozambique at the end of the civil war in 1994.

Academics and NGO practitioners have generally been more sceptical, emphasising the danger of NGO dependence on the state and loss of autonomy. Tvedt (1998: 18) has pointed out that 'The contradiction between formal constitutions and regulations claiming independence and self-rule, on the one hand, and the growing dependence on state money, on the other, is apparent across the board.' Edwards and Fowler (2002: 369) have taken a similar tack, stressing that, over the course of the 1990s, 'the proportion of official, tax-derived funds in the NGDO total has increased from about 20 to about 50 per cent'; and that, as a result, 'NGDOs have become more tied to official aid and, hence, more exposed to changes in its policies and priorities.' Hulme and Edwards (1997: 3) have set out the dilemma even more starkly, asking 'whether NGOs are getting so close (in terms of interests, values, methods, priorities and other factors) to Northern-government donors...that important elements of their potential contribution to development have been lost or weakened.' They recognise that 'popularity is pleasant' but wonder:

> ...does it reflect genuine recognition or does it accrue because NGOs have now been socialised into the establishment – the 'development industry'? Are NGOs being valued because of the different questions they ask and approaches they adopt? Or are they valued because they now have the social grace not to persist with awkward questions and the organisational capacity to divert the poor and disadvantaged from more radical ideas about how to overcome poverty? (Ibid)

The second norm involves the increasing professionalisation of NNGOs over the last two decades or so and is both a cause of the first trend (more professional NGOs will attract more support from the state) and a consequence of it (closer relations with government encourage more professional structures and operations). The term 'professionalisation' here refers to the adoption of a more accountable approach and a set of structures, procedures and techniques that respond to the demands of their increasingly target-driven central governments. This process of state-led professionalisation has been widely commented upon in the NGO literature, notably in relation to Anglo-American NGOs. Thus, writing with reference to the American non-profit sector, Froelich (1999: 256) has affirmed that 'Overwhelming evidence points to government-driven professionalization, bureaucratization, and loss of administrative autonomy.' This point is echoed by Wallace *et al.* (1997 and 2006) who, with particular reference to British NGOs, have noted how development techniques are being standardised, destroying some of the very features which made NGOs attractive to the state in the first instance. They emphasise that 'There are, within the UK NGO sector, undoubted moves towards more formalised project planning, including the adoption of LFA [logical framework agreement]; a growing use of strategic planning tools; and a rise in evaluation work in order to prove effectiveness and efficiency' (Wallace *et al.*, 1997: 58).

The trend towards state-led professionalisation and performance-based accountability has been viewed by Wenar (2006: 16) as 'potentially useful' and by Beaudoux (1996: 9) as 'a dynamic mechanism for everyone involved more or less directly in an operation'. Fowler (2000: 93) has taken a harder line, arguing that professionalisation can often lead to an alignment with government technocratic and evaluation procedures, many of which can seriously compromise the autonomy of NGOs and lead to 'mission creep.' Relatedly, Edwards and Hulme (1995: 31) have concluded that 'the formal, linear, mainstream approach to development planning (which is part and parcel of donor funding) is more of a threat to the development aspirations of some NGOs...than a growing dependence on donor funds *per se*.' Adopting an even more critical posture, Murphy (2000: 330) has claimed that NGOs have all too readily traded 'their essential values for technical professionalism' and are, in the process, losing 'their place as part of a transformative movement for social justice.'

This brings us to the third, and in many ways the most debatable, trend identified in the literature, namely the growing readiness of NNGOs to drop their critical stance and act as *service delivery agents* or *vectors* on behalf of their central state. This apparent evolution, though hard to show empirically and vigorously denied by some NGOs (BOND, 2007), has nonetheless been widely commented upon, most notably in the case of Anglo-American NGOs. In this context, Tvedt (1998: 62) has stressed that

> The US Government has used and contracted NGOs for policy purposes since World War II.... It is not difficult to show that US organizations have not only co-operated with the government, but have willingly functioned as a cover-up for espionage and clandestine policies.

Minear (1987: 208) has similarly contended, in relation to American PVOs that

> Though it need not, acceptance of substantial US government funding frequently does limit the independence of PVOs and their willingness to engage in education and advocacy. Among American PVOs which accept government resources, there are doubtless more which also accept the government's development priorities and strategies than are willing to challenge these when and where necessary.... The 'P' in PVO is thus in real danger of coming to represent 'public' or 'parastatal' rather than 'private'.

For his part, Fowler (2002: 383) has observed how British NGOs are often treated by their own government as 'a particular type of development contractor, rather than civic entities with autonomous agendas.' He goes on to claim that 'reform to donor funding "windows" for NGDOs – the Civil Society Challenge Fund and Participatory Partnership Agreements – are premised on applicants having a sufficiently similar agenda to the DFID itself.'[8]

This trend has not been viewed negatively by all commentators. Thus, for example, Lewis (2001: 69) has claimed that 'For many NGOs implementation and service delivery have been areas of relative success. For example, in agriculture NGOs may be engaged in the delivery of services to people in "unreachable" areas such as the fragile, complex or risk-prone lands for which government outreach is poor.' For his part, Smillie (1999: 10) has observed that

> Nobody forced NGOs to take government funds; nobody forced them to become contractors. Some have resisted the temptation or have passed byelaws restricting the amounts of government funding they will accept. Others have knowingly and willingly maximised their government income, believing that they can retain sufficient control over it to carry out their prime mandate, whether it is emergency assistance or the provision of development assistance to poor communities....

Most commentators are more critical. Tvedt (1998: 212–32) has expressed concern that NGOs are becoming 'development diplomats' and maintaining a quasi-official presence in countries where it is awkward for Northern states to be active. Fowler (1993) has seen them as 'agents of democratisation', exporting donor-led development prescriptions and Western modes of governance. Others have voiced concern that NNGOs now act as 'ladles for the global soup kitchen' (Fowler, 2000: 60), 'handmaidens of capitalist change' (Temple, 1997) and as 'little more than vectors through which to continue [neo-liberal] policies by other means' (Pech and Padis, 2004: 6). NNGOs are, in effect, accused of serving to palliate the negative effects of the capitalist system on the poorest peoples; and of thereby stifling dissent and perpetuating a fundamentally unfair system. In this context, Manji and O'Coill (2002: 15) have contended that

> NGOs are acknowledged today as 'the preferred channel for service provision in deliberate substitution for the state'..... Development NGOs have become an integral, and necessary, part of a system that sacrifices respect for justice and rights. They have taken the 'missionary position' – service delivery, running projects that are motivated by charity, pity and doing things for people (implicitly who can't do it for themselves), albeit with the verbiage of participatory approaches.

It should not, of course, be inferred from this, or any of the above trends, that NNGOs have all simply given up their autonomy and identity to become 'government-paid development diplomats' or 'propagandists for a triumphant West' (Tvedt, 1998: 1). Most authors have, in fact, been wary of any sweeping generalisations about developments across the NNGO sector. Thus, for example, Fougier (2004) has stressed that many large and medium-sized NNGOs are now at the forefront of the 'anti-globalisation' or *alter-mondialiste* movement.[9] The Overseas Development Institute or ODI , for its part, has noted that NNGOs have exerted significant 'reverse influence' on states (ODI, 1995), whilst Edwards and Hulme (1995) have observed that, in many cases, NGOs refuse to go along with state policy priorities or demands for bureaucratic professionalisation. Other writers, such as Themudo (2002: Conference Abstract), have even argued that 'NGOs can and often do pursue strategies to maintain their independence even in conditions of high reliance on state or donor funding. Under the right conditions NGOs can "bite the hand that feeds them" and participate in monitoring the state.' Others still, such as Wallace *et al.* (1997: 3), have stressed that the potential for state influence often boils down to the make up of individual NGOs. These organisations are said to contain 'different interest groups and coalitions', some of which 'are more open to responding to donor demands than others' and some of which 'are more committed to the original mandate and ideology than others'. In a similar vein, Hulme and Edwards (1997: 275) have been anxious to point out that 'simple generalisations about the nature of these relationships are not feasible', that 'different things are happening in different places' and that 'institutional histories and national and local contexts shape events as much as more generalised, indeed globalised, factors'). Taking this argument further, Fowler (2000: 192) has claimed that

> the degree of influence a state exerts through its funds depends on the nature of the political system. Unlike two-party majority rule, proportional representation seems to exert a tempering influence on the propensity of states to interfere with the non-profit-making organizations they fund. The development foundations in Germany and the Netherlands enjoy substantial autonomy despite significant government funding that can amount to 95 per cent of their total.

Honing in on the French case

It will not be the aim of this book to seek to establish empirically whether or not the above trends have any broad validity across the NNGO sector. For our purposes, it should suffice to note that these tendencies have been widely commented upon in the literature and, above all, in writings which focus on Anglo-American NGOs (e.g. Wallace *et al.*, 1997 and 2006; Robinson, 1997; Froelich, 1999; Warkentin, 2001). Yet can these observations be equally valid in the case of NNGOs which have not been raised in a liberal Anglo-American tradition? Can they, more specifically, be said to apply to French NGOs, which have emerged in a context that is indelibly marked by 'the ideological weakness of liberalism' (Hazareesingh, 1994: 23) and the power of a 'quintessentially strong state' (Hayward, 2003: 35)?

There are at least two obvious reasons for assuming that French NGOs may, indeed, have fallen in line with the putative international trends outlined above. The first is that these non-governmental actors are firmly embedded in an international landscape that has come to be 'oligopolistic' in nature and increasingly 'dominated by a handful of "giants" in the US and Europe... [which] account for the lion's share of aid resources, and set the terms of debate for the rest of the community' (Stoddard, 2003: 1).[10] French NGOs liaise increasingly with these other civil society actors, whether in global social forums or in European lobby networks, such as the *Confédération Européenne des ONG d'Urgence et de Développement* (CONCORD). They are, as such, prone to the effects of institutional isormorphism, all the more so since they are (or rather their head offices are) based in a rich, democratic country, which has one of the largest voluntary sectors in the world (Archambault, 1997: 224). The second reason is that French NGOs are now operating within a domestic context, which is more favourable towards them than in the past. As will be demonstrated in later chapters, the French state – under pressure from the European Union, reformist French politicians and its own civil society – has offered a number of legal, fiscal and financial concessions to French NGOs, the most significant of which being the introduction, in 1996, of the 'new contractual arrangements' (*la nouvelle contractualisation*). This innovative measure introduced a new longer-term official funding mechanism for NGOs designed, among other things, 'to encourage the state to take more of a back-seat, regulatory role and to urge NGOs to take on more fully the role of service provider' (*Commissariat Général*, 2002: 104).

At the same time, however, there are also grounds for doubting that French NGOs will have fallen in line with wider trends. The first is that French NGOs work within a legal and political climate, which has been shaped by the tenets and ideology of French Republicanism and which is still less propitious than other contexts, notably those obtaining in Anglo-Saxon and Nordic countries, to accommodating NGOs and encouraging them to act as intermediaries between the state and its citizens. Against such a backdrop, it seems likely that there will still be some mutual suspicion and residual tensions between France's secular, Jacobin state and French NGOs, particularly faith-based actors. The second reason to be sceptical relates to the long history of 'exceptionalism' in French cultural and political life.[11] While this exceptionalism is gradually becoming a thing of the past (Milner and Parsons, 2003), it is nonetheless said by Archambault (1999) to remain a feature of French non-profit organisations as a whole. For this author, the

French non-profit sector does not fit comfortably into any of her four distinct models. It has very little in common with the 'Rhineland model' (Germany, Austria, Switzerland, Belgium, Holland), which includes strong political foundations and powerful, often federal organisations, tied in closely to the state; the Scandanavian or 'social democratic' model (Norway, Sweden, Denmark, Finland), which is marked by NGOs that have close links with a strong welfare state and that are, generally, neither ideologically driven nor church-related; or, indeed, the Anglo-Saxon or 'liberal model' (United States, Canada, United Kingdom, Australia, New Zealand), which is characterised by strong voluntary, philanthropic and primarily Protestant organisations operating in a context where the welfare state is weak or in decline. It is closer to, but also quite distinct from, the 'Mediterranean model' (Italy, Spain, Portugal, Greece), which is associated with mainly Catholic countries, where there has been no separation of Church and state and where conflict between these two powerful actors has significantly restricted the development of the non-profit sector (Archambault, 1999).[12]

Echoing Archambault's findings to some extent, Wieviorka (2003: 141) has observed, in relation to French NGOs and pressure groups associated with the *altermondialiste* movement, that there appears to be a 'French model' for lobbying against the ravages of the global free market; and that this draws on the long history of anti-liberalism, which has marked both Catholic and Marxist NGOs in France. Referring specifically to French NGOs involved in international development and relief work, Condamines (1989: 13) has simply noted that 'In many respects, here as elsewhere, the French set up appears exceptional...'.

The literature on French NGOs

So how far, then, have French NGOs gone in following the trends outlined above, that is, in collaborating more closely with their own central state, in professionalising their operations and in taking on more of a service delivery role on behalf of the state? Surprisingly, given the importance of NGOs as part of the social fabric, moral barometers and major sources of 'social capital' (Putnam, 2002), this question has not been explicitly tackled in any of the general writings on French NGOs (discussed below) or, indeed, in the more sector-specific studies (reviewed briefly in Chapter 2). Nonetheless, insights into these questions can be gleaned from this literature, notably from cross-national surveys, overviews of French NGOs and their relations with the central state, studies of the modus operandi of these NGOs, and analyses of the priorities and motivations of these actors.

To begin with cross-national studies, the most detailed of these have explored the contours of the Northern voluntary sector as a whole (Salamon and Anheier, 1996; Halba, 2003). They have, as such, been primarily concerned with non-governmental actors, whose main concern is with domestic issues and the social welfare of the people in the country of origin of the NGO. Other surveys have focused on developmental and humanitarian NGOs but have often taken the form of international directories broken down by country. These cross-national 'lists' of NGOs have been prepared by the OECD (various years) and the Union of International Associations (annually).[13] They have supplied invaluable comparative statistical data but have not sought to analyse this information or focus on collective trends. A few substantive surveys have offered a broadbrush comparative overview of NNGOs active in international development and relief. The OECD study *Partners for Development* (1988) was one of the first works to offer explicit comparisons of specific features of NNGOs. Its findings have been complemented by an OECD-led survey by Woods (2000), which provides some cross-national statistical data on European NGOs, and two others – by Smillie and Helmich (1993) and Smillie *et al.* (1999) – which offer brief comparative analyses of NNGO–state relations. Writing for the *Commission Coopération Développement* (CCD), Potevin (2000) has compiled an impressive comparative overview of the key features of European NGOs, highlighting, in particular, their different funding relationships with the state. Finally, Smith (1990) has produced an ambitious comparative survey of American, Canadian and European NGOs in which he contends that the former are the least radical and the latter the most. While valuable, however, many of the above texts are now either very dated or quite prone to gloss over the specificities of French NGOs.

This latter criticism cannot, of course, be levelled against overviews of French NGOs, even if many of these have not examined NGO relations with the state in any great depth. In this context, Joly, in his 1985 study of French NGOs and their various developmental philosophies, has not even explored the implications of these various ideologies for the relationship between NGOs and the state. Beigbeder (1992) and Condamines (1989) have looked at links between French NGOs and the government; but they have done so only briefly and as part of much wider surveys of NGO relations with their environment. The same is true of a lengthy study by Deler *et al.* (1998) and an insightful text by the CCD (1999: 5), each of which has touched only very briefly upon the issue of whether NGOs can be an alternative, or merely a complement, to official aid.

A number of studies have bucked this trend and focused in more detail on NGO-government relations. Yet these have tended to be reports written by official or semi-official bodies and aimed essentially at convincing officials and politicians to channel higher levels of foreign aid through NGOs (RPR, 1994) or to offer greater fiscal concessions to fund-raising NGO (*Commissariat Général du Plan*, 2002). Also included in this category are reports prepared by Parliamentary rapporteurs, such as Stéphane Hessel (1990, unpublished), who recommended the creation of a 'High Council' of NGOs, Bernard Husson (1991), who called for a 'contractualisation' of NGO–state relations, and Roland Blum (2005) who proposed that the French state should pass legislation to distinguish the top 20 or so French NGOs from the many thousands of associations governed by the same founding law (the *Loi de 1901*).[14] While providing valuable insights into the uneasy nature of the NGO–government relationship, these reports have been primarily concerned with finding ways of enabling French NGOs to cooperate more closely with the French authorities. They have, as such, been normative and polemical; and they have begun with the assumption that such collaboration is self-evidently a desirable goal, which may, of course, not always be the case.

Turning to studies of the modus operandi of French NGOs, there have, in fact, been a number of analyses of the growing professionalisation of these actors. Some have deplored this trend, suggesting that it can involve an ill-advised shift away from original NGO values (*Centre Tricontinental*, 1997). Other surveys have been more approving and welcomed the rise in the qualifications of staff (Haddad, 2002), improvements in recruitment and training (Dauvin *et al.*, 2002), reforms to the organisational structure and management of NGOs (Deler *et al.*, 1998) and the emergence of new fund-raising, financial management and evaluation techniques (Blum, 2005). While all of these analyses have been insightful, they have generally been premised upon the assumption that professionalisation along any lines, including the more 'bureaucratic' version recommended by the state, is necessarily a good thing. They have not always spelt out precisely what they mean by professionalisation or how such a process has or should come about. Nor have they sought to establish whether it has been pressures from the state, initiatives by forward-thinking NGO managers or demands from commercial companies and other private funders, which have been the principal drivers behind this evolution in French NGO working practices.

The third category of study has looked at the policy and operational priorities of French NGOs and sought to explain the rationale for these. Most surveys have glossed over the reasons why NGOs adopt particular policies or projects or simply assumed that their motives are altruistic (*Coordination SUD*, 2004). This is particularly true of the primary literature produced by NGOs themselves, whether in the form of fund-raising fliers, self-congratulatory annual reports or promotional newsletters such as *Faim et Développement* (CCFD) and *Le Défi* (*Terre des Hommes-France*). Scholarly texts have provided a more balanced assessment of the driving forces behind NGO actions. Thus, for example, Condamines (1989) has highlighted the commercial and political considerations of French NGOs, while Joly (1985) and Mabille (2001: 179–232) have honed in on the desire of these actors to spread Christian or secular values. Other studies have pointed to a more pragmatic concern with acquiring funding to survive and expand operations (Dardelet, 1995). Others still have revealed ideological – often Marxist – motives driving French NGOs, such as their desire to contest the capitalist world order (*Centre Tricontental*, 1997), to change the rules of the capitalist game (Rouillé-d'Orfeuil, 1984) and to establish a new global civil society (Rouillé-d'Orfeuil, 2006).

Taken together, these writings have offered a broad understanding of the motivational factors at work across the French NGO sector. But none of these texts has provided a theoretical framework with which to explain the recent evolution of French NGO policy and practice. This is not, of course, to suggest that there has been no theoretical work carried out whatsoever on these actors. Piveteau (2004) has, for example, used market failure theory (discussed in Chapter 3) as part of his quest for a suitable model for evaluating (mainly French) NGOs, while Szarka (2002) has, for his part, employed policy networks and advocacy coalition theory to shed light on French environmental pressure groups. However, the fact remains that theoretical analysis of French NGOs has not moved much beyond 'the most rudimentary of stages' (Ryfman, 2004: 6).

To sum up, while the literature does include incisive, valuable and often first-hand insights into the work of French NGOs, it is of variable quality, Franco-centric and, at times, anecdotal and superficial. There is clearly a need for a rigorous up-to-date survey, which seeks to describe and explain, using both empirical evidence and a theoretical framework, the recent evolution of the French NGO sector.

Aims and focus

This book aims to plug these gaps in the literature. It seeks, in particular, to establish whether French NGOs have aligned themselves with wider international trends (towards rapprochement, professionalisation and service delivery) over the global era. It also strives to identify a theoretical framework which can explain the recent evolution, or lack of evolution, of French NGOs in the direction of these trends.

Given the ambitious nature of these objectives, it is vital to tighten the focus of this research. For a start, this book does not seek to demonstrate that French NGOs are exceptional, that they are operating in line with a highly distinctive French 'model', or that they represent, from a comparative perspective, a 'most different system' or case study of NNGO behaviour.[15] Such an assertion could only be made on the basis of a vast cross-national survey of French and other NGOs operating across all the member states of the OECD. It would, moreover, be premised upon the assumption that NNGO sectors in countries other than France have simply adopted a uniform stance towards emerging international 'norms' and that these individual sectors do not have their own specificities. This assumption is palpably incorrect. The fact is that most NGO sectors have distinctive traits. This is particularly true in Japan, where – even though their situation has improved since their high-profile role in the 1995 Kobe earthquake (Smillie, 1999: 14) – NGOs are often treated with disdain by government officials who prioritise social harmony over diversity (Lancaster, 1999: 177–8). It is, equally, the case in Germany, where the NGO scene is heavily marked by political foundations, which are explicitly linked to national political parties, and by faith-based NGOs, which benefit from 'church taxes' levied by the state on individual taxpayers. Similarly, specificities are to be found in Eastern Europe where NGOs are very underdeveloped; and in Spain and Italy, where a large proportion of official monies for NGOs are channelled through regional authorities.

Furthermore, this book does not endeavour to evaluate the effectiveness of French NGOs, either in terms of their developmental or social impact. These issues have already been touched upon in the literature (Piveteau, 2004; Dauvin *et al.*, 2002; CCD, 1999) and must remain the domain of development economists and sociologists. Relatedly, this survey does not argue that French NGOs should necessarily fall in line with international norms. Such a blanket recommendation would be based upon normative, even polemical, judgements and ideological considerations about the merits and demerits of working more closely with, and aligning priorities with those of, the state. It might, of course, be possible to find evaluations and other data, which suggest that NGOs are more developmentally effective when they move closer to the state. But, even if such information were available, it would not provide any insights into the resulting loss of socio-political impact in terms of, say, NGO advocacy campaigns.

Lastly, this study does not focus on all French non-state actors. For reasons which will be set out in Chapter 2, it does not devote any substantial space to domestic voluntary organisations (e.g. *Les Restos du Coeur*, soup kitchens set up by the French comic Coluche in 1985), para-public agencies (e.g. the *Fonds de Coopération de la Jeunesse et de l'Éducation Populaire* or FONJEP) or social movements (e.g. the ecologist, feminist and *altermondialiste* movements). Nor does it hone in on Southern NGOs (SNGOs), that is to say, non-governmental actors originating and based in the Southern hemisphere, or, for that matter, on French pressure groups, such as the *Association pour la Taxation des Transactions Financières et l'Aide aux Citoyens* (ATTAC).[16] Nor, indeed, does it give any detailed consideration to humanitarian NGOs, such as MSF and Médecins du Monde (MDM), even though their prominence internationally and their predominant share of total French NGO funding make them impossible to ignore completely. Instead, the focus will be on an important, but under-researched, set of actors, namely developmental and volunteer-based NGOs, such as the CCFD, the *Secours Catholique-Caritas France* (SC-CF), TDH, *Frères des Hommes* (FDH), the Protestant Missionary Service known as DEFAP and the *Délégation Catholique pour la Coopération* (DCC). All of these organisations have long been operational throughout most of the developing world and they remain primarily active in the world's poorest region, sub-Saharan Africa.

Methodology

Having narrowed down the aims and focus of this research, it is time to ask how these objectives have been achieved. A number of research methods have been employed. For a start, an extensive survey has been carried out of the primary and secondary literature in order to identify any evolution in the policies and practices of French NGOs towards wider international trends. This search has drawn on campaign and fund-raising documents, financial statements, annual reports, directories, guides, periodicals and websites prepared by French NGOs. This, and other, documentation has been collected mainly from the larger NGOs, since these are the only actors which keep reasonable and accessible archives (the CCFD and DEFAP along with MSF and MDM have particularly good resource centres). But attention has also been accorded to the records of smaller NGOs, where these have been available via internet sites and the 80 RITIMO (*Réseau d'Information Tiers Monde des Centres de Documentation pour le Développement*) centres across France (see Chapter 6). Given the heterogenous nature of most documentation, special consideration has been given to OECD listings of NNGOs and, above all, to the directories and financial accounts prepared for the French NGO sector as a whole by bodies such as the CCD.

Furthermore, almost 40 semi-structured interviews have been undertaken in France and Cameroon (see Annex A). These have involved a broad range of actors: officials working for the French Foreign Ministry, the *Agence Française de Développement* (AFD) and their missions in Yaoundé; representatives of French local authorities, the European Commission and the Cameroonian state; not to mention French and Cameroonian civil society actors, such as pressure groups, academics, consultants, trades unionists and, of course, NGOs. Every effort has been made to ensure that the NGOs interviewed are representative, and discussions have been held with developmental NGOs with partners overseas (e.g. the CCFD and SC-CF), those without such contacts (e.g. the *Association Française des Volontaires du Progrès* or AFVP), those which specialise in a single sector (e.g. AIDES), volunteer organisations (e.g. the DCC and DEFAP), development education centres (e.g. RITIMO) and federations (e.g. *Coordination SUD*). Interviews have even been conducted with senior figures within emergency NGOs, such as MSF, MDM, *Action Contre la Faim* (ACF) and *Handicap International*, whose size alone has meant that they cannot be airbrushed out of this study. Needless to say, the bulk of the interviews have been carried out with representatives of larger NGOs, since these are the ones which have the institutional capacity to respond to requests for data and which generally have 'the most to say' (Wallace *et al.*, 1997: 11). This bias can be justified by the fact that resources are now so heavily concentrated in the hands of so few organisations: the top 20 French NGOs garnered 78.2 per cent of total resources in 2005 (CCD, 2008: 10).

Whilst interviews have provided first-hand insights into the thinking and workings of French NGOs, they have painted only a partial, and often a highly personalised, picture of the driving forces behind these organisations. They are of limited value in explaining any broad, collective shifts in the policy and operational priorities of French NGOs. For this, there is a need to identify and deploy an appropriate theoretical framework. This book has – after a review of relevant economic, international relations and organisational theories – identified, as a suitable perspective, Resource Dependence or RD theory (Pfeffer and Salancik, 1978). According to this theoretical framework, all organisations, including NGOs, operate essentially in line with the rational choice paradigm and are driven both by a need to acquire resources and a desire to minimise any awkward dependencies, which these resources may generate.

Finally, a case study approach has been used to test whether the evolution of French NGO practice in the field can be explained in terms of RD theory. The value of the case study approach is widely appreciated. The question which arises relates to the number of cases to be examined. A large number may have the advantage of giving wider explanatory power to a theoretical model. But it can also lead to 'vacuous description or superficial analysis' (Shalev, 1980: 40), particularly where (as was the case with this study) the funding was not available to undertake more than one detailed independent evaluation of NGO project work in the field. It follows that a small number of cases, or even a single case study, has the distinct advantage of permitting more intensive analysis of the actors involved, their motivation and the context in which they operate. It is this approach that has been adopted in our penultimate chapter, which focuses upon a joint French NGO–state programme to bolster civil society in Cameroon. Our criteria for choosing this critical and informative case study are set out more fully in Chapter 9.

Outline of the study

Having set out the aims, scope and methodology of this research, this study will focus in Chapter 2 on issues surrounding the definition of NGOs. It will hone in on developmentally focused organisations, explaining why these actors are worthy of a study in their own right. On the basis of a review of existing theories, Chapter 3 will identify the RD perspective as the most useful framework for explaining recent developments in the French NGO sector. Chapter 4 will sketch out the resource environment which French NGOs have faced over the global era and will demonstrate empirically that the 'critical resource' for these actors is not the French state but rather the donor public and grassroots activists.

Chapters 5 to 7 will seek to establish whether French NGOs have fallen in line with wider trends in the NNGO sector. An assessment of whether there has been any significant improvement in terms of the relationship between French NGOs and the state will be undertaken in Chapter 5. This chapter will also look at whether these ameliorations are enough to lay the bases for a new partnership. Chapter 6 will examine whether French NGOs have undergone professionalisation along the lines recommended by the French authorities or whether they have held on to their core militant profile. Chapter 7 will seek to establish whether French NGOs have become service agents or vectors for the French state or whether they have preserved their autonomy of action.

Chapter 8 will explain recent developments in French NGO–state relations in terms of RD theory. It will assess how far ideological and other constraints have impeded NGOs in their strategic decision-making and their use of resource stabilisation techniques. Chapter 9 will then focus on a case study of French NGO–state collaboration in the field in Cameroon and will ask whether French NGO behaviour in this specific instance is consistent with, and explained by, RD theory. Finally, the concluding chapter will examine whether French NGOs are, in the future, likely to move closer to the state and to wider international trends or whether they are destined to reject such compromises and hold on to their utopian aim of building 'another world' (Cassen, 2003).

Conclusion

This chapter has suggested that the dilemma of how closely to work with the state has come to the fore in the global era. It has argued that three broad trends emerge from the literature: a general improvement in the terms and conditions of the relationship between NNGOs and their central governments, a growing professionalisation, and an increasing tendency for NGOs to act as service providers on behalf of the state. The implication of much of this literature is that these trends apply widely, not just in Anglo-Saxon countries, but also in countries with very different political and social traditions. This book tests this assumption by focusing on French NGOs, which, despite being part of one of the largest voluntary sectors in the world, are also steeped in a socio-political culture that is renowned for its 'exceptionalism'. The existing literature on French NGOs does not shed much light on whether or not these actors have fallen in line with wider trends. Nor does not it explore in any detail the driving forces behind any changes or lack of changes in these NGOs. These questions will be at the core of this survey. Before undertaking this detailed analysis, however, this study must explain what is meant by the term 'NGO' and which actors, in particular, are under examination in this book.

2
Zooming in on French NGOs

Although they have existed in various forms for many centuries, NGOs were not defined or labelled as such until 1945, when the UN officialised the term by writing it into its Charter (Article 71).[1] Even today, the acronym NGO remains, in the words of Martens (2002: 272), 'terra incognita', with uncertainties persisting as to 'what this phrase actually encompasses'. This lack of agreement is, as Vakil (1997: 2057) argues, more than a 'mere nuisance'. The confusion makes it difficult to draw cross-national comparisons and even to put a ballpark figure on the number of NNGOs operating in the international development field, with estimates ranging from around 5,000 (Senarclens, 2001) to 20,000 (Smouts *et al.*, 2003).[2]

This chapter seeks to clear up some of this conceptual confusion by outlining the different approaches to defining NGOs and singling out the self-definitional approach as the most useful. It notes, however, that this latter method still covers, in the French context alone, over 450 NGOs active in international development and relief. It explores ways of breaking this NGO sector down into manageable units of analysis and hones in on an activity-based classification system, which distinguishes between French pressure groups, emergency NGOs and developmental organisations. Finally, it zooms in on this last category of actors and explains why it is worthy of a study in its own right.

In search of a definition

NGOs have been defined, with varying degrees of precision, as 'voluntary associations' (Cernea, 1988), 'organisations which serve as channels for aid' (Piveteau, 1998: 271) and 'self-governing, private, not-for-profit organizations that are geared toward improving the quality of life of disadvantaged people' (Vakil, 1997: 2060). There have, in fact, been so many attempts at pinning down the meaning of this umbrella term that it is possible to identify at least five different definitional approaches, each of which has its own strengths and drawbacks.

The first is the *juridicial approach*, which defines NGOs by their legal status, as recognised either by national legislation (Belgium and Quebec are unusual in providing a distinct legal status for international NGOs) or by various international bodies. The latter include the UN, whose Economic and Social Committee (ECOSOC) offers consultative status; and the European Council, which guarantees the same legal rights to all NGOs belonging to countries that are signatory to the European Convention on the Recognition of International NGOs.[3] The juridicial approach is valuable in that it offers explicit criteria for deciding what is and is not an NGO. Yet, this method has drawbacks. Thus, national legislation can be too inclusive and can mask real differences within the NGO sectors of particular countries (Martens, 2002). To illustrate, the 1901 Charity Law in France lumps together not only developmental and humanitarian NGOs of all shapes and sizes, but also tens of thousands of other domestic voluntary associations. International legal recognition can also be too all-encompassing, with, for instance, ECOSOC status being open, not just to NGOs but also, to non-state actors, such as commercial companies. It can, equally, be too exclusive, with, for example, legal recognition from the European Council not being available to NGOs outside Europe (Ibid).

The second is the *sociological approach*, which defines NGOs in terms of what they are not. Thus, Lador-Lederer (1963: 60) notes that 'NGOs are non-governmental, non-profit-making and not-uninational'. Similarly, Willetts (1996: 5) declares that NGOs are 'any non-profit-making, non-violent, organized group of people who are not seeking government office'. This approach is useful in distinguishing NGOs from other non-state actors, such as companies, quasi-NGOs (QUANGOs), local authorities and national political parties. But it has shortcomings. Thus, as Martens (2002: 279) has argued, the claim that NGOs are 'non-violent' is problematic insofar as some perfectly legal NGOs have occasionally engaged in violent action in opposition to, say, Genetically Modified Foods or in favour of issues, such as animal rights. Equally, the assertion that NGOs are not 'uni-national' is questionable given that many NGOs, notably in the development education field, operate solely in the national context, but with an international dimension to their activities (e.g. the various RITIMO centres across France). Furthermore, the assumption that NGOs are 'non-governmental' and, in fact, according to the UN System of National Accounts, can only be counted if they receive less than 50 per cent of their funding from the state, could rule out internationally recognised NGOs, such as CARE and CRS, which are heavily financed by the American government (Tvedt, 1998: 31). But the biggest drawback of this approach is that it is negative – in Chinese, the term NGO is translated as 'anti-government' – defining NGOs by what they are not rather than by what they are and do (Martens, 2002: 278).

The third method is referred to by Tvedt (1998: 15) as the functional definition and emphasises the 'organizational principle of voluntarism' (Bratton,

1989: 574). The functional approach compensates for the negativity of socio-logical approaches but overemphasises the voluntary function, idealism and attachment of NGOs to good causes. It 'focuses on highly normative criteria that are difficult to apply vigorously in different countries and at different times' (Tvedt, 1998: 15). It also fails to account for the process of profes-sionalisation, which has led so much of the NNGO sector to recruit more permanent staff and employ lucrative marketing techniques borrowed from the commercial sector.

The fourth definition is a *structural-operational* one devised by scholars taking part in the John Hopkins Comparative Nonprofit Sector Project, launched in 1990 to identify the key features of NGOs and the 'third' sectors in which they operate.[4] According to Salamon and Anheier (1997: 33–4), the non-profit sector is made up of organisations, which are private, institution-alised, non-profit distributing, self-governing and voluntary. This compre-hensive definition incorporates many of the features of the aforementioned approaches: a stress on rules (juridicial), an explicit emphasis on non-governmentalism (sociological) and a focus on voluntarism (functional). But it has been criticised for neglecting to include the large number of NGOs that are not formally constituted or registered and for failing to distinguish between voluntary sector organisations and NGOs, the former essentially active in domestic welfare and the latter focusing on international develop-ment and relief (Tvedt, 1998: 17–18).

Finally, the self-definitional approach is the method employed by those bodies which compile NGO directories on NGOs. Thus, for example, the OECD, which collates data on all its industrialised member states, uses a 'flexible definition' of the term NGO, which is based on the 'singular trad-itions' of different Western civil societies involved in sustainable develop-ment (Woods, 2000: 10). The CCD adopts a broadly similar approach for its directories of French NGOs. In effect, it lists all those NGOs which respond to a standardised questionnaire sent out every three years.[5]

Needless to say, this method can never be completely foolproof or pre-cise. Indeed, almost any organisation could claim to be an NGO and could conceivably benefit from government monies and tax breaks in the process. Conversely, numerous organisations which – either because they do not have time for, do not know of, or do not receive, the questionnaire – could find themselves omitted from these figures and, hence, from this defin-ition. In addition, as the OECD itself admits, this approach 'inevitably requires accepting different cultural, legal and ideological interpretations of what constitutes an "NGO"' (Woods, 2000: 10). In this context, it might be noted that Canada includes in its official statistics for NGOs, universities, professional organisations and trade unions. Scandanavian countries also count trade unions, Japan lists many parastatals and Germany incorporates political foundations (Smillie, 1999: 16; Potevin, 2000: 6–7). That said, how-ever, the organisations compiling these publicly available directories are

vigilant as to the omission of any key actors; the inclusion of any organisations which are clearly not 'non-governmental' organisations or, indeed,
the double-counting of NGOs which are both national and transnational
organisations.

It will be argued here that the self-definitional method is the most useful for this study of French NGOs and their linkages to wider Northern
trends. For a start, it corresponds to the perceptions of the actors themselves in this milieu and allows for the inclusion of many organisations,
which are willing to be listed in national and international directories but
which do not normally refer to themselves as 'NGOs'. There are, according
to Najam (1996), 47 different terms around the world for NGO, with non-
governmental organisations in the United States, for example, preferring
to call themselves 'Private Voluntary Organizations' and those originating
in the United Kingdom labelling themselves (international aid) 'charities'.
The term *Organisation Non-Gouvernementale* is beginning to be used more
widely in France.[6] But it remains less popular than more positive-sounding
terms, such as *Associations de Solidarité Internationale* (ASI) and *Organisations
de Solidarité Internationale* (OSI).[7] It also provokes a particularly lukewarm
response from faith-based actors, such as the DEFAP and SC-CF, which see
themselves less as 'NGOs' and more as 'arms' of their respective churches.

Clearly this self-definitional approach has the advantage of not listing,
and hence excluding from the category of NGOs, a host of non-state actors,
which are either profit-making (e.g. private companies) or focused on the
self-interest of their membership (e.g. trade unions). It also rules out organisations, which are too diffuse in terms of their organisational structures
(e.g. 'new' social movements) or which are simply too close to the state
or to power (e.g. political parties and quasi-governmental agencies, local
authorities, para-governmental bodies, official aid agencies).[8] This method
also screens out most SNGOs, as well as any NNGOs whose head office or
affiliates are not based in France.[9] It does, moreover, leave out actors which
operate solely in the French domestic social context or in what is variously
referred to as the 'voluntary' sector (*le bénévolat*) or the social economy
(*économie solidaire*). These organisations are said by Archambault (1997:
191) to include cooperatives (member-oriented non-profit organisations,
such as agricultural cooperatives and cooperative banks that are engaged
in some form of commercial activity); mutualist societies (insurance funds
and related schemes offering coverage beyond that provided by the state
social security system); and the 800,000 or so French associations formed
as part of the 1901 Law, the majority of which are active in health, education and welfare in France itself. This should not, however be taken to
imply that the French NGOs listed in the OECD and CCD directories do
not ever focus on domestic voluntary issues. MSF, MDM and SC-CF are
all, in fact, particularly active in terms of both international and domestic
welfare work.[10]

Making sense of the French NGO sector

While useful, this self-definitional approach still leaves the potential analyst focusing on a vast number of French NGOs active in the field of international development and humanitarian work. The exact figure has been variously estimated at between 458 (CCD, 2000) and 800 (www. ibiscus.fr). But it could be much higher. Indeed, as Hatton (2002: 153) observes, 'Nobody knows whether this figure needs to be multiplied by three, by six, by eight or by ten or more to know the true number...'.

Given the sheer number of actors concerned, consideration needs to be given to finding a classification system, which can break down the French NGO sector into more manageable units of analysis. Many of the existing taxonomies go beyond the remit of this study and map out the entire non-profit sectors of specific countries (Salamon and Anheier, 1997; Archambault, 1997). Others are, however, more directly relevant to this analysis, and their advantages and drawbacks will be discussed below.

Perhaps the most obvious way to categorise NGOs is by size: their number of staff, fee-paying members, local affiliates or, more usually, the value of their resources. This latter criterion is used by the CCD in its directories and financial overviews of the French NGO sector, which is divided into nine bands of NGO, ranging from those with income above M€100 to those with revenue below €500,000 (CCD, 2008: 52). This method is objective, non-judgmental and easy to measure empirically. It serves to reveal two specificities of the French NGO sector. The first is the sheer proliferation of small NGOs, which make up, in numerical terms, an estimated 54 per cent of the 159 French NGOs covered by the most recent CCD survey (CCD, 2008: 3). The second relates to the absence of any truly large NGOs in the French context: the most resource-rich actor, MSF, with a budget of M€144 in 2006 (MSF, 2006: 1) is small by comparison with the American branch of World Vision, which collected around US$900 million in the same year (Zimet, 2006: 48). This method of categorisation by size is, however, much less useful as a tool for comparing trends in different NNGO sectors, given that there is no yardstick for determining what is large or small, in terms of personnel or resources, across different countries. Significantly too, this approach glosses over very real differences between NGOs within particular income bands and fails to take into account whether the revenue of these non-governmental actors has come from private or official sources.

Another general method of classification is by *proximity to the state*. This approach has been employed by Kuhnle and Selle (1992), who draw up a typology of relationships between Northern non-profit sectors and the state, which are said to range from 'separate autonomy to 'integrated dependence'. It also forms a key component of the methodology used by Brown and Korten (1991), who distinguish between service-delivery agencies, development-catalyst organisations, sector-support and networking organisations, public service contractors and people's organisations. While this system of categorisation focuses on what is often the most important relationship for many NGOs, namely their ties with the state, it does concentrate on this relationship at the expense of all others. It has also been criticised by Tvedt (1998: 32) for falsely distinguishing between 'the fundable "good" NGOs... [and] the "bad" NGOs', for neglecting 'historical and cultural differences in these relations from society to society and from time to time' and for failing to recognise that 'what is regarded as antigovernment in some countries may be seen as pro-establishment in other countries and vice versa' (Ibid). Tvedt has even claimed that 'The enormous differences in character of state formations and the size and character of the "third sector"... make any classification of NGOs in regard to relations with government or state very difficult, if not impossible' (Ibid: 34).

Another widely recognised system of categorisation focuses on the *strategic orientation* of NGOs. Based on the influential work of Korten (1987), this approach distinguishes between (originally three but now) four generations of NGOs, each with a different development strategy. The first generation involves NGOs which are at an early stage of their evolution and give priority to meeting immediate needs through relief and welfare work. The second enjoys a growing awareness of 'development' issues and may engage in small-scale, self-sustaining local development work. The third has a much more explicit concern with the sustainability of their work and has moved from an essentially service delivery function towards the role of catalyst for socio-economic change. Finally, the fourth generation aims to support the governments and civil societies of developing countries on major issues at a national or global level (e.g. the defence of human rights, environmental protection). This schema captures the dynamic nature of NGOs and their propensity to learn over time. It seems particularly well adapted to the evolution of larger Anglo-American NGOs, such as OXFAM, World Vision and CARE, all of which have moved away from their initial, near-exclusive focus on emergency relief work towards a much broader stance which includes a strong concern with long-term development issues.[11] Yet, there are question marks associated with this model. For a start, it assumes that all NGOs will, and perhaps even should, go through these generational changes over time. In so doing, it ignores the fact that 'some development NGOs are "reverting" to becoming "first" generation NGOs because there are official funds easily available in this area' (Tvedt, 1998: 34). Korten's typology is, moreover, a highly subjective form of classification and one which does not fit comfortably with broad trends in the French NGO sector, where, as will be discussed below, developmental NGOs have come to be eclipsed by humanitarian organisations and where the leading emergency NGO, MSF, prides itself on the overriding priority it continues to accord to short-term relief work in the immediate aftermath of a crisis (Interview with MSF Board member, 2003).

Another approach to categorisation hones in on the *philosophy* of NGOs, whether it be their ideological or their religious leanings. As will be suggested in Chapter 7, one of the main divisions in the French context has tradition-ally been between radical Left-leaning, *tiersmondiste*, developmental NGOs, such as the CCFD and FDH, and more libertarian, pragmatic humanitar-ian NGOs, inspired, at least initially, by MSF. Another fault line has been between faith-based NGOs, such as SC-CF or ACAT, and secular NGOs, such as *Terre des Hommes-France* and the *Comité National de Solidarité Laïque*. These distinctions have become less relevant since the late 1980s, when the very public battle between *tiersmondistes* and the foundation *MSF-Liberté* was resolved in the latter's favour and when radical Left wing and church-led NGOs began to form a coherent alliance in the battle against a global free market. With some exceptions (notably the emergence of Islamic NGOs, such as *Secours Islamique*), there has, over many years, been a process of secu-larisation taking place in the French NGO sector (Ryfman, 2004: 9). There has, equally, been a general relegation of ideological positions and proselyt-ising missions to more of a backseat role. This process is particularly true of the CCFD, France's largest developmentally oriented NGO, which openly recruits non-Catholics and seeks to help people of any religion through its work. While this organisation was, in the 1960s, heavily influenced by the Vatican, it has over recent decades moved into a strong secular phase.[12] Indeed, according to the former head of the NGO research unit Solagral, 'the only truly significant faith-based NGO in France is the CCFD, and, since the CCFD has adopted more of a progressive stance...the distinction between faith-based and secular organisations is no longer particularly rele-vant' (Interview, 2003).

A particularly insightful cataloguing technique, developed by Hatton (2002: 154) with the French NGO sector specifically in mind, involves breaking NGOs down into six distinct categories. The first are those which were set up at the behest of the state, including the *Comité Français pour la Solidarité Internationale* or CFSI, formed in 1960, and the AFVP, founded, in 1963, at the instigation of the French Development Ministry.[13] The second are NGOs created upon the initiative of private organisations. Thus SC-CF was established following a decision by the Episcopate of French Catholic Bishops, while the CCFD emerged, in 1961, as a result of an initiative by various Catholic action movements. The third are organisations created by domestic French 'associations', which wished to add an international dimen-sion to their activities. This applies, in particular, to youth and educational movements, such as *Éclaireurs* or *Éclaireuses de France, Scouts* or *Guides de France* and the *Ligue Française de l'Enseignement et de l'Éducation Permanente*. The fourth category relates to NGOs established by people in a specific pro-fession: *Pharmaciens Sans Frontières* (PSF) and *Reporters Sans Frontières* (RSF) are only two of many examples. The fifth grouping includes bodies founded by private French citizens, such as *Échanges et Consultants Techniques*

Internationaux, AGIR ABCD and the *Groupement des Retraités Éducateurs Sans Frontières*. The final category relates to organisations set up at the instigation of individuals living in France, who are from immigrant families and who aim, among other things, to help towns and villages in their country of origin. These *Organisations de Solidarité Internationale issues des Migrations* (OSIM), which have now created their own federation in France known as FORIM, are primarily oriented towards the countries of the Maghreb.

For Hatton, a further distinction can be drawn in terms of management structures. He notes that the first three categories of NGO are run by 'boards made up of representatives of legal entities with institutional mandates'. Thus, the French Foreign Ministry has a determining influence over the AFVP board, whilst the positions of the Episcopate and the Protestant Federation of France are 'taken into account on international relations issues by the Directors of the SC-CF and *Comité Inter-Mouvements Auprès Des Evacués* (CIMADE), even if these latter structures do have real autonomy in their management' (Ibid: 154). By contrast, the last three categories are deemed to be 'associations created at the behest of private persons' (Ibid). They have leadership structures made up of private individuals, who are normally elected at the time of general assemblies, to which all members of the association are invited. Hatton's method of classification sheds valuable light on the origins of French NGOs and into the managerial structures which have guided them. However, it is not clear how easily this Franco-centric approach could be extended to other NNGO sectors or used as the basis for cross-national comparison. It is also unlikely that this system could cope with the very different evolution of some NGOs with broadly similar origins; or, for that matter, with the propensity of some privately formed NGOs (e.g. *ATD Quart Monde*) to refuse most government assistance and of others (e.g. the *Groupe de Recherches et d'Échanges Technologiques* or GRET) to accept high proportions of official funding.

Perhaps, however, the most commonly used system of categorisation, and the one employed in this study, is by *function*. Focusing on NGOs in general, Clark (1991) identifies six activity-based categories of NGOs: 'relief and welfare agencies' (e.g. CRS); 'technical innovation organisations' (e.g. the Grameen Bank in Bangladesh); 'public service contractors', which work closely with governments in the Southern hemisphere and official aid agencies (e.g. CARE); 'popular development agencies', which help build grassroots democracy (e.g. the Bangladesh Rural Advancement Committee or BRAC); 'grassroots development organizations', which are membership bodies (e.g. the Self-Employed Women's Association in India) and 'advocacy groups or networks', which have no field projects but carry out lobbying (e.g. the World Development Movement in Britain). Such activity-based classifications can, of course, involve a high degree generalisation. They can lump together into single categories NGOs of different sizes and with distinct philosophies, origins, histories and relationships to the state. These approaches can also run into problems because 'many organizations increasingly carry out a range of different types of activities' (Lewis, 2001: 35). This is particularly true of large Anglo-Saxon NGOs but it also applies to many French NGOs, which are described by Blum (2005: 14) as 'very polyvalent' and 'multi-specialist'.

The weaknesses of the activity-based approach are nonetheless outweighed by their strengths. Thus, while this method of classification does not fully capture the hybridisation of NGO activities, it can be used to distinguish between the core functions of most small- and medium-sized NGOs, which still operate within a limited range of sectors. It can even be relevant to some of the largest NGOs in the world, which are still primordially associated with specific sectors such as child sponsorship (World Vision) and sanitation (OXFAM) (Stoddard, 2003). Furthermore, the functional approach has the distinct advantage that it breaks the sector down in ways that are easy to grasp for outsiders, meaningful to NGO practitioners, and compatible with the thematic and sectoral priorities, around which NGOs have formed their main federations and networks (see below). It is, above all, for the accessibility that it offers that an activity-based categorisation will be used in this study. The distinction drawn here will be between three types of organisation: pressure groups, humanitarian NGOs and developmental NGOs, with the latter category being the main focus of this book. Before, however, honing in on these developmental organisations (henceforth abbreviated to NGDOs to distinguish them from French NGOs as a whole), it is first important to set out the key distinguishing features of pressure groups and emergency NGOs; and to explain why they will not be central to this survey.[14] Finally, the main characteristics of NGDOs will be elaborated, and an explanation provided as to why these actors are worthy of a separate study.

Pressure groups

Pressure groups are voluntary organisations which engage in lobbying or advocacy work. They do not aspire to a service delivery role on behalf of the state or, indeed, any formal positions of power within parliament or the government. They do, however, seek to exert influence on official policymakers. Some do so by becoming 'insider groups' and enjoying regular access to the state at the risk of some loss of autonomy. Others do so by acting as 'outsider groups' and criticising, or remaining aloof from, positions adopted by their central government. Many of these organisations are referred to as 'sectional' or 'interest' groups, since they advance or defend the demands of a particular category of people or section of society (e.g. their own members in the case of a trade union). However, there is also another category of pressure or advocacy group, which promotes a specific ideal or cause and which 'breaks with the usual rules of the game by supporting the interests of people outside the movement itself and eschewing a conventional logic of self-interest' (Walters, 2003: 10). This latter type of organisation is especially active on issues such as human rights, the environment and overseas economic development.

The leading French groups on the environment tend to be close to political actors, such as the Green Party, and are often offshoots of major Anglo-Saxon actors, such as Greenpeace and the World Wide Fund for Nature or WWF.[15] On economic matters, French pressure groups are in the forefront of the *altermondialiste* movement (Fougier, 2004). The best known organisation is ATTAC, which was created in 1988 and now has a mass following of 30,000 members in France (Walters, 2006: 142). Its core function is to lobby for a Tobin tax on international financial transactions, partly to prevent currency speculation and partly to liberate funds to promote development. Turning finally to French pressure groups on human rights, these have been eclipsed by Anglo-American giants, such as Human Rights Watch and Amnesty International. They do, nonetheless, include organisations with long histories, such as the *Ligue des Droits de l'Homme* (which was formed at the height of the Dreyfus Affair in 1898 and helped form the international grouping, the *Fédération Internationale des Droits de l'Homme* or FIDH in 1922).[16] Other human rights groups are of more recent origin and are more hard-hitting. These include *Agir Ici*, which has, since its creation in 1989, undertaken around four wide-ranging campaigns a year; and *Survie*, which has, since its foundation in 1984, published numerous critical studies of French African policy and become embroiled in several major lawsuits (see Chapter 8).

It goes without saying that pressure groups cannot simply be airbrushed out of this study. These actors generally share the same legal status as NGOs (namely, the 1901 Law) and are also included in the CCD Directory of French NGOs. Equally, they engage in activities, which overlap with and complement, or even inspire, actions undertaken by developmental NGOs. To illustrate, they frequently take part in the same social forums as French NGDOs and they belong to the same ecological, feminist and *altermondialiste* movements. They also share a concern with awareness-raising and advocacy work at the international level; and they have been collaborating with NGDOs on the international diplomatic scene ever since the Rio Earth Summit (1992). In fact, according to the President of the *Centre de Recherche et d'Information sur le Développement* (CRID), the main federation of French NGDOs,

> There has been a rapprochement with environmental organisations in France, such as Greenpeace and Friends of the Earth; it became particularly pronounced at the time of the Johannesburg summit, at which point we created a joint platform to prepare this summit on sustainable development.... So we can no longer separate out issues, such as human rights, development and the environment. (Interview, 2003)

Significantly, however, pressure groups will not be a central focus of this book, as they are quite distinct from developmental NGOs in a number of respects. For a start, the former tend to be membership-based, whereas the latter usually have a relatively limited number of members (Edwards and Fowler, 2002: 198). Second, French pressure groups generally work in France (*ici*) or, in some instances, in major capitals, such as Brussels, Washington DC and New York. They may, in some cases (e.g. the FIDH) pay visits to developing countries (*là-bas*); but they are not, unlike NGDOs, permanently based or fully operational in those countries. Nor do they enjoy the kind of organic links which French developmental NGOs have with overseas partner organisations, such as indigenous cooperatives, women's and 'peasant' associations. Third, pressure groups specialise in lobbying policy-makers to change their policies, whereas NGDOs often combine advocacy work with action in the field. Fourth, lobbyists, such as the FIDH and the French section of Amnesty International, do not receive official subsidies but see it as their *raison d'être* to challenge the state. By contrast, NGDO federations, development education centres and many individual NGDOs often find themselves quite reliant on funding from governments and international organisations. Fifth, pressure groups tend to be more outspoken and to 'attach more weight to the whole gamut of militant activism' than do NGDOs (Ryfman, 2004: 47). Sixth, some advocacy groups simply do not see themselves as NGDOs. Thus, the French section of Amnesty International actually chose, in 1999, to have itself taken off the CCD directory (CCD, 1999). In other instances too, pressure groups have kept their distance from developmental NGOs, so much so that Ryfman (2004: 45) has commented that 'outside of major international conferences, ties remain strained and several joint initiatives have failed'.

Finally, pressure groups have also attracted their own distinct literature. In the French context, most writings hone in on individual organisations like the *Ligue des Droits de l'Homme* (Perrotin, 2003), *Agir Ici* (Boisgallais and Fardeau, 1994), ATTAC (Walters, 2006) or Greenpeace (Auger and Ferrante, 2004). Other surveys cover pressure groups within wider studies of social movements (Walters, 2003) or specifically in the context of the *altermondialiste* movement (Wieviorka, 2003: 141–54).

Humanitarian NGOs

Humanitarian or emergency NGOs are often referred to in the French context as *urgenciers*. These actors have a long ancestry dating back to the Order of Malta (*Ordre de Malte*), formed during the Crusades in 1099. They are, more usually traced back to the International Committee of the Red Cross (ICRC), created in 1863, and the French Red Cross (*Croix Rouge Française*), founded in 1864. However, most of the largest and best known are of more recent origin. The most famous of all is MSF, which was set up, in 1971, by a group of French doctors, led by Bernard Kouchner and Claude Malhuret.

The latter were disillusioned by the failure of Western governments and of the ICRC to provide humanitarian relief to the victims of the Biafran war without the prior permission of one of the warring parties, the Nigerian Federal Government. MSF won the Nobel Peace Prize in 1999 and is now the largest French NGO in terms of resources (see above). It has sections in 19 countries as well as international offices in Brussels, Geneva, New York and the United Arab Emirates.[17] With high-profile interventions in Afghanistan (1980), Ethiopia (1984), Rwanda (1994) and Darfur (2004), MSF has laid down a blueprint for other *urgenciers* to follow after their own fashion. It has, above all, stressed its neutrality and its 'duty' and 'right' to intervene, with or without the approval of host states, in any situation where human life is threatened.[18] It has also claimed for itself a *droit de témoignage*, that is, a right to speak out wherever systematic human rights abuses occur, even if this precipitates the expulsion or withdrawal of MSF from the territory concerned.[19]

The next three most resource-rich NGOs are all *urgenciers* and generally enjoy an annual income of between €50 and €100 million (CCD, 2008: 53).[20] MDM is the second largest French NGO. Also active in the medical domain, it was formed in 1980 by Bernard Kouchner after a rift with MSF over a major operation to highlight the plight of the Cambodian boat people.[21] MDM is much more 'French' in its outlook, with a militant activist and volunteer base, a longer-term focus and more substantial operations at home (notably its *Mission France*, which was set up in 1986). The third biggest French NGO, *Action Contre la Faim* (originally *Action Internationale Contre la Faim*) was founded at the time of the Soviet Union's invasion of Afghanistan in 1979. It focuses upon providing emergency food relief to victims of crises and tackling 'food security' and other medium-term nutritional issues.[22] The fourth largest is often *Handicap International*, which was created in 1982 to help amputees with prosthetic limbs and which won the Nobel Peace Prize in 1997 for its role in the recent international campaign to ban landmines. Other humanitarian NGOs tend to be medium-sized and either rooted in the medical field (e.g. *Aide Médicale Internationale, Pharmaciens/ Infirmières/ Vétérinaires Sans Frontières*) or more technical, even technocratic, in their focus (e.g. *Ingénieurs/ Électriciens Sans Frontières*).

It goes without saying that emergency-related NGOs cannot be altogether excluded from this study. The fact is that many of the official statistics provided in later chapters have simply not been disaggregated to distinguish between *urgenciers* and developmental NGOs. Furthermore, numerous analysts have argued that the distinctions between these two types of NGO are no longer valid. Thus, Hatton (2002: 160) has claimed that it is 'quasi impossible' to differentiate the two, whilst others have contended that the distinction is 'scarcely relevant' (Ryfman, 1998), 'barely used' since the mid-1990s (Hours, 1998) or even a 'source of confusion' (Ryfman, 2004: 39). These assertions are based upon a number of arguments and observations.

The first is that it is now increasingly difficult to distinguish between these types of organisation in terms of the time spectrum of their field operations. As Ryfman (2004: 39) notes, 'So-called "emergency" NGOs also engage in medium to long-term programmes', whilst 'so-called "developmental NGOs" put in place ... programmes offering immediate relief to refugees and displaced persons'.[23] In a similar vein, Hatton (2002: 160) observes that *urgenciers* are increasingly involved in 'long-term actions against the AIDS pandemic', whilst Blum (2007) points out that NGDOs, such as the CCFD and SC-CF, were actively involved in relief work relating to the recent South Asian tsunami.[24]

The second argument is that it is no longer easy to draw a hard and fast distinction between the way in which these actors now work in the field. Thus, *urgenciers* are no longer content to send out highly paid expatriate specialists to take over from indigenous organisations. Instead, they are beginning to espouse the notion of 'partnership' with local organisations, which has, of course, long been the approach favoured by most *développementalistes* and volunteer agencies.[25] This new approach is welcomed by the CRID, whose president acknowledged that

> Humanitarian NGOs now also work with the idea of partnership in mind ... even if MSF sends out expatriates following an earthquake, it will also look out for local organisations which can subsequently take over its work .... There will be efforts to construct partnership-like relations, something which simply did not happen ten years ago. (Interview, 2003)

The third contention is that it is increasingly difficult to differentiate between *urgenciers* and *développementalistes* in terms of their advocacy work. Indeed, humanitarian and developmental NGOs have begun to work much more closely together on raising awareness about human rights (particularly economic, social and cultural rights) and in campaigning for the introduction of new international bodies and treaties. They even shared a joint platform at, for example, the 2002 UN summit in Johannesburg. This prompted a senior figure within the CRID to assert: 'We are witnessing a very clear rapprochement between emergency and developmental NGOs ... the cleavage which existed ten years ago ... is now much less visible' (Interview, 2003).

The final observation is that it is becoming ever more difficult to draw a clear legal distinction between *urgenciers* and NGDOs. These humanitarian and developmental NGOs have, of course, long been governed by a common founding law, namely the *Loi de 1901* on associations. But they are also now equally covered by a raft of more recent legislation. This includes various fiscal directives and labour codes, as well as ministerial decrees and laws relating to overseas volunteer work or *le volontariat* (see Chapter 5).

Without wishing to contest the underlying basis of many of the above claims, it is, nonetheless, argued here that the differences between humanitarian and developmental NGDOs are only gradually breaking down and are, in fact, still meaningful today. The continuing relevance of these distinctions is recognised by Potevin (2000: 12), who notes that 'the separation between emergency and development work remains a key characteristic of the French scene, even if there are attempts under way to ensure that there is continuity between emergency, rehabilitation and development work'. Potevin's assertion can be supported by a number of observations. The first is that, whilst *urgenciers* are increasingly involved in longer-term activities and even in some preventative action, they tend to be first and foremost concerned with emergencies and with the short- to medium-term consequences of those crises. The same is not true of NGDOs, which are primarily interested in tackling longer-term development issues and in dealing with the underlying politico-economic causes of crises, often in countries marked by a good deal of stability. These developmental organisations tend, moreover, to intervene in emergencies only occasionally; and they do so at the request of, and indeed often through the medium of, their local partners (Interview with CCFD, 2003).

A second observation is that the priorities of these two types of organisation are not the same. Thus, according to the CCD (1999: 32), 'for emergency NGOs, the emphasis is on the individual who suffers...; for developmental NGOs, account has to be taken of the whole social organisation governing the population at large'. A third point is that, while the lines are blurring between the way in which humanitarian and developmental NGO intervene in developing countries, this distinction does still remain broadly valid. In other words, leading *urgenciers* continue to expatriate primarily French staff who are high-cost specialists, whilst developmental NGOs still prefer to work through indigenous NGOs or to send out low-paid volunteers on local contracts.[26]

A fourth indicator is the fact that *urgenciers* and NGDOs perceive themselves differently. This point is acknowledged by Ryfman, who notes (2004: 40) that 'It would obviously be wrong to suppose that these NGOs are identical: on top of their own histories and cultures, the specificities, areas of expertise and competence of each are not the same. They are, moreover, clearly marked out.' That French NGOs continue to see their principal activity as being of defining importance can be inferred from their membership of federations, with *développementalistes* finding a natural home in the CRID and *Groupe Initiatives* (see Annex B), and with emergency NGOs preferring to join *Coordination d'Agen* and – admittedly alongside developmental volunteer agencies – the *Comité de Liaison des ONG de Volontariat* (CLONG-V).

A further sign that emergency and developmental NGOs are still distinct lies in the way that these actors are viewed by others. That these organisations are perceived differently can be inferred from the fact that they enjoy different levels of private donations, often at different times of any given year (see Chapter 4). They also receive the bulk of their official resources from different French government bodies and different units within international organisations. Thus, many French *urgenciers* have secured most of their official income from the French Foreign Ministry division known as the *Délégation à l'Action Humanitaire* (DAH), and from the European Commission Humanitarian Office (ECHO). French NGDOs have, by contrast, received most support from the Foreign Ministry unit known, until recently, as the *Mission pour la Coopération Non-Gouvernementale* (MCNG), and from EuropeAid (discussed in Chapter 4).[27]

Finally, urgenciers have been treated separately from, and in more detail than, NGDOs in the wider the literature on French NGOs. These writings have focused, *inter alia*, on the recent evolution of French humanitarian organisations (Ryfman, 2001); on their growing collaboration with the French state and military (Rufin, 1994; Weissman, 2003); on their changing recruitment practices (Dauvin *et al.*, 2002); and on their degree of professionalism in responding to the December 2004 South Asian tsunami (e.g. Blum, 2007).

Developmental NGOs

Turning to developmental NGOs or NGDOs, these actors will be at the core of this book and need only brief treatment in this chapter. They can be broken down into *développementalistes* or *développeurs,* on the one hand, and volunteer agencies (*volontariat*), on the other.

As for *développementalistes*, these engage primarily in medium- to long-term development activities, such as rural development, education, social development and local capacity-building. They comprise two main types of organisation, namely those which emphasise financial support and operate indirectly through local partners, and those which send out their own staff on (short-term) contracts and provide their own technical expertise, often in the form of consultants. Most of the better known *développeurs* fall into the first category and were either born around the time of World War II (CIMADE in 1939; SC-CF in 1946) or in the immediate wake of France's decolonisation of Africa in 1960 (e.g. CCFD, CFSI, *Frères des Hommes, Terre des Hommes-France*).[28]

With the emergence of a whole generation of *sans-frontiériste* NGOs in the 1970s and 1980s, *développementalistes* gradually lost their status as the leading actors on the French NGO scene. But they continued to include, within their ranks, a number of important organisations. This is particularly true of the CCFD, which is generally reckoned to be the largest developmental NGO and the fifth largest French NGO of all. While significantly smaller than the top *urgencier,* the CCFD does boast an annual income of M€39 (2006) and can lay claim to 1,500 local groups and to donations from an average of 350,000 donors a year.[29] This NGDO has, unsurprisingly, become a crucial source of funding for the peasant associations, NGOs, churches and other local partners, through which it operates in developing countries.

The other leading *développementaliste* is the *Secours Catholique-Caritas France*, which is the French branch of the international Catholic movement, *Caritas Internationalis*. This non-governmental actor is actually bigger than the CCFD, when account is taken of the domestic charity work carried out by the *Secours Catholique* in France.[30] The SC-CF is, however, always ranked as being smaller for two main reasons. First, it devotes fewer resources to overseas development work; and second, it does not have the same range of partnerships, preferring to operate exclusively through its own local church networks in developing countries. A similar philosophy of partnership also governs Protestant NGOs, such as the CIMADE, secular organisations, such as TDH, and, for that matter, all of the 50 or so organisations belonging to the federation of *développeurs*, the CRID (see Annex B).

The other main category of *développementaliste* takes the form of technical organisations, which send out specialist French staff, offer professional advice on finance and undertake expert evaluations. These consultancy-type NGDOs act essentially as operators, even if they do try to include, and seek to bolster, local expertise in the process. Many of these developmental NGOs form part of the federation known as *Groupe Initiatives*, whose leading members include the GRET, the *Centre de Coopération pour le Développement International* (CICDA) and the *Institut de Recherches et d'Application des Méthodes de développement* (IRAM).

Other NGDOs which do not fit comfortably into either of the above categories include fair trade NGOs, such as the *Fédération Artisans du Monde*, development education centres, such as RITIMO and the various French NGO federations. None of these actors is actively engaged in field operations overseas, but they all clearly play an important role in awareness-raising and in advocacy work on overseas development matters. They do so, for example, by offering training services (usually in France) to Northern and Southern NGOs, by engaging in advocacy campaigns which 'educate' the wider public about international development issues and by providing briefing packs for future volunteers.

Turning to the other main type of developmental NGOs, volunteer agencies, these send out *volontaires de développement* to developing countries. These volunteers operate on poorly remunerated local contracts ranging from one year to a maximum of six years. They can, as such, be distinguished from *volontaires d'urgence*, who often perform better-paid short-term specialist work in crisis or post-crisis situations. Volunteer associations have in common with *développementalistes* the fact that they work to a logic of 'autonomisation' rather than 'substitution'. In other words, they only send out volunteer staff at the behest of their partners in the Southern hemisphere and they seek to build local capacity through their exchanges with these organisations.[31] The largest of these agencies are accredited by the French Foreign Ministry and are, in many cases, members of the federation known as CLONG-V (see Annex B).

Volunteer associations trace their origins back to various missionary movements. Among the earliest on the French scene were the Catholic organisation, the *Délégation Catholique à la Coopération* (DCC), and its Protestant counterpart, the *Département Évangélique Français d'Action Apostolique* (DEFAP). In the post-colonial era, these faith-based actors took charge of posting, on behalf of the French state, large numbers of *coopérants*, that is to say young French men, who opted to become volunteers rather than doing their military service (see Chapter 5 for details). While this source of recruits dried up after the end of national service in 1996, the DCC has nonetheless continued to expatriate a huge number of overseas volunteers (some 697 or 38.5 per cent of the total in 2002). The DEFAP, for its part, has continued to send a reasonable number (some 58 or 3.2 per cent in the same year) (Godfrain, 2004: Annex 1).[32]

The other leading volunteer agency is the *Association Française des Volontaires du Progrès*. While this organisation only sent out 284 volunteers in 2002 (*Cour des Comptes*, 2005: 41), it is nonetheless the largest developmentally focused volunteer organisation, both in terms of its financial income (M€13 in 2008) and its human resources (40 permanent staff).[33] The AFVP does not have any true partners in developing countries, and, partly for this reason, it pays volunteers a much higher rate than other developmental volunteer organisations (which offer 'stipends' rather than salaries).[34] While, the AFVP did initially enjoy considerable autonomy in its own decision-making actions, its room for manoeuvre is now strictly limited. It has acted, since 2005, almost exclusively as a service provider for the French state.

Having narrowed down the focus to *développementalistes* and volunteer agencies, it is worth noting that this study will not examine every single organisation, which could be included within these categories and which is listed in the CCD directory as an NGO. It will not, for example, give any detailed consideration to NGOs, based in France, which are affiliates of large Anglo-Saxon organisations. These NGOs, which include CARE-France, WWF and *Amnesty International-Section Française*, are almost certain to have been moulded by quite different socio-political cultures and traditions. Nor will it focus on OSIM, that is, NGOs set up by immigrants who now live in France and who wish to channel their support to the people of their home towns in North Africa and other parts of the developing world. These NGOs have clearly been forged out of different historical experiences and they are as much focused on integrating (Muslim) immigrants into France's secular society, as they are concerned with international development. Although these associations of immigrant workers have been authorised to engage in overseas development work since 1982, they have only recently come to prominence, and, even now, their relations with the French state continue to be marked by strong mutual suspicion.[35]

Finally, two other categories of actors listed in the CCD Directory will not be a major focus of this study. The first is foundations such as the *Fondation de France,* the *Fondation Max Havelaar* and other members of the *Centre Français des Fondations* (created in 2001). While active in international development, these bodies should generally be viewed as sources of revenue for NGDOs (see Chapters 4 and 8). They are, in fact, different from developmental NGOs in a number of respects. To begin with, they are governed by different legislation (notably the 1987 law on the development of sponsorship) and face tighter regulation by a powerful statutory body, the Council of State. Furthermore, they tend to give priority to domestic issues, such as poverty and medical research, over international development concerns.[36] They also enjoy different rights. To illustrate, foundations, unlike most NGDOs, can own property other than the minimum which is strictly needed for premises and they are, moreover, automatically entitled to public utility status (discussed in Chapter 5). Above all, they are underpinned and driven by a different logic: they have no members, are formed following a philanthropic gift of funds, and finance their activities through the interest generated by their investments. Most NGDOs, on the other hand, do at least have some members. They also operate on the basis of a minimum reserve of funds and are, as such, constantly engaged in a quest for more donations (Blum, 2005).

The other set of actors which will not be studied here are regional French NGOs. These organisations do engage in activities broadly similar to those of national French NGOs and some have even set up their head offices in Paris. The vast majority are, moreover, governed by the same 1901 Law on associations, with the only exception being NGOs based in Alsace-Lorraine, which are subject to a local civil code. Regional associations can also, occasionally, operate on a par with national NGOs by establishing networks, such as RESACOOP in the Rhône-Alpes region and similar groupings in some 16 other regions. Overall, however, local and regional NGOs are a highly dispersed set of actors, who are hard to quantify and pin down: separate directories exist for regions such as Languedoc-Roussillon but not for most others.[37] These regional actors are also, nearly always, smaller affairs than national NGOs, with limited expertise in international relations, and with a primary official funding relationship with local or regional government. They are, as such, less likely to be fundamentally concerned by the core relationship, which is at the heart of this study, namely NGDO relations with French central government.

Why study developmental NGOs?

Having identified French developmental NGOs as our main focus, it is worth asking why these organisations are worthy of their own study. The first reason is that very little research has been done on these actors. As Joly (1985: 13) has noted, they constitute a social phenomenon 'which remains largely unknown outside of a narrow circle of NGDO activists and government officials'. This is, no doubt, a reflection of the fact that most of these associations are small, underdeveloped and engaged in activities, which are less headline-grabbing than the emergency relief work of *urgenciers*, such as MSF, or, indeed, the hard-hitting advocacy of pressure groups, such as ATTAC.

Against such a backdrop, it is hardly surprising that *développementalistes* and volunteer associations have been neglected in the literature on non-profit organisations. There have, of course, been exceptions to this rule, such as the works of Joly (1985), the CCD (1999), Deler *et al.* (1998), Potevin (2000) and Blum (2005). Yet, while these studies have singled out *développementalistes* for special attention, the first three are now quite dated, whilst the latter two are not so much scholarly analyses as insightful, advisory reports to official bodies (the CCD and Foreign Affairs Committee). Other texts have looked at *développementalistes* through the eyes of practitioners. These have taken the form of interviews with leading NGO figures (Holzer, 1994) and case studies of NGDO practice in the field (*Terre des Hommes*, 1998; Rouillé d'Orfeuil, 1984). Another set of surveys has honed in on French volunteer agencies, with Le Net and Werquin (1985) exploring the traditional sociopolitical make up of French and other Northern volunteer organisations; and with the CCD (2001) providing an upbeat assessment of the response of France's *volontariat* to the many challenges it faces. Other analyses have concentrated on specific 'volunteer associations', such as the DCC (Mabille, 2001: 179–232) or the AFVP in Cameroon (Kenmogne, 2003). Others still are vocational guides, which present an almost entirely positive image of these organisations and are designed to attract future volunteers (RITIMO, 2002; Gloaguen, 2002). Needless to say, whilst all these studies provide valuable first-hand insights into the internal workings of key NGDOs, they are often polemical, overly personalised and self-congratulatory accounts, which say little about how NGDO relations with the French state have been evolving.

A second reason for studying these organisations is that, despite their neglect in the literature, NGDOs are an important part of the French socioeconomic fabric. They form an integral part of a non-profit sector that employed, in 1994, an estimated 1.3 million people and which made up, in 1991, 4.2 per cent of the total French work force (Archambault, 1997: 123 and 115). Whilst NGOs operating in international development only represent a small share of this sector, they do nonetheless offer work-related opportunities to a very large number of voluntary staff. Indeed, one estimate puts the number of *bénévoles* (or volunteers working in France) at 150,000 and equates this to some 88,000 full-time jobs.[38] Significantly too, French NGOs enable large numbers of young French people to undertake assignments as volunteers (over 300,000 people over the last 30 years) (Ponsignon, 2002). In so doing, they enhance notions of citizenship, promote a wider understanding of Republican, and indeed Christian, values, and strengthen social capital, cohesion and trust. This latter role was acknowledged by Charles Josselin, former French Minister for Development and *Francophonie*, who remarked that 'Volunteer work overseas is a crucible, which will make for citizens who are active and responsible.... It is also a contributory factor to social cohesion, in both the North and South'.[39]

Third, French NGDOs make up a preponderant share of the NGO sector in terms of their numbers. In 1987, NGDOs were estimated to represent 58 per cent of all French NGOs (CCD, 1987: 120). In 2004–05, some 85 per cent of the 159 NGOs surveyed by the CCD claimed to engage in some kind of overseas development work, with 25.2 per cent undertaking development activities only (CCD, 2008: 3–5).[40] These large numbers do not, of course, automatically mean that NGDOs enjoy a preponderant share of overall NGO resources. It must be recalled here that the top four NGOs are all *urgenciers* and, collectively, these leading humanitarian organisations account for about a third of total French NGO revenue (CCD, 2008). Yet, whilst many NGDOs are indeed tiny (with some 99 of the smallest NGOs, mainly developmental ones, receiving only M€36.9 or 4.8 per cent of total NGO resources in 2004–05), they have nonetheless included some much larger players within their ranks. Indeed, around half of the top 20 French NGOs can claim to be developmental in their focus.[41]

Fourth, French NGDOs engage in activities which are important in terms of the development of some of the poorest countries in the world. While French NGOs as a whole may not have all that much to spend (4.4 billion francs in 1999, a derisory sum compared to the 12 billion exchanged daily on the Stock Market (CCD, 2001: 13), this has been enough for them to undertake important advocacy and development education on issues, such as debt cancellation. It has also enabled them to carry out thousands of operations designed to promote the economic and socio-political development of scores of developing countries. French developmental volunteer organisations have, for their part, been annually responsible for sending some 2000 volunteers to 90 different countries. The largest *développementaliste*, the CCFD has, alone, engaged in 500 projects a year in 76 countries across Africa, the Indian Ocean, Latin America, the Caribbean, Asia, the South Pacific, as well as Central and Eastern Europe.[42] Significantly too, French NGDOs can play an important role by their mere presence in a developing country. They signal the interest of the North in creating a global civil society. They also promote democratic values and can be important sources of revenue (through tax returns and customs duties). Finally, they are also key employers of local personnel, with one estimate suggesting that French NGOs as a whole employ around 20,000 local staff across the developing world (Ryfman, 2004: 66).

Finally, French NGDOs offer valuable insights into the wider NGO sector in France and, indeed, other OECD countries. They are almost all members of NGO federations, and some 87 per cent are estimated to be involved in some kind of European or international network (World Bank, 2001: 44–5). To illustrate, the CCFD is part of the *Coopération Internationale pour le Développement et la Solidarité* or CIDSE (which includes leading Catholic NGOs, such as *Misereor* in Germany and *Développement et Paix* in Canada), whilst the CIMADE is a member of APRODEV, which incorporates Protestant organisations, such as Bread for the World.[43] For its part, FDH belongs to a federation of the same name, with affiliates in ten developed countries, and is, at the same time, part of a European advocacy network known as Eurostep. Following a similar logic, French child sponsorship agencies, such as *Écoliers du Monde-Aide et Action,* have joined Action Aid Alliance, which is present in six European countries, while *Enfants et Développement* is part of the Save the Children Alliance, which includes associations from 30 countries (*Commissariat Général,* 2002: 164).

French NGDOs are also members of other advocacy units at the European and national level. They are, for example, affiliated to CONCORD (formerly known as the *Comité de Liaison des ONG de Développement auprès de l'Union européenne* or CLONDG-UE), which is a Europe-wide grouping that includes over 1,600 NGOs from 27 European member states.[44] In the national context, French NGDOs are, moreover, members of numerous federations (*collectifs*), clusters (*plateformes*) and consortiums. The most significant of these is *Coordination SUD.*[45] This is the overarching French NGO federation, which was created in 1994 and now includes some 129 member organisations (see Annex B). *Coordination SUD* incorporates six smaller federations, three of which are of particular relevance to developmental NGOs: the CRID, which was formed in 1976 and now incorporates over 50 NGOs engaged in awareness-raising and overseas development work; the CLONG-V, which was formed in 1979 to promote the interests of volunteer agencies and includes 14 member organisations; and *Groupe Initiatives,* which was created in 1993 and comprises seven technical NGDOs, which offer, between them, a network of 270 professional staff for work throughout the developing world (see Annex B).

Other important federations include *Coordination d'Agen,* which was established in 1983 at the instigation of the *Guilde Européenne du Raid* and which incorporates 12 national level developmental and emergency NGOs;[46] the *Comité pour les Relations Nationales et Internationales des Associations de Jeunesse et d'Éducation Populaire* (CNAJEP), which was founded in 1969 and provides a forum for dialogue between the state and over 70 associations active in youth education work (Hatton, 2002: 164); as well as FORIM, the most recent federation, which was created in 2002 by immigrants who have settled in France and which brings together 29 organisations in France, with links to around 700 associations active in 20 developing countries (CCD, 2007: 14–15).[47]

French NGDOs have also formed geographic clusters of non-governmental actors concerned with particular countries (South Africa, Mexico, Palestine, Columbia, Madagascar and Burkina Faso), or with specific regions, such as South East Asia (*France-Pays du Mékong*), Central Africa (*Réseau France Afrique Centrale*) and Eastern Europe (*Comité pour les Partenariats avec l'Europe Orientale*). They have, equally, created thematic groupings. These include *Plateforme Dette et Développement*, which campaigns for massive multilateral and bilateral debt cancellation, *Plateforme de l'Éthique sur l'Étiquette*, which seeks to protect workers' rights and pushes for greater corporate social responsibility and *Plateforme d'Éducation au Développement et à la Solidarité Internationale* (EDUCASOL), which strives to enhance the effectiveness of development education work. Other coalitions include, *Plateforme Ensemble, Luttons contre le Sida en Afrique* (ELSA), which aims to improve North–South and South–South cooperation in the fight against AIDS; *Plateforme pour le Commerce Équitable*, which endeavours to promote fair trade and institute a charter for best practice; and *Plateforme Française: Publiez ce que vous Payez*, which calls on international mining companies to publish how much they pay in taxes and questionable commissions to the governments of the developing countries in which they are present. There are also groupings on poverty (*Action Mondiale contre la Pauvreté-France*) and movements supporting a stronger 'social economy' (*Le Mouvement pour l'Économie Solidaire*). Finally, there are consortiums of French NGDOs, established to deal with specific events, such as *Le Collectif Jo'Burg*, which brought together NGDOs and environmental groups to help prepare for the 2002 Johannesburg Summit on Sustainable Development.

Conclusion

This chapter has assessed the main methods used in defining 'NGOs' and has opted for a 'self-definitional' approach, as employed by international directories. Having explored the various techniques used to break down the non-profit sector into manageable units for analysis, this survey has argued that the most useful categorisation is by activity. The main distinction has been drawn between pressure groups, humanitarian NGOs and developmental NGOs. The latter category (*développementalistes* and volunteer agencies) have been identified as the main focus of this book. They are worthy of a separate study on a number of grounds: they are under-researched, an important part of the French social fabric, vital in terms of their advocacy and field work, and well placed – thanks to their membership of numerous international networks and national NGO forums – to shed light on wider trends in the French NGO sector and, indeed, the Northern non-governmental community as a whole. Whether or not French NGDOs do reflect and conform to wider NGO trends will be the subject of later chapters. First, though, there is a need to identify a theoretical perspective which can explain the recent evolution, or possibly non-evolution, of French NGDOs in the direction of these international trends. This quest for an analytical framework will be the main focus of Chapter 3.

3
The Quest for a Theoretical Framework

Northern NGOs active in the field of overseas development are value-laden organisations, which are driven by a host of different internal and external forces. It is, no doubt, because of their complexity and diversity that developmental NGOs in general and French NGDOs in particular have usually been discussed in the literature without reference to a theoretical framework. This should not, however, be taken to imply that this study is being written in a vacuum or that there have been no theoretical writings on Northern non-profit organisations or the voluntary sector as a whole. This chapter will draw on this literature to produce a brief review of the main theoretical approaches to non-profit organisations, namely market and government failure theories, historico-cultural approaches, International Relations (IR) perspectives and organisational theories. It will assess the value of each of these to this study of French NGDOs and will suggest that the most useful framework is Resource Dependence (RD) theory. It will conclude by laying down a working assumption on how Northern and, indeed, French NGOs might be expected to behave if they are acting in line with the RD perspective.

Useful theoretical perspectives

To begin with *market and government failure theories*, these functionalist perspectives represent the dominant paradigm in theories of the non-profit sector. These perspectives contend that non-profit organisations emerge because of the failure of the market or the state to provide goods or services at the level required by segments of the community. They take various forms and include public goods (or 'performance failure') theory (Weisbrod, 1974). Here, the focus is on products or services like clean air that are enjoyed by everyone for free. Clearly, if these goods were to be channelled through the market, they would not attract many customers, as non-profit actors would emerge who could supply these items free of charge. Alternatively, if these products were distributed through government agencies, this would fail to meet the demands of voters who had a greater than average demand for these products. Non-profit organisations would arise in this context to satisfy this residual demand.

A closely related perspective is 'contract failure' theory. According to Hansmann (1981), non-profit organisations are formed where ordinary contractual mechanisms do not provide consumers with adequate means to assess the services that firms' offer. Here, the idea is that for some services, such as care for the elderly, the purchaser is not the same as the consumer. In these circumstances, the normal workings of the market, which are based on informed consumer choice, do not apply and there is a need for an intermediary, namely the non-profit organisation, which can verify quality and reassure the purchaser, who is not the recipient of what he buys. A more politicised variant of 'failure' theory has been elaborated by Douglas (1987), who suggests that non-profit actors emerge, since they have scope to take on politically risky tasks that governments would rather avoid. In so doing, these organisations are said to ensure a more diverse society and a more legitimate government. This latter claim is, however, contested by Seibel (1990), who has argued that non-profit organisations help shield governments from responsibility for risky political programmes. They disguise but cannot solve the real problem.

Perhaps the main advantage of these functionalist perspectives is the fact that they are based on economic laws and hence are empirically testable. They have, moreover, been used to good effect to shed light on NGOs active in developing countries. Drawing on Douglas' work, Brown and Korten (1991: 47) argue that NGOs are 'particularly relevant' in developing countries 'as remedies for market failure' and as 'flexible antidotes' to the problems of state failure. 'Failure' theories do, however, have drawbacks which make them less useful for this study. First, they overstate the extent to which the emergence of a non-profit sector is a reactive and inevitable process. Indeed, Tvedt (1998: 4) even goes so far as to claim that developmental NGOs are not 'the natural outcome of state and market failures' but actually 'a product of deliberate state policies'. Second, these theories fail to account for significant variations in the nature and size of NNGO sectors (Tvedt, 1998: 58). Third, they understate the extent to which NNGOs operate increasingly alongside, rather than in place of, official aid agencies. Finally, they do not give enough consideration to the historical and cultural processes by which these actors come into being.

An alternative to the above perspectives is the *historico-cultural* (or *national style*) *approach*, which views NGOs as part of the organisational landscape of a specific country and as 'a reflection of its cultural and historical characteristics rather than as a functional product of market and state failures' (Tvedt, 1998: 59). This approach provides a mechanism for honing in on NGOs from a particular country and serves to counter the tendency in much of the literature 'to produce generalizations of "African NGOs", the "Asian NGO scene"' or, for that matter, the NNGO sector (Ibid: 60). It does, however, have drawbacks. To begin with, it is more like a typology than a theory, and is better suited to describing the character, rather than explaining the evolution, of the NGO sector. Furthermore, it tends 'to encourage superficial descriptions ... and create stereotypes' (Ibid). Relatedly, it focuses exclusively on the national context, ignoring key aspects of institutional isomorphism and the influence of international mega-trends in the donor community (Ibid: 64). It simply cannot explain why small NGOs in one country can be influenced by larger ones in another; and it is not, as such, well suited to explaining the propensity of French NGDOs to follow or ignore wider trends in NNGOs.

Tvedt (1998: 76) seeks to get round these shortcomings by combining this perspective with systems theory and viewing NGOs as an integral part of an 'aid channel' or social sub-system, which includes government actors and is clearly subject to wider international donor-led pressures. While complex, this approach works well in the case of Norway, where NGOs are marked by 'corporatism' and can be 'lumped together' with the state without too much difficulty. However, it may be of less value in the case of the French NGDO sub-sector, which has not traditionally enjoyed warm relations with the state.

Turning to *IR theories,* the realist school has traditionally neglected non-governmental actors and focused instead on states and 'high politics', notably security issues, as the key to international relations.[1] Keohane and Nye (1972) were the first to seriously challenge the realist paradigm and emphasise the need to analyse non-state actors alongside states. They developed a theory of 'world politics' and argued that NGOs 'internationalise' domestic politics and encourage international pluralism by linking together national interest groups within transnational structures. Putnam (1988) builds on these ideas by using 'two-level games' theory to explain the complex interaction between international diplomatic negotiations and pressures from domestic coalitions of NGOs and other actors. Risse-Kippen (1995) similarly focuses on questions of interdependence and attempts to identify the conditions under which transnational coalitions of non-state actors can successfully change government policies. Other theorists seek to explain the growing interdependence of non-state and state actors in terms of comparative advantages. The main strength of NGOs is said to lie in their political legitimacy (Willetts, 1982), their level of commitment (Clark, 1995: 510) or their understanding of human rights issues (Weiss and Gordenker, 1996). For Keck and Sikkink (1998), it is their detailed knowledge and their ability to frame, package and distribute information in effective ways across national frontiers which enable NGOs to ensure that states do not monopolise the debate on many issues.

International Relations theories are clearly valuable insofar as they shed light on the emerging role of NGOs within an international policy arena hitherto dominated entirely by states. They also underscore the growing phenomenon whereby NGOs engage, via transnational networks, in global advocacy campaigns designed to ensure a fairer system of global governance (e.g. the 1994 'Fifty Years is Enough' campaign by NNGOs which challenged the legitimacy of the World Bank and International Monetary Fund (IMF) to set the rules of the international economic system). Ultimately, however, most IR theories are less concerned with understanding NGOs than with explaining the complexity of the state-centric world of international relations. They examine NGOs in terms of their implications for national sovereignty (Cameron and Mackenzie, 1995) or global governance (Weiss and Gordenker, 1996). They also ignore variations in the size and strength of particular NGOs or non-state sectors and pay scant attention to differences in the nature of the NGO–state relationship in different national contexts. At the same time, they neglect to say much about the actions of small- to medium-sized NGOs (the vast majority in France), whose contact with the state and with supranational organisations is often limited. Finally, they fail to shed much light on why NGOs evolve, or choose not to evolve, over time. These questions cannot be ignored by this study. .

Turning finally to *organisational theories*, the focus here will be on the three perspectives singled out for attention by Powell and Friedkin (1987: 180–92) in a ground-breaking study by the former scholar (Powell, 1987). The first focuses on the 'dynamic qualities of organizations and their internal sub-systems' and explains organisational change in terms of reactions to internal conditions – in particular, growth, decline and crisis (Ibid: 181). Researchers in this tradition have shown how the growth in the structure of an organisation can necessitate changes in its management (Chandler, 1977) and how the procedures and goals of an organisation can be altered by staff pursuing personal ambitions or blindly following 'standard operating procedures' (Selznick, 1957). While this approach could offer valuable insights into the inner workings of NGOs, as well as the evolution of their structures and goals, it fails to take account of the external environment in which organisations operate and upon which they depend for vital resources. It is, no doubt, better suited to an in-depth analysis of a single organisation than to a survey of trends in the NGDO sub-sector as a whole.

The second theoretical perspective hones in on the external dimension and sees organisational change as a result of 'institutional isomorphism' or, as DiMaggio and Powell (1983) put it, 'processes that lead organizations in specific organizational fields to become more similar to one another over time, without necessarily becoming more efficient'. In effect, organisations working in particular institutional sectors interact more frequently with each other and come to see certain actors and their practices as dominant. These latter organisations serve as role models and help establish field-wide norms, to which all organisations should either adhere or face sanctions. Needless to say, this approach could be potentially relevant to this study, which asks whether French NGDOs have moved into line with trends in the NNGO 'organisational field'. But this theoretical tradition is ultimately better at describing than explaining organisational change. It also overplays the extent to which NGOs may be aware of any 'mega' trends or, indeed, of the benefits or penalties associated with field-wide norms. This is likely to be particularly true of the French NGDO scene, which is marked by a plethora of small, widely dispersed and relatively uninformed organisations.

The third perspective is RD theory, as developed by Pfeffer and Salancik (1978). This explains organisational change in terms of the propensity of organisations to alter their structures and goals with a view to obtaining the resources needed to survive. The RD perspective uses an open systems framework and, at its core, is the view that organisations will (and should) respond to the demands of those groups in the environment that control critical resources. They should, according to Pfeffer and Salancik (1978: 260), 'seek stability and certainty in their own resource exchanges' in order to 'ensure the organization's survival'. In other words, because organisations are not internally self-sufficient, they require resources from their wider context; they become, as such, dependent upon those elements that provide the most needed forms of support. The challenge is to secure stable resources whilst avoiding any awkward dependencies that these may generate.

The RD framework will be used in this study of French NGDOs. It obviates many of the problems associated with the theoretical perspectives outlined above. Thus, it is not too descriptive or overly concerned with processes of national and international governance, unlike, say, historico-cultural approaches or IR theories. Furthermore, it does not ignore internal value systems or the external environment, as 'failure' theories, in the former case, and some organisational perspectives, in the latter instance, are inclined to do. Instead, RD theory explains the actions of developmental and other NGOs in terms of their dynamic quest for resources. It hones in on these NGOs as actors in their own right and emphasises not only external factors, such as the resource environment, but also the internal dynamics of these organisations and their attachment to their original values.

A number of possible objections could be raised in relation to this theoretical framework. The first is that the RD perspective overstates the extent to which developmental and other NGOs are driven by resource acquisition. As Tvedt (1998: 132) observes 'Many NGDOs are based on strong ideological orientations, be they political or religious. They are value-rational rather than means-rational.' They would, therefore, reject comparisons between themselves and profit-driven companies, claiming that their primary concern lies not with resource acquisition but with improving quality of life, both spiritually and materially, in the poorest countries. These assertions are not without foundation, but they ignore the basic fact that all organisations are fundamentally driven by the need to acquire resources. For Pfeffer and Salancik (1978: 2), these are 'the key to organizational survival.' Fowler (2000: 53) makes the point even more starkly, stressing that

> Resources steer organisations. How you raise the resources you need, and from which source, has a strong influence on what an organisation is and what it can be. ..... The underlying point is that success at resource mobilisation is the standard by which NGDOs should be judged. This is the ultimate 'bottom line'. No resources means no organisation.

The second criticism is that RD theory exaggerates the extent to which NGOs act rationally in pursuit of their own economic self-interest. Thus, whereas private companies are unashamedly profit-driven and free 'to switch product lines, discontinue services, buy or sell other companies, all in the pursuit of greater financial return', the non-profit organization's mission – be it charitable, educational or cultural – places 'much greater limitations on its flexibility of action' (Powell and Friedkin, 1987: 180). This criticism is, however, misplaced, given that RD theory, although based on the rational choice paradigm, does not assume that organisations will act with 'perfect rationality'. Indeed, Pfeffer and Salancik (1978: 92) actually identify constraints on rational decision-making and they stress that some organisations 'may misread interdependence, misinterpret demands, remain committed to past practices, or fail to see the various conflicts in demands.' They add that 'Many organizations have gotten into difficulty by failing to understand those groups or organizations on which they depended for support or by failing to adjust their activities to ensure continued support' (Ibid: 19). Needless to say, those organisations which are unable or unwilling to 'enact', that is to say interpret correctly, their resource environment are likely to fail or fare less well than 'effective' organisations, which correctly read their context, showing a readiness 'to bend and shift with the prevailing political and economic winds' (Powell and Friedkin, 1987: 180).[2]

A third concern is that RD theory overstates the capacity of NGOs to engage in strategic behaviour and exert influence over their environment. Analysts subscribing to 'complexity theory' (e.g. Brown and Eisenhardt, 1998) contend that today's rapidly changing markets and political environments do not allow organisations to plan ahead strategically and force them merely to react to events. There is certainly some truth in this observation in the case of business organisations operating in competitive 'free' markets. Non-governmental organisations, too, lack the critical mass required to think long term, and NGO managers rarely have the luxury of time to engage in detailed forward planning. These organisations do, however, operate in 'markets' which are not quite as cut-throat as those of profit-making enterprises; and they do also benefit from substantial official funding alongside private donations. For these and other reasons, NGOs have enjoyed some scope for developing – consciously or intuitively – strategies to stabilise resource interdependencies. That they have this capacity can perhaps be seen most clearly in their increasing use of sophisticated strategic management and forward planning techniques (see Chapters 7 and 9).

The fourth, and in many ways the most telling, criticism is that RD theory is too uni-directional and tends to focus essentially on the resource-dependent actor (in this case, French NGDOs) and to assume that all the power and influence lies with the resource-rich actor (here the French state). He who pays the piper is deemed to call the tune. Yet, while the RD perspective does not offer any specific mechanism for explaining the actions of the resource-rich actor (a question which will be touched upon in subsequent chapters), it does, nonetheless, provide the tools for analysing how developmental and other NGOs can, using various resource stabilisation strategies (see Figure 3.1), seek to exert 'reverse influence' on the state and, for that matter, other resource-rich actors.

A final concern is that RD theory is really designed for analyses at the organisational unit level rather than for studies of collective trends across a whole sector. It is true that some of the earliest applications of the RD perspective involved in-depth surveys of individual organisations. Thus, Pfeffer and Salancik (1974) focused on the budget of one American university, whilst Powell and Friedkin (1986) honed in on a single American television station. More recent work has, however, shown that the RD framework can easily be extended from single organisations to sets of organisations, as well as to whole sectors and sub-sectors. It has, in fact, been used to shed light on the revenue diversification techniques of organisations across the American non-profit sector (Froelich, 1999). Equally, it has been applied to the resource 'partnerships' between NGOs in the Northern and Southern hemispheres (Hudock, 1999). RD theory has even been employed by Fowler (2000) to make some broad generalisations about the resource-related behaviour of all NGOs active in international relief and development.

A resource dependence model

The work of Alan Fowler and, in particular, his insightful study entitled *The Virtuous Spiral*, is particularly valuable for our purposes, as it includes a RD model of the behaviour of NGOs and their inter-relationships with their resource environment. Fowler's RD schema (2000: 63) usefully identifies the various resources and strategic 'options' available to these non-governmental actors, as well as the 'trade-offs' associated with different types of resource mobilisation. It has been drawn on in the conceptualisation of the RD model depicted in Figure 3.1. But it has also been adapted in two main ways. First, it has been streamlined to avoid this survey becoming embroiled in any detailed categorisation of the individual characteristics of different NGOs. Second, Fowler's model has been strengthened to include aspects of Pfeffer and Salancik's theory, which have been neglected in the RD

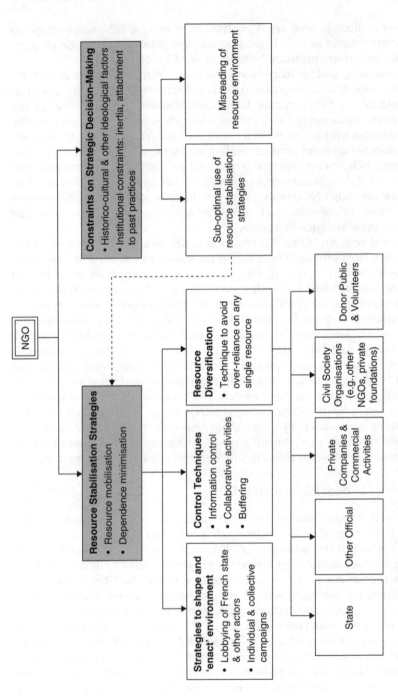

Figure 3.1 Resource dependence model of NNGOs and their environment

Source: Adapted from the work of Pfeffer and Salancik (1978) and Fowler (2000: 63).

literature, notably their focus on constraints on strategic decision-making and resource stabilisation strategies other than revenue diversification.

Our variant of the RD model is underpinned by four assumptions. The first is that resources may be financial or non-financial, but that the former are generally preferred by NGOs, given that they are more fungible (Fowler, 2000: 63). This point will not, however, be overplayed in this study, lest it should detract from the more important concept of 'criticality'. A 'critical resource' for any organisation is one without which it would find it difficult, in some cases impossible, to function. This may take the form of money, but it can also involve, for example, the efforts of unpaid volunteers.

The second assumption is that the different features of NGOs can affect the various strategies which these organisations adopt towards resource acquisition. In this context, Fowler (2000: 98) has spelt out six key characteristics of individual NGOs in relation to the resources they covet. These are autonomy, sensitivity, vulnerability, compatibility, consistency and criticality. In short, the more sensitive and vulnerable the NGO and the more critical the resource, the more likely the organisation is to be dependent on that revenue stream. Conversely, the more autonomous the organisation and the more consistent and compatible the resource is with the NGO's existing activities, the less likely it is to generate dependence. While insightful, this categorisation is too detailed for the purposes of this survey, which is not so much concerned with distinguishing between individual French developmental NGOs, as with identifying broad trends in their relations with the state, their procedures and their priorities. A key distinction, which should, nonetheless, be borne in mind, is between French NGDO autonomy from, and dependence on, the French government.

The third assumption requires more detailed elaboration. It contends that the characteristics of resources, and of the organisations offering them, are likely to affect the way in which these resources are pursued by NGOs. This point will be developed in further detail in Chapter 8, which will examine the advantages and drawbacks of all the key official funders and private donors, with specific reference to French NGDOs. For now, it should suffice to note that the main distinction, which is generally drawn in the nonprofit literature, is between resources that come from the state and those that emanate from private sources, above all the general public.

Drawing on reviews by, among others, Froelich (1999) and Fowler (2000), it is clear that *resources from the state* tend to be viewed with some suspicion by Northern and other NGOs. They are often deemed to lead to 'mission creep' and goal displacement (Liebschutz, 1992), especially where state initiatives are underfunded (Gronbjerg, 1993) or where there are funding delays; or, following a change of government, a reversal of earlier policies, which requires NGOs to plug the gaps with their own revenue (Ibid). State support is widely thought to lead to 'changes in the internal processes and ultimately in the structures of nonprofit organizations'; and to subject them to 'burdensome accountability procedures' and 'increased centralization' (Froelich, 1999: 257). As Froelich observes (Ibid: 256), 'In essence, the non-profit organization risks losing its unique character as it increasingly mirrors the structure and behavior of a government agency.'

At the same time, however, resources from the state – whether in the form of fiscal concessions, financial assistance or technical expertise – have real advantages, not least from a RD perspective. Above all, they are generally stable, secure, predictable and relatively long term (Gronbjerg, 1993). They are also more accessible than monies from, say, private foundations (Gronbjerg, 1991), and they are believed to help NGOs enjoy 'greater outreach and scale of operation; improved continuity to ongoing work; or reverse influence on the funder' (Fowler, 2000: 121). And while government support can impact upon NGO autonomy, it need not necessarily undermine the legitimacy of these actors in the eyes of private donors. Thus, as Froelich notes (1999: 236), 'government funding has been associated with both increases and decreases in private contributions'.

Turning to *private resources*, these are, by contrast, viewed much more favourably by non-profit actors. As Froelich (Ibid: 250) points out, 'Private contributions are revered in non-profit organisations as they provide not only income but indicate support for an organization's mission among constituents, thus representing legitimacy.' Private support may emanate from the general public, private foundations, commercial companies and revenue-generating activities. The most favoured forms of contribution are arguably funds from the donor public and the unpaid or underpaid contributions of volunteers. In part, this is because these donations of time and money, when aggregated together, usually offer a much larger flow of resources than any other private contribution. In part, it is also because, as Fowler (2000: 121) rightly remarks, 'Access to funds from civil society creates the least problems for NGDO identity' and offers 'better economic and civic rooting'.

However, there are also real drawbacks linked to private resources. In the case of the donor public, the disadvantages relate to volatility as a result of the fickleness of individual donors and the susceptibility of the entire sector to negative publicity, particularly in cases where unethical practices and other scandals are unearthed. Gronbjerg's 1992 and 1993 case studies describe the unpredictability and instability of individual donations, while Froelich (1999: 249), for her part, has noted how 'acquiring donations absorbed considerable staff, board, and volunteer effort, diverted attention from other vital functions, and steered selection of board members to those with personal networks for solicitation targets'. Another concern relates to goal displacement, which occurs when aims and activities are modified to satisfy the wishes of contributors, especially wealthy philanthropists.[3] As Froelich (Ibid: 250) has observed, 'a variation of goal displacement that is referred to as *creaming* involves shifting an organization's programs into areas that have greater appeal to donors'. She goes on to note that this can lead to a proliferation of projects that evoke emotions of sympathy and 'the inadvertent creation of stereotypes' as well as 'the shifting of priorities to match somewhat faddish funding criteria' (Ibid). Yet another unsolicited consequence of private donations can be changes to NGO procedures. Thus, as Fowler (2000: 121) has made clear, 'Finance from individuals creates a stronger demand on NGDOs to demonstrate adequate performance in relation to fund-raising messages. It also calls for cost control and good "marketing" in relation to the issue of overheads'.

The final assumption underpinning our RD model is that organisations – in this case NGOs – are primarily engaged in strategies to stabilise resources (especially critical resources) and to control, as far as possible, their environment. These strategies tend to be referred to interchangeably, in writings on the non-profit sector, as 'resource mobilisation' and 'dependence minimisation' techniques. In reality, of course, the former is really a supply-led strategy designed to secure resources available in an environment, irrespective of any dependencies which that process might create (Fowler, 2000). By contrast, dependence minimisation is a demand-led approach aimed at limiting demands and dependencies created by resource acquisition (Ibid). It should, nonetheless, be clear that the two strategies are not only inextricably entwined, but also deployed simultaneously by NGOs. The clearest illustration is perhaps the use by NGOs of resource diversification techniques which are, at one and the same time, an effort to mobilise resources and to avoid over-reliance on any single source.

In line with conventional thinking in NGO circles, it will be assumed in this survey that resource mobilisation and dependence minimisation are two sides of the same coin, that is to say, part of a general strategy which is designed to stabilise resource flows. Needless to say, this approach can take various forms or, as Fowler puts it, offer up several different 'options'. One such option is for NGOs to seek to shape their environment by lobbying their own state or other official actors. NGOs may campaign for more official funding or strive to alter the norms by which their projects are evaluated by the state. They may also endeavour to alter the context in which they operate either by engaging in development education work, which should help generate higher donations and secure future volunteers for NGOs, or by effecting a shift in the locus of their activities towards, say, more emergency relief work or longer-term development work.

A second approach involves controlling demands on the organisation. This can involve attempts to 'co-opt' funders (e.g. through an exchange of personnel between NGOs and the state); or through a process known as 'buffering', where NGOs emphasise their 'unique selling point' or particular specialism, which cannot be easily replicated elsewhere in the sector.[4] It may also include NGO efforts to control, even manipulate, the information they disclose, not least about activities such as failed projects or critical evaluations of their programmes. Finally, it may revolve around collaborative actions, whereby NGOs join with other non-state actors, either to protect themselves from excessive demands by funders or to share expertise which will help them improve or simply 'scale up' their operations. In some cases, NGOs may even endeavour to 'contractualise' their relations with funders over a number of years in order to guard against short-termism.

The last method, resource diversification (RDVN), involves efforts to ensure 'proportionality' and avoid 'excessive reliance on a single source of funding not controlled by the organisation.' As Pfeffer and Salancik (1978: 272–3) argue

> Dependence diminishes through diversification .... By having numerous interests make demands on the organization, the organization reduces its need to respond to any specific interest because each represents only a small part of the total organization and its activities. While there are still resource acquisition consequences of not complying, the effects are diminished.

Conclusion

This chapter began by reviewing the main theoretical perspectives that have been applied in the context of NNGOs. It suggested that, while many of these theories could be used to shed light on the workings and evolution of French NGDOs, they all suffer from important drawbacks. Resource dependence theory was also found to have shortcomings, but these were shown to be easily overcome and outweighed by the strengths of this approach. This perspective and the model elaborated above were said to be based on a number of assumptions about the nature of resources, the characteristics of the organisations providing those resources, and the strategies adopted by NGOs in pursuit of this revenue and other forms of support.

Having set out our interpretation of the RD model, it is worth asking how Northern and, indeed, French NGOs might be expected to have evolved over the global era if they have, indeed, been adhering to the basic tenets of RD theory. There are no clear-cut answers to this question in any of the writings on the non-profit sector which employ the RD framework. Needless to say, this literature does warn of the dangers of co-optation by the state (Fowler, 2000: 102–8; Froelich, 1999: 254–7). It does, relatedly, highlight the dilemma inherent in the 'state funding paradox', namely the fact that the state's resources are attractive but can also threaten autonomy (Themudo, 2002; Hudock, 1999). However, on balance, the literature tends to suggest that, from a RD perspective at least, NGOs might normally be expected to seek out and embrace government support. In this context, Gronbjerg (1993) has shown how state finance is more predictable and stable than other types of income. Themudo (2002) has argued that that 'because of its reliability, state funding reduces resource uncertainty and frees [up] NGOs to pursue their mission'. For his part, Fowler (2000: 122) has contended that 'Finance from government is a legitimate claim for NGDOs to make. In negotiating agreements, NGDOs can complement or collaborate with government agencies'. Finally, as Froelich (1999: 259) has put it

> A revenue strategy anchored by government funding exhibits low revenue volatility. Furthermore, a stable relationship with government can allow scope for reverse influence. In general, the pressure on NGDOs to seek out and/or accept funding is considerable.

It would appear from the above discussion, and from our earlier overview of the relative benefits and drawbacks of resources from the state and from private sources, that there is a strong RD-related case for anticipating that NGOs might normally gravitate closer to the state and actively seek out the kind of long-term, micro- and macro-level resources which it offers. At the risk of grossly oversimplifying, this crude working assumption would certainly seem to be borne out by what appears from our opening chapter to be happening in much of the NNGO sector, where there is evidence of NNGOs moving closer to the state (as a resource-rich actor), professionalising (as a means of better accessing government resources) and undertaking more of a service delivery role on the part of the state (as a potential paymaster). But can the same be true of French NGDOs and their relations with the French authorities? Have they, as RD theory might suggest, been moving closer to the state and actively pursuing the resources it offers? Or have they been prioritising a different critical resource, whose demands may even conflict with those of the state? This question will be central to Chapter 4 and, indeed, to the rest of this study.

4
French NGDOs and their Resource Landscape

It is now a commonplace in the literature on NGOs to note that 'he who pays the piper calls the tune'. In line with this thinking, it was suggested in the last chapter that NNGOs, if acting in line with RD theory, might normally be expected to move closer to the state. This crude working hypothesis was based upon the assumption that the state offers stable, predictable resources and either is, or has the potential to become, a critical resource for NGOs. Whether or not this assumption holds true across the NNGO sector is a question which lies beyond the remit of this study. Suffice it to note, however, that the evidence presented in our introductory chapter does suggest that many NNGOs are willing to move closer to their central governments and that Northern states are increasingly prepared to take on the role of 'a', or even 'the' critical resource.

Yet, how accurate is this working hypothesis in relation to French developmental NGOs and the resource environment in which they operate in the global era? Can French NGDOs now rely on the state for substantial support and is the latter now a critical resource for these actors, with all the potential compromises and dependencies that government monies can entail? Or, do French NGDOs look elsewhere for support and cater for the demands of a quite different critical resource? This question will be at the heart of this chapter, which will provide information on the key French NGDO sources of revenue, namely the French central state, other official sources and private actors.

Before undertaking this survey, it is worth making two preliminary points. First, this chapter will only present raw data on the resources secured by French NGOs, with the full implications of these revenue streams not being explored until our RD analysis in Chapter 8. Second, the statistics provided here have not been disaggregated to separate out revenue acquired by developmental NGOs, *urgenciers* and pressure groups. Hence the term NGO will be used more frequently than NGDO throughout this chapter.

The French central state

To begin with the French central state, the most important point to note here is that this is not 'the' or even 'a' critical resource for most French NGOs. As Table 4.1 demonstrates, the French state has, in some years, provided as little as 7.3 per cent of total NGO resources. Its share of NGO revenue has, moreover, fallen over recent years, slipping from 13.3 per cent in 1991 to 8.2 per cent in 2004–05. The exceptionally low level of French support for NGOs is brought out more clearly through comparison with the levels of assistance offered by other Northern states. Thus, France has consistently channelled a lower percentage of its official aid budget to NGOs than any other 'Western' European state: less than 1 per cent, compared to a European average of around 5 per cent.[1] In some years, the French government has provided as little as 0.6 per cent of its overseas programme, which is the lowest level of support of all OECD countries and ten times less than the percentage figure offered by Denmark and Holland.[2]

While the French central state has remained far from generous, it has recently promised to double the amount of assistance routed through NGOs between 2004 and 2009 (*Cour des Comptes*, 2005). It has also begun to mount some semblance of a defence of its record on aid to NGOs.[3] It has, for example, pointed out that its funding has increased from M€46.2 in 1991 to M€56.1 in 2004–05, a rise of 21 per cent in absolute terms. The French government has, moreover, argued that it has performed better in terms of its aid to NGOs than its own figures suggest. Its level of financial support is, in fact, understated for a number of reasons: the absence of any agreed consolidated approach for calculating aid from different ministries; the tendency to count assistance from local government separately and the failure to include some support offered by embassies, whether in the form of officially sponsored projects (*projets d'état*) or projects financed through the Social Development Fund.[4] Indeed, one estimate suggests that, in 1999, central government assistance to NGOs should have been recorded as 500 million francs rather than 373 million.

A small amount of this French state assistance has emanated from the Ministries for Social Affairs, for Youth and Sport, and for Culture. The Ministry for Education has given more substantial support, significantly increasing, between 1994 and 1999, its aid for international development education activities carried out by French 'counties' or *académies*.[5] In 2000, it also funded the International Development Awareness Week to the tune of €68,600, with some of these monies going directly to French NGDOs (*Commissariat Général*, 2002: 138). Equally important has been the Ministry for Regional Development and the Environment, which has financed NGO development projects and awareness-raising activities, as well as

Table 4.1 Overview of official and private resources of French NGOs

	1991	1993	1995	1997	1999	2000–01	2002–03	2004–05
French state M€	46.2	37.2	43.5	52.9	48.3	57.7	53.4	56.1
French state %	*13.3*	*8.9*	*8.8*	*10.5*	*7.3*	*8.1*	*8.1*	*8.2*
Other Official M€	73.5	136	165	171	210	222	189.5	211.3
Other Official %	*21.2*	*32.5*	*33.5*	*33.9*	*31.6*	*31.3*	*28.7*	*30.8*
Private Actors M€	227	246	284	280	407	430	417.4	419.7
Private Actors %	*65*	*59*	*58*	*56*	*61*	*61*	*63*	*61*
Total	347	420	493	504	666	710	660.5	687.1

Source: Adapted from CCD (1992, 2001a, 2003, 2005, 2008). Note that, as with all the tables in this chapter, the data for 2004–05 has been brought into line with funding in previous years through the exclusion of the extra monies generated by the December 2004 South Asian tsunami.

contributing to the cost of NGO preparations for, and participation at, international conferences (Ibid: 139). It is not, however, always easy to work out how much of this Ministry's funding relates directly to developmental NGOs and how much goes to *urgenciers* and other associations. The same is true of assistance from the Ministry of Agriculture and Fisheries. While this Ministry has offered support to NGDOs, such as the CFSI (e.g. in 2000, almost €11,000 were granted towards the cost of organising a World Food Day), it appears to have channelled most of its aid to *urgenciers*, such as ACF (Ibid). It has even – in an effort to minimise bureaucratic delays to emergency food relief work – provided ACF with a structural subsidy every year since 1999 (Ibid: 118).[6]

A more important and growing source of funding has been the *Agence Française de Développement*. This aid agency reports to the Finance and Foreign Ministries and is geared towards productive investment projects. It has traditionally dealt directly with the governments of developing countries, according them grants and loans and leaving it to their discretion as to whether they employ French NGOs in a service delivery role. Over the last decade or so, however, the AFD has become more proactive in promoting the services of French NGOs to aid recipient governments, especially in areas of recognised NGO excellence, such as micro-credit. The AFD has also begun to provide more innovative forms of support, particularly since the late 1990s, when this agency inherited responsibility for health and education from the former Development Ministry. To illustrate, the AFD introduced, in 2001, the concept of 'investment partnership' projects. These provide legal and financial safeguards to French NGOs by ensuring that a contractual agreement is signed between the NGO providing the service and the host government benefiting from that service (*Commissariat Général*, 2002). The AFD also established, in October 2001, the first ever French government–NGO partnership framework agreement. This partnership is between the AFD and *Écoliers du Monde- Aide et Action* and seeks to develop, over time, primary education in West Africa and Madagascar. It is based on shared responsibility: *Écoliers du Monde* funds the 'social development' activities, while the AFD finances the infrastructural work, notably the building of schools. For all its innovations, however, this French government agency remains a comparatively small source of revenue for French NGOs. In 2005, it provided only M€4.4, which is less than 8 per cent of French central state support (CCD, 2008: 23). It also offered assistance to only 21 NGOs, most of which were medium-sized or large (Ibid).[7]

A much more significant source of funding has been the French Foreign Ministry, which, together with overseas embassies and aid missions, made up a massive 83 per cent of the total French central and local government budget for NGOs in 2004–05 (CCD, 2008: 22).[8] Some of this support has come from units which will not be central to this study. These include the *Délégation Humanitaire*, which was established in 2002 as a sub-division of the Foreign Ministry and which has focused almost exclusively on emergency assistance, giving 90 per cent of its funding to *urgenciers* (Interview with the *Délégation Humanitaire*, 2003). Other such units include French embassies and aid missions overseas. While these latter organs provided M€5.2 in 2005 in the way of decentralised credits, a large proportion of these monies was directed towards projects carried out by indigenous NGOs (CCD, 2008: 22).

Rather than looking at overseas missions or units dealing with emergency relief, the main focus of this survey will be on the 'International Development Division' of the Foreign Ministry. The *Directorat-Général de Coopération Internationale de Développement* or DGCID is all that remains of the French Development or 'Cooperation' Ministry after the Jospin aid reforms of 1998 – hence the appearance of 'zero entries' in Table 4.2. Within this Division, by far the largest source of funding for NGDOs has been the *Mission pour la Coopération Non-Gouvernementale* or MCNG, referred to as such throughout this book, even though it was restructured and renamed the *Mission d'Appui à l'Action Internationale des ONG* (MAAIONG) in March 2006. As will be seen in subsequent chapters, the MCNG has given logistical, technical and financial support, above all in the form of co-funding for development education, volunteering activities and overseas projects. It has also begun, under the terms of the 'new contractual arrangements', to provide more 'liberal' forms of backing to NGDOs involved in larger scale development programmes. Equally, the MCNG has offered 'window funding', whereby it identifies a priority (e.g. the AIDS pandemic in Cambodia or the political crisis in Haiti), sets up a thematic or geographic fund and then encourages NGOs to put forward suitable funding proposals. As a rule, however, this Foreign Ministry unit has continued to favour more restrictive forms of support, allocating most of its financial assistance to classic short-term projects, which are generally small, low-budget and easy to manage.

Other official sources

Turning to 'other official sources', these have risen dramatically over the global era from M€73.5 or 21.2 per cent of total NGO resources to M€211.3 or 30.8 per cent in 2004–05 (see Table 4.1). One such source is French local government (regional authorities, *départements*, *communes*). Needless to say, there could be a case for simply amalgamating the assistance provided to NGOs by France's local or 'territorial' authorities with the aid allocated by the French central government. However, it has been decided not to do so here for a number of reasons. To begin with, the income collected by France's territorial authorities comes from locally rather than centrally collected

Table 4.2 French central state funding of NGOs in M€ and in percentage terms

	1991	1993	1995	1997	1999	2000–01	2002–03	2004–05
Foreign Ministry M€	5.2	5.6	12.2	10.1	35.4	38.5	43.2	46.6
Foreign Ministry %	*4*	*3*	*6*	*4*	*14*	*13.8*	*18*	*17.5*
Development Ministry M€	31.3	23.6	24.9	29.7	0	0	0	0
Development Ministry %	*26*	*14*	*12*	*13*	*0*	*0*	*0*	*0*
Other ministries M€	4.3	5.8	1.7	3.1	5.5	4.4	4.6	9.6
Other ministries %	*4*	*3*	*1*	*1*	*2*	*1.6*	*1.8*	*3.6*
Other sources	5.5	2.1	4.7	10.1	7.5	14.8	5.8	4.5
Other sources %	*10*	*12*	*8*	*9*	*11*	*12.2*	*2.3*	*1.7*
Total central state M€	46.2	37.2	43.5	52.9	48.3	57.7	53.4	56.1

Source: Adapted from CCD (1992, 2001a, 2003, 2005, 2008). The 'other sources' are not specified by the CCD but they relate to central government funding for public bodies, such as the *Agence de l'Environnement et de la Maîtrise de l'Énergie*, the FONJEP and the *Fonds d'Action Sociale* (CCD, 1992: 32).

taxes. Furthermore, local authorities, particularly when they are dominated by political opposition parties, often have a quite different perspective on overseas development from that of the central state. Finally, local authorities in France are often viewed by French officials as being closer to French civil society than they are to the state apparatus (Interview with MCNG, 2003).[9] This can be inferred from the fact that the MCNG has traditionally provided co-funding, not only for NGDO projects, but also for 'decentralised cooperation' or local level overseas development work carried out by French local authorities. It is also clear from the French government's decision to include local authorities in the *Haut Conseil de la Coopération Internationale* (HCCI), a civil society advisory body to the French state established in 1999 (see Chapter 5).

As can be seen from Table 4.3, the revenue from French territorial authorities has risen from M€5.3 in 1991 to M€12.8 in 2004–05, with some regions, such as Île-de-France, being particularly proactive in this domain. Yet, while this form of assistance has been greatly under-reported, the actual sums involved have remained small, especially in the case of French *départements* and *communes*. In fact, even if local government aid were added to revenue from the central government, the total amount of French official assistance would still not represent a 'critical resource' for French NGOs. The bottom line is that local government funding has never made up more than 4.8 per cent of official funding for the NGO sector as a whole (see Table 4.3). It has, moreover, only been a significant source of revenue for small NGOs,

Table 4.3 French local government funding of NGOs in M€ and as percentage of total official resources

	1991	1993	1995	1997	1999	2000–01	2002–03	2004–05
Regions M€	–	–	–	–	–	–	3.7	3.75
Regions (% official resources)	–	–	–	–	–	–	*1.8*	*1.4*
Départements M€	–	–	–	–	–	–	0.9	1.7
Départements (% off. res.)	–	–	–	–	–	–	*0.4*	*0.7*
Communes M€	–	–	–	–	–	–	0.8	1.5
Communes (% off. res.)	–	–	–	–	–	–	*0.4*	*0.6*
Total local authorities M€	5.3	4.3	6.9	7.6	9.6	6.6	8.2	12.8
Total % official resources	*4.4*	*2.5*	*3.3*	*3.1*	*3.7*	*2.4*	*3.5*	*4.8*

Source: Adapted from CCD (1992, 2001a, 2003, 2005, 2008). No breakdown of figures available for 1991 to 2000–01 inclusive.

constituting around 30 per cent of total official funding for NGOs with an income below €200,000 (CCD, 2008: 24).

A much more important official source of revenue has been bilateral and international donor agencies. Taken together, these represent the second largest source of funding for French NGOs overall. As can be deduced from Tables 4.1 and 4.3, these agencies now make up over a quarter of overall French NGO resources and around three-quarters of all official income. The amount they are providing has almost tripled from M€66.8 in 1991 to M€198.6 in 2004–05 (see Table 4.4).[10]

Turning first to bilateral donors, these actors have dramatically increased their contribution to French NGOs from M€1.1 in 1991 to M€42.4 in 2004–05. Although a precise breakdown is not available, official statistics show that the United States is the largest single donor, giving M€14 in 2005. European states, such as the United Kingdom, Switzerland, Germany, Sweden, Italy and Holland, have supplied some M€16, while other countries, such as Canada and Japan have provided the remaining M€14.8 (CCD, 2008: 27).

Taken collectively, international organisations (IOs) are an even more important source of revenue. One of the least generous of these bodies from the perspective of French NGOs has been the World Bank. While the Bank, together with the main regional banks for Africa, Asia and the Americas, has increased its contribution to French NGOs since the start of the millennium (from 1 per cent to 5.9 per cent of international resources), its funding actually fell from 29 to 10 million francs between 1991 and 1999 (CCD, 2001a: 12). Furthermore, according to a major World Bank study, only 21 of the 76 French NGOs surveyed were found to have already collaborated on the ground with the Bank (World Bank, 2001: 46). The same report (Ibid: 48) also indicated that only 11 French NGOs had enjoyed co-funding from the Bank for 'classic' development projects, that no more than 12 had benefited from Bank Trust funds and that only two had received support with the cost of publications.[11]

As for the UN, this is normally the second most important provider of international resources to French NGOs. Its share of these resources has risen from 9.8 per cent in 1993 (M€11.1) to 11.9 per cent (M€23.6) in 2004–05. Traditionally, the UN has channelled most of its assistance through *urgenciers*. Thus, in 2004–05, it concentrated 85 per cent of its allocation to the French NGO sector on only five organisations, most of which were essentially active in humanitarian assistance. In the same year, the UNHCR focused its support on ten French NGOs and the World Food Programme on six organisations, most of which were, once again, *urgenciers* (Ibid). Other UN agencies such as the UNDP, UNICEF and the United Nations Industrial Development Organization (UNIDO) have, however, attenuated this trend by spreading their aid more evenly across 37 French NGOs, many of which were developmental in their focus (CCD, 2008: 26).[12] These same agencies

Table 4.4 International funding of French NGOs in M€ and as a percentage of international resources

	1991	1993	1995	1997	1999	2001	2002–03	2004–05
DG Development/EuropeAid M€	–	19.2	34.6	27.8	32.6	22.1	33.1	49.7
DG Development/EuropeAid %	–	*17*	*25*	*17*	*18*	*12*	*20.3*	*25*
DG External Relations M€	–	–	4.7	5.3	6.7	23.7	2.3	0
DG External Relations %	–	–	*3.5*	*3*	*4*	*13*	*1.3*	*0*
ECHO M€	–	48.6	59.6	55.3	77.8	67.4	65.6	62.2
ECHO %	–	*43*	*43.5*	*34*	*43*	*36*	*40.3*	*31.3*
Other EU M€	–	13.6	7.3	38.3	10.7	10.4	8.3	5.4
Other EU %	–	*12*	*5*	*23.5*	*6*	*5.5*	*4.8*	*2.7*
EU sub-total	**50.9**	**81.4**	**106.3**	**126.7**	**127.8**	**123.6**	**109.3**	**117.3**
EU as % of official funding	–	*72*	*77*	*77.5*	*71*	*66.5*	*67*	*59.1*
UNHCR M€	2.7	9.6	11.6	4.7	9.5	7.8	6.9	4.3
UNHCR %	–	*8.5*	*8.5*	*3*	*5*	*4*	*4*	*2.2*
WFP M€	–	–	1.1	6.9	8.4	1.3	4.6	10.2
WFP %	–	–	*1*	*4*	*5*	*1*	*3*	*5.1*
Other UN M€	1.5	1.5	2.3	5.2	5.3	18.1	5.9	9.1
Other UN %	–	*1.5*	*1.5*	*3*	*3*	*10*	*3.5*	*4.6*
UN sub-total M€	**4.3**	**11.1**	**15**	**16.8**	**23.2**	**27.2**	**17.4**	**23.6**
UN sub-total %	–	*9.8*	*10.9*	*10.3*	*13.0*	*14.6*	*10.6*	*11.9*
Other (e.g. World Bank) M€	4.4	1.4	1.2	2.3	1.5	2.4	7.3	15.3
Other (e.g. World Bank) %	–	*1*	*1*	*1.5*	*1*	*1*	*4.5*	*7.7*
Bilateral donors M€	1.1	18.9	14.8	17.7	26.7	32.9	29.4	42.4
Bilateral donors %	–	*16.5*	*11*	*11*	*15*	*17.5*	*18*	*21.3*
International sources M€	**66.8**	**112.8**	**137.3**	**163.5**	**179.2**	**186.1**	**163.4**	**198.6**
International sources (% total official)	–	*65.1*	*65.9*	*73.0*	*69.4*	*66.5*	*67.3*	*74.3*

Source: Adapted from CCD (1992, 2001a, 2003, 2005, 2008). Figures for 1991 and 1993 are incomplete. 'Other EU' refers to other Directorates within the European Commission and includes monies from the *Fonds Social Européen* and the Leonardo programme. The emergence of EuropeAid as a unitary aid channel accounts for the zero entry alongside DG External Relations in 2004–05.

have also stepped up their assistance considerably from M€1.5 in 1991 to M€9.1 in 2004–05 (see Table 4.4).

By far the most important source is the European Union (EU), or more specifically the European Commission, which has seen its contribution to French NGOs more than double from M€50.9 in 1991 to M€117.3 in 2004–05. In recent years, it has typically represented between two-thirds and three-quarters of total international funding and just under half of all official income received by French NGOs (CCD, 2001a: 12). The levels of EU support rose particularly sharply following the creation, in 1992, of the European Commission Humanitarian Office (ECHO), which directs assistance (M€57.5 in 2005) exclusively to NGOs engaging in humanitarian relief and rehabilitation work. This organisation has, moreover, shown its capacity to step up its aid dramatically in times of crisis (e.g. the 1994 Rwandan genocide, the 1999 Kosovo war and 2004 South Asian tsunami). It has not, however, been the only part of the EU to provide large quantities of resources to the French NGO sector. The other main funders have been the Directorate-General (DG) for External Relations and, above all, the DG for Development, operating through the budgetary line B7-6000. These latter units have offered substantial levels of support (some M€49.7 in 2004–05) to developmental and other French NGOs.[13] They have, in fact, now been combined to form a single channel for delivering aid, namely EuropeAid (Cooperation Office), which was established in January 2001 as part of a reform of the European external assistance programme (see Table 4.4).[14]

Private sources

As can be seen from Table 4.1, private support makes up the preponderant share of total French NGO revenue. While this type of funding has fallen slightly as a percentage of total NGO resources (down from 65 per cent in 1991 to 61 per cent in 2004–05), this is really only an arithmetic consequence of two main factors. First, income from international sources has risen so dramatically over the last 15 years that it now makes up around 30 per cent of overall NGO revenue. Second, official statistics for 2004–05 have been adjusted to exclude the massive boost in private funding generated by the South Asian tsunami. The underlying truth is that private resources have held up well over the last decade or so, with the rate of growth averaging 10 per cent a year between 1991 and 1999 (CCD, 2001) and with total income almost doubling from M€214 in 1991 to around M€443 in 2005.

The three broad categories of private support will be taken here to be: private companies and consumers of NGO commercial activities; private foundations and other civil society organisations; and, lastly, the donor public and the grassroots activist base of NGOs. This last grouping will be seen to constitute the critical resource.

Private companies and consumers of commercial products

To begin with private companies, whether they are French or multinationals based in France, these can provide support in the form of sponsorship of events (*le parrainage*), the transfer of staff and technical expertise (*le mécénat*) or in-kind benefits (advertising space, toll free phone lines or, indeed, price reductions on plane tickets, insurance and vaccinations for volunteers).[15] In some cases, longer-term support is available in the form of partnerships between French companies and NGOs, notably *urgenciers* and environmental NGOs. Recent examples include partnerships between ACF and *Magasins U* and between WWF-France and the cement manufacturer Lafarge.[16]

Overall, support from companies represents a growing proportion of total income. It has increased from around 2 per cent of private resources in 1991 to 5.8 per cent in 2005 (see Table 4.5). This type of assistance is also now more widespread and benefits some 57 NGOs in total (CCD, 2008: 15). As a rule, however, French corporate contributions to NGOs involved in international development remain small compared to the sums allocated to *urgenciers* and to the sponsorship monies directed towards French educational, cultural and sporting associations. The paltry nature of this form of support can best be gauged by comparison with the volumes of money available from commercial firms in Anglo-American NGOs. By way of illustration, corporate donations to French voluntary associations as a whole approximated to M€340 in 2000, compared to a staggering \$9 billion for their American counterparts in the same year (Rubio, 2004: 280).

Turning to consumers of NGO 'commercial' services and products, this category is, in many ways, hard to distinguish from the 'donor public' in general. The somewhat artificial distinction, which will be drawn here, will be between, in the former case, individuals and organisations effecting the immediate purchase of a specific good or service at, or above, the market rate; and, in the latter case, individuals or other actors making a donation, either in the form of cash, a legacy or a direct debit, in exchange for a much vaguer promise of well doing by NGOs at some point in the future. The first of these two exchanges involves something approximating to a commercial transaction; and may, as such, be governed by different fiscal rules and legislation. Examples include the sale of fair trade products at the hundred or so outlets of the *Fédération Artisans du Monde* (Ibid: 177), as well as the various ethical savings schemes offered by NGDOs, such as the CCFD, SC-CF, *TDH-France*, FDH, CIMADE, in conjunction with cooperative banks, such as the *Crédit Coopératif*. These latter schemes revolve around

Table 4.5 NGO revenue from private sources in M€

	1991	1992	1999	2000	2001	2004	2005
Cash donations	131.1	141.9	247	247.1	270.4	234.6	259
Cash donations (%)	*61.4*	*60.2*	*60.6*	*58.9*	*61.5*	*59.4*	*61.3*
Legacies, gifts	10.8	7.7	12.8	14.2	14.6	15.3	17.7
Legacies, gifts (%)	*5.1*	*3.3*	*3.1*	*3.4*	*3.3*	*3.9*	*4.2*
Other support from the public	–	–	19.4	38.2	29.3	31.4	30.3
Other support from the public (%)	–	–	*4.8*	*9.1*	*6.7*	*7.9*	*7.2*
Sub-total donor public	**141.9**	**149.6**	**279.2**	**288.9**	**314.3**	**281.3**	**307**
Sub-total donor public (%)	***66.4***	***63.4***	***68.5***	***68.9***	***71.4***	***71.2***	***72.6***
Other civil society organisations	11.1	12.9	22.8	30.4	27.3	55.7	68.8
Other civil society organisations (%)	*5.2*	*5.5*	*5.6*	*7.2*	*6.2*	*12.0*	*14.4*
Companies (sponsorship etc)	4.2	3.8	26.5	16.1	14.2	17.5	24.6
Companies (sponsorship etc) (%)	*2.0*	*1.6*	*6.5*	*3.8*	*3.2*	*4.4*	*5.8*
Consumers of NGO products & services	9.4	11.4	8.9	20.5	11.4	8.3	8.5
Consumers of NGO products & services (%)	*4.4*	*4.8*	*2.2*	*4.9*	*2.6*	*4.2*	*3.9*
Membership fees	2.6	2.7	2.6	5.4	5.4	7.2	7.7
Membership fees (%)	*1.2*	*1.1*	*0.6*	*1.3*	*1.2*	*1.8*	*1.8*
Financial products	10.6	11.6	10.4	8.6	9.3	17.7	20.8
Financial products (%)	*5.0*	*4.9*	*2.6*	*2.1*	*2.1*	*4.5*	*4.9*

(Continued)

Table 4.5 Continued

	1991	1992	1999	2000	2001	2004	2005
Sub-total of consumer purchases	**22.6**	**25.7**	**21.9**	**34.5**	**26.1**	**33.2**	**43.9**
Sub-total of consumer purchases (%)	*10.6*	*10.9*	*5.4*	*8.2*	*5.9*	*8.4*	*9.9*
Exceptional products	–	–	4.8	4.5	4.5	7.3	6.9
Exceptional products (%)	–	–	*1.2*	*1.1*	*1.0*	*1.8*	*1.6*
Other resources & write-back of provisions	33.9	38.8	52.2	54.5	53.5	–	–
Other resources & write-back of provisions	15.9	16.5	12.8	13.0	12.2	–	–
Total private resources	**213.6**	**235.8**	**407.4**	**419.4**	**439.9**	**395.0**	**444.3**

Source: Adapted from CCD (1992, 2001a, 2003, 2005, 2008). 'Other support from the public' relates to revenue raised by concerts, fairs and the sale of recycled products. 'Other civil society organisations' are NGOs and foundations. 'Consumers of NGO products' include private educational and health establishments. 'Financial products' relate to ethical investments. 'Exceptional products' are surpluses carried forward from the previous financial year. 'Write-back of provisions' (where data is available) relates to the recovery of monies set aside for contingency purposes. The incomplete figures for 1991 and 1992 have been converted at the rate of one French franc to €0.143 and €0.144, respectively (http://fxtop.com/en/cnvhisto.php3).

ethical investment products, such as *Faim et Développement* and *Épargne Solidaire* (where savers forego a proportion of the interest earned by unit trusts, and where the trusts themselves are usually made up of government bonds rather than company shares).[17] Many other products are harder to classify and include NGO membership fees and revenue from the sale of magazine subscriptions, greetings cards, books, badges, recovered items and various training services supplied to other NGOs by federations, such as *Coordination SUD*.[18]

Overall this 'commercial' income represents for most, though by no means all NGOs, a minor share of French NGO revenue: in 2005, it amounted to M€43.9 or 9.9 per cent of total private resources.[19] This figure can be seen to be particularly small when compared with the amounts raised by OXFAM, which, with over 400 shops in the United Kingdom alone (Rubio, 2004: 184), generated some £75 million in trading income in 2006–07.[20]

Private foundations and other civil society organisations

As for revenue from civil society organisations, this can, for example, come from French and other NNGOs. It may include financial support to help smaller NGOs muster together the minimum stake required by the Foreign Ministry before it is prepared to co-fund a project proposal. The scale of this civil society support is hard to ascertain, given how poor NGO records are on this matter. The figures are further confused by the fact that some of the resource transfers offered by 'donor NGOs' were, in the first instance, monies received by them in the form of state subsidies (*Cour des Comptes*, 2005). Overall, however, this would seem to be a marginal resource for the vast majority of French NGOs. Thus, according to the CCD (2008: 14), a single (unnamed) organisation benefited from M€48.3 in 2005, leaving the rest of the NGO sector to share the remaining M€12.4.

Another source of civil society funding takes the form of private foundations. In the French context, these include the *Fondation de France*, which financed, in 2005, some 68 projects, 39 of which were carried out by associations (Blum, 2007: 50), and the *Fondation pour la Recherche Médicale*, whose main focus is on research into pathological illnesses affecting populations in both the Northern and Southern hemispheres. Other important foundations are the *Fondation Abbé Pierre pour le Logement des Défavorisés*, which fights social exclusion in the North and South, the *Fondation Raoul Follereau*, which tackles leprosy in all its physical and social forms and, finally, the *Fondation Max Havelaar*, which is now, as will be seen in Chapter 7, the leading fair trade NGO. Total NGO revenue from these bodies was estimated at around M€8 in 2005 and has remained relatively stagnant over the years.[21] This is somewhat inevitable given the small number of such foundations in France and given that such bodies are not deeply entrenched in French traditions. To illustrate, with only 486 legally accredited foundations, France finds itself well behind countries, such as the United States, with 12,000, the United Kingdom, with 3,000 charity trusts, and Germany, with 2,000 foundations, some of which dominate the NGO scene (Blum, 2005: 9). A similar observation can be made about the philanthropic in-kind support provided by celebrities. There have, of course, been French figures from the entertainment industry involved in international humanitarian causes. Thus, for example, the French actresses, Isabel Adjani and Adriana Karembeu offered support, respectively, to campaigns for ACF in 1985 and the French Red Cross in 2002. There has, however, been no equivalent on the French scene to the likes of Sir Bob Geldoff, Bono or Princess Diana, and nothing that quite approximates to the kind of highly mediatised, even sensationalised campaigning and fund-raising activities that are common in the United Kingdom and the United States.

The donor public and NGO volunteer base

The donor public and grassroots activist base will be taken here to represent the critical resource of French NGOs. The former represents, collectively, the single largest proportion of their income, while the latter constitutes a pool of human resources, without which NGOs could not perform at anywhere near their current levels.

Revenue from the donor public can come in many different financial formats. These include cash donations, legacies, gifts and donations in kind (a format which is no longer actively encouraged by most NGOs because of the problems associated with finding compatible beneficiaries for gifts of specific medicines, Western clothing items and second-hand books).[22] As will be demonstrated in Chapter 6, these monies are collected by a variety of means, including church collections (especially by the likes of the CCFD and SC-CF), fund-raising in the street (e.g. *Fondation Raoul Follereau*), mail-shots (the most common method), telethons (notably the annual fund-raising event by *Association Française contre les Myopathies*) and other appeals (e.g. *SidaAction*).[23]

As can be seen from Table 4.5, these individual donations amounted cumulatively to M€307 in 2005 and represented 72.6 per cent of total private resources (CCD, 2008: 12). The actual percentage figure is higher than this given that the year-on-year statistics have been harmonised by the CCD to exclude exceptional events, such as the South Asian tsunami. This natural catastrophe generated an additional M€60.3 in NGO private funding in 2004 and a further M€207.7 in 2005 (CCD, 2008: 50).

As for the contributions by the NGO activist base, it is extremely difficult to quantify the actual cost of services by an estimated 250,000
NGO members or *adhérents*.[24] It is even harder to calculate the financial
value of the efforts of *bénévoles,* that is, the tens of thousands of volunteers based in France, who make their services available on a sporadic
basis (CCD, 1995: 49).[25] Similarly, it is not easy to put a figure on the
unpaid overtime by 2,000 paid French NGO staff or indeed the potential loss of earnings of around 2,000 'development volunteers', or of a
further 2,000 'emergency volunteers', most of which work overseas on
stipends or salaries that are below the market rate (CCD, 2008: 35). These
unpaid and underpaid efforts are part of the capital or *fonds propres* of
French NGOs and they represent the very 'core and foundation of associative life' (Blum, 2005: 11). The contribution of *bénévoles* alone was
estimated by the CCD to equate to unpaid work worth at least M€155 in
2005 (CCD, 2008: 34). However, as the CCD itself admits, this guessti-
mate massively underestimates the true figure, as it is based only on the
efforts of volunteers based in head offices and not in France's myriad of
local and regional groups.

While the exact worth of such contributions may be hard to compute, what
is clear is that the scale of this voluntary base is huge. To take, for example,
the CRID, which is the federation of NGDOs operating through partners in
developing countries, this alone comprises a network of some 7,500 local
groups involving 180,000 volunteers (*bénévoles*).[26] For its part, FDH has 25
local groups, *TDH-France* has 40, *Solidarité Laïque* has 54 regional delegations
and the CCFD and *Secours Catholique* each have around 100 committees or
delegations in different dioceses across France (Hatton, 2002: 159). Overall,
it should be added that French NGOs have the highest percentage of volunteers in the whole of Europe. With an estimated 99 per cent of all personnel
being voluntary, France has a far higher proportion of volunteers than, say,
Britain (74 per cent), Sweden (56 per cent) or Austria (3 per cent) (Woods,
2000: 19).

Conclusion

This chapter began by recalling our crude working assumption that if
NNGOs are adhering to the tenets of RD theory, they might be expected
to move closer to the state as a source of stable long-term resources. It wondered whether such a claim could be meaningful in the case of French
NGOs and set out briefly the resource landscape of these actors. It found
that the critical resource for French NGOs as a whole is not the state but
the donor public and their own grassroots activists. Needless to say, the
latter are more militant and likely to impose demands on NGOs, which

conflict with those of the state and which make closer collaboration with central government more problematic. Whether or not this overall balance of resources has played a determining role in the recent evolution of French developmental NGOs will be the key question addressed in our RD analysis in Chapter 8. For now, however, it is imperative to turn to the empirical data and to establish whether or not French NGDOs have fallen in line with the wider international trends outlined in our introductory chapter. This issue will be central to Chapters 5 to 7.

5
French NGDOs and the State: Paving the Way for a New Partnership?

Our introductory chapter suggested that three broad trends have marked the NNGOs sector over the last decade and a half. The first of these involved a general improvement in the terms and conditions of the relationship between NNGOs and the state. Whether or not such a development has taken place widely across the NNGO sector is a question which must ultimately be left to future researchers. For the purposes of this survey, it should suffice to note that this trend has been widely observed in the non-profit literature and that it has even formed the subject of seminal studies by Hulme and Edwards (1997) and Smillie *et al.* (1999).

Yet, how true is such an observation of French NGOs and their relationship with the state? Is the French Foreign Ministry right to boast (on its website) of a 'regular and sustained dialogue' now under way between French NGOs and the state.[1] Are French NGOs correct to claim that 'the conditions are in place for the French authorities and French NGOs to reach a certain maturity in terms of their partnership'.[2] How real, in fact, is this rapport? These questions will be the central concern of this chapter, which will begin by showing briefly how the legal, financial and consultative basis of ties between the French state and NGOs, particularly developmental NGOs, were poor in the decades following France's decolonisation of much of black Africa. It will go on to demonstrate how the French government has made overtures towards French NGOs as a whole over the global era. It will then hone in on French NGDOs and show how these actors have welcomed recent concessions from the state, whilst seeing them as insufficient to lay the basis of a genuine partnership. Finally, it will conclude by pointing to some possible implications of these findings for our RD analysis in Chapter 8.

Before undertaking this survey, it is imperative to set out some caveats. The first is that it is misleading to talk of the 'state' as if it were a monolithic entity, with a single unified approach towards NGOs. As noted in Chapter 4, the French state is a hydra-headed actor, which comprises a range of ministries and other government organs, many of which provide funding to, and enjoy some kind of relationship with, French NGOs.

The second proviso is that it is hard to generalise about the attitude of French developmental NGOs towards closer cooperation with the state. As demonstrated in Chapter 2, French NGOs generally and French NGDOs specifically are diverse and densely populated. There is, quite simply, no such thing as a 'typical NGO' (Beigbeder, 1992: 7), as these actors range in size from miniscule to large and often have very different origins and traditions.[3] There is, moreover, no uniform or 'model' relationship with the state. Indeed, relations are likely to vary depending upon whether an NGDO is at a rudimentary or advanced 'stage of development' (Fowler, 2000: 122), whether the focus is on the NGDO's head office in France (*ici*) or its staff in the field (*là-bas*) and whether the NGDO in question is financially dependent on the state or largely 'autonomous' in terms of its funding.[4] Two extremes are represented by the most resource-rich volunteer agency, the AFVP, and the leading *urgencier*, MSF. The former was created by the French state and is 100 per cent funded by official sources, enjoying its own designated line in the French Development/ Foreign Ministry budget. The latter has, over recent years, set down an alternative system to dependence on the state and has refused all forms of central government funding, moving towards a position where 90 per cent of its actions are now financed by small or individual donors (Interview with MSF, 2003).

The final caveat is that it is extremely difficult to demonstrate empirically any direct causal link between the actions of the French state and the evolution of French NGDOs. The latter may well be effecting changes independently of the state and may, indeed, be responding either to internal pressures or to the demands of other actors in their wider environment. They may even be exerting a 'reverse influence' on the French government and modifying the policies it adopts towards them and towards overseas development issues. This type of 'reverse agenda' is not fully captured by the RD framework, which is geared towards explaining the effect of the resource-rich actor (the French authorities) on the resource-dependent organisation (the French NGDO sub-sector). This is a point which this study will return to in subsequent chapters.

Early French NGO–state relations

The historically poor relationship between French NGOs and the state can be broken down into three components: legal/ fiscal relations, financial/ non-monetary links and consultative ties. Each of these will be discussed in turn.

French NGOs as a whole did not, historically, enjoy a favourable *legal* context. Indeed, the French state's restrictive treatment of non-governmental actors can be traced all the way back to the French Revolution and the Chapelier Act of 1791.[5] This Act, together with the Allarde Decree of the same year, suppressed guilds and other groupings, thereby ruling out freedom of association and slowing down the evolution of French associations relative to their counterparts in more liberal, Anglo-American countries.[6] Inspired by Jean-Jacques Rousseau's concept of the 'social contract', this law also prohibited 'all forms of association that stood between citizen and State' and held that 'there was no common or collective interest separate from the State and the unified nation that it embodied'.[7]

The legislation relating to NGOs was only relaxed at the start of the twentieth century, when associations were accorded legal recognition by the French state. The 1901 Law on associations made it easy to form an NGO in France and afforded like-minded individuals the chance to establish themselves either as *associations non-déclarées*, *associations déclarées* or *associations reconnues d'utilité publique*. The former are simply groupings of individuals, with no legal rights, while 'declared associations' are those which have been registered at a French *préfecture* or *sous-préfecture* and which are legally entitled to sign contracts, possess property and engage in various commercial transactions. As for 'public utility associations', these are accredited by the French Council of State and enjoy privileged status: they have, in particular, the right 'to own real estate, to receive legacies... [and] to engage in profit-making' (Archambault, 1997: 56).

It should not, however, be thought that the 1901 Law signalled a new liberal approach by the French state towards NGOs. In fact, this legislation remained restrictive, defining associations 'in contradistinction to companies' and imposing constraints on the commercial, property-owning and fund-raising activities of the vast majority of NGOs. The Law did not, of course, discourage NGOs from applying for 'public utility status' but it did nothing to help them meet the strict conditions associated with this form of accreditation.[8]

On the *fiscal* front, too, French NGOs did not traditionally enjoy any 'privileged' treatment from their own government. As Archambault (1997: 69–70) has observed: 'For a long time, until the 1980s, there was only a symbolic exemption on the income tax/corporation tax by physical persons or organizations to well-defined associations or foundations'. Indeed, up until 1984, the maximum tax deduction granted by the French state stood at only 1 per cent of disposable income (Ibid). This low level of fiscal relief, coupled with a complex and arcane tax system, served inevitably to constrain the levels of donations which French NGOs received from private individuals and companies over these years. To illustrate, in 1985, total tax-exempt donations to French NGOs amounted to only 510 million francs, which is less than one per cent of household income after tax (Ibid: 70–1). By contrast, in Anglo-Saxon countries, private donations regularly reached between two and three per cent of disposable income (Collard, 1978).

Turning to *financial* relations, here, too, French NGOs, especially developmental actors, typically enjoyed little in the way of state support. This is not to say that the government assistance they received was of little interest or entirely negligible: it made up, in the mid-1980s, the majority (some 55 per cent) of their total official funding, with the Foreign and Development Ministries providing three-quarters of this share (CCD, 1987: 72). The bottom line was, however, that French NGOs received less in the way of financial aid from the state than any of their counterparts in the Northern hemisphere. With 1.1 per cent of official aid channelled through French NGOs, these actors found themselves on a par with Japanese NGOs and way behind the OECD average of 4.3 per cent (OECD, 1988: 93). They lagged far behind NGOs in the United States (4.4 per cent), Belgium (5.4 per cent), Germany (5.9 per cent), Holland (6.1 per cent), Canada (8.7 per cent), New Zealand (8.9 per cent) and Switzerland (13.6 per cent) (Ibid). They also fared worse than NGOs in other developed countries in terms of co-funding from the state. In the mid-1980s, some 39 per cent of French NGOs did not receive any official co-funding for their projects (CCD, 1987: 45); and those that did were offered terms which were at the less generous end of the spectrum for international donors.[9] Against such a backdrop, it is perhaps not surprising that the vast majority of French NGOs relied primarily on private sources, which made up 72 per cent of their total funding in the mid-1980s (Ibid).

French NGOs fared little better in terms of the *non-monetary support* which they received from the state. The French Foreign Ministry did offer technical advice on project proposals within joint NGO–state forums, such as the CCD (discussed below); and it did provide, via its vast diplomatic network, a political safeguard to NGOs establishing themselves in overseas territories. Overall, however, these forms of support were extremely limited. The one exception to this rule was the role played by the French government as a *conduit* for volunteers in the form of *coopérants*, that is, young French men, who opted to do their national service in a non-military capacity, often in the field of overseas development. The French state channelled many of these *volontaires du service national actif* through NGOs, such as the AFVP and the DCC, and it paid all of their national insurance costs. In 1986, the French government routed some 4,600 *coopérants* through volunteer associations and it offered a subsidy of 16,200 francs per head (Condamines, 1989: 73; Barrau, 2001: 55).

Turning finally to *consultative ties*, French NGOs did not enjoy much access to government during the early post-colonial decades. They had little direct contact with the state outside of specialised advisory forums, such as the *Commission Nationale Consultative des Droits de l'Homme* (formed in 1947), which explored various human rights issues and which was presided over by the French Prime Minister. As from the mid-1970s, they did begin to develop tentative links with the *Bureau de Liaison des ONG* (BLONG) in the Development Ministry, which was set up in 1976 to inform NGOs about developments in French aid policy and to organise occasional meetings between senior French officials and NGO representatives.[10] It was not, however, until the first socialist government of the French Fifth Republic and the creation, in 1983, of the CCD that NGOs were integrated formally into discussions with the state. This latter body, usually referred to as the CCD or the COCODEV, was a joint structure, presided over by the Development Minister and comprising an equal number of NGO and official members. The CCD played a key role in facilitating dialogue between NGOs and the state about overseas development. But it was, ultimately, only one unit within a small department (the BLONG) of a junior Ministry (the *Ministère de la Coopération*). Needless to say, neither the BLONG nor the Development Ministry enjoyed much influence over the higher echelons of government, which themselves had no mechanisms for dealing with NGOs and no interest in creating such instruments.

Overall, French NGOs had historically poor relations with the French government, and these did not improve significantly over the early post-colonial era. These NGOs, particularly faith-based and Marxist NGDOs, were chronically underfunded and frequently ignored by a secular French state, steeped in Republican and anti-clerical traditions (Hazareesingh, 1994). For Walters (2003: 60), this situation arose largely out of the thinking of officials of the French Republic, who viewed non-state actors as 'negative particularist elements that divided society and subverted the general interest ... [and which,] emerging freely within society, ... escaped public authority and transcended processes of political regulation and control'. For Cohen (2004: 2), it was the result of 'fears of mutual exploitation' as well as of a state ideology that was said to be

> rooted in the highly centralizing tradition of French foreign policy-making, which had little patience for any intrusion of civil society in foreign affairs and in the political culture of the non-profit sector, marked by a libertarian nature and a resistance to any compromise with the diplomatic corps....

Towards a new rapport: overtures by the state

Over the global era, the French state has expressed a much clearer interest in establishing closer relations with French NGOs. To this end, it has made overtures to French NGOs on the legal/fiscal, financial/non-monetary and consultative front.

Legal and fiscal relations

To begin with *legal* measures, the French authorities have endeavoured to create a more favourable environment for all French NGOs. They have effected two main changes. The first has involved a relaxation of the restrictions on the money-making activities of NGOs and other *assocations de 1901*. One example of this is the legal directive of 15 September 1998, which allows NGOs to engage in some profit-related activities without sacrificing the privileges associated with their charitable status (*Commissariat Général,* 2002: 70–1).[11] In line with this directive, French NGOs are now able to claim tax relief on commercial activities, such as the sale of clothes, provided that the items are bought by individual members of the public and not by professional clothes retailers (Ibid: 71).[12] Another example of the French state's more relaxed stance is the July 1987 law on sponsorship. This permits NGOs other than 'public utility associations' to elicit donations directly from the public; to raise funding in the form of legacies; and to enjoy exemption from inheritance tax or probate duty. The main beneficiaries of this concession have been *associations de bienfaisance,* variously defined as 'charities acting in the public interest' or associations 'whose exclusive goal is charity or whose main activity involves scientific/ medical research' (Théry, 2007: 55–6).

It is, however, in the second area, namely *le volontariat,* that the state has carried out the most significant changes. It has, in this context, passed four important pieces of legislation over the last two decades. The first was a ministerial decree of 15 March 1986, which accorded volunteer agencies their own legal status as *associations de volontariat.* In so doing, it brought France more into line with other European countries and ensured that volunteers benefited from some kind of basic social protection; some help with reintegration into the world of work upon their return to France; and some assurances that time spent abroad would count towards pension rights. At the same time, this legislation also created a new Commission for Volunteer Organisations (*Commission du Volontariat*), which comprised three NGO representatives and three officials from the Development Ministry (Condamines, 1989: 73).

The second measure was a further decree, passed on 30 January 1995, which aimed to shore up the status of volunteers working in developing countries. In effect, the French state agreed to pay the lion's share of the social cover for volunteers of any age working for accredited associative structures, such as local African associations, hospitals and faith-based organisations. More specifically, the French government agreed to cover 60 per cent of the cost of training volunteers, 37 per cent of the administrative price-tag attached to running volunteer programmes and the full amount of both the end-of-mission allowance and the bonus given to help volunteers reintegrate themselves into professional life in France (Godfrain, 2004: 16). In exchange for this official support, the decree formalised the responsibilities of French volunteer organisations and their partners in the Southern hemisphere. It charged these non-governmental actors with providing volunteers with a subsistence living 'wage' (€152 a month), decent meals and accommodation (by local standards), travel costs, third party insurance and technical help for volunteers returning to work in France (Ibid: 9–10).

Faced with continuing pressure from volunteer organisations anxious to ensure that the above decrees were not revoked, the French state has pushed through two further pieces of legislation. The first, a law passed on 14 March 2000, was designed to encourage young people aged between 18 and 28 – who were, as from December 1996, no longer obliged to do any form of military service – to undertake a voluntary civilian form of national service (or *volontariat civil*). This piece of legislation sought to bolster the rights, not just of volunteers sent out by NGDOs, but also those expatriated by companies and the French state itself. It fixed the duration of the work at between 6 and 24 months and, somewhat injudiciously, guaranteed volunteers a minimum monthly wage of around €527 (Barrau, 2001: 55). In so doing, the 2000 law set the price of taking on a volunteer too high for French volunteer agencies active in international development, most of which were chronically under-funded and operating through local partner associations that were even more cash-strapped. A second law was, therefore, passed on 23 February 2005, which sought to balance the concerns of volunteer agencies and the needs of volunteers. To this end, it recommended a stipend of up to €400 a month but did not impose a minimum wage for volunteers. It also enhanced some of the benefits associated with 'civilian' forms of volunteering. In particular, it promised full social cover and pension rights to volunteers and extended the age limit for former volunteers wishing to sit entrance competitions for French civil service posts. Furthermore, it provided validation for the experience acquired by volunteers and even offered meal tickets as a form of non-financial payment.

On the *fiscal* front, the French state has introduced a range of tax incentives to encourage private donors to increase their donations to French NGOs. On 1 August 2003, for example, it introduced a law on sponsorship, which allowed companies and commercial foundations providing support to NGOs to claim 60 per cent tax relief on their donation, substantially more than the 33 per cent which was previously permitted.[13] More significantly still, the French authorities have progressively stepped up the level of fiscal concessions they offer to the donor public. They introduced, in this context, the Coluche Law of 24 June 1996. This allowed individual donors to claim 60 per cent tax relief on any donations they made (up to a maximum of €407) to NGOs offering help to the needy in France and overseas.[14] Anyone donating to other types of French NGO was entitled to ask for 50 per cent tax relief, up to a ceiling of 10 per cent of their income. Since then, the French state has promulgated a further law, on 1 August 2003, which enables individuals donating to the first set of organisations to claim back 66 per cent of their donation (up to €414), whilst permitting anyone giving to the latter type of association to reclaim 60 per cent (up to a maximum of 20 per cent of their income). More recently still, in 2005, the limits were raised yet again to 75 per cent (up to a maximum of €470) and 66 per cent (up to 20 per cent of income), respectively, thereby placing the French fiscal regime at the more generous end of the tax spectrum in Europe.

Financial and non-monetary links

The French authorities have, equally, stepped up their *financial* support to the French NGO sector as a whole. As noted in the Chapter 4, the French state has increased financial assistance to NGOs in absolute terms from M€46.2 in 1991 to M€56.1 in 2004–05. It has also pledged to double aid to NGOs between 2004 and 2009 (*Cour des Comptes*, 2005). In addition, it has improved the terms of its co-financing of NGO projects and programmes under the rubric of a major new initiative known as 'the new contractual arrangements' or *la nouvelle contractualisation*. This scheme, introduced in 1996, involves the signature of a contract between the MCNG and a large French NGO or a group of non-governmental actors, represented by a single coordinator or *chef de file*. These 'new contractual arrangements' offer more flexible, pluri-annual (three to four year) funding on highly favourable terms, with the French state often providing 75 per cent of the cost of a programme, compared to a maximum of 50 per cent prior to 1996. This *contractualisation* initially revolved around schemes known as *conventions d'objectifs, programmes concertés* and *programmes prioritaires* (*Commissariat Général*, 2002). But these early forms of cooperation have since given way to *conventions programmes* (where one NGO develops a coherent ensemble of similar projects, seminars and training schemes), *programmes inter-associatifs* (which bring together different NGOs to work on a specific programme) and *programmes concertés pluri-acteurs* (which may involve trade unions, local authorities and other actors alongside associations).[15]

These 'new contractual arrangements' have signalled a readiness on the part of the French authorities to become more than just a 'cash dispensing' machine for NGOs and to play a proactive role in supporting larger scale NGO initiatives. These new funding mechanisms have also provided the government with a real incentive to enhance the quality of its technical feedback on NGO project proposals; and, to this end, the state has devolved responsibility for the running of a number of these new co-financing arrangements to French missions in the field (e.g. in Senegal and Mali).

As regards the *non-monetary* support now offered by the French authorities, this may take the form of food aid, military back-up in conflict zones and logistical support to coordinate humanitarian relief efforts. While these types of assistance are directed primarily to *urgenciers*, other forms of support are of a more general nature and include measures to encourage NGO professionalisation (see Chapter 6) and initiatives designed to raise the profile of specific NGOs, such as CCFD, which was granted 'leading national cause' (*grande cause nationale*) status by the French Prime Minister in 1993. Other examples of non-monetary support from the state include: in-kind assistance in the form of staff transfers; help with the recruitment of young people via France's youth employment scheme; and the granting of office space to NGOs at a discounted rate. In this latter context, the GRET has been located free of charge within the premises of the French government-funded *Institut de Recherche pour le Développement* (*Cour des Comptes*, 2005).[16]

Arguably, however, the most important forms of non-monetary assistance for NGOs have come in two main areas. The first is volunteer work. Here the French state has, on top of the subsidies it provides to volunteer organisations, also offered logistical support to help them recruit overseas volunteers (*volontaires*). It has established, with the support of the Ministries of Finance and Trade, the *Centre d'Information sur le Volontariat International* (CIVI), and it has instructed this body to launch campaigns, provide advice and evaluate applications from potential volunteers. The French authorities have, moreover, made it easier for NGOs to recruit the other main category of French volunteer, namely *bénévoles*. It has, in this context, imposed a legal requirement on companies and other organisations to grant a period of leave to any employee wishing to engage in work related to international development.[17]

The second area of non-monetary support has involved official guidance on funding bids. Here, the French Foreign Ministry has provided technical advice aimed at enabling French NGOs to submit more effective applications to the French state and to multilateral donors. It has co-financed training courses on the workings of 'the new contractual arrangements' and has compiled, in consultation with French NGOs, a two-volume guidance note or *Vade Mecum*, which provides extensive advice on how to access all major sources of Foreign Ministry funding. Equally, it has set up a cell designed specifically to enable French NGOs to access multilateral funds. The French state has also, through its permanent representation in Brussels, prepared a full directory of all the budgetary lines available from the European Commission (Blum, 2005: 18); and it has become much more proactive in impressing upon the European Commission the merits of French NGOs (Interview with HCCI, 2003).[18]

Consultative ties

Finally, on the issue of consultation, the French state has become much more accessible to the NGO sector as a whole over the global era. In this context, Cohen (2004: 3) has noted how there are now 'many less formal contacts between the authorities and human rights NGOs as well as those working in sustainable development'. Others have pointed to a trend in which French NGOs are increasingly consulted by the French government ahead of important international conferences (Interview with the CRID, 2003). As will be shown in Chapter 7, French NGOs have enjoyed meetings, in recent years, with the French President (e.g. ahead of the June 2003 G8 Evian summit). They have discussed debt cancellation with officials from the Africa cell of the *Elysée* and the Finance Ministry; and they were invited to visit the French Trade Ministry ahead of the World Trade Organisation (WTO) summit in Cancun in September 2003.

The French government has, above all, sought to encourage more sustained dialogue within designated NGO-government forums. In 1990, for example, it included NGOs for the first time in bilateral *commissions mixtes*, that is to say, meetings between the French state and their recipient governments in developing countries.[19] Subsequently, over the course of the 1990s, the French authorities widened their consultations with NGOs by encouraging the CCD to create a number of new thematic commissions; and by helping it to establish, in August 2006, its own Joint Steering and Programming Committee (*Comité Paritaire d'Orientation et de Programmation*). Composed of six officials and six NGO representatives, this latter body is designed to examine 'the evolution of the new contractual arrangements between the Foreign Ministry and associations' and to promote 'a continuous dialogue about the procedures and volumes of budgetary allocations granted each year to NGOs by the French authorities' (*Commissariat Général*, 2002, Annex 6).

The French state has, equally, set up, in consultation with French NGDOs, a number of new forums. The first of these, the HCCI, was formed in February 1999, in the wake of the 1998 reforms of the aid administration conducted by French Prime Minister, Lionel Jospin. The HCCI is an independent body with its own headquarters located within the Prime Minister's office. It was initially composed of some 60 members appointed by the Prime Minister and drawn from NGOs, local authorities, universities, trade unions and businesses. Its remit is to 'encourage regular consultation between official and private actors about international development' issues, to raise public awareness of these questions and generally 'to make better known the views of civil society as a whole regarding the [government's] development assistance policy' (World Bank, 2001: 19). The HCCI submits an annual report to Parliament via the Prime Minister. It also issues regular 'opinions' and recommendations on aid-related issues, as well as organising formal and informal debates on international development. It acts mainly as a think tank and leaves the operational side of development projects to the CCD.[20]

Another new consultative mechanism is the *Club des OSI* or 'NGO Club', created in November 1999 by the AFD. Under the co-presidency of the Director of the AFD and the President of *Coordination SUD*, the Club includes a handful of senior ranking officials and around 15 NGO representatives. It meets three or four times a year to develop closer ties between NGOs and the AFD and to explore precise courses of action and themes of common interest. It also aims to refine procedures for financial partnerships and to share experiences of dealing with issues, such as micro-finance, health sector reform and support for the informal sector. As a result of the work of the *Club des OSI*, the operational relationship between NGOs and the AFD was clarified, in March 2001, in a document entitled *Relations Opérationnelles OSI-AFD, Règles du Jeu* (*Commissariat Général*, 2002: 139).

Finally, the most recent collaborative forum is the Steering Conference on Strategy and Programming (*Conférence d'Orientation Stratégique et de Programmation or* COSP). This consultative body, which was formed in July 2004, is an offshoot of the *Comité Interministériel de la Coopération Internationale et du Développement* (CICID). It meets annually under the chairmanship of the French Development Minister and includes, within its membership, a representative from the main French federation, *Coordination SUD*.[21]

A measured response from French NGDOs

French NGDOs, together with many other French NGOs, have long been calling for the kind of legislative, financial and consultative measures that the state has taken over the global era. But, while they have welcomed many of the above initiatives, they have not seen these 'concessions' as substantial enough to form the basis of a genuine NGDO–state partnership.

Major legislative changes or too little too late?

French NGDOs have welcomed the recent relaxation of *legal* restrictions on profit-making and fund-raising as a measure which they have long been demanding within forums, such as the CCD. They have also approved of the French state's recent move to extend the benefits of 'public utility status' to a wider range of French associations. Indeed, some French NGDOs have even been proactive in their pursuit of this form of accreditation, seeing it as a 'benchmark of excellence' (*Commissariat Général*, 2002: 52) and as a way of distinguishing themselves from the many thousands of other *associations de 1901*. Significantly too, most NGDOs have welcomed recent government legislation on *le volontariat*, which they see as a direct response to lobbying by volunteer organisations within the *CLONG-Volontariat* and the *Commission du Volontariat*. Volunteer organisations, in particular, have appreciated the fact that their separate legal status is now enshrined in law, and 27 of these organisations have already sought formal accreditation from the Development/ Foreign Ministry.[22]

French NGDOs have, equally, embraced the recent *fiscal concessions* offered by the government to incentivise company sponsorship and donations from the general public. They have seen these measures as going some way towards meeting the tax-related demands which they have long voiced through the *Conseil National de la Vie Associative* and which they have, more recently, articulated through the *Commissariat Général du Plan* (2002).[23] French NGDOs have, moreover, viewed these changes as a real fund-raising opportunity and have, accordingly, brought these tax-relief measures to the attention of private donors by providing guidance notes in their newsletters and posting electronic tax claim forms on their websites. In so doing, they have helped to bring about more than a fourfold rise in the value of fiscal concessions from the state from M€250 in 1991 to €1.16 billion in 2005.[24]

At the same time, however, most French NGDOs have continued to protest about the overall legal environment in which they operate, focusing particularly on the 1901 law on associations. While most accept that this legislation has been invaluable in facilitating the creation of 'a diverse and dynamic NGO sector' and many 'believe it allows them to rest upon a militant base' (Blum, 2005: 7), other NGDOs have seen 'the limited legal capacity of the 1901 Act...[as] an obstacle to fundraising, investing, borrowing, acquiring real estate, in a word to normal economic activity' (Archambault, 1997: 212). Some NGDOs have expressed concern that within this single legal category are found extremely diverse structures, including associations of fishermen and commercial companies (Blum, 2005: 8). Others have actually favoured a revision to this founding law to distinguish between larger NGDOs and the vast number of much smaller and less 'professional' associations. A few have even questioned whether this century-old legislation is now appropriate. Thus, as Blum makes clear,

> Developmental NGOs believe that there is a need for some kind of accreditation...which will allow them to compete better with the arrival of foreign NGOs, especially American ones, on the French fund-raising scene. Some NGOs regret for example that it is impossible for two associations to merge, the only possibility for growth being absorption of one organisation by another, in the way that the *Centre International de Développement Agricole* (CICDA) was absorbed by *Vétérinaires Sans Frontières* (VSF) to become VSF-CICDA. (Ibid)

At the same time, a number of French NGDOs have honed in on another negative aspect of the 1901 law, namely the restrictions which this imposes on commercial activities. They have bemoaned the fact that they are, unlike their Anglo-American counterparts, only allowed to engage in profit-making 'when the activities performed to reach the organization's goals happen to generate profits, or when the making of profit is part of an educational or social process' (*Commissariat Général*, 2002: 41). They have also regretted the fact that 'public utility status', and the numerous advantages it brings, is still only obtainable at the end of a long and difficult road and after the association has undergone rigorous scrutiny by the *Cour des Comptes* and the French Interior Ministry. Equally, they have complained that this status and the lesser title of 'charities acting in the public interest' (accorded for five years in the first instance) are still not widely available. Indeed, only one in 35,000 associations in France enjoy public utility status and, as the *Commissariat Général* (2002: 78) has observed, 'Of the 18 top NGOs involved in international development and relief which amass nearly 80 per cent of all resources, seven have not received, in 1999 or 2000, a single legacy and have neither benefited from public utility status nor from the lesser status of "charity"'.[25]

Even the main beneficiaries of recent legislative changes, French volunteer organisations, have remained critical of the limitations, or lack of appropriateness, of the state's approach. While welcoming the government's readiness to modify relevant decrees and laws, they have nonetheless regretted the length of time and sheer level of effort it has taken to work towards a viable legislative framework. They have, for example, had to reiterate their concerns over the tenuous nature of ministerial decrees, age limits on volunteers, and the need for more support for volunteers returning to France. In particular, they have complained that the law of 24 March 2000 was tailored to the needs of *Francophonie* agencies and companies sending out volunteers and that it was totally unsuited to volunteer agencies active in overseas development. These latter organisations operate on a shoe string; neither they nor their local partners could possibly afford to pay the level of stipend stipulated in this law (Interview with CLONG V, 2003).

At the same time, most French NGDOs have not seen recent fiscal measures as paving the way for a new partnership with the state. They have continued to grumble that the French tax system is 'as ineffective as it is opaque' and that relief measures are still less favourable than those available in Anglo-Saxon countries (*Commissariat Général*, 2002: 187). As Blum (2005: 7) makes clear: 'They complain regularly, some for having to pay taxes on salaries, others for not being able to recover VAT; and they vaunt the merits of the British system [of charities] in this context'. Some have bemoaned the fact that, while tax exemptions are granted for profit-making activities in areas of marginal concern to most NGDOs, such as the sale of clothes, they are not available in one of the areas in which French developmental NGOs are heavily engaged, namely fair trade products. Others have protested that the fiscal situation (notably in relation to the Coluche law) has infringed the Republican ideal of equality of treatment of associations and arbitrarily benefited some, such as the *Restos du Coeur*, at the expense of others, such as smaller NGDOs involved in development education work.[26] Others have taken the view that the French state has abused its fiscal powers by offering tax relief directly to private donors in its own recent fund-raising appeals (specifically for the Lebanon and Northern Israel in 2006). Finally, a few organisations have even expressed concern that the French administration is taking away fiscal concessions from NGDOs (e.g. on the sale of their newspapers) and seeking to 'tax everything they do' (Interview with *TDH-France*, 2003).[27]

New-found generosity or yet more penny-pinching?

French NGDOs have, unsurprisingly, welcomed recent increases in *financial aid* by, and pledges of further assistance from, the French authorities. They have viewed these extra monies as, in many ways, a direct response to their own lobbying through federations, such as the CRID and *Coordination SUD* (see Chapter 8). They have also been more than happy to take advantage of better co-financing terms, particularly under *la nouvelle contractualisation*, which again was something for which they had long campaigned and over which a full consultation exercise with the state had been undertaken.[28] In some cases, they have even shown themselves willing to become financially dependent upon French government funding and to take on the role of service provider on its behalf (see Chapter 7).[29]

French NGDOs have also welcomed *non-monetary support* from the state in its various forms. They have, for example, gladly accepted subsidised rent on officially owned premises, as well as secondments of staff from various state organs, who are 'placed freely at the disposal of NGOs' and who represent 'an indirect subsidy which can be quite considerable (worth €800,000 a year for the GRET for example) (*Cour des Comptes*, 2005: 6). They have, moreover, greatly appreciated, and actively participated in the preparation of, the three-yearly NGO directories and biannual financial reports, which have been produced by the CCD since the mid-1980s.[30] In the case of volunteer agencies, they have been happy to take advantage of the administrative and other services offered by state-funded bodies such as the CIVI and the FONJEP. French NGDOs have, in addition, recognised the value of official advice on ways of producing better bids for funding from the French state and the European Commission (Interview with the CRID, 2003). Indeed, the leading NGO federation, *Coordination SUD*, has, with the help of the *Agence des Micro-Projets de la Guilde* and with monies from the Foreign Ministry, recently laid on a series of courses and a programme of technical support to help smaller NGOs gain greater access to official funding.[31]

Ultimately, however, French NGDOs have not seen this financial or non-monetary support as being sufficient to lay the basis for genuinely close cooperation with the government. As Potevin (2000: 6) tactfully puts it, 'They sense a discord between the state's political discourse in favour of French civil society actors active in international development and the realities of budgetary constraint.' On the financial front, they have bemoaned the fact that French government aid to NGOs has remained paltry and is still the lowest in Europe, outside of the accession states. Thus, as can be seen from Table 5.1, French NGOs received, in 1998, only 0.65 per cent of total French foreign aid and around 0.9 per cent of French bilateral assistance, which was significantly less than NGOs from Luxembourg (which enjoyed 11.6 and 27.9 per cent, respectively), Holland (which secured 9.8 and 14.1 per cent) and Denmark (which received 7.3 and 41.4 per cent). While this situation is beginning to change (see Chapter 10), very low levels of assistance were still a feature of the early years of this century. In this context, the Parliamentary rapporteur, Roland Blum (2005: 16) noted that, in 2001, the share of official aid transiting French NGOs still represented 'less than one per cent', compared to a European average of 5.1 per cent and, indeed, 30 per cent in the case of the United States.[32] More recently still, the *Cour des Comptes* reported that French government assistance to NGOs

Table 5.1 Aid from European States to NGOs in 1998 in M€ and as a percentage of their overall and bilateral aid budgets

Donor country	Volume of support to NGOs (M€)	Share of NGO support as % of total aid budget	Share of NGO support as % of bilateral aid budget
Austria	15.9	3.89	6.08
Belgium	65	7.25	13.39
Denmark	123	7.25	41.41
European Commission	143	3.11	–
Finland	27	7.6	14.5
France	33.1	0.65	0.87
Germany	88.8	1.77	2.8
Italy	17	0.84	2.71
Luxembourg	11.5	11.62	27.9
Holland	268.6	9.8	14.1
Spain	70	6	9.31
Sweden	103	6.8	10.31
Switzerland	40.1	4.8	6.87
United Kingdom	102	3.15	5.62

Source: Potevin (2000: 4).

was 'very low, representing €53 million in 2005, barely 0.7 per cent of the €7.2 billion of credit allocated to official aid'.[33] Whilst these aid figures are understated in a number of ways, as demonstrated in Chapter 4, they are also inflated in at least one major respect. Thus, for example, they include substantial French government subsidies to organisations, such as the AFVP and FONJEP, which are, strictly speaking, service agents of the French state rather than NGOs *per se* (see Chapter 7).

French NGDOs have also continued to harbour doubts about the French government's co-financing mechanisms. Some have taken the view that the whole system needs to be overhauled, as it is too preoccupied with imposing pre-evaluation constraints on project proposals. Thus, for example, *Coordination SUD* believes that co-funding, as it is practised today, 'amounts to an *a priori* evaluation' and wants to see the system replaced by 'an *a posteriori* control of co-financed actions... [which]... probably means thinking about structures and generating formulas which would allow a greater say to private actors in the management of the official aid programme' (Blum, 2005: 16–17). Others have remained concerned that it takes six to seven months to finalise approval of a bid for co-funding and that there are often delays associated with rolling forward official funding from one year to the next.[34] These slippages have, at times, obliged NGDOs to go to their banks to seek bridging finance and have, in fact, prompted *Coordination SUD* to call upon the French Foreign Ministry partially to guarantee short-term overdraft facilities to NGOs, which are due to receive state subsidies.

Other commentators within the NGO movement have pointed out that the average amount of co-funding allocated to projects is actually quite low in the French context, standing at around €100,000 per project (*Commissariat Général*, 2002: 103). This is fine for small- to medium-sized organisations but less interesting for NGOs of international proportions, which have access to larger multilateral funding sources. A few observers have voiced their concern that the most generous official funding of all, which comes in the form of programmes 'under order' or 'under convention' – where the state may provide 75 per cent of the cost of the project – has only been available to NGOs which fit stringent government criteria.[35] Other critics from across the NGO sector have simply noted that *la nouvelle contractualisation* has remained only a minor part of overall state support to NGOs, amounting to less than 20 per cent of all project funding in the year 2000 (*Commissariat Général*, 2002: 110).[36] These same detractors have, in fact, complained that the new co-funding arrangements fall well short of their original demands and, above all, of their proposal in the early 1990s that all government assistance to the NGO sector should be jointly managed by the state and by NGOs themselves via a 'A Public Interest Group on International Solidarity' (Devin, 1999: 72).

Finally, French NGDOs have tended towards the view that, when it comes to *non-monetary support* from the state, they are poor cousins compared to *urgenciers* and French local authorities that engage in overseas development work (Devin, 2002: 76). As a senior figure within *TDH-France* makes clear (Interview, 2003), 'we have had to fight for any concessions, whilst the French state cuts short our supply sources or forces us to spend more'. These comments reflect a growing concern at the prospect that non-monetary forms of aid from the government will start to be withdrawn, tightened up or even exaggerated as a way of presenting a better picture of overall French state support to NGOs. The need for all official assistance to NGOs to be properly calculated and publicly declared has, in fact, already been highlighted by a recent *Cour des Comptes* (2005) report, which stressed that French NGOs should not be exempt from the demands which are imposed on other actors receiving financial assistance from the government.

Meaningful consultation or pure window dressing?

On the *consultative front*, French NGDOs have acknowledged the new openness of the French government. Thus, for example, as a former President of the HCCI, has noted: 'the whole of French civil society is more and more consulted on international questions' (Interview, 2003). For his part, Bernard Pinaud, Head of the CRID, has spoken of 'a much more sustained dialogue with the state' and a move away from 'mechanical dialogues purely about co-financing' (Interview, 2003). French NGDOs have also welcomed their inclusion in bilateral *commission mixtes*: they took part, between 1990 and 1994, in around 20 of these, half of which led to the setting up of *programmes prioritaires*, joint operations or working groups (*Commissariat Général*, 1992: 95). They have also participated enthusiastically in more extensive consultation exercises undertaken by the CCD through its creation of eight working committees. These latter forums, established between 1998 and 2001, were designed to focus on questions ranging from volunteer work through to debt cancellation and civil society capacity-building. (Ibid: 147).

French NGDOs have, moreover, been keen to be involved in the activities of newly created consultative bodies, such as the *Club des OSI*. Within this forum, they have willingly exchanged views with the AFD on themes, such as health, micro-finance, support for companies and French bilateral debt relief (Ibid: 152). Equally, they have been happy to be involved in the COSP and to exert influence through this body on the strategic direction of French aid policy. They have, above all, been active within the HCCI, participating in the many thematic commissions created by this civil society body and contributing to the 20 or so 'opinions' handed down by the *Haut Conseil* during its first three-year mandate.[37]

Ultimately, however, many French NGDOs have wondered whether these state-led consultation processes are genuine or largely a façade. Thus, whilst they have had greater access to all levels of the French government, they are still mainly in contact with relatively junior ministerial units, such as the MCNG. They also remain primarily active in relatively powerless forums, such as the CCD, which is simply 'not consulted...over the work and/or agenda of the CICID', that is, the main inter-ministerial committee steering the French aid and development programme. This situation has prompted Hubert Prévost, a former president of *Coordination SUD*, to remark that 'Although much listened to by the authorities, even at the highest level, NGOs question whether they really are being heard'.[38]

This observation applies equally to consultation within recently created joint NGO–state forums. Thus, within the framework of the *Club des OSI*, French NGDOs have only been able to discuss general themes and have not had the option of raising concerns relating to ongoing projects. In the case of the COSP, NGDOs have been able to attend these annual gatherings, but not the two-monthly meetings of the CICID, whose discussions are deemed too politically sensitive.[39] Finally, in the context of the HCCI, French NGDOs have felt that their views have carried little weight with the government. Thus, as the *Commissariat Général* (2002: 95) has noted, the HCCI 'would like its recommendations to be followed through more in practice'. In a similar vein, the OECD has observed that 'lessons born of the experience of the International Solidarity Organisations (OSIs) are not, however, really being put to good use by the public authorities' (OECD, 2004: 18). This tendency to ignore the *Haut Conseil* does inevitably beg questions as to the genuineness of the French state's consultation processes. The fact is that the French authorities weakened the HCCI at the time of its creation by attaching it to the Prime Minister's office, *Matignon*, rather than to one of the organs of government that have a determining say over foreign and development policy, namely the *Elysée* (the Presidential office), the Foreign Ministry or the Finance Ministry. Then, in 2001, the government of Jean-Pierre Raffarin further curtailed the influence of this forum by cutting down representation on the HCCI from 60 to 45, by according a much greater say to local authorities within this civil society body and by encouraging the HCCI to concentrate less on ambitious policy reforms and more on low-level operational questions (Interviews in Paris, 2003).

Conclusion

This chapter has focused on the first of three trends outlined in Chapter 1. It has demonstrated how the French state has taken steps to improve its relations with French NGOs and how the latter have welcomed these measures, while deeming them insufficient to form the basis of a genuine rapprochement. It has noted, in particular, how French developmental NGOs have continued to complain about the restrictive nature of their legal and fiscal context, how they have deplored the continuing low levels of government assistance, which are 'scarcely defensible' and how they have questioned the credibility of the government's commitment to the consultation process.[40] Overall, as the *Commissariat Général du Plan* (2002: 97) has observed, NGDO relations with the French authorities are still 'marked by a certain distance and stiffness' and by 'quarrels about legitimacy [and] debates on objectives and modes of action'.

It will be left to chapter 8 to determine whether the behaviour of French NGDOs vis-à-vis the state is consistent with RD theory. For now, however, it should suffice to note that these non-governmental actors do appear to be acting broadly in line with the logic of RD. Thus, for example, they have generally pushed for, and taken advantage of, the extra resources and concessions which have been offered by the French government on the legislative, fiscal, financial, non-monetary and consultative front. They have not, however, gravitated closer to the French authorities in circumstances where the state has offered insufficient incentives or where the risk of accepting government monies has simply been too high. The greatest danger in closer association with the French authorities has, of course, been that NGDOs become 'tainted' and lose legitimacy in the eyes of their critical resource, that is to say, their millions of individual donors and tens of thousands of militant activists, whose demands might be expected to take precedence over those of the French state.

6
Towards Professionalisation?

The term 'professionalisation' is variously understood in NGO circles. For many, it is simply equated with professionalism (Ryfman, 2004: 41), while for other it involves a more business-like orientation with 'the application of managerial practices and structures adopted from the commercial sphere' (Haddad, 2002: 51). For our purposes, it will be taken to refer to a process that brings NGOs closer into line with the systems and workings of the state. This type of professionalisation is referred to pejoratively by Wallace *et al.* (1997) as 'the standardisation of development' and by Fowler (2000: 105) as the creation of a bureaucratic 'development monoculture'. For Korten (1991: 36), it means 'enhancing technical and managerial capabilities and installing improved control systems so that NGOs can function more like the technical agencies of government. Professionalism in this context is sometimes treated as the antithesis of voluntarism'.

This movement towards professionalisation across the NNGO sector was the second putative international trend to have been identified in Chapter 1. Whether or not NNGOs have, indeed, standardised their development practices is a question for future analysts. Here, it will suffice to note that allegations have been made to this effect by various prominent scholars (Smillie and Helmich, 1993; Wallace *et al.*, 1997; Lewis, 2001). Yet how accurate are these claims in relation to French NGOs, particularly *développementalistes* and volunteer agencies? This chapter will begin by outlining the militant, even amateurish, profile of French NGDOs in the early post-colonial decades. It will then set out briefly what the French state has done over the global era to encourage professionalisation. Subsequently, it will show how French NGDOs have edged closer to this state-led conception of professionalisation, whilst at the same time holding on to their core militant profile. Finally, it will conclude by asking whether the behaviour of French NGDOs appears broadly consistent with RD theory.

Before undertaking this analysis, it is worth laying down a few caveats. The first is that it is hard to identify any single view of professionalisation across the entire French state system. Indeed, even within the Foreign Ministry, which has done the most to advance its thinking on this issue, there are differences of emphasis. Thus, the *Délégation Humanitaire*, which deals with *urgenciers*, prefers rapidly devised, internal and informal evaluations of performance (Interview, 2003), whereas the MCNG, which provides most of its funding to NGDOs, stresses lengthier and more formal procedures, often involving its own evaluation department or independent consultants employed by the F3E (discussed below).

The second proviso is that it is difficult to generalise about professionalisation taking place across all French NGOs or, even, across all French NGDOs, given that these actors are at various stages in their life cycles and have different origins, funding sources and objectives. Clearly, there are differences between smaller, more militant French NGOs and larger ones, some of which have 'become very professionalized, [and] ... are increasingly perceived as "bureaucratic" and self-interested' (Cohen, 2004: 3). Another distinction, which is gradually breaking down, is between *urgenciers*, which are generally composed of highly trained professionals and specialists, and developmental NGOs, whose staff, although increasingly qualified, are often generalists. Yet another fault line might be discerned within the ranks of French *développementalistes* themselves. Thus, for example, there are clear differences between associations, such as the CCFD, which has its 'roots in society' and which foregrounds 'the pedagogical and militant dimension' of its actions, and 'more technical' NGDOs, such as the GRET, which are 'not unlike consultancies and 'oriented towards a professional service delivery role' (Devin, 1999: 73).[1]

The final caveat is that it is hard to draw any clear correlation between French state actions and any professionalisation, or lack thereof, by French NGDOs. The question of causality is complicated by two factors. The first relates to the role of pressures from the corporate sector. The fact is that the state's new demands have largely had their origins in the world of business and theories of 'new public management', whilst many innovations in French NGDO fund-raising, communication and marketing practices have also come directly, rather than through the intermediary of official pressures, from the commercial sector.[2] The second is that, while the French government has, no doubt, exerted influence over NGDOs in the direction of greater professionalism, it has by no means been the only actor pushing for change and has had to compete with the 'rival' conceptions of professionalisation propounded by other actors, such as far-sighted NGDO managers, company sponsors, IOs and, even, the donor public. It follows, then, that the French state has held greater sway over NGDOs in relation to some aspects of their professionalisation than others. The areas where government influence would appear most likely are as follows: the staffing profiles of NGDOs, their institutional structures and their approaches to evaluation, feedback and learning. The aspects of non-governmental behaviour which would seem, *a priori*, less susceptible to state influence include: (private) fund-raising techniques, micro-level, internal management processes and approaches to advocacy/campaigning work. These latter elements of NGDO operations will not be a major focus of this analysis but do need a brief mention at the start of this survey.

Professionalisation along 'non-standard' lines

To begin with private fund-raising (as opposed to the quest for official resources, which was discussed in Chapter 5), this is one dimension of French NGDO working practices over which the French authorities are unlikely to have much direct influence. Thus, whilst the French state can facilitate NGDO fund-raising by relaxing fiscal measures, it cannot ensure that any extra revenue generated by these concessions is used towards professionalisation. Nor, indeed, can it guarantee that this additional income does not serve to discourage professionalisation, by allowing some NGDOs to persist with ineffective approaches to fund-raising and overseas development.

There are nonetheless ways in which the French government has been able to affect directly the private fund-raising practices of NGDOs. The first of these has been through its increasingly rigorous demands for greater financial accountability and transparency on the part of NGDOs (discussed later in this chapter). The second has been through its chronic neglect and under-funding of NGDOs. This approach by the state has, perhaps unintentionally, served as a spur to professionalisation and forced French NGDOs to be more self-reliant, to diversify their resource base, and to adopt more effective approaches in pursuit of private resources.[3]

There have, of course, been limits to this professionalisation of fund-raising techniques. Thus, for example, developmental NGOs have so far steered clear of the lucrative advertising techniques pioneered by *urgenciers*, which emphasise the dependency of the peoples of the developing world rather than portraying them positively as partners in the development process.[4] Nevertheless, the general trend in French NGDO fund-raising has been to adopt more professional approaches, many of them borrowed from Anglo-American NGOs. These new methods have led the costs involved in raising donations to increase over time, rising from 5 per cent of total NGO expenditure in 1991 to 8.7 per cent in 2005 (CCD, 2001: 17; 2008: 37). They have included a much more extensive use of internet websites, direct debits and facilities for accepting funds via text messages (Rubio, 2004: 180). They have also involved the introduction of the first annual telethon (discussed below), cold calling (an approach which is still rarely used in France) and 'house-to-house canvassing'. Equally, these professional techniques have included a rise in 'street fund-raising', which is 'regulated' to some extent by *ONG-Conseil*, an association that coordinates allocation of pavement space and trains those involved in collecting funds and signatures (Blum, 2005: 24). Finally, they have been discernible in a growing tendency of NGDOs to appoint fund-raising officers, to publish guides that encourage the public to donate 'sensibly',[5] to conduct surveys on the motivations of the French donor public[6] and to call upon the services of public relations agencies (e.g. Euro RSCG C&O, TBWA), which charge for their technical advice whilst offering advertising space for free. A few NGDOs are even thought to have attended the October 2004 International Congress on Fund-Raising, which charged an entrance fee of €1,500 (Ibid).

With regard to internal management processes, these can be taken to include the policies of individual NGDOs on human resources, target-setting and strategic planning.[7] These practices , will be touched upon briefly in Chapter 9 of this study. But they will not be the main focus of this book, which is concerned with broad trends in the French NGDO sub-sector rather than with the myriad of internal procedures employed by hundreds of different NGOs. This should not be taken to imply that these management processes have been free from the influence of the French state. But it does suggest that where the state has made demands for professionalisation, it has done so at the level of the NGO sector as a whole rather than getting involved in micro-management issues or prescribing particular approaches to the internal running of organisations of which it has extremely limited knowledge.

Turning finally to their approach to lobbying and campaigning, this is clearly an area where French NGDOs have become much more sophisticated. This is evident from the way they have created directories of Parliamentarians with an interest in the developing world (*Agir Ici*, 1993), developed closer ties with MPs and senators (aided greatly by the HCCI, with its dozen or so nationally and locally elected representatives) and built up coalitions with trades unions and other actors within European and World Social Forums. NGDO progress in the field of lobbying can also be discerned in the much more systematic use of internet-based and other strategic campaigns, timed to coincide with elections in France.[8] It is also apparent from the creation of advocacy departments, even by conservative NGDOs such as the *Secours Catholique*, from the development of transnational NGO networks, such as the European NGO platform, CONCORD and from the increasing tendency for NGDOs to seek common positions ahead of major international conferences. However, the professionalisation of lobbying activity will not be a major focus here for two main reasons. The first is that, as a rule, advocacy work, particularly of a critical nature, is something, which NGDOs themselves want to do, rather than something, which the state necessarily wants to encourage. As Devin (1999: 73) puts it, the French authorities 'baulk at subsidising professional lobbyists' and are unlikely to wish to help non-governmental actors to improve their capacity to engage in lobbying, which could involve criticisms of the French state or its policies. The second is that it is hard to know what constitutes professionalisation in the context of advocacy campaigns. Indeed, as Alan Hudson has observed, 'NGOs are hard-pressed to know what they have achieved in their advocacy work, and hence what they should be accountable for' or, for that matter, whom they should be accountable to'.[9]

As for the areas where the French state has had more scope for direct influence over NGDOs, these fall into three categories: staffing and structures, financial management and accountability, and operational approaches in the Northern and Southern hemispheres. These will be discussed below, with the focus being initially on the early post-colonial decades and, subsequently, on the global era.

Early militancy and amateurism

It is commonplace to note that French NGDOs were characterised by militancy and amateurism in the early post-colonial decades. Generally, they did their 'own thing' and were given little encouragement by the state to 'professionalise', restructure or evaluate their own operations. On the staffing front, French NGDOs were marked both by a relative absence of permanent personnel, including at the level of their directors, as well as by an excessive emphasis on voluntary staff (Woods, 2000). This reliance on volunteers was incompatible with, or at least 'no guarantee' of, 'professionalism or continuity', given the 'episodic availability' of these actors (Beigbeder, 1992: 23), many of whom were young and engaged in their first work experience (CCD, 1999: 88). The priority of these NGDOs lay less with the qualifications and expertise of their recruits and more with their levels of commitment; be they religious, ideological or simply altruistic (Dauvin *et al.*, 2002). The result was that French developmental NGOs were often accused by *urgenciers* of ideological *dilettantisme* and a refusal to tackle the real challenges of the developing world. As one observer noted, 'In the 1960s, involvement in an NGO was all about motivation and activism' (Interviews in Paris, 2003). Similarly, Haddad (2002: 58) has argued, with reference specifically to the CCFD, that 'it was militants who ran the show:...enthusiastic and non-specialist staff were co-opted from within the ranks of the militants, thereby forming a good old band of friends'.

In these years, too, French NGDOs were marked by weak structures, at both an individual and a collective level. They were overwhelmingly small: some 76 per cent of the 158 NGOs in the first financial survey by the CCD (1987: 34) had an annual income of less than 3 million francs. They also had little scope for specialisation of staff or departments, as well as fairly manageable overheads, averaging around 14 per cent of total expenditure in 1985 (CCD, 1987: 108). They were said by Haddad (2002: 51) to display a classic non-profit structure, with volunteers, no clear management hierarchy or division of labour. While a few NGDOs were organically tied in to wider international networks (e.g. the CCFD, SC-CF, TDH-F, FDH), many were not and most were only just beginning 'a long process of maturing'

(Herlemont-Zoratchik, 2002: 209). The majority of NGDOs were, moreover, only just adjusting to the idea of federations, the most important of which, in the developmental domain, were not set up until the mid- to late 1970s.[10] It was not, in fact, until June 1982 that the first attempt was made at forming an overarching national federation, the *Intercollectif*, which comprised some 72 associations grouped together in six federations.[11] This was largely succeeded, in 1988, by the *Comité de Liaison des Organisations de Solidarité Internationale* (CLOSI). The CLOSI remained, however, a grossly understaffed entity, with only one part-time employee (Verschave and Boisgallais, 1994: 100) and a very light structure, which delegated major tasks to existing, smaller scale federations.[12]

As regards the financial management of NGDOs, here there were some examples of professional practice over the post-colonial decades. Thus, for example, public utility associations would submit their accounts to the scrutiny of regulatory bodies, such as the *Cour des Comptes* (see Chapter 5), whilst NGOs employing more than 50 staff, or securing more than 20 million francs in annual revenue, would nominate their own chartered accountant (Rubio, 2004: 102). However, the majority of NGOs did not have public utility status, did not submit their accounts to any official regulatory body, and did not, in fact, have any 'specific obligations in terms of accounting practices' (Ibid). Unsurprisingly, this slipshod approach meant that the quality of financial accountability to donors, both public and private, was generally low and marred by poor levels of transparency. This, in turn, contributed to a number of scandals. These included, in the 1970s and 1980s, the alleged funding by the CCFD of Marxist liberation movements in Latin America (Algrin, 1988); and, in 1993, the corruption scandal surrounding the cancer research NGO, the *Association pour la Recherche sur le Cancer* (ARC).

A similar lack of professionalism marked the approach of French NGDOs to projects and other operational work in the Northern and Southern hemispheres. To begin with their activities in industrialised countries, the main focus here will be on their development education efforts in France. While dozens of NGDOs engaged in such activities, few specialised in them and many saw awareness-raising either as the responsibility of the 'omnipotent' French state or as a by-product of their advocacy campaigns and their work in the field.[13] Development education was at quite a rudimentary stage in these years and was highly localised in its focus, often involving tiny, atomistic events, such as small-scale walks and talks, usually little reported by the media, and without much in the way of coordination across regions or at the national level. There were exceptions, such as the annual telethon, which began in 1987 and involved a 34-hour televised fund- and awareness-raising exercise for the *Association Française contre les Myopathies*. Another exception took the form of the development education activities undertaken by RITIMO, a vast network of documentation centres located in every region of France. Formed in 1985, RITIMO engaged in advocacy work, provided information to the general public, and offered information packs to potential volunteers.

Turning finally to NGDO projects, programmes and other operations in the South, these were often marked by amateurism, with emphasis being placed less on planning, coordination or results, and more on the personal conviction and engagement of French activists and volunteers. Commitment to the cause and good intentions were enough and often took precedence over any kind of measurable developmental impact. Considering themselves to be on a mission to help their fellow man materially and, often, spiritually, French NGDOs were reluctant to engage in self-criticism, soul-searching or evaluation. Indeed, evaluation was traditionally seen as a form of 'neo-colonial control' (Interview with CRID, 2003) and was 'considered both to be a type of interference and a useless, costly practice externally imposed by donors' (Ryfman, 2004: 42). There was, moreover, no clear commitment to learning or feedback mechanisms, prompting one expert commentator to note that 'French NGOs make little effort to draw lessons from their experience'.[14]

There were, no doubt, many reasons for this lack of professionalism in French NGDOs. It was partly a consequence of the lateness with which freedom of association emerged in France (Archambault, 1997), as well as the fact that there were (thanks to the 1901 law) so many non-governmental actors chasing after such a limited supply of French state resources. It was also partly a function of the anti-conformist, anti-capitalist leanings of many early NGDO leaders, who had grown up supporting the liberation struggles of the Third World and who were often Marxists and unreconstructed *soixante-huitards* (Dauvin *et al.*, 2002). It was, moreover, partly a result of an ideological mindset within French government circles, which baulked at the idea of encouraging the development, or the professionalisation, of unelected intermediaries between France's eternal, omnipotent state and its citizens.

In line with this thinking and with a general predilection to rely on official aid channels, the French state did little to push NGDOs to professionalise their approach in any of the aforementioned areas. To begin with the staffing question, the French government made only token gestures to promote higher levels of expertise. For example, it financed a handful of induction courses for volunteers going overseas with the AFVP and other volunteer agencies. It also set up, in 1985, the *Fonds de Développement de la Vie Associative* (FNDVA) as a mechanism which would fund the training of volunteers (*bénévoles*) based in France. Equally, the French state covered the bulk of the cost of courses offered by bodies, such as the *Institut Bioforce Développement* (BIOFORCE), which was created in 1983 to provide training to NGO logisticians, administrators and programme managers. However, the government limited its assistance in all these areas and did nothing to help resolve one of the most important staffing questions facing NGDOs during these years, namely the legal restrictions on remunerating their full-time or part-time directors (Archambault, 1997: 82).

The French state also did little to help NGOs build up their structures over the post-colonial era. It did make some attempt to bring developmental NGOs together through the creation, in 1960, of a civil society umbrella organisation known as the *Comité Français Contre la Faim* (CFCF).[15] It did, equally, provide some financial and other forms of support to federations, such as the CNAJEP (formed in 1968) and the CRID (established in 1976).[16] But it was far from wholehearted in its commitment and generally left NGDOs to their own devices, sometimes with unhappy consequences: for instance, the first overarching NGO federation, the CLOSI, imploded only a few years after its creation.[17]

The French government was equally lacklustre in its approach to NGDO financial management. As a rule, it only actively encouraged a handful of NGOs, specifically those enjoying public utility status, to submit detailed financial information to any regulatory authority.[18] It was not much more supportive when it came to development education work by NGDOs. The French administration did open up, to the general public, documentation centres in official bodies, such as the French Development Ministry. It did also provide funding for awareness-raising work by RITIMO and various NGO federations, and it did offer financial incentives to encourage these bodies to establish benchmarks of excellence in their activities and publications. But the French state made no systematic attempt to monitor or evaluate the quality of NGDO development education work. In fact, its support for awareness-raising activities remained one of the lowest in Europe, prompting some commentators to question whether the French administration even saw this type of work as its responsibility (OECD, 2000).

Finally, the French government was not proactive in pushing NGDOs to enhance the impact of their fieldwork. It did provide feedback (based on consultations with embassies and aid missions) on project proposals. But it made no attempt to introduce a more formal system of NGDO project evaluation. This reticence is perhaps not surprising, given that the French state itself was widely criticised for the lack of effectiveness of its official aid programme (Lancaster, 1999: 120–3) and was not, as such, well placed to insist that French NGDOs formalise their lesson-learning procedures.

Promoting 'bureaucratic' professionalisation

The French state has, over the global era, done much more to promote 'bureaucratic' forms of NGDO professionalisation. It has felt compelled to do so, partly to assuage the concerns of a donor public shaken by NGDO financial scandals, such as the ARC affair, and partly to reassure itself, and its critics, that official assistance to NGDOs was being used in a transparent manner and towards agreed ends. This latter concern has heightened in the last decade or so for a number of reasons. First, the French government has had to contend with high levels of domestic unemployment and the budgetary constraints imposed by the European Stability Pact (which places a ceiling on the public deficit of 3 per cent of Gross Domestic Product). Second, it has had to deal with allegations by the *Cour des Comptes* (2005) that the French Foreign Ministry has little control over the taxpayers' money it channels through NGOs. Finally, the French state has been its own hardest task-master, introducing, in 2001, the *Loi Organique relative aux Lois de Finances* or LOLF, a rigorous and far-reaching process of reform of all official spending.[19]

Faced with these pressures, the French government has, unsurprisingly, become more proactive in encouraging NGO professionalisation in the various areas discussed above. It has, for example, done more to encourage staff development by part-funding a much wider range of training courses. These are now offered by federations, such as *Coordination SUD*, by specialist bodies, such as BIOFORCE and by more established centres, such as the *Institut International de Recherche et de Fédération Education au Développement* (IRFED), founded by Father Lebret in 1958. The French state has also sought to raise levels of NGDO expertise by introducing, in January 2002, a system for validating the work experience of *bénévoles* who have devoted over 2,400 hours to an international cause (Rubio, 2004: 49). It has, moreover, helped NGDOs to enjoy more stable and strategic forms of management by authorising them, under the 2002 Finance Law, to remunerate directors who are working full-time.

Significantly too, the French government has been much more vigorous in its efforts to bolster NGDO structures. It has, for example, shored up the institutional capacity of individual NGDOs by concentrating the bulk of its assistance on a comparatively small number of large- to medium-sized organisations.[20] Equally, the French state has facilitated the development of more 'bureaucratic' NGDO structures by paying above-average levels of overhead costs for the projects it co-funds. To illustrate, France covers 10 per cent of these expenses, placing her in the top five European donors, behind Switzerland (10–14 per cent) but ahead of countries with a stronger record of support for NGOs, not least Holland (7.5 per cent) and Germany (4 per cent) (Potevin, 2000: 14).

At the same time, the French government has aimed to strengthen NGDO structures at a collective level. Thus, the Foreign Ministry unit, the MCNG (part of whose remit is to build up the structure of the non-governmental sector) has provided NGDOs with financial incentives for putting together joint funding bids and for taking on the extra administrative burden of coordinating inter-associative and other programmes co-financed under 'the new contractual arrangements' (see Chapter 7). Equally, the MCNG has offered technical support and guidance for the formation and development of federations and other coalitions capable of negotiating authoritatively with the French government. It has recently contributed €610,000 a year towards the total operational cost of the main federations, with around a third of this sum being channelled specifically to *Coordination SUD* (Ibid: 20).[21] Lastly, the MCNG has even supported French NGO efforts to develop their links with other national networks. It has, most notably, offered specific support to *Coordination SUD* in the elaboration of a three-way agreement with the Brazilian and Indian federations, Associação Brasileira de ONGs (ABONG) and Voluntary Action Network India (VANI) (DGCID, 2002).

In the case of financial management, the French authorities have stepped up their efforts to ensure greater NGDO accountability. Whereas in the past, it was only resource-rich NGOs and those with public utility status that were subject to financial checks by the *Cour des Comptes*, the French state has now passed a series of legislative measures tightening up these official controls. The first, on 10 August 1991, was a law requiring all NGOs which make nationwide funding appeals to the donor public to prepare financial accounts and to deposit these at the French *Prefecture* for inspection by the *Cour des Comptes* (Rubio, 2004: 102). Then, on 28 May 1996, legislation was promulgated that required NGOs active in health-related work to make their accounts available to the *Inspection Générale des Affaires Sociales* (IGAS). More recently still, on 1 August 2003, a law was passed that gave the *Cour des Comptes* the right to check, should it wish to, the accounts of any NGO benefiting from tax relief (Blum, 2005: 26).

Finally, the French authorities have provided NGDOs with greater incentives to professionalise their development education activities and their operational practices in the field. Toning down its earlier opposition to integrating development education into the school syllabus, the French state has begun to co-fund NGDO work aimed at preparing pedagogical tools and teacher training courses on overseas development issues.[22] The French government has, moreover, demonstrated a new-found willingness to co-finance NGDO awareness-raising work, at least in the case of well-coordinated, national-level campaigns, such as the *Semaine de la Solidarité Internationale*, *Acteurs Solidaires* and *Demain le Monde* (discussed later). It has also been keen to ensure that many of these development education activities should be properly evaluated via the *Fonds pour la Promotion des Études préalables, Études transversales et Évaluations* or F3E (examined below).

As regards NGDO operations overseas, here the French state has been particularly keen to promote best practice. It has, in the context of 'the new contractual arrangements', required French NGDOs to spell out, in their funding bids, their commitment to feasibility reports and to strategic management tools such as the logical framework.[23] More generally, the French government has pushed NGDOs to place greater emphasis on evaluation, feedback and learning. With these goals in mind, it played a key role in the creation of the F3E in 1994. This evaluative and training body was set up to improve the quality of French NGDO action and to give the sector the capacity to undertake its own evaluations.[24] The F3E, which is funded to the tune of 80 per cent (around €400,000 per year) by the French Foreign Ministry, allows for a 70 per cent state subsidy on most evaluations and feasibility reports; and this figure rises to 90 per cent for cross-cutting evaluations, which simply could not be undertaken without substantial external funding (Blum, 2005: 31). This unit also seeks to promote lesson-learning and the pursuit of best practice by requiring NGDOs to make their evaluations available to all member organisations. In so doing, it builds upon the work of other state-funded forums, such as the CCD and the *Inter-Réseaux développement rural*, each of which offers NGDOs the opportunity to engage in dialogue and advance their thinking on specific thematic and sectoral issues.[25]

Towards a 'development monoculture'?

In response to these recent overtures from the government, French NGDOs have undertaken some 'bureaucratic' forms of professionalisation. But they have stopped well short of becoming 'technical agencies of government' (Korten, 1991: 36) or, for that matter, 'development monocultures' (Fowler, 2000: 105). Instead, they have sought to hold on to something of their earlier militancy, not least in their approach to staffing, financial management and operational issues.

Staffing and structures: professionalisation 'with borders'

On the staffing front, French NGDOs have recognised the need to respond to the state's criticism of the relatively amateurish profile of their personnel. French *développementalistes* have, for example, come to the view that 'good will, the desire to help is no longer enough in itself' and that 'nowadays it is essential to have real skills in order to work for an NGO' (Haddad, 2002: 50). Voluntary agencies, for their part, have reached similar conclusions and given up on 'the missionary model where desire to be "of service" used to take precedence over the question of expertise' (Ibid).

One of the main ways in which French NGDOs have addressed these perceived shortcomings has been through recruiting better qualified personnel. This is clear from Table 6.1, which shows how the qualifications of volunteers for overseas placements have risen significantly over the global era. In effect, in 1989, 43 per cent of recruits did not have degrees (BAC+3) and only 17 per cent had a postgraduate qualification higher than a Master's. By 1999, however, only 27 per cent of volunteers did not have degrees and 28 per cent had doctoral qualifications. More recent statistics confirm this trend. Thus, a 2003 IPSOS survey noted that the overwhelming majority of those volunteering to work overseas (76 per cent) are now graduates, whilst

Table 6.1 Percentage of volunteers qualified at various levels

	CAP/ BEP	BAC	BAC+1 or 2	BAC+3 or 4	BAC+5 or more
1989	5	5	33	40	17
1998	3	3	21	44	28

Source: CCD (2001b: 82). Note that the BAC or *baccalauréat* equates roughly to A-level qualifications; the CAP or *certificat d'aptitude professionnelle* is a vocational aptitude certificate; and the BEP or *brevet d'études professionnelles* is a technical school certificate.

only 19 per cent of the French population can lay claim to this level of education.[26] Furthermore, 39 per cent of NGDO recruits 'have come from one of France's top business schools or studies at the doctoral or Master's level', whilst almost half of the overseas programme managers working for the largest *développementaliste*, the CCFD, now have a level of BAC+5 (that is, five years of study after 'A-levels') (Interview with the CCFD, 2003).

At the same time, a parallel phenomenon has been the recruitment of highly skilled staff, sometimes from IOs or the world of business and sometimes from other NGDOs – Jean-Marie Fardeau, for example, was lured away from the pressure group *Agir Ici* to become director of CCFD (Ryfman, 2004: 72). There has also been a new-found willingness to raise salaries in cases where NGDOs have a need for specialist expertise (e.g. fund-raisers) or for older, more experienced staff, who may need to be offered expatriate salaries to encourage them to undertake longer-term missions (Blum, 2005).

Not only have French NGDOs effected major changes to their staffing profile, but they have also done so in a relatively seamless fashion. They have been helped in this 'up-skilling' process by a number of factors. The first was the high level of unemployment in France, particularly among young graduates in the 1990s (Haddad, 2002). The second was the end of French national service on 1 January 1997. This allowed volunteer agencies to move away from their past practice of accepting applicants whose main motivation was often the avoidance of military service. It also paved the way for more applications from female candidates, as well as for a more competitive selection process, based explicitly on the qualifications of applicants (Interview with CLONG-V, 2003).[27] The third factor was internal to NGDOs themselves and involved a change in attitude towards recruitment and training (Dauvin *et al.*, 2002). This new thinking can be seen in the way that French NGDOs now systematically post job advertisements on internet sites, such as the *Coordination SUD* and F3E websites. It is, moreover, apparent from the raft of recent NGDO guides which have been produced to encourage better qualified young people to engage in volunteer work.[28] It can, equally, be discerned in the greater readiness of French NGDOs to provide specialist training, undergraduate courses and postgraduate qualifications to young people interested in international development and humanitarian work. In this context, NGO practitioners have, for example, developed, together with a Paris-based business school, a diploma in fundraising offered by the *Union pour la Générosité*. They have also worked closely with the *Groupement d'Intérêt Scientifique pour l'Étude de la Mondialisation et du Développement* (GEMDEV), which offers over 30 postgraduate and development courses on globalisation and development economics across different universities in Paris (Blum, 2005).[29] Equally, they have established links with the Catholic University in Paris (whose students are often members of ATTAC), and with the University of Paris I (which proposes PhDs in NGO management).

This changing mindset is also evident in the greater commitment of developmental NGOs to on-the-job and other types of training. NGDOs have been keen to take advantage of, and send their staff on, the much wider range of training schemes that are currently available on overseas development matters. The latter include, accounting, strategic and personnel management courses offered by the prestigious *École des Mines*, the training on micro-credit issues available from the *Agence des Micro-Projets de la Guilde* and the informative sessions on human rights issues provided by *TDH-France*. A wider range of schemes are also now available from established training bodies, such as BIOFORCE and IRFED, whilst a new set of courses are on offer from NGO federations. In this latter context, the CRID currently coordinates the annual 'summer university', whilst *Coordination SUD* provides training in the area of capacity building and – under a scheme known as *Thunderstorm* – acts as an 'honest broker' by putting French NGDOs, and any of their local partners who require training, in touch with suitable course providers.

At the same time, French NGDOs have come to recognise the validity of the state's criticisms regarding their lack of institutional capacity. Aided by steadily rising levels of income from official and private sources, a number of leading French NGDOs have grown in size and taken on more permanent staff. In this context, for example, the CCFD has increased its number of employees based in France from 90 in 1988 to 184 in 2004, whilst the DCC and GRET have raised their number of permanent staff over the same period from 9 to 17 and 45 to 56, respectively (CCD, 1988 and 2004). Many French NGDOs have, moreover, 'come to recognise the emergence of specific career paths within their organisations' (Ryfman, 2004: 72) and have developed new areas of expertise, such as civil society building. Others have created specialist posts for fund-raisers or have set up new departments focusing exclusively on advocacy (as in the CCFD and even the *Secours Catholique*) or communications (as in MSF).

Significantly too, French developmental and other NGOs have engaged in more concerted efforts to structure themselves collectively. Leaving behind many of their old inter-associative disputes, they formed, in 1994, the first cohesive national federation, *Coordination SUD*.[30] They gave this a mandate to promote NGO interests in discussions with the state and helped it to bring within its fold all the main federations (see Annex B). French NGDOs have also created or helped to form, over the last decade or so, a host of other NGO 'platforms', specialised units, consortiums, networks and federations (see Chapter 2 for details).[31] They have, moreover, used these groupings as a means of engaging in more effective lobbying (see Chapter 7), as a way of developing expertise (notably in areas such as debt and microcredit) and as a springboard for collaborative bids for state funding under 'the new contractual arrangements'.

That said, however, it would be misleading to suggest that French NGDOs have remodelled their staff profile and structure simply to cater to the demands of the state. Most NGDOs have, in fact, viewed the rapid rise in the qualifications of recruits 'with circumspection' (Blum, 2005: 12). For some, this increase in staff qualified in often theoretical, high-level courses may simply end up serving the careerist ambitions of some new recruits, who will quickly leave the non-profit sector to take up better paid posts in international organisations. For others, it may result in a decline in the number of volunteers posted (Interview with MDM, 2003) or it may deny opportunities to enthusiastic young applicants with no formal qualifications and, perhaps even, to candidates with more practical qualifications (Interview with CLONG-V President, 2003).[32] For others still, particularly senior managers, the overriding concern is that this rise in qualifications might lead to a loss of NGDO identity and might even fuel a trend towards higher salaries.

Low pay levels have long been a feature of French NGDOs. They can be attributed 'to the small scale of the organizations, to the lack or weakness of trade unionism in the non-profit sector and to the fact that many workers accept over-exploitation because they share the ideals' of the association (Archambault, 1997: 210). Equally, they are 'due to a structural effect, as the labor force in associations is mostly female and more part-time than in any other sector' (Ibid). They are, moreover, the result of a deliberate strategy on the part of NGDOs, which harbour an ethical aversion to high salaries. As Blum (2005: 12) has pointed out, French NGDOs, unlike their Anglo-Saxon counterparts, have 'moral qualms about recruiting professionals and paying them in line with market rates'. Many feel the need to keep salaries low to maintain their links to the poorest people in developing countries, to distinguish themselves from private companies and to underscore the fact that they are not simply making a career out of other people's misfortune. In other words, they are living 'for' and not 'off' humanitarian action (Ryfman, 2004: 71–2). Indeed, according to the ACF logistician, Philippe

Sallet: 'Modest stipends enable us to remain militant. No-one is afraid to lose his job. We are as such free to say what we think.'[33]

In line with this thinking, French NGDOs have, despite considerable changes within the profession, maintained average salaries 30 to 50 per cent below market rates (Ryfman, 2004: 73). They have done so, equally, in terms of their remuneration of NGO directors, which has been much lower than in Anglo-Saxon countries. They have also been quick to criticise any non-governmental actors that are deemed to be paying comparatively high salaries. In this context, Sylvie Brunel, former ACF President, publicly complained about alleged 'freewheeling lifestyles' in this organisation where 'the salary level is incompatible with the act of appealing to the generosity of the public'.[34] There have also been criticisms levelled against NGDOs which pay their directors, not by following the restrictive terms laid down by the 2002 law, but through alternative channels. One such method is for a highly mediatised, but unpaid, figure to be appointed as president, whilst a salary is paid to a director-general, who assumes the day-to-day management of the organisation (Blum, 2005: 14). In other cases, the president may be remunerated through another association with a legal link to the NGDO in question; but, in such instances, the NGDO is often condemned by its peers for engaging in a form of 'hypocrisy ... a sort of device for getting round the law' (Ibid).

It has been partly out of fear of this type of criticism from fellow NGDOs that many non-governmental actors have been reluctant to take on the kind of fully fledged bureaucratic structures which state-led demands for professionalisation might require. Thus, while the top ten or so French NGDOs have grown and become more bureaucratic over the global era, the vast majority (89 per cent) of developmental NGOs have remained small- to medium-sized, with an annual income below M€10 (CCD, 2008: 52). They have, as such, had little scope to create specialised units or to take on additional salaried staff: some 51 per cent of French NGOs have, in fact, less than five employees and 72 per cent less than 10, this latter figure being well above the European average of 61 per cent (Woods, 2000: 19). Most small- to medium-sized NGDOs have been particularly wary of taking on too many permanent staff. Thus, while the sector as a whole now employs 2,231 full-time employees in France (CCD, 1998: 35), over 1,000 of these salaried personnel are concentrated in the 12 largest French NGOs (*Commissariat Général*, 2002: 31). Significantly, too, one of the biggest employers, the CCFD, does not even consider its staff to be 'permanent' and imposes an eight-year time limit, after which employees should, in principle, look for work elsewhere.

It follows that most NGDOs have remained strongly attached to their voluntary profile. Indeed, the overwhelming majority of personnel working for the French NGO sector have been *bénévoles*. According to the latest CCD survey (2008: 35), this type of volunteer made up the equivalent of 7,579 full-time posts out of a total of 41,198.[35] In terms of actual numbers, the

CCD estimated that there were 88,592 *bénévoles* in France in 2001, which made up 76 per cent of the total staff (CCD, 2003: 9–10). While these estimates are substantially lower than those of many other commentators, they are broadly consistent with the findings of an extensive World Bank study (2001: 40) which noted that 'three quarters of the NGOs questioned had between one and a hundred voluntary staff [based in France], which is above the European average'.[36] In a similar vein, Blum (2005: 13) has commented that

> French NGOs still rely very heavily on voluntary staff which ensures that the ideals of commitment and disinterest remain central and that costs are kept down. This results, however, in an image of French NGOs as being still largely artisanal and amateurish or at least non-professional compared, in particular, to Anglo-Saxon organisations.

This impression of amateurism tinged with militancy is particularly clear in the case of the most cash-strapped NGDOs, whose 'lack of means leads them to recruit poorly trained and badly paid staff, on short term contracts and/ or within the framework of the French youth employment scheme' (Ibid: 36).[37] It is also true of some of the smallest NGOs, which 'boast that they can do without the process of professionalisation' (Ryfman, 2004: 41) or refuse to accept the state's 'right to take a critical look' at them (CCD, 1999: 83). It is, equally, a feature of some French volunteer agencies, which do not 'see themselves as having a part to play in this vast movement towards professionalisation' (Ryfman, 2004: 41). While this amateurish image has been tempered by the emergence of new NGO federations, which have served as a catalyst for professionalisation, there are still many small- and medium-sized NGDOs which have simply not participated in the work of these collective groupings. The non-governmental actors in question have frequently been too preoccupied by a culture of immediate action and too constrained by shortages of staff, money and time. Operating in a legal climate which limits the working week of many of their staff to 35 hours, these organisations have had little choice but to 'free ride' and allow federations to take on advocacy or development education work in areas of concern to them. They have had to view these collective structures as a secondary priority, well behind the demands of their own NGO (Interview with the CRID, 2003).

Financial accountability versus bad habits

French NGDOs have, at the same time, responded to demands from the state and other sources for greater financial accountability. Most have recognised the need for 'a certain transparency' (CCD, 1999: 88) and have begun to send their annual reports to all their members, as well as putting these, together with their charters and a full breakdown of their accounts, on the web.[38] A total of 18 of the top French NGOs have gone further and formed, in 1989, the *Comité de la Charte de Déontologie*. This NGDO 'financial watch-dog' has drawn up a best practice charter on the duties and rights of NGOs and has promised to provide the donor public with the information they need if they are to 'give with confidence'. It has made commitments that go further than NGDOs are legally required to and it has sought to establish 'ethical and transparent rules' (Blum, 2005: 28). The focus of this charter has been on 'the transparency of documents placed at the disposal of the donor... the honesty of messages disseminated as part of appeals... and the rigour of modes of seeking and collecting funds' (Ibid). The *Comité de la Charte* has required its signatories to open up their books to public scrutiny and obliged any organisation wishing to use its logo to seek accreditation (for a three-year period), to agree to undergo an annual inspection and to pay a membership fee, which will vary according to the size of the organisation (Blum, 2005, 28).

As well as introducing this charter, French NGDOs have also engaged in their own internal audits and have, in some cases, signed up to a new system of certification, based on the Anglo-Saxon scheme, Charity Navigator (www.charitynavigator.org). The French version is run by the *Bureau Veritas Quality International* (BVQI) and involves a full on-site audit of procedures and other tests of NGDO financial and management practices before a certificate is awarded for a three-year period. The initial full-scale audit is subsequently backed up by interim controls such as annual or six-monthly check ups and even visits by mystery donors.[39]

Yet, while French NGDOs have undoubtedly improved their financial accountability, some have not gone nearly as far as others down this road. In some cases, this may be attributable to a lack of capacity, but in others it reflects a different set of convictions and priorities. Thus, many NGDOs have retained a continuing belief in the unquestionable rightness of their cause and an unwavering dislike of any external scrutiny of their accounts. As the CCD (1999: 83) makes clear, French NGDOs, 'having laid out their stall on the side of the critics, have long thought that they could not themselves be subjected to criticism.... Who had the right to criticise the critic?'. And while it is true that a number of NGDOs have signed up to an ambitious *Comité de la Charte*, it is unclear whether their motive for this initiative has been an innate desire to tighten their own internal rules or a more pragmatic concern to obviate the need for further rigorous controls by regulatory bodies, such as the *Cour des Comptes*. The truth probably lies somewhere between the two, as NGDOs have come to appreciate how imperative it is both to reassure their critical resource and to distance themselves from financial scandals, which can break out anywhere and at any time across the non-profit sector. The ARC affair has already been cited, but it was by no means a one-off. It was, for example, followed in 2002 by revelations, in an enquiry by the French Ministry for Social Affairs, that the *Fondation Raoul-Follereau* had apparently been using private donations, not for the declared purpose of eradicating leprosy in all its forms but, to subsidise conservative Cardinals in the Vatican and to fund productive investment projects in the Ivory Coast.[40]

Whatever their motivation for, and level of commitment to, tighter financial management, French NGDOs have been keen to keep their involvement in such self-regulatory schemes voluntary.[41] As Blum (2005: 28) puts it

> Even though the *Comité de la Charte* has laid down ethical criteria which are common to all associations, this remains a self-styled elaboration by NGOs of common standards. These organisations accord a quality-label for good conduct, which is insufficient given that those who engage in checks are volunteers and the only sanction available is the withdrawal of the kitemark…. It is also not clear that donors know how to distinguish between requests for donations from an organisation which sports the *Comité de la Charte* logo and one which does not.

The same author goes on to note, with respect to the NGO certification scheme, that 'here once again the system shows its limitations insofar as every agency [involved in the certification process] has its own system for marking and certification, and insofar as NGOs are bound to be all too easily tempted to opt for the system which is most likely to secure them the highest mark' (Ibid).

Given the voluntary nature of these financial management schemes, it is perhaps not surprising that French NGDOs have fallen short of government expectations in two recent official reports. The first was written by the *Cour des Comptes* (2005) and found that, while French NGDOs were not guilty of any major waste or abuses, they were marked by serious dysfunctionings and inadequate budgetary controls.[42] It pointed to failures in financial reporting and noted that, for projects co-funded by the state, travel and other receipts were often not produced on time, if at all, and the cost of NGDO expertise was often overvalued. It also suggested that, because of the lack of transparency in their reporting procedures, French developmental NGOs could be suspected of diverting state subsidies for purposes other than those for which they were accorded. It complained that NGDOs under-reported state subsidies by omitting, for example, the cost of telephone calls, electricity and water charges and so on. It also bemoaned the fact that French NGDO control over the salaries of their 'expatriate' and locally recruited overseas staff was marked by 'a certain laxness, with … additional payments accorded in a very opaque manner … and expatriate allowances at a level which is sometimes higher than contractually agreed' (Ibid: 9). It went on to deplore the fact that, in the case of the local partners of French NGDOs based in developing countries, 'Receipts are not checked or are poorly controlled, with fairly superficial checks carried out by local auditors, [and] an absence of any in-depth audits…' (Ibid). It added that there have even been instances where monies have been disbursed 'for intellectual services, without any assurance that these services will be carried out' (Ibid). Finally, it expressed concern that personal usage of NGO property and equipment is often implicitly or even, in the case of *Eau Vive*, explicitly permitted, despite the potential costs to the organisation of breakdowns, accidents, liabilities and general wear and tear.

The second report was a Parliamentary mission of enquiry (Blum, 2007), which focused on the use by French NGOs of private and public funds donated in the wake of the South Asian tsunami of December 2004. It was initiated following concerns – first signalled, in July 2005, by MSF – that the unprecedented volume of donations in response to the tsunami was greater than anything that French NGOs could possibly absorb and, hence, might end up being misspent or allocated to other tasks. Though focused essentially on emergency NGOs, this enquiry also looked at the CCFD and the SC-CF, which were present before, during and after this crisis. It corroborated many of the findings of the *Cour des Comptes* report and, indeed, of an earlier study by Blum, which had pointed to 'make-shift management' and 'a certain lack of professionalism' across the French NGO sector (Blum, 2005: 34). The 2007 Blum report noted with regret that French NGOs had been reluctant to help with this Parliamentary scrutiny and that they had viewed it as a constraint on their operational activity. It complained that they had refused to follow the advice of their own *Comité de la Charte*, namely to provide maximum transparency and to use a common 'grid' (developed in January 2005) for presenting financial data. Instead, 'NGO accounts were only submitted after several reminders and were produced in formats which were often hard to understand and impossible to compare from one institution to the next' (Blum, 2007: 10). Furthermore, questions from the mission of enquiry were often not answered or were answered erroneously, with mistakes amounting to several million euros in the case of the *Secours Populaire Français* and some €50,000 in the case of the CCFD. Finally, it claimed that respondents had used jargon and a plethora of data to give the impression of being accountable without actually explaining to their donors what they were doing and why. Indeed, it even contended that 'French NGOs do not know how to, or do not want to, hand over their accounts; they do not feel themselves accountable to their donors' (Ibid: 11 and 15).

Operational approach: pursuing quality or preserving militancy?

Turning finally to their operational approach, this is yet another area where French NGDOs have taken steps to respond to criticisms from the state and other actors. To begin with their development education work, here NGDOs have made a real effort to move away from their earlier localised, uncoordinated and amateurish practices towards a more professional form of awareness-raising that is destined, not only to reach a wider public, but also to portray a consistently positive image of the peoples of the developing world and to produce a message that is free from contradictions. With a view to professionalising their development education activities, they have employed a number of techniques, many of which are quite innovative. The first has involved the drawing up of charters. One of the most significant of these, entitled 'A Shared Set of Ethics', was prepared by *Coordination SUD* in 1997. This document, which has to be signed by all members of this federation, lays down a set of guidelines on ethical behaviour, some of which relate directly to development education work.[43] Another important charter, which was subsequently drawn up by the CRID in the late 1990s, focuses specifically on awareness-raising activities and stresses the need for all campaigns to convey to the public the complexity of the economic development process, the interdependent nature of North–South relations and the diversity and creativity of the developing world.[44]

A second method has revolved around the use of quality benchmarks or 'labels'. The pioneer of this concept was arguably the RITIMO network, which set up commissions in the mid-1980s to approve the quality of its publications and other outputs. The idea of 'quality-labelling' has since been taken further by NGDO federations, such as the Federation for Ethical Labelling (*Collectif de l'Éthique sur l'Étiquette*), which was formed in 1995, partly to establish a social or ethical kitemark for fair trade goods produced and sold in France and partly to make consumers, companies and the government aware of the ethical issues involved in the production and sale of these goods. The concept has also been used by the CRID, which introduced, in 1996, an initiative known as *Acteurs Solidaires* or 'Actors Working Together'. This latter scheme has involved the awarding of 'labels' to high-quality campaign work undertaken by NGDOs and has been geared towards encouraging these organisations to look beyond isolated activities and engage in joint awareness-raising initiatives at the regional level. *Acteurs Solidaires* has, to this end, co-financed, with Foreign Ministry support, various collaborative ventures by French NGDOs in the field of development education. It has, moreover, organised workshops and colloquiums, disseminated strategy papers and produced other informative tools designed to stimulate reflection.

A third technique to enhance the quality of development education work has been to offer training and other expert support to NGDOs involved in awareness-raising activities. This approach underpins the work of a new thematic NGO coalition known as the *Plateforme d'Éducation au Développement et à la Solidarité Internationale* (EDUCASOL), which was created in March 2004 at the initiative of 22 French associations and federations. Above all, this grouping provides training in the methodology of development education, as well as technical support, via its databases of pedagogical tools. As to the fourth approach, this has involved harnessing technology to ensure a more effective and widespread dissemination of information to the general public. One example of this has been the work of the RITIMO network in setting up, in 1988, a major bibliographical database which includes all the key resources from its various sites. This electronic tool has facilitated the process known as 'mutualisation', whereby books can be borrowed by members of the public on inter-library loan across any of RITIMO's 80 affiliated centres across France. An even more obvious example relates to the recent creation of internet sites by nearly all the main French NGDOs. The pioneer in this field has no doubt been *Coordination SUD*, which has set up a huge website that serves as a gateway to the sector as a whole and that includes reports, archives and links to all member organisations.[45] The CRID, too, has built up an impressive website, with archives of numerous high-quality reports, a raft of campaign literature and various newsletters (e.g. *Les Cahiers de la Solidarité*).

The fifth method has simply involved 'scaling up' awareness-raising activities. The clearest example of this is perhaps the efforts of NGDOs to have development education activities integrated into the French school syllabus, whether through Third World School Days (*Journées Tiers Monde à l'École*), their development of pedagogical tools for particular age groups or their endeavours to identify and set out the training required for teachers in this domain.[46] But other examples abound. These include the annual awareness- and fund-raising campaign, 'Future Planet' or *Terre d'Avenir*, which was first launched by the CCFD in 1992 and which is now a three-day event involving some 60,000 people, who come to visit around 500 stands devoted to issues relating to overseas development.[47] Then there is the 'International Development Awareness Week', coordinated by the CRID, which was launched by French NGOs, with French state backing, in October 1997.[48] This week-long event is now an annual fixture, which has in recent years, involved over 700 different activities and 200,000 people and which has offered NGOs the opportunity present their solutions to the challenges of the developing world.[49] It is complemented by a number of more targeted initiatives. Some of these have focused on specificgroups. Thus, the 'Student Solidarity Programme' (*Programme Solidarités Étudiantes*), which has, since 1993, informed students about international development issues, provided support to student associations active in this field and helped young people to secure work in this sector. Others have honed in on particular themes. To illustrate, 'The World of Tomorrow' (*Demain Le Monde*) was formed, in 1994, by a grouping of French developmental NGOs and trade unions with a view to raising awareness of specific themes, such as water, hunger, education for all, the environment, sustainable development, international migration and health. Similarly, the 'Fair Trade Fortnight' (*La Quinzaine du Commerce Équitable*) is a nationwide campaign organised annually in May by the NGDO 'Platform for Fair Trade'. It involves debates, exhibitions and stands selling a range of fair trade products. Its success can be measured by the fact that it organised over 3,000 activities in 2006 and saw the percentage of the French public claiming to be aware of this event rise from 9 per cent in

2000 to 74 per cent six years later (CCD, 2007). Finally, *Alimenterre* is annual European campaign, which includes some 160 French associations.[50] These organisations undertake, in around 20 towns across France, awareness-raising activities, which include debates, pedagogical campaigns and food markets, all designed to stress the importance of the 'right to food' and to food self-sufficiency. Events take place throughout the year, with the high point being the organisation of a World Food Day in mid-October (Ibid).

The final innovation has been the new-found readiness of French NGDOs to subject their awareness-raising activities to external scrutiny. This approach has been particularly encouraged by the organisers of *Terre d'Avenir* (see above), which was set up, at least partly to encourage exchanges, learning and systematic evaluations of development education activities. But other French NGDOs active in this field have also been prepared give up their unquestioning *militantisme* and allow evaluations to be carried out – usually by consultants from the F3E – on some of the larger development education programmes.

Alongside these innovations in their awareness-raising activities, French NGDOs have also taken steps to professionalise their fieldwork in the Southern hemisphere, as well as in Eastern and Central Europe. Here again, they have gone along, at least to some extent, with the 'template' for professionalisation laid down by the French state. They have, for example, adapted their project proposals, notably those falling within the remit of *la nouvelle contractualisation*, to take on board the guidelines and advice offered by the French authorities on funding applications. They have, in this context, pooled their expertise with other NGDOs and submitted the kind of large-scale collaborative bids which these new contractual arrangements are designed to finance (see Chapter 7). They have also integrated into their project proposals the type of strategic management tools which are regarded as a benchmark of quality by the French state, notably feasibility studies (which are a form of pre-evaluation of the likely impact of a programme) and the logical framework (which is a mechanism for agreeing at the outset of a project measurable targets and outcomes).

French NGDOs have, moreover, begun to see some value in persistent state-led demands for evaluations of their project work. Some have even come to view evaluation as 'a pragmatic and worthwhile measure' (Ryfman, 2004: 42) and have started to conduct their own limited, internal evaluations. French developmental NGOs were also just as keen as the Foreign Ministry on the establishment of the F3E as an independent consultancy and advisory unit on NGO evaluation matters. By 2006, some 55 NGDOs had signed up to this mechanism, paying their membership fee (initially 3,000 francs) and investing their energies in the running of this body.[51] They have formed their own 'general assembly'; elected, on an annual basis, a seven strong bureau, which examines requests for co-funding; and created a technical secretariat to implement the evaluation programme. NGDOs seeking to have their project evaluated have willingly incurred the costs of putting together a bid and have even covered part (usually 20 per cent) of the cost of the actual study. Indeed, in total between April 1994 and April 2002, some 33 feasibility studies, 50 evaluations and 7 cross-cutting studies were carried out by this body.[52]

French NGDOs have, moreover, fully recognised the importance of another of the government's main concerns, namely with learning and the creation of institutional memory ('capitalisation'). French NGDOs have themselves long been interested in learning, whether through word-of-mouth lessons or through feedback from volunteers, local staff and overseas programme managers. But they have increasingly begun to formalise these processes. In particular, they have viewed the F3E as a much needed source of learning and institutional memory. Thus, as the CCD (1999: 81) has noted,

> Thanks to dialogue with the permanent secretariat of the F3E..., [its] timely and sustained support in the drafting of the terms of reference of a study, ... [and its] training days offering technical advice on evaluation, the members of the F3E learn to subject their action to the scrutiny of an independent expert.

Furthermore, by joining this forum, NGDOs have agreed to a number of basic conditions. They have accepted that the findings of any evaluation must be open to all member organisations as a source of potential learning. Equally, they have endorsed the policy of focusing heavily on cross-cutting evaluations, which are deemed to benefit the largest possible swathe of organisations. Finally, they have agreed to take part in themed study days and restitutions whereby, one year after the evaluation, they provide feedback on what they have learned.

At the same time, French NGDOs have not seen the lesson-learning process as being confined to evaluation work. They have, for example, also sought to learn and exchange ideas through their participation in thematic commissions within the CCD, as well as in the working groups set up by CONCORD. They have also sought to guard against loss of institutional memory, and the problems associated with high staff turnover, by forming broad federations and by pooling their expertise within specialised thematic coalitions. The latter include, *Plateforme Dette et Développement* (the French civil society grouping on overseas debt), CERISE (a specialist NGDO network on micro-credit) and *Groupe Initiatives* (a federation of technical NGDOs, which serves as an invaluable memory bank on issues of international development).[53] In addition, many NGDOs have endeavoured to bridge gaps in their knowledge by developing closer links with independent research bodies. Indeed, over half of all French NGOs now claim to collaborate with French or foreign research centres and with universities on specific issues (*Commissariat Général*, 2002).

In parallel with these actions, French NGDOs have also taken greater care to store lessons, whether in the form of electronic archives on the internet or in NGO documentation centres, such as those managed by the DEFAP, the CCFD and UNICEF. The lessons learned are also disseminated across the French NGDO sub-sector by way of best practice guidelines (e.g. the *Vade Mecum* on funding bids), survey reports (e.g. the September 2003 CLONG-V/ IPSOS survey on volunteers returning to France) and regular updates on advocacy campaigns (e.g. *CRID Échos*). Other guidelines are circulated by means of manuals (e.g. F3E handbooks on evaluation), training courses, newsletters and even blogs. Most of the aforementioned material is produced by bodies, such as the F3E, the *Guilde Européenne du Raid*, *Coordination SUD*, the CCD, the HCCI and the CRID.[54]

It follows that French NGDOs have clearly altered their working practices in the Northern and Southern hemispheres quite significantly. Yet it would be wrong to think that they have routinely adapted their operational approaches to accommodate the wishes of the French state or, indeed, any other official or corporate donor. Thus, their development education activities can still be uncoordinated, localised and lacking in expertise. This is, in some ways, a systemic problem and an inevitable consequence of the ease with which French NGOs can be set up and then orient themselves towards development education work: some 146 organisations claimed to be involved in such activities in 2007 (CCD, 2007). It is equally linked to the rather unplanned way in which much awareness-raising has expanded. Thus, even national networks, such as RITIMO, are ultimately only a collection of highly localised centres, each with its own specialist interests, opening hours and library lending policies. This lack of coordination is, at the same time, also a reflection of a more deliberate strategy on the part of many NGDOs, which continue to see awareness-raising work as a militant activity and a spontaneous act of solidarity. This thinking is reflected, at least partly, in the way that some French NGOs have refused to sign up to the various innovations in development education work outlined above. For example, while the development charter drafted by the CRID has had real resonance for many NGDOs, it has been much less binding on *urgenciers*, many of which have continued to rely on emotive awareness-raising techniques. Significantly too, while some NGDOs have accepted the value of quality kitemarks, others have questioned whether development education activities can, in fact, be measured. These latter organisations have simply not attended the kind of methodological training courses offered by EDUCASOL and have taken the view that awareness-raising techniques cannot be learnt, since this type of activity is all about conviction and an activist spirit.

While most French NGDOs have, of course, taken advantage of new technologies, some have been less enthusiastic. Thus, many of the smallest NGOs and even some larger ones, such as the DEFAP, which sees itself more as a 'service of the Church' than an NGO *per se*, still have no website. Furthermore, French developmental NGOs have not made as much use of the audio-visual media as their counterparts in Anglo-Saxon countries. It remains a very rare thing indeed, outside of coordinated appeals at the time of extreme emergencies, for NGDOs to diffuse television advertisements to inform the public or raise money. This latter point is, at least partly linked to the reluctance or inability of some developmental NGOs to ratchet up their awareness-raising activities from a local to a regional level – a recurring criticism in recent evaluations.[55] Finally, whilst French NGDOs have been prepared to see their recent, large-scale development education activities evaluated, they have had neither the capacity nor the desire to see the vast majority of their work in this field subjected to external scrutiny.[56]

A similar set of observations could be made regarding NGDO operations overseas. Here again, it would be misleading to suggest that these actors have simply professionalised their fieldwork in the manner recommended by the French state. Thus, while they have certainly submitted more sophisticated bids for project funding, they have not always matched the discourse in these applications with effective and professional collaboration in the field. Indeed, many of the initial attempts at coordinated multi-actor projects, such as the 'priority programmes' in Vietnam and Palestine, the first *Programme Concerté Maroc* in Morocco, and the *Dotation au Partenariat* in Cameroon, had quite disappointing outcomes (Interviews in Yaoundé, 2004). And while some NGDOs have integrated strategic planning and logical frameworks into their project proposals, many others have refused to do so, considering these tools to be too time-consuming, too mechanical and too ill-adapted to the kind of holistic and participatory approaches favoured by French *développementalistes* and volunteer agencies.

In line with this logic, many French NGDOs have also continued to harbour doubts about evaluations. They have, in particular, questioned whether the Anglo-Saxon style of evaluation being recommended, with its emphasis on measurable targets and standardised criteria, can truly capture the participatory, affective and sometimes 'spiritual' nature of their social development work, let alone their wider efforts to promote empowerment, self-reliance and sustainability. As Blum (2005) has noted,

> NGDOs...consider that...it is impossible to generalise about the same type of experiences, with each terrain and each action being different. Furthermore they wonder who might have the right, as well as the necessary means, to draw up a framework for evaluation and then evaluate NGO actions in line with this framework.

Volunteer organisations, for their part, have also opposed the standardisation and measurement which evaluation implies, seeing each volunteer situation as a different exchange. Thus, according to the CCD (2001b: 22):

> They refuse to envisage a standardisation of humanitarian interventions...in the name of a quest for efficiency.... Rather, they affirm that

the success of their actions cannot be measured on the basis of cold and rigid norms. This success depends heavily on the quality of the work carried out in common by individuals whose exchanges take place in specific contexts...

The reflections of these organisations have been strengthened by the work of 'militant' experts based in French consultancy NGDOs, such as the GRET, IRAM and the *Centre International d'Études pour le Développement Local* or CIEDEL (i.e. the very bodies, which do most of the evaluation work for the F3E). These organisations have formed a federation, *Groupe Initiatives*, which examines issues surrounding the evaluation of social projects. Their work on participatory evaluation has run in parallel to that of *urgenciers* (specifically those belonging to the *Groupe Urgence Réhabilitation Développement*).[57] Both French NGDOs active in *Groupe Initiatives* and the *urgencier* think-tank have questioned Anglo-Saxon attempts, as typified in the Sphere Project (1997), to lay down a definitive set of measurable criteria for evaluating NGO effectiveness.[58] They have also militated in favour of a more holistic conception of development effectiveness, based at least partly on the quality of relationships between civil society actors and other empirically unmeasurable criteria. They have gone so far as to argue that a project may be judged successful if many people are involved, even if it does not achieve material or concrete results (Interviews in Paris, 2005).

Where French NGDOs have had to undergo formal evaluations, they have, in many cases, continued to see this as an imposition. Their culture simply has not leant itself to evaluation and, as Blum (2005: 31) has observed,

> In reality, it is often the Foreign Ministry which pushes NGOs to engage in a process of evaluation, particularly before renewing its funding or agreeing the next tranche of monies. The whole point of the F3E is to get beyond this sense of obligation by encouraging NGOs and the Foreign Ministry to look beyond a policy based entirely on penalties and put in place one based on joint learning and dialogue, drawing on the recommendations of independent experts (Ibid).

Blum has further remarked that 'there are few NGOs whose project proposals contain a budgetary allocation specifically for evaluation';[59] He has, equally, noted that French NGDOs have not always embraced the spirit of state, or indeed other official, demands in this context. Thus,

> Whilst NGDOs have accepted financial checks on their accounts, they have been less inclined to put in place systems for monitoring and evaluation. Among those who have done, many very often confine themselves to measuring effectiveness accurately, that is to say, to comparing the results achieved with the objectives laid down; sometimes they try to

measure efficiency, which consists of comparing results achieved with resources mobilised. But they rarely seek to assess the relevance and durability of their actions, with a view to measuring impact... (Ibid)

Relatedly, they have often taken steps to limit the risk of any negative reports. In cases where independent evaluations have been carried out, and where findings are critical, efforts have been made to bury, conceal or rubbish any damaging conclusions (Interviews in Paris, 2003). In other cases, they have undertaken self-evaluations which are inevitably on a much smaller scale given that they are self-financed (Interview with CCFD, 2005). The findings of such studies also tend to be quite flattering. As Blum (2005: 29) has argued,

> The majority of NGOs are prepared to undertake a form of self-evaluation by producing narrative accounts or activity reports, which are sent... to their members, at the same time as financial reports, which are to be found on their internet site. There can nonetheless be no doubt that NGOs are, in such instances, more inclined to congratulate themselves, all the more so since these reports often serve as a form of advertising.

In other cases, they have eschewed truly independent evaluators and opted for more sympathetic consultants, who are known to them or already familiar with the project. As the *Cour des Comptes* (2005: 10) has pointed out, 'NGOs, such as the GRET, and groupings, such as IRAM or the F3E..., are, at one and the same time, given funding to carry out projects and employed as evaluators of other projects'. These actors may not be objective, since they are bound to be affected by the 'links which exist between evaluators and operations on the ground'. They are also likely to be influenced by the 'prospect of being themselves judged in turn in the future' (Ibid).

Needless to say this lukewarm attitude of French NGDOs towards evaluation has had a negative impact on their ability to learn, store and disseminate formal lessons. It could be argued that they have not generally viewed evaluations as a true source of learning, that is to say, as a way of exposing weaknesses, which could subsequently be rectified. Instead, they have considered evaluations as a means of providing public and private donors with a string of success stories and as a mechanism for pulling the wool over the eyes of observers, rather than with getting to the heart of any problems. The F3E is, in part, an attempt to get round this issue, but its evaluations are only accessible to member organisations and its activities are premised upon the questionable assumption that those organisations are all genuinely prepared to have their shortcomings identified and made known to the rest of the membership.

It follows, then, that there are few instances of NGOs drawing lessons from past evaluations, establishing formal feedback loops or disseminating lessons widely across the NGDO sub-sector. There is also little evidence of any systematic attempt by French NGDOs to learn, to store lessons or build up institutional memory. They have, in fact, been constrained in these tasks by a number of factors. These have included the action-oriented culture of NGDOs, which tends to assume that lessons are constantly changing and that there is, as such, a need to operate exclusively in the 'here and now' (Mowjee, 2001: 174). A second obstacle has been staff shortages and the lack of capacity of NGDOs to maintain up-to-date archives. A third impediment has involved the absence of organic or systematic links with universities and research centres (Interview with the HCCI, 2003). A final constraint has been the high proportion of voluntary personnel (both *volontaires* and *bénévoles*). The rapid turnover of these staff, together with the short period of time they often work for an NGDO, have militated strongly against long-term evaluations or the build up of institutional memory. As Blum (2005: 31) has noted, 'Young people... tend to use NGOs as a kind of on-the-job apprenticeship before taking on the world of work. Undertaking only one NGO mission, the latter cannot... build on their experience and draw lessons from past failures'.

Conclusion

This chapter has shown how French NGDOs have gone some way towards the 'bureaucratic' forms of professionalisation advocated by the French authorities. It has stressed, however, that they have also held on to their militant profile and that this can still be discerned in their staffing, structures, financial management and operational approaches at home and overseas.

It will be left to Chapter 8 to examine in detail whether French NGDO behaviour in this context has been in line with RD theory. Without wishing to pre-empt our subsequent findings, it is worth pointing out that the actions of these non-governmental actors do appear to fit broadly with the RD perspective. Thus, French NGDOs have altered their working practices wherever the state has offered tangible incentives, whether in the form of technical advice, logistical support or financial assistance. They have, however, stopped short of allowing their organisations to become bureaucratic 'monocultures' or to be marked by what Chambers (1994) has referred to as 'normal professionalisation'.[60] In so doing, they might be accused of missing out on opportunities for additional resources from the state. In reality, however, they would appear to be correctly reading their environment and recognising that their priority lies, not so much with the state, which is a relatively marginal resource, as with the donor public and their activist base, which represent their critical resource.

With this perspective in mind, it is not difficult to understand the behaviour of French NGDOs. Thus, while these actors are all too aware of how censorious the French public can be in the face of corruption scandals, they have also realised that this donor public has a very different conception of professionalisation from the kind of 'development monoculture' advocated by the French authorities.[61] They have recognised that the public does not want to see its donations used towards the development of more robust NGO structures or reporting procedures and that it equates professionalism essentially with action, immediate results and the avoidance of delays. This mindset is described by Lewis (2001: 9) as the 'widespread view, particularly among the public and donors, that NGOs should use almost all their funds for working with poor people and should not spend money on administrative overheads or waste too much time on administrative questions'. In a similar vein, Smillie (1995: 151) has suggested that there is a 'powerful public myth that development should be "cheap" which has led, in some quarters, to a tendency to take low NGO administrative overheads as one of the main criteria for judging success'.

At the same time, French NGDOs have also been aware of the need to take on board the views of their grassroots activists. They have been all too conscious that their militant supporters do not share the French state's enthusiasm for professionalisation. Indeed, many of these volunteer activists have rejected this process altogether, seeing it as a form of private sector managerialism that will lead the NGO movement to lose touch with the poor, become indistinguishable from commercial companies and sacrifice its original mission. These core supporters have opposed what they see as a process of standardisation and 'a homogenizing "tyranny" around demands for the use of specific tools and techniques, irrespective of the NGDO's own competences and context' (Edwards and Fowler, 2002: 17). Some have taken the view that professionalisation may be a threat to their 'conviction-based culture' (Ryfman, 2004: 70) and their 'ethos of solidarity' (Blum, 2005: 13). Others have even seen it as undermining the very qualities of innovation and flexibility, which first attracted donors to NGDOs and to the services they had to offer. It is to this role of service provider on behalf of the state, and to the dilemma it poses for French developmental NGOs, that this survey now turns.

7
Working for or Working on the State?

The third trend highlighted in our introductory chapter involves a possible alignment of the priorities and activities of NNGOs with those of their respective central states. This particular trend is especially problematic in that it suggests that NNGOs are willing not only to strike up a rapport with the state and professionalise their working practices, but also to embrace the government's priorities and act as agents in the delivery of its policies. Whether or not NNGOs have, indeed, taken on more of a service delivery role is a question which will require detailed empirical research by future scholars. For the purposes of this survey, it should suffice to recall that accusations have been made to this effect by respected analysts and NGDO practitioners, such as Wallace *et al.* (1997), Fowler (2000) and Hulme and Edwards (1997).

Yet, can these allegations be seriously levelled at French NGDOs? Have they aligned their prerogatives with those of the French state and agreed to serve as agents in the delivery of its policies or, indeed, as vehicles in the dissemination of the government's message to a wider domestic and international audience? These questions will be central to this chapter, which will begin by demonstrating how the operational and policy priorities of the French authorities and those of French NGDOs diverged in the early post-colonial decades. It will then set out briefly the French state's prerogatives over the global era or, more specifically, since the pivotal moment in the mid-1990s, when the government introduced the 'new contractual arrangements'. Next, it will assess how far French NGDOs have been prepared to align their core objectives with those of the state and to act as a service provider or vector on its behalf. Finally, it will ask whether, *a priori*, the behaviour of French NGDOs in this context appears broadly consistent with RD theory.

Before undertaking this survey, it is worth stressing that the caveats outlined in previous chapters are particularly relevant here. The first is that it is extremely difficult to show any clear-cut causal connection between policy or operational shifts by the French state and changes in the priorities of NGDOs. As Hulme and Edwards (1997: 195) have argued, 'there are the inevitable questions of causality: if an NGO suddenly allies itself to donor policies how do we disentangle the influences of donor finance...from a change in leadership of the NGO?' How, it might equally be asked, can it be determined that the direction of causality has not been the other way round and that it has not, in fact, been French NGDOs, which have exerted a determining influence over the French state? This whole question is further complicated by the fact that many of the financial statistics, particularly on the NGO side, are both incomplete and presented in formats, which are barely comparable over time. This point is perhaps most clearly illustrated by a recent CCD report, which was unable to identify the geographic region in which 35 per cent of French NGO project monies were spent or, indeed, the particular sector, in which 47 per cent of NGO revenue was disbursed (CCD, 2003: 19 and 20).

The second proviso is that it is hard to generalise about the priorities of the French state or to assume that it is a monolithic unit with a homogen-ous policy on overseas development. This latter actor does not have just one set of easily identifiable prerogatives but multiple aims arising out of a number of quite distinct institutions, which include the *Elysée*, the Prime Minister's office, the AFD, the Treasury and, above all, the Foreign Ministry. Since 1999, the diverse views of a dozen ministries interested in foreign aid issues have been distilled within an inter-ministerial forum, the CIDIC, and fed straight back to NGOs via the COSP (see Chapter 5). While it will be assumed here that the policy pronouncements of the CIDIC and the MCNG (the main NGO contact within the Foreign Ministry) are broadly represen-tative of the views of the French authorities, it should not be forgotten that the French state's priorities in relation to NGDOs and overseas development are never easy to pin down. This problem is exacerbated by the fact that rhetorical statements by ministers (e.g. on the need for more aid to be chan-nelled through NGDOs) are rarely followed up, and by the way that the state's own prerogatives changed quite significantly over the course of the 1990s. There is, indeed, now some confusion, on the part of commentators, as to where the French government's true priorities lie. In this context, the OECD (2004: 10) has noted how French development policy has 'several key principles' but 'no unified vision'. It has called for 'an overview of the direc-tions for ODA [overseas development assistance]...in order to rank goals by order of importance, clarify geographic, sectoral and thematic choices, and determine the role of different institutions and instruments...'.

The final caveat is that it is virtually impossible to cover all, or even most, of the myriad of priorities of a range of actors as diverse as French NGDOs. Instead, it has been decided here to focus only on core operational and policy prerogatives. In the case of the former, the emphasis will be on broad sectoral and geographic preferences, that is, the key fields of activity and continents in which NGDOs are active. It is recognised, of course, that this approach cannot do justice to the range of operational priorities espoused by different non-governmental actors, some of which are generalists operating globally (e.g. the CCFD, SC-CF) and others of which are specialists active only on a single continent (e.g. *Afrique Verte*) or even in a single sector (e.g. AIDES). As regards policies, here the focus will be on the core prerogatives of French NGDOs for the political and economic development of the developing world. Once again, it is accepted that this way of proceeding excludes other important NGDO issues (such as the environment, AIDS and women's empowerment) and glosses over ideological differences, which have, historically, been a source of division within the French non-governmental sector. One such divide, which has subsided since the end of the Cold War, has involved Marxist NGDOs, on the one hand, and Christian organisations, on the other. While both sets of actors were firmly located within the *tiersmondiste* camp (a loosely defined grouping of anti-imperialist, left-leaning organisations, which sought to protect the developing world from the ravages of capitalism) and while they were bound together by their concern for social justice and their links to the anti-colonial liberation movements, they did, nonetheless disagree over the solution to the problems of the 'Third World'. The former adopted a radical, class-based and secular rhetoric calling for an overhaul of the capitalist system, whereas faith-based NGDOs were more concerned with placing man, specifically the poor peasant, at the centre of the development process and were less implacably opposed to the free market, which was ultimately seen as a lesser evil than atheistic communism (Joly, 1985). Another division, which came to the fore in the mid- to late 1980s, was between left-leaning, *tiersmondiste* developmental NGOs and more libertarian *urgenciers*, led by the *Fondation MSF*. Although the rift between these actors has become less visible since the defeat of the former by the latter, it can still be discerned in relation to particular issues. On human rights, for example, former *tiersmondiste* NGDOs have continued to focus mainly on collective economic and social rights, while *urgenciers* are still primarily geared towards the defence of individual civil and political rights.[1] These organisations have, equally, differed in their stance vis-à-vis the anti-globalisation movement. To illustrate, large developmental NGOs, such as the CCFD, have always been more closely tied in to the *anti-* or *alter-mondialisation* movement than leading humanitarian non-state actors.[2] Indeed, the largest *urgencier* of all, MSF, has, with the possible exception of its recent campaign with OXFAM to demand reductions in the price of life-saving drugs, kept a safe distance from this movement (Fougier, 2004).[3]

Early French state priorities

To begin with the priorities of the French state during the early post-colonial decades, these were linked to its *realpolitik* ambitions and afforded little scope for French NGDOs to take on any kind of service provider role. Indeed, the French authorities were deeply suspicious of these non-governmental actors, some of which were Marxist-leaning and others of which were close to the Church and, hence, not organisations, which the secular French Republic might normally be inclined to finance.[4] The French government also did not feel the need to rely on NGDOs given that it had its own extensive network of embassies, aid missions and technical assistants deployed across the developing world. It even doubted whether these developmental NGOs, with their unmeasurable participatory and holistic approaches, were professional or large enough to implement the kind of macro-level programmes which the French aid administration liked to fund. Finally, the French state was all too aware of the potential problems associated with relying on NGDOs as service agents, given how incompatible its own operational and policy priorities were with those of French non-governmental actors.

So what, then, were the operational priorities of the French authorities in the years before *la nouvelle contractualisation*? These clearly revolved around macro-level programmes much more than local, micro-level projects.[5] The state's emphasis was on large infrastructural development projects (which generated substantial revenue for French companies) and productive economic programmes (which shored up French investments). Its focus was also on mechanisms to promote macro-economic stability (e.g. budgetary support and programme aid), as well as on measures to preserve French influence (e.g. high levels of assistance to tertiary education and university sponsorships for the children of ruling elites in developing countries) (see Figure 7.1). The French state did, of course, take some interest in social development work. Thus, it devoted around 60 per cent of its co-funding to the NGO sector to issues such as basic healthcare, primary education and rural development (see Figure 7.2). Yet, the total volume of this assistance was low, at around 55 million francs, and the French government's emphasis was less on basic needs and more on ways of exporting Western medicines, mechanised agricultural techniques and the French language.

As to the French state's geographic prerogatives in these years, these were concentrated on the former empire (see Figure 7.3). Its main focus was on maintaining a sphere of influence in Africa; and, to this end, 54 per cent of bilateral aid was reserved for sub-Saharan Africa (particularly for better-off former colonies, such as Senegal, the Ivory Coast and oil-rich Gabon), with a further 10 per cent set aside for North Africa and the Middle East. By contrast, only a comparatively small proportion of assistance was allocated to continents, such as Asia (10 per cent) and Latin America (6 per cent), where France had fewer historical connections (see Figure 7.3).

As regards the French state's policy priorities, these were underpinned more by its realist ambitions than by any overriding desire to find economic or political solutions to the challenges of the 'Third World'. Its proposed remedies for developing countries were, as such, unlikely ever to be

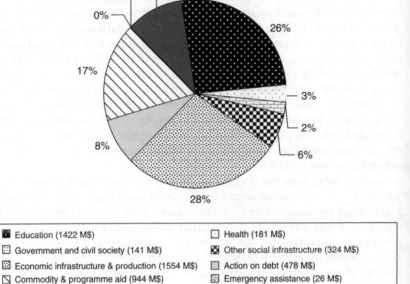

Figure 7.1   Sectoral breakdown of French state aid in 1991–92
Source: OECD (2004: 81). Figures are in millions of dollars (US) and relate to gross bilateral aid.

supported, let alone propounded, by value-driven organisations, such as French NGDOs. Two examples should suffice to illustrate this point. The first was the French state's espousal in the 1970s, of Rostowian theories of economic growth, which assumed that donors could, by using aid to plug skills and capital shortages, enable developing countries to enjoy the kind of rapid growth experienced by Western Europe in the wake of the Marshall Aid Plan.[6] This approach was, of course, never likely to win much backing from French NGOs, partly because it did not deliver the levels of growth it had promised and partly because it presupposed an acceptance of what was, for many NGDOs, an unjust capitalist mode of exchange. The second example involved the French government's adoption, in 1981, of the *Doctrine d'Abidjan*, which linked French bilateral aid to the signature of World Bank-led, neo-liberal economic recovery programmes. In theory, this policy shift might have created space for French NGDOs to collaborate closely with the French authorities and play a greater role in alleviating the negative social effects of the transition by developing countries to a market-led economy. In reality, however, no such collaboration ever took place, partly because the

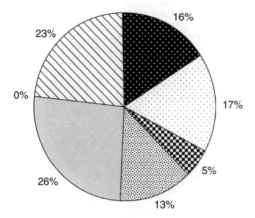

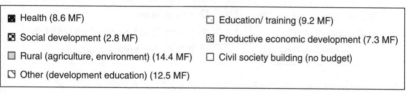

Figure 7.2 Sectoral breakdown of French state co-funding of NGOs in 1993

Source: *Ministère de la Coopération* (1995: 50). Figures are the earliest available in the public domain and are in millions of French francs. They relate only to French Development Ministry co-funding of NGO projects and development education work. Assistance to volunteer associations is not included.

French government had its own doubts about World Bank-led programmes and partly because French NGDOs rejected the underlying logic of structural adjustment and refused to help to perpetuate the capitalist system.

The French authorities did seek to bring NGDOs more on board in the immediate post-Cold War period by introducing measures, such as the Social Development Fund (discussed in Chapter 4), which sought to alleviate the negative social consequences of structural adjustment. They also won some backing from NGDOs by linking French bilateral aid, as from President Mitterrand's 1990 speech at La Baule, to progress by developing countries on democracy and civil and political liberties. Ultimately, however, the French state continued to advocate what were essentially market-led solutions to the problems of the developing world. Thus, for example, it introduced, in 1993, the *Doctrine Balladur*, which re-affirmed France's commitment to tie its bilateral aid to adherence by developing countries to World Bank/IMF recovery programmes. Then, in 1994, the French government appeared to signal its support for market-led remedies south of the Sahara by presiding

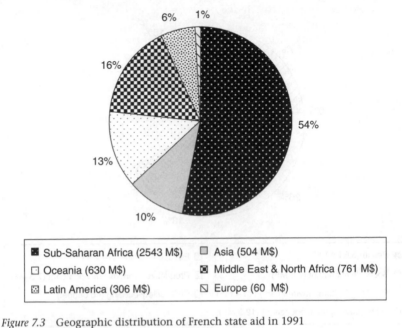

Figure 7.3   Geographic distribution of French state aid in 1991

Source: OECD, *Development Cooperation Peer Review Series: France*, OECD, Paris, 1994, p. 14. Figures are in millions of dollars (US) and refer to gross bilateral aid.

over the 50 per cent devaluation of the African (CFA) franc. On the political front too, the state adopted a stance that was unlikely to be fully endorsed by NGDOs. In particular, it pushed for minimalist, top-down forms of electoral democracy, with a strong emphasis on strengthening the institutions of state (the judiciary, the police, the civil service) and on making it politically accountable, not so much to the people as to the donor community. Needless to say, this approach left only limited scope for collaboration with NGDOs, which were primarily interested in participatory democracy and economic and social rights (see below).

Early NGDO priorities

Against such a backdrop, it is hardly surprising that French NGDOs were either not interested in or were strongly opposed to taking on the role of service providers or vectors on behalf of the state. While there were notable exceptions, such as the AFVP and FONJEP, whose status was always closer to that of public contractors than that of NGOs, the vast majority of NGDOs were wary of serving as agents of a French state, which they viewed as self-interested and neo-imperialist. Most French NGDOs were, moreover, unable to see a way of bridging the divide between the state's vision and approach and their own long-standing operational and policy priorities.

On the operational front, French NGDO priorities diverged widely from those of the French administration. NGDOs rejected the state's techno-cratic, substitutive and 'professional' methods and preferred their own participatory, holistic and self-sustaining solutions to the challenges of the developing world. They saw their approach as distinct from, rather than complementary to, the French government's efforts, with their emphasis being, not on macro-level programmes, but on small, isolated projects; on partnerships with local NGOs and on building up the autonomous cap-acity of indigenous communities and populations. They believed in adopt-ing methods, which were adapted to local needs, and they employed these carefully tailored techniques to all of the sectors which they considered to be priorities. The productive or commercial sector in developing countries was not one of these. Indeed, French NGDOs, taking a different tack from their own government, ignored or neglected the role of this sector, consider-ing *entrepreneurs* to be 'predators' and finding profit-making reprehensible. According to the CCD (1999: 10),

> For a long time, French NGDOs privileged the social sector at the expense of the productive sector.... Indeed, up until the 1980s, many NGOs felt a kind of repulsion towards a commercial sector which accumulated profit, all the more so since this was for the benefit of the few. Only an intro-spective economy, which reinjected profits back into the collectivity, was worthy of support.

In line with this thinking, French NGDOs concentrated, above all, on social sectors, such as primary education, basic healthcare and rural devel-opment. In matters of education, they sought to 'set aside the Western model in favour of an alternative policy of education', such as that advo-cated by the statutes of the *Institut Coopératif Inter-Universitaire* (Joly, 1985: 41). Their focus was, as such, on promoting a pedagogy, which emphasised active participation by pupils, rather than more formal styles of learning (Ibid: 16). In the case of healthcare work, here the stress was on 'medicine adapted to local needs', particularly in the years after the influential Alma-Ata Conference, organised by the World Health Organisation in 1978. As the CCD (1999: 15) observed, 'The aim was to devise a medical practice that was better adapted to the level of local development: there was no point in exporting unusable "high-tech" medicine; it was better to train non-specialised local agents, who could respond locally and pragmatically to core medical concerns'.

Finally, as regards rural development, here the aim of NGDOs was to ensure 'sovereignty' in terms of food production and to set to one side the Western model, which was geared towards cash-crop export production.

The CCD (1999: 11–12) has explained this strong rural focus in terms of a natural agrarian bias in French and Southern NGOs at this time. It has also argued that

> The interest of NGOs in the rural sector corresponded to a certain vision of poverty. The 'forgotten ones' were those living in the countryside who were far from the traditional poles of development, the towns. On the other hand, the city-dwellers were 'the privileged ones', benefiting from their proximity to institutions which were supposedly geared towards meeting their needs (Ibid).

It should not, however, be inferred from the aforementioned that French NGDOs were engaged in a conscious strategy to do things differently from the French authorities at all costs. They were, in fact, quite prepared to accept the state's lead and establish themselves in countries where there was already a strong French diplomatic presence or historical connection. Their geographic priorities were, as such, quite close to those of the French authorities in the years before the introduction of *la nouvelle contractualisation*. Thus, as can be seen from Figure 7.4, French NGOs were, like the state, heavily present in the countries of the former empire, most notably sub-Saharan Africa (which attracted 47 per cent of total NGO expenditure), with a further 10 per cent of expenditure being reserved for North Africa and the Middle East. In this context, the CCD (1987: 123) has pointed to 'the massive concentration of private aid on the African continent (504 million francs or 66 per cent of the total spent on overseas projects)'. It has even labelled this geographic overlap as a form of 'tracking' or 'mimicking' by NGDOs of the state (Ibid). There is no doubt an element of truth in this observation. Thus, for purely pragmatic reasons, French NGDOs found it easier to establish themselves in countries, which already had French official aid missions and embassies, a strong French community and a largely Francophone population.

Yet, there is a need to relativise this finding. For a start, there were differences in the geographic distribution of private and official aid. Wary of being accused of a neocolonial bias, French *tiersmondiste* NGDOs did, unlike the government, set aside a reasonable proportion of their revenue for projects in Asia (15 per cent) and Latin America (10 per cent) (see Figure 7.4). They also allocated substantial funding to non-Francophone countries, such as Brazil (15 million francs) and India (25 million francs), both of which were key players in the 'Third World' (CCD, 1987: 125). There were also instances of NGOs, primarily *urgenciers*, undertaking missions in countries where the French state had no visible presence (e.g. MSF in Afghanistan after the December 1979 Soviet invasion). Furthermore, even though French NGDOs were heavily implanted in France's former empire, particularly sub-Saharan Africa, this should not be read as a sign that they were prepared

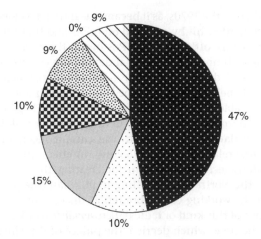

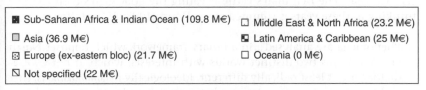

Figure 7.4 Geographic breakdown of French NGO expenditure in 1991

Source: CCD (2003: 19). Note that the figures for sub-Saharan Africa include the Indian Ocean territories. Figures are in millions of euros.

to act as service providers or to do the bidding of the French state in these countries. Far from it. Their priorities were very different and had less to do with promoting the national interest than with meeting basic needs. As the CCD (Ibid: 124) has pointed out, 'If Africa attracted so much attention from NGDOs, it was because the latter wanted, above all, to help countries which were among the poorest and most vulnerable on the planet'. Indeed, it could be argued that the strong presence of French NGDOs in the former empire may have had less to do with any meeting of minds with state officials and more to do with historical issues (some NGDOs had become embroiled in the liberation struggles of developing countries), language barriers (the lack of language skills in French NGOs made Francophone territories more attractive) and religious factors (NGDOs often went where church networks were already firmly established, as in Africa and Latin America) (Ibid).

Turning finally to the *policy prerogatives* of French NGDOs, these diverged sharply from the French state's priorities in the 1970s and 1980s, making any notion that these actors could serve as vectors for the French government's policies completely unthinkable. The discourse and agenda of French

NGDOs radicalised in the 1970s, as it became clear that developing countries were among the hardest hit by external oil crises and that their economies were not going to 'take off' in the way Rostowian theories predicted. These NGOs moved away from any notion that developing countries were simply experiencing 'lagged' development (*sous-développement*), whereby they were economically well behind, but launched on a growth-led trajectory that would one day enable them to catch up. Instead, they began to denounce what they referred to as 'wrong-headed development' or *mal-développement*, arguing that 'the flaw was intrinsic to the current mechanism for international economic relations' (Joly, 1985: 44). In effect, they began to condemn the capitalist economic system for creating the South's structural dependence on the North and for failing to put man (the poor farmer, the good citizen or the working class labourer) at the core of the development process. A flavour of this kind of radical, *tiersmondiste* thinking is clear from the slogans of the time, which decried 'the pillage of the Third World' and claimed that 'The rich man's cattle is eating the poor man's corn'. NGDO thinking in these years is summed up by Hours (1998: 35) as follows:

> Phenomena are analysed... in a binary framework which opposes North and South... as two distinct worlds with interests, which, if not contradictory, are at least radically different. Ideologically *tiersmondisme* is, first and foremost, about this division between rich and poor, erected almost as an ontological barrier that has to be broken down.... The surpluses of the rich must go to the poor living in the Southern hemisphere.

For French NGDOs, the policy solution lay in negating the capitalist system and in promoting alternatives to the market approach. To these ends, they took part, alongside other NNGOs, SNGOs and various states, in a major North–South debate, which was launched by the UN in 1974 and which aimed to ensure a fairer redistribution of global wealth through the establishment of a New International Economic Order. French NGDOs also advocated approaches, which were intended to shelter the populations of developing countries from the ravages of market forces and to discourage them from becoming even more dependent on, or integrated into, the liberal economic system. These strategies, which included 'endogenous' and 'self-directed' development (*développement endogène* and *développement auto-centré*), stressed the importance of agricultural self-sufficiency and of local resources, such as indigenous workers, raw materials and produce from the land. The aim of these economic doctrines was to satisfy 'the basic needs of indigenous peoples by developing exchanges appropriate to the region or country rather than the types of externalised exchanges inherited from the colonial era'.[7]

If anything, the distance between French NGDO and state priorities widened in the 1980s, with the collapse of the North–South debate, the emergence of the Third World debt crisis and the shift by the international donor community towards advocacy of structural adjustment. French developmental NGOs began openly to criticise their own state and the wider donor community for these neo-liberal austerity measures, which were deemed to ignore participatory forms of development, lack transparency and neglect the specificities of individual developing countries. These approaches were also accused of hurting local populations, particularly the poorest people, without actually achieving the levels of growth promised.[8]

By the time the Cold War had ended, French NGDOs were beginning to tone down some of their more radical economic and political prescriptions for the developing world. This watering down process was probably an inevitable consequence of the collapse of the communist bloc model and of the defeat of *tiersmondistes* in public debates with *urgenciers* in the late 1980s. It was also, no doubt, a response to changes in the French state's own policies in the immediate post-Cold War period (discussed above). Whatever the cause, the fact was that French NGDOs felt able, in this slightly more propitious context, to modify their stance on overseas development in ways which opened the door to closer cooperation with the state. On the economic front, they began to adopt policy positions, which were more compatible with the French government's proposed 'remedies' for the developing world. Thus, in the words of Lechervy and Ryfman (1993: 61), they 'returned to a greater degree of pragmatism in their proposals', largely dropping their rhetoric on 'endogenous' and 'self-directed' development and openly acknowledging the need for some 'extraversion' of developing economies. Relatedly, they toned down their advocacy of agricultural self-sufficiency and food sovereignty in favour of much more moderate and manageable demands for 'food security' (Interview with *Solagral*, 2003). They also began to shed their visceral hatred of entrepreneurial activity, and some even sought to harness the dynamism of the market to their own ends. To illustrate, some NGDOs engaged in partnerships with companies (see Chapter 8) whilst others invested more heavily in alternative approaches, such as micro-credit projects, ethical savings programmes and 'fair trade' schemes (see Chapter 6 for more details).[9]

Also in the early 1990s, French NGDOs began to modify their political prescriptions for the developing world in ways which brought them closer to the new-found priorities of the state, namely democratisation and respect for civil liberties. Hitherto, French developmental NGOs had focused predominantly on economic and social rights, particularly those of communities rather than individuals; and they had tended only to take part in campaigns for civil and political liberties at a very low level or in a slightly more concerted manner in extreme cases, such as the struggle against apartheid in South Africa. They had, moreover, espoused a logic of *autonomisation*, whereby it was for developing countries to find, devise and put into practice their own modes of governance, independently of the wishes of their former colonial 'masters'. French NGDOs had, as such, often turned a blind eye to autocratic forms of government. As Joly (1985: 45) has observed,

> Far from imposing their own thinking, NGOs do not exert any pressure on local governments which could be construed as external interference. They do not allow themselves to call into question the existing political, economic and social system, even if they do not approve the bases or consequences of it; at the very most, they take it upon themselves to pass on to the authorities criticisms of some state practices (the expulsion of foreign workers by the Nigerian government, for instance), or of some large projects which seem to go against the interests of local peoples.

In the immediate post-Cold War era, however, French NGDOs toned down their earlier insistence on *autonomisation* and moved towards a stance, which was slightly more interventionist and more compatible with the French state's official position on the promotion of multi-party democracies and human rights. In line with this shift, established NGDOs, such as the CCFD and CIMADE, began to list the promotion of human rights among their core activities in the 1995 CCD Directory. By the time of the 2007 *Répertoire*, the number of such organisations had, in fact, risen to 32, whilst 45 NGOs also claimed to be engaged in democratic capacity-building work or *appui institutionnel* (CCD, 2007: 221). Needless to say the most active in this domain were pressure groups, such as *Agir Ici, Survie, Amnesty International-France* and FIDH, which produced a raft of reports and campaigns. A prominent role was also played by *sans-frontiéristes*, such as *Reporters Sans Frontières*, and medical *urgenciers*, whose insistence on 'bearing witness' or *témoignage* meant that they had a self-appointed duty to denounce major human rights abuses. Nonetheless, developmental NGOs also got involved in lobbying the French state to do more to promote democracy, notably in countries such as Zaire (now the Democratic Republic of the Congo) and Togo.[10] Some also became involved in observing elections (e.g. the SC-CF), in voter education work (e.g. the CCFD in Latin America) and in the promotion of civil and political liberties. In this latter context, *Juristes Solidarités* set up, in Latin America, a mobile legal school to raise awareness of citizens' rights, whilst the CCFD funded an NGO, Outreach, to inform people in Cambodia of their rights (CCD, 1999: 38–42).[11]

It would, however, be wrong to suggest that French NGDOs had, in the early 1990s, simply bought into the French state's economic and political prescriptions for the developing world. On the economic front, they remained wary of taking on the role ascribed to them by France and much of the donor community, namely to palliate the negative social effects of the liberalisation of developing economies. They were still as deeply opposed as ever to market liberalism and they believed that this underlying objective had not changed for the donor community or indeed France, which had, under the premiership of Edoaurd Balladur, toughened its pro-market remedies for developing countries in the early 1990s (see above). On the political front, they remained unconvinced by the French state's new-found enthusiasm for democratic reform. Along with advocacy groups such as *Agir Ici*, French NGDOs launched a number of campaigns, which condemned the French state for its failure to apply pressure on some leaders, particularly Francophile African dictators, to democratise. They also remained sceptical about the emphasis placed by France and the donor community on minimalist forms of democracy and highly contestable, periodic, top-down elections. Instead, they persisted in their advocacy of grassroots participatory democracy, involving bottom-up pressures from communities and peoples. As *Frères des Hommes* put it,

> Democracy is not an automatic by-product of the collapse of communism. It seems to be universally held that free elections and multi-party systems should be enough in themselves. We believe that there is a need, instead for... the emergence of a true civil society and of the freedoms associated with citizenship.[12]

In a similar vein, French NGDOs continued to question the French state's and the donor community's minimalist approach to human rights, with its focus on civil liberties (effectively rights *from* state repression) and its neglect of economic, social and cultural rights (rights *to* various goods and services supplied by the state). These *droits économiques, sociaux et culturels* or DESC were to become, by the mid-1990s, a major focal point for many NGDOs, particularly *Terre Des Hommes* and *Peuples Solidaires*.[13]

The state's new-found prerogatives

While the French state and French NGDOs clearly showed little interest in working together during the early post-colonial era, they have become more receptive to the idea of closer collaboration over the last decade or so and, particularly since the introduction of 'the new contractual arrangements' in 1996. The state, for its part, has explicitly declared its interest in using developmental and other NGOs both as service providers in the delivery of its policies and as vehicles for the dissemination of its message, whether through advocacy or development education work. It has done so for a number of reasons. First and foremost, it has recognised the efforts, which NGOs as a whole have made to professionalise, to pool their expertise in inter-associative networks and to adopt an agenda that is more 'pragmatic' than in the past (Pech and Padis, 2004: 86). The French government has also become increasingly aware of the important role which both private secular and faith-based NGOs can play in promoting human rights and Christian values to parts of the world that are prone to the spread of Islamic fundamentalism (Interview with MDM, 2003).[14] Equally, it has come to accept the fact that NGOs can, not only perform tasks more cheaply than government operators (an important consideration at a time of budgetary restraint imposed by membership of the euro zone), but they can also operate in countries where the French government's presence might be politically awkward (e.g. in Rwanda after the 1994 genocide) or where there is no functioning host government (e.g. Haiti as from 2003).[15] As Cohen (2004: 5) observes,

> NGOs do work that states like France no longer want to do. Their presence allows the state to justify its withdrawal and to delegate tasks to the non-profit private sector while keeping a certain control over development aid projects via co-financing. And they cost less than the private sector, a factor of no small importance.

Cohen goes on to note that

> NGOs are now perceived as another avenue of French influence throughout the world. They are in a position to convey the French viewpoint effectively in international forums, and they can advocate France's position in international volunteer circles, thus limiting the influence of American and British NGOs, many of which make no bones about defending their government's positions. (Ibid)

In line with this new thinking, the French authorities have made overtures to try to bring developmental and other NGOs more on board, both as service providers and as vectors for the propagation of French ideas. The French state has, for example, encouraged NGOs to take on more of a service delivery role by improving the terms of its funding (see Chapter 5) and by providing incentives for professionalisation (see Chapter 7). It has also promoted closer cooperation in the field by instructing its diplomatic posts to draw up an annual report, the Partnership Framework Document or *Document Cadre de Partenariat*, in which the actions undertaken by key NGOs in particular countries are explicitly acknowledged (Blum, 2005: 25). The French Foreign Ministry has also urged aid missions or *Services de Coopération et d'Action Culturelle* (SCAC) to 'engage in dialogue' with these non-governmental actors (Ibid) and has directed ambassadors to take better account of the growing importance of these organisations.[16]

The French state has further sought to enlist the services of developmental and other NGOs by adapting some of its own sectoral priorities in ways that facilitate cooperation (see Figures 7.1 and 7.5). In line with a recent paradigmatic shift in its overall aid priorities in the direction of poverty reduction, the French administration has begun to decrease its emphasis on the productive sector (down from 28 per cent in 1991–92 to 11 per cent

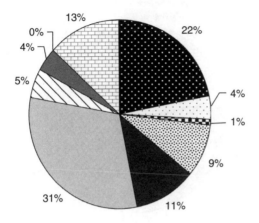

Figure 7.5 Sectoral breakdown of French state aid in 2001–02

Source: OECD (2004: 81). Figures are in millions of dollars (US).

in 2001–02). It has also honed in on social development priorities, such as healthcare (with some M€300 being accorded, in 2007, to the Global AIDS, Tuberculosis and Malaria Fund), primary education (with the launch of an 'Education for All' initiative) and debt cancellation (with 31 per cent of the aid budget being allocated to this task in 2001–02) (see Figure 7.5).[17] Significantly too, as can be seen from Figures 7.2 and 7.6, the French Foreign Ministry has increased the share of its co-funding to NGOs operating in the health sector from 15.9 per cent in 1993 to 17 per cent in 2002. It has, equally, introduced a new prerogative, namely civil society capacity-building, an activity which enjoyed some M€3.8 or 12 per cent of Foreign Ministry funding in 2002 (DGCID, 2002: 84).

At the same time the French state has modified the geographic prerogatives of its aid programme in ways that facilitate greater collaboration with NGOs (see Figure 7.7). It has, for example, extended its list of priority aid recipients (now termed the *Zone de Solidarité Prioritaire*) to some of the poorest countries in the world (e.g. Tanzania, Malawi) and it has promised to reach the UN target of 0.15 per cent of aid for Least Developed Countries by 2012.[18] Above all, the French government has stressed that top priority will

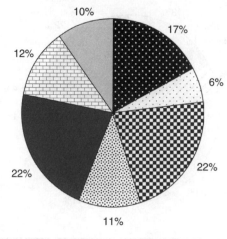

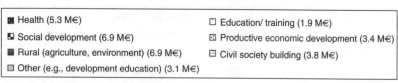

Figure 7.6   Sectoral breakdown of French state co-funding of NGOs in 2002

Source: DGCID, *Rapport d'Activité 2002*, French Foreign Ministry, Paris, 2002, p. 84. Figures (in millions of euros) relate to Foreign Ministry funding of overseas projects and development education by NGOs and local authorities. Assistance to volunteer associations is not included.

be given to sub-Saharan Africa, which has seen its share of bilateral aid rise from 54 per cent in 1991–92 to 59 per cent in 2005–06 (Figures 7.3 and 7.7).[19] Indeed, the former French President, Jacques Chirac, promised, at the 2002 Johannesburg Summit, that French development assistance would reach the UN 0.7 per cent of GNP target by 2012 and that at least half of this proposed doubling of aid would be directed towards Africa. The French state has, equally, attached priority to this continent in its co-funding of NGO programmes, almost two-thirds of which are now focused on Africa.[20] Indeed, 5 of the top 15 NGO projects approved by the French Foreign Ministry in 2002 and 4 of the top 15 in 2003 were focused explicitly or exclusively on Africa.[21] This was far more than Latin America, which benefited from three projects in 2002, and one in 2003, and Asia, which did not attract any of the largest NGO projects in these years.[22]

The French state has not, of course, confined itself to encouraging NGOs down a service delivery route. It has, at the same time, taken active steps to seek to capitalise on the legitimacy of these non-governmental actors and use them as a vehicle for the transmission of France's culture, language and ideas. This new approach is spelt out by the *Commissariat Général* (2002: 10), which notes that one of the aims of the recent aid reforms carried out under

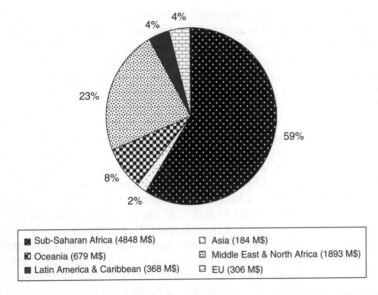

Figure 7.7 Geographic breakdown of French state's aid expenditures in 2005–06

Source: OECD, *Development Cooperation Report 2007*, OECD, Paris, 2007, p. 83. Note that 675 M$ are not attributed to any region or, indeed, included in the above pie chart. All figures are in millions of dollars (US) and relate to gross bilateral aid.

French Prime Minister Jospin was to bring about 'a renewal of NGOs which are also a vector for French influence'. The Head of the French Development Division within the Foreign Ministry makes a similar point, advising of the need to align French policy with that of 'better organised countries' and to 'attach more worth to, and make better use of, the specific contribution of NGOs, particularly in mobilising public opinion'.[23] That the French government has taken this advice seriously can be inferred from a number of measures it has adopted recently. First, it has begun regularly inviting NGDOs and other NGOs to take part in the preparation of major international conferences. Second, it created and financed, ahead of the UN Rio summit in 1992, a new state-funded post of NGO coordinator to bolster the presence of French NGOs at these venues.[24] Third, the French authorities have continued to devote the highest share of aid funding in Europe to volunteer agencies which, by their very nature, are likely to serve as vectors for the dissemination of France's language and values.[25] Finally, the French government has, over the last decade, adapted its own economic and political prescriptions for the developing world in ways that are likely to make them more palatable to developmental NGOs.

On the economic front, the French state has moved away from its earlier market-led prescriptions towards a stance with which French NGDOs, not to mention neo-Colbertist and neo-Gaullist elements within the

French political establishment, are likely to be more comfortable. It has, for example, become quite vociferous in its calls for stricter market regulation and a greater role for governments in the overseas development process. In so doing, it has reflected its growing concern at the social consequences of the global free market and Anglo-Saxon liberalism; rising unemployment, de-localisation, a deepening North–South divide, and a diminishing of France's language, culture, social democratic model and place in the world.[26] The French state has, moreover, rendered its policy on overseas development more palatable to NGDOs partly by linking itself rhetorically to unorthodox NGDO-inspired proposals, such as the Tobin Tax and a duty on airline tickets, and partly by making poverty reduction the overarching priority of its aid programme.[27] In this latter context, the French government has subscribed to the UN Millennium Development Goals (to halve global poverty by 2015), as well as to the various instruments recommended for the achievement of these targets. These include France's adoption, in 1999, of World Bank-led Poverty Reduction Strategy Papers (PRSPs) as from 1999; its pledge to reach the UN aid target of 0.7 per cent of GNP by 2012; and its support for substantial debt cancellation measures (notably the multilateral Highly Indebted Poor Countries Initiative and its own bilateral mechanism, the *Contrat de Développement et de Désendettement* or C2D (discussed in Chapter 9).[28]

As regards its political prescriptions for the developing world, the French state has toned down its earlier calls for a minimalist, top-down form of electoral democracy, based upon periodic (often flawed) multiparty elections. It has, at the same time, edged closer to NGDO thinking on political reform and called for more participatory, bottom-up forms of democracy, backed up by a strong civil society. Equally, the French government has broadened its policy on the promotion of human rights in the developing world. In particular, it has moved away from its earlier, narrow focus on the defence of civil and political liberties and begun to adopt more of a 'rights-based' approach, which recognises all human rights (including economic, social and cultural rights) and which requires states in both the Northern and Southern hemispheres to invest more heavily in education, healthcare and other social concerns. In line with this logic, the French authorities have recently expressed 'great interest' in 'global public goods' (i.e., 'commodities', such as drinking water, education and energy, which everyone should be able to access, with proper support from states and international institutions). Together with Sweden, France has even co-funded a working party to report on the implications of global public goods.[29]

A cautious welcome from French NGDOs

These overtures by the state have not been lost on French NGDOs, which have gone some way towards taking on a greater service delivery role, whilst stopping short of serving as agents or vectors on behalf of the French authorities.

Agents of the state or prickly partners?

French NGDOs have generally shown a greater readiness to act as service providers on behalf of the state. Not without some exaggeration, Lancaster (1999: 128) has noted how 'Nearly all [French] NGOs are service deliverers, still new to political advocacy and often reliant on the French government for funding'. Blum (2005: 34) has likewise pointed out that

> [While] some authors even go as far as to label them as public contractors…, French NGOs are, first and foremost, service providers who respond to tenders from donors and who, by dint of this fact, must sign up to a strategy for intervention drawn up by public policy-makers. Only a few leading NGOs in France can define projects and finance them out of their own resources, essentially drawing on donations from the general public.

In some cases, French developmental NGOs have indeed been little more than public contractors. This is true wherever NGDOs act 'under convention', that is, when they respond to a precise order from the French state and where the latter is prepared to pay the majority of the costs. In such instances, the norm is for a service agreement to be drawn up, which then makes the activities of NGDOs 'easier to track' and cost out (*Cour des Comptes*, 2005: 49). The term 'service agent' applies equally in the case of QUANGO-like bodies, such as FONJEP, which received, in 2003, 12.4 per cent of total French Foreign Ministry assistance to NGOs for managing government subsidies to French volunteer agencies;[30] and the AFVP, which secured 20.4 per cent of state funding in the same year and has no private monies of its own.[31] It can also be said to apply largely to the 15 non-state actors listed in Table 7.1, each of which receives at least two-thirds of its funding from the state.

The label 'service provider' cannot be attached to, but does have some resonance in the case of, a further 10 or so NGDOs, which receive over half of their funding from the French state. These include federations, such as *Plateforme Française pour la Palestine* (62.5 per cent) and *Coordination SUD* (57.9 per cent), as well as the 'multi-specialist' NGO the *Guilde Européenne du Raid* (53 per cent) and the volunteer agency *Service de Coopération au Développement* (50.6 per cent). There are also NGDOs, which receive high volumes of government assistance but which can honestly claim that these contributions only represent a small percentage of their overall resources. To illustrate, the SC-CF and ENDA-TM secured around €875,000 and €690,000, respectively, in 2003, yet this income only constituted 3 per cent and 7.4 per cent of their overall resources (see Table 7.2). In other instances,

Table 7.1   Most heavily subsidised French NGOs in percentage terms

Name of organisation	French official (%)	International (%)	Private (%)
Humatem	96.0	0.00	3.98
CORAIL – *Codéveloppement Rhône-Alpes International*	92.3	3.79	3.90
ACAUPED – *Association pour la Coordination d'Aides Utiles aux Pays en Développement*	83.2	0.00	16.81
AARASD – *Association des Amis de la République Arabe Sahraouie Démocratique*	80.9	0.00	19.13
IIFARMU – *Institut International de Formation en Anesthésie Réanimation et Médecine d'Urgence*	80.1	–	19.9
ACFL- *Amitié-Coopération Franco-Laotienne*	80.0	–	20.0
PFCE- *Plateforme pour le Commerce Équitable*	78.7	–	21.3
Le Sillage	78.4	–	21.6
Étudiants et Développement	76.9	–	23.1
GRDR – *Groupe de Recherche et de Réalisations pour le Développement Rural*	76.2	14.8	9.0
FAFRAD – *Fédération des Associations Franco-Africaines de Développement*	75.1	–	25.0
JDM – *Jardins du Monde*	75.0	–	25.0
AFVP – *Association Française des Volontaires du Progrès*	74.5	11.0	14.5
VET – *Villes en Transition*	72.3	7.2	20.5
Vietnam Plus	68.4	0.00	31.6

Source: CCD (2008: 29–32). Note that, although all listed as NGOs in the most recent CCD financial report, some of the above are semi-public bodies (AFVP), university hospitals (IIFARMU) and local authority-type agencies (CORAIL). French official figures include local as well as central government.

French NGDOs may deliberately understate the volume of assistance that they are receiving from the French authorities. This point has been made convincingly by the *Cour des Comptes*, which noted that while organisations, such as the GRET, *Agriculteurs Français et Développement International* (AFDI) and *Eau Vive* claim on their websites only to rely on the French government for 14.4, 59.5 and 20.2 per cent, respectively, of their overall budgets, the reality is that they are really much more dependent. This watchdog body has since recalculated the true value of state support and estimated this to

Table 7.2 Most heavily subsidised French NGOs in monetary terms

NGO	State funding in 2003 (€)	Total budget for 2001 or 2002 (€)	State subsidies as % of NGO overall budget
AFVP	11,192,000	23,782,000	47.1
GRET	1,180,684	8,202,000	14.4
CCFD	1,024,853	28,508,000	3.6
Inter Aide	899,910	6,505,800	13.8
SC-CF	875,485	28,886,000	3
VSF	762,245	4,800,000	15.9
FERT	737,702	1,768,500	41.7
ENDA-TM	689,908	9,316,000	7.4
AFDI	668,219	1,123,000	59.5
CICDA	593,300	3,157,000	18.8
Initiative Développement (ID)	558,918	3,257,000	17.2
Handicap International	491,549	54,880,000	0.90
F3E	445,000	4,847,000	9.2
Eau Vive	423,046	2,100,000	20.2
ADER	413,761	1,434,600	28.8

Source: Cour des Comptes (2005: 41–2). Figures in euros. The glossary provides the full name of all the above-mentioned organisations, with the exception of *Formation pour l'Épanouissement et le Renouveau de la Terre* (FERT), *Environnement et Développement du Tiers Monde* (ENDA-TM) and *Association pour le Développement Économique Régional* (ADER).

represent, for the same year, M€6.3 (51 per cent) for the GRET, M€1 (67 per cent) for *Eau Vive* and M€1.4 (79 per cent) for AFDI.

French NGDOs have had many reasons for becoming more amenable to playing the role of service provider. These include their chronic shortage of (both public and private) funding, their need to pay for increasingly bureaucratic structures, and their inherent desire to expand their operations and do 'more good'. But another equally important reason has been their perception that the French state has been shifting its sectoral and geographic priorities more clearly into areas which have long been NGDO prerogatives. This is particularly true of the following sectors: health, where some 127 NGOs now claim to be active (CCD, 2004: 226); rural development, where the figure stands at approximately 106 (Ibid: 219); education/ training, where 189 NGOs have some kind of activity (Ibid: 220–1); and civil society capacity-building, where 36 NGOs – mainly *développementalistes*, with local partner associations in developing countries – are operational (Ibid: 217).[32] The fact that French NGDOs were already so active in, or well adapted to all of the aforementioned social sectors has, no doubt, facilitated their bids for co-funding from the state and made it easier for them to justify the acceptance of such monies to their own critical resource, that is, the donor public and their activist base. They have, in effect, claimed to be accepting state funding for projects, which they would have carried out in any case with their 'own' money.

At the same time, French NGDOs have broadly welcomed their government's decision to place more emphasis on Least Developed Countries and above all the world's poorest continent, Africa. They have, of course, been particularly well placed to take advantage of any increases in funding to Africa, given that this continent has long attracted the largest share of French NGO expenditure (see Figure 7.8) and the greatest number of French NGDOs and volunteers. Thus, according to the CCD, 74 per cent of the French NGOs it surveyed were active in Africa, whilst the top 18 organisations all saw sub-Saharan Africa specifically as a priority and devoted 65 per cent of their operational expenses to this part of the world (CCD, 2008: 45). In addition, some 52 per cent of all volunteers go to Africa, almost 14 times more than the number being posted to better-off states in Central and Eastern Europe (Godfrain, 2004).

It would, however, be wrong to think that French NGDOs have, over the last decade, completely aligned their operational priorities with those

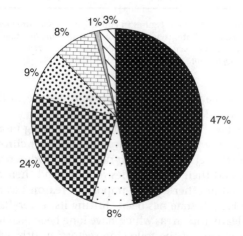

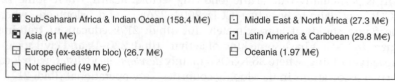

Figure 7.8   Geographic breakdown of French NGO expenditures in 2003

Source: CCD (2005: 27). Activities in Eastern Europe have mainly been the work of French *urganciers*. The unspecified figure includes M€11.3 of spending in France. All figures are in millions of euros.

of the state or, indeed, taken on the role of service delivery agent. Fearing co-optation by the government, a loss of credibility vis-à-vis their core supporters, and a reduction in their responsive capacity (as they align themselves increasingly with bureaucratic state procedures), most NGDOs have been keen to affirm their operational independence. *Coordination SUD* has asserted that 'French NGOs are not public contractors implementing government policies. They are happy to develop partnerships with the French authorities on joint programmes, but they wish their scope for initiative as non-governmental actors to be recognised'.[33]

With a view to underscoring their autonomy, French NGDOs have stressed that they do not, for the most part, receive more than a minority share of their funding from the central state. Thus, some 75 of the 159 NGOs surveyed in the 2008 CCD financial directory enjoyed less than 10 per cent of their income from French official sources, with 53 of them securing less than 5 per cent and 21 receiving none at all. This category of largely autonomous NGOs includes all the top *urgenciers*; most *sans-frontiéristes*, which take a particularly hard line on government funding; and some developmental NGOs, such as *ATD Quart Monde* and *Emmäus International*, which have sought significant autonomy from state funding (CCD, 2008, 29–30).[34] Crucially too, French NGDOs have affirmed that, even where they have accepted very uneven levels of co-funding from the state, they have often continued to enjoy a considerable, even a determining, say over projects.[35] The *Cour des Comptes* (2005: 4) acknowledges this fact, noting that

> Whilst those projects that the state has placed 'under convention' or 'under order' do correspond to priorities of the Ministry, those which benefit from specific subsidies are not the result of a deliberate choice on its part. It is the NGOs themselves which present the projects, from which the DGCID selects a certain number, which seem to it to fit within its policy. The Ministry becomes [in such instances] simply a funding mechanism.

A similar observation could be made in relation to most of the larger schemes financed under the 'new contractual arrangements'. Thus, whilst NGDOs applying for such co-funding can be dependent upon the state to put up 75 per cent of the costs, they have retained a major role in the decision-making process. NGDOs have, in effect, usually been the ones drafting the original bids, appointing consultants and pushing for participatory, community-based techniques (see case study, Chapter 9).

French NGDOs have also asserted, with some justification, that they have not been the ones who have aligned their sectoral priorities with those of the state. Indeed, it has, if anything, been the government which has followed their lead and taken on board 'reverse lobbying' by NGOs in forums, such as the CCD and the COSP (Chapter 5). Whatever the truth of these claims, the fact is that French NGDOs were, indeed, heavily involved in social and poverty-related work long before the state. They have, moreover, continued to mark out their differences from the French authorities in these sectors (see Figure 7.9). For example, French NGOs as a whole have devoted around 39 per cent of their own funds to healthcare and nutrition, whereas the French state itself has only allocated around 4 per cent of its overall aid budget to this sector, with only 1 per cent being earmarked for basic healthcare (OECD, 2004: 81). Equally, NGOS have set aside 10 per cent of their own monies essentially for primary education, whereas the French authorities have only allotted 4 per cent of their aid specifically for this purpose (Ibid).[36] French developmental NGOs have, moreover, displayed a much clearer bias than the state in favour of the poorest and most excluded populations, notably those living in the countryside. Thus, according to the World Bank (2001: 37), 71 per cent of the associations it surveyed were active in the rural sector and some 11 per cent were only operational in the rural milieu. By contrast, the French state only allocated, in 2001, some M€201 or 5 per cent of its bilateral aid to agriculture, forestry and fishing (OECD, 2004: 81).

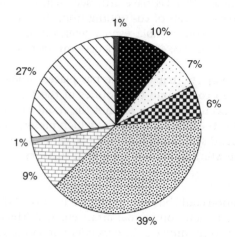

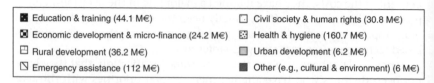

Figure 7.9   Sectoral breakdown of French NGO spending in 2004

Source: CCD (2008: 43–4). These figures exclude M€55, which were not attributed to any particular sector. All figures are in millions of euros.

Vectors or free-thinking agents?

French NGDOs have given a similarly mixed response to the idea of serving as a vector on behalf of the French state. They have, in the past, somewhat reluctantly, played the role of 'informal ambassadors' for France overseas. Thus, for example, during the Cold War years, leading French *urgenciers*, such as MSF and MDM, conveyed to the wider world a positive and dynamic image of French medical expertise and, arguably, of France itself. Similarly, French volunteer agencies served, wittingly or unwittingly, as harbingers of the free world and vehicles for the dissemination of France's culture and language. As Blum (2005: 21) has observed,

> NGOs contribute through their behaviour to the propagation of French influence in the world, even in spite of themselves. The cultural conduct of expatriates is very different depending upon their nationality. They present an image of France... [particularly] in fields of recognised excellence, such as 'the French doctors'.

While French NGDOs have continued to resist any form of instrumentalisation by the authorities, they have, over the last decade or so, become considerably less hostile to the idea of serving as a vehicle for the transmission of the French state's message and policies. Thus, as Blum (2005: 22) has noted,

> Apart from a few misfits, they are more and more prepared to act as vehicles for the message of the French state when it has been spelt out to them and when they have taken part in elaborating it. They can as such be precious vectors for influence in multilateral forums.

French NGOs as a whole have taken on this new function most clearly in the context of international conferences. Thus, for example, they have participated in meetings of inter-ministerial 'follow up' committees, established to monitor progress on measures agreed at UN conferences (e.g. the Population and Development summit in Cairo, 1994; the Social Development summit in Copenhagen, 1995; and the Conference on Women in Peking, 1995). *Handicap International* went a step further and was included in the French official delegation during negotiations, in 1996 and 1997, on the Ottawa Treaty to ban landmines. Similarly, in June 1999, *Coordination SUD* was part of the French official representation at a special session of the UN General Assembly on the issue of population. More recently, French NGDOs have accepted invitations from the French Foreign Ministry regarding the preparation of international conferences (e.g. the 2002 UN Johannesburg summit), whilst some 40 NGOs welcomed the opportunity to meet President Chirac for two hours ahead of the G8 Evian summit in 2003.[37] Significantly too, French NGDOs have, in the course of these international conferences, issued statements, adopted arguments and engaged in advocacy activities, which have, in some ways, complemented the French state's positions on key international development issues.[38]

There are many reasons why French NGDOs now disseminate a message that chimes in more closely with the French government's vision. These include the fact that French NGDOs have enjoyed much greater access to the French authorities and have come to appreciate the need for advocacy work and coalition-building at the international level if they are to serve as a critical force (a *contre pouvoir*) in world politics. As Zimet (2006: 40) has observed, 'Developmental NGOs have realised that operations in the field are no longer enough: they now have to take action in the North, in rich countries, to influence the policies which have an impact on the countries of the South in areas, such as agriculture and trade policy and in G8 and WTO summits.' Having equipped themselves, as from the mid-1990s, with their own advocacy units, many of the larger NGDOs have also come to the realisation that US-led international organisations, such as the World Bank, IMF and WTO, should be the prime target for their lobbying, given that these financial institutions have a greater say over global development issues and are arguably even less sympathetic to their 'world vision' than the French authorities. Perhaps the most salient reason for the change in the discourse of French NGDOs has been their perception that the French state itself has moved away from its earlier neo-liberal political and economic prescriptions for overseas development and begun to espouse prerogatives, which are much closer to long-standing NGDO priorities. These include poverty eradication, which has, from the outset, been the core function of most developmental NGOs, and participatory democracy, which has, for some years, been a fundamental aim of many *développementalistes*. Needless to say, the fact that the French authorities appear to have effected this paradigmatic shift has made it easier for French NGDOs, not only to sing broadly from the same 'hymn sheet' as the government, but also to do so without carrying out any major revisions to their own core policy objectives.

It would, however, be wrong to suggest that French NGDOs have become mere vectors on behalf of the French state, disseminating the latter's message or supporting its wider objectives, notably its pursuit of 'the national interest'. As Blum (2005: 34) has remarked, large numbers of these NGOs 'still refuse openly to fly the flag for France, unlike their American counterparts, who serve as standard-bearers for American interests'. There are many reasons for this continuing reticence on the part of NGDOs. These include their fear of being instrumentalised and their suspicion that they are not being 'listened to' (see Chapter 5). They also relate to the fact that their whole identity has been forged in a counter culture. Indeed, as Blum (2005: 21) has argued, 'Having structured themselves ideologically against the state, French NGOs are careful not to let themselves be sucked into France's discourse and operations overseas; they refuse above all to see themselves confused with the bilateral actions carried out by the government.' Another important explanatory factor is the fact that French *développementalistes* have considered themselves to be vectors primarily for the peoples of the South and more of a counterweight to, rather than a vehicle for, the French state. Yet, perhaps the main reason is the fact that French NGDOs have continued to discern significant divergences between their economic and political policy priorities and those of the French administration.

To begin with economic prerogatives, French NGDOs have continued to harbour doubts about the French state's whole approach to overseas development. Some have simply remained sceptical as to the genuineness of the French administration's commitment to poverty reduction as the overriding priority of its aid programme. As the CRID has noted, the French Finance Ministry 'has continued to prioritise trade and investment', while the state as a whole has remained 'obsessed with France's place in the world'. Given this, it wonders 'how are we to interpret the [government's] discourse on the fight against poverty and inequality? Does it stem from a true concern with solidarity, a politically correct attitude or from a desire to develop markets and potential customers?'[39] In light of these doubts, French NGDOs have felt the need to campaign heavily to keep the attention of the French state focused on the importance of higher levels of more concessionary aid and speedier debt cancellation, free from elaborate conditionalities.[40] The most famous such campaign was *Pour l'An 2000, Annulons la Dette!*, which was launched as part of the International Jubilee 2000 campaign by nearly 60 French NGOs in February 1999 and which gathered an unprecedented 520,000 signatures in a matter of months.[41] Building on its success, around 40 French NGOs and trade unions formed, in January 2005, a coalition known as *2005: Plus d'Excuses*, which called on the French government and donor community to do more to eradicate world poverty, speed up debt cancellation, improve aid effectiveness, introduce fairer trade rules and abolish tax havens.[42]

At the same time, French NGDOs have also had reservations about the terminology, targets and other mechanisms employed by the French state in pursuit of its new economic priorities. While NGDOs themselves have used the term 'poverty' in their discourse, they have preferred to talk more about 'exclusion' and 'inequality' (CCD, 1999: 14). They have also been reluctant to single out a category known as the 'poor', the 'poorest' or for that matter the 'poverty-stricken', not least since this type of labelling flies in the face of their whole commitment to portraying the peoples of the South in a positive light. Significantly, too, French NGDOs have been reticent about the use of poverty-reduction targets by France and other donors. Many of these *développementalistes* and volunteer associations have considered the acts of 'solidarity' in which they engage to be unmeasurable. They have also questioned the donor community's view that 'poverty' or 'exclusion' can be regarded as a discreet problem, which is susceptible to technical solutions or indeed to target-driven approaches, such as the Millennium Development Goals.[43] Instead, they have deemed poverty and 'marginalisation' to be political matters, which require uncomfortable answers that will, in turn, involve major changes to the existing capitalist mode of exchange.

In a similar vein, French developmental NGOs have also been reluctant to endorse other mechanisms advocated by the French state, not least PRSPs. For French NGDOs, these World Bank-led PRSPs do not do what they promise: they do not ensure genuine consultation between the population of developing countries and their own governments over poverty-reducing priorities. In particular, these strategy papers are accused of focusing mainly on the demands of urban elites and neglecting the views of poor people living in the countryside. Significantly too, PRSPs are criticised on the grounds that they can be vetoed by the World Bank and IMF, thereby perpetuating the alleged domination of North over South and rendering it impossible for the peoples of developing countries to truly 'own' these poverty-reduction plans.[44]

Finally, most French NGDOs have taken the view that, even if the French state is genuinely committed to its new economic priorities, it simply does not go far enough in terms of its proposals. In adopting this stance, French developmental NGOs have distanced themselves from OXFAM and other 'moderate' elements within the *altermondialiste* movement and placed themselves in the 'radical' camp, alongside other organisations, which see the existing capitalist system as the underlying cause of global poverty and inequality.[45] While steering clear of violent elements within this movement and refusing to call for the dismantlement of leading international financial institutions, French NGDOs have, nonetheless, been at the forefront of those organisations calling for 'another' type of globalisation and a 'better world'.[46] In this context, they have campaigned for much greater regulation of the global market, for trade barriers to be brought down in the North and remain raised in the South, for measures to ensure food security and for rigorous prohibitions on dumping.[47] Equally, they have called for a Tobin tax on international financial transactions (CRID, 2002: 7), for price guarantees for certain commodities, for 20 per cent of official aid to be used towards tackling issues of exclusion and even, in some cases, for a return to economic strategies based on 'self-directed development'.[48] Needless to say, many of these measures go way beyond anything which the French state could support, even in a non-committal rhetorical fashion or through the kind of 'gesture politics' at which French diplomacy excels.

Turning to political prerogatives, here NGDOs have questioned the French state's rhetorical commitment to the promotion of democracy and human rights, particularly in former colonies and other developing countries, which are deemed to serve France's wider geopolitical interests. They have launched campaigns, hosted counter-summits and produced publications, exposing the French state's collusion over recent years with African despots, such as Presidents Robert Mugabe of Zimbabwe, Paul Biya of Cameroon and Gnassingbé Eyadéma of Togo.[49]

At the same time, French NGDOs have tended to see the French state's view of democracy and human rights as too restrictive and too close to the minimalist neo-liberal version espoused in Anglo-Saxon countries. Thus, according to the CRID (2002: 5–6), 'The issue of democracy is vital … and … cannot simply be boiled down to a new dogma, one which identifies democracy with the market'. French NGDOs have, for their part, aspired to a much more radical political agenda, which seeks ultimately to establish a global system of democratic governance that is capable of genuinely representing the views of civil societies of both the North and South. The mechanism for this would be the UN, given that this is the international organisation, which is deemed to be the most representative and the most clearly based on human rights covenants.[50] The UN and its agencies (notably ECOSOC) would take precedence over the World Bank and IMF, which would see their powers curtailed and their activities independently evaluated. There would also be a UN 'General Assembly' of NGOs, which would help to oversee the introduction and enforcement of a Tobin Tax, a policy on 'global public goods' and a system for ensuring that that all states recognise economic, social and cultural rights, that is, the right of individuals and communities to food, healthcare, a proper education and a decent living wage.[51] Needless to say, these NGDO demands, with their implied loss of sovereignty for the state in favour of some vaguely defined IOs and unelected civil societies, have gone well beyond anything which a Jacobin French Republic could ever accept.

Conclusion

This chapter has focused on the third putative trend outlined in our introduction. It has demonstrated how the French authorities and French NGDOs had very different operational and policy priorities in the early post-colonial decades. It has also shown how the French state has, over the last decade or so, recognised the potential value of NGOs as service providers and vectors and adapted its operational and policy prerogatives in ways which facilitate closer collaboration. French NGDOs have responded positively to these overtures but have stopped short of taking on the role of public contractor or voice piece for the French government, preferring to hold on to many of their own traditional operational prerogatives and to retain a critical stance towards many of the state's policies.

Whether or not French NGDO behaviour in this context has been consistent with RD theory is a question which will be addressed in Chapter 8. For now, it should suffice to note that French NGDOs have, in line with the RD perspective, been quite prepared to take on the role of service provider or vector on condition that the state funding has been available and that the objectives of the government have been broadly compatible with their own. Where, however, these conditions have not obtained, NGDOs have eschewed a service delivery role. In such circumstances, they have often preferred to rely on other sources of funding and to undertake operations in pursuit of their own long-standing prerogatives. These include programmes to improve 'food security', projects to promote community-led development and advocacy campaign activities designed to tackle the underlying causes of poverty.[52] On the face of it, French NGDOs could be accused of not doing enough to tap into the potential for further state resources, which service delivery work can offer. But they have, it would seem, been demonstrating a deeper appreciation of their wider environment and a recognition of the need to respond less to the exigencies of the French administration, whose funding for NGDO service provision remains limited, and more to the demands of their own core supporters, whose political and economic policy prescriptions are generally more radical than, and often conflict with, those of the French state.

8

A Resource Dependence Perspective

French NGDOs have, over the global era, clearly moved some way into line with the wider trends outlined in our introductory chapter. But they have also been careful to ensure that their relationship with the French authorities should not become 'too close for comfort' (Hulme and Edwards, 1997), that their modus operandi should not be overly bureaucratic and that they should not find themselves labelled as mere agents or vectors of the government. By imposing limits on their collaboration with the state, French NGDOs might appear to be undermining our working assumption, which contended that NGOs that adhere to RD theory, should normally be proactive and flexible in their pursuit of central government resources. Yet, have French NGDO been acting out of line with the logic of RD and missing out on valuable funding opportunities from their central state? Or, have they been correctly interpreting their resource context, but operating in a climate which simply does not promote closer NGDO-government cooperation? These questions will be central to this chapter, which will begin by examining the evidence that French development NGOs have misread their resource opportunities, before constructing our main argument, namely that they have been 'enacting' (i.e., correctly interpreting) the resources available from the state and other actors in their environment.[1]

Misreading their resource environment?

The case for saying that French NGDOs have been misreading their resource context is built upon the idea that they have simply faced too many constraints on their capacity for strategic decision-making, and that they have, as a result, not engaged sufficiently in the kind of dependence minimisation strategies which might allow them to garner more state resources without generating awkward dependencies.

Constraints on decision-making

The constraints facing French NGDOs include historico-cultural, ideological and institutional factors. These can skew NGDOs' interpretation of the world and inhibit a utilitarian or 'rational' reading of their resource environment. Taking historico-cultural and ideological constraints together, these are closely interrelated, involving an excessive attachment to the past and to the ideology and values of the early years of the NGDO movement, notably the 1970s, when radical *tiersmondiste* ideas about the intrinsically unjust nature of the capitalist system came to predominate (see Chapter 7). This ideology is underpinned by 'romanticised views of poverty' (Whaites, 2002: 11) and the idealistic notion that spontaneous and selfless acts of generosity by French NGDO activists should not be sullied by contact with the state or, for that matter, other leading actors in the profit-driven capitalist system (e.g. private companies and international financial institutions). According to this mindset, NGDOs ought to disdain and steer clear of the adoption of commercial or managerial techniques, even where these could enable them to 'do more good'. They should avoid too close an association with the state as the handmaiden of the free market, even where the objectives of central government and NGDOs are broadly compatible. This visceral and excessive mistrust is masterfully understated in a report by the French centre-right party, the *Rassemblement Pour la République*, which notes how French NGDOs are 'marked by a different culture from their European counterparts' and 'view collaboration with the state in quite a specific and ultimately somewhat less than positive manner' (RPR, 1994: 10). It is spelt out more candidly by commentators, such as Pech and Padis (2004: 83), who liken closer cooperation with government and private enterprise to signing 'a pact with the devil'.

This often-exaggerated fear of co-optation is a central concern of militant activists within the French NGDO movement. While there has been little sociological analysis of the composition, motivation or staff profile of NGDOs, it would appear from this research that these organisations continue to be influenced by individuals who might best be described as second-generation *soixante-huitards*.[2] This old guard includes leaders, who rose through the ranks of the NGDO movement following the liberation struggles of the colonial era and during the Cold War, when many leant much more towards Marxism or revolutionary notions of social justice than they did towards 'freewheeling' market capitalism. This hard core has been said by Ryfman (2004: 75) to include

> Veterans of the anti-colonial struggle seeking to carry on the fight on behalf of the Third World, orphans of the post May 1968 era..., ex-communists or activists from the far Left who broke away from their party or respective movements after revelations about the Gulag, right-wing sympathisers disappointed by their party's policies once in power;

NGOs have commonly served (and continue) to serve as a safe haven for former political activists.

Described by some as 'anti-conformist addicts' (Ponsignon, 2002), many of the above actors have come to be joined by a younger breed of militant activists, some of whom have emanated from social movements and groups, such as ATTAC. This new generation has generally defined itself in opposition to the Establishment, demonstrated a visceral dislike of the Anglo-Saxon, particularly the American, free-market model of development and forged links with more radical elements of the 'alter' or 'anti-globalisation' movement (see Annex C). Some of these activists have been quite hard-line, prompting the Head of CLONG-V to intimate to the author that 'one of the big problems in the world of NGOs is to ensure that it is not flooded by extremists' (Interview, 2003).

Turning to institutional constraints, these include entrenched practices, bureaucratic inertia and a general lack of capacity of NGDOs to glean information and resources from their wider environment. These structural and procedural shortcomings can be attributed to a number of factors. First, they are a direct function of the small size, disparate nature and sheer proliferation of French NGDOs. Second, they are an indirect consequence of long-standing policies by the French state, which has chronically underfunded NGDOs and limited their development via legal measures ranging from restrictions on directors' salaries through to the introduction, in January 2000, of a 35-hour working week (which has effectively limited the time that staff can devote to NGDO federations and other activities outside their organisations).[3] Third, these institutional weaknesses are often a function of the failure of developmental NGOs as organisational structures to overcome the personal ambitions and prejudices of their charismatic leaders, activist supporters and, in some cases, 'trustees' (Dauvin *et al.*, 2002). In this context, Devin (1999: 72) has commented that 'The world of French NGDOs is fragile. When it is not racked by personal ambitions, it has to face the challenges of its lack of capacity and unity.'

Finally, these organisational shortcomings are also the result of stubborn choices and irrational fears on the part of non-governmental actors themselves. Pfeffer and Salancik (1978) have observed that some organisations display an excessive, nostalgic and even superstitious attachment to practices that have worked in the past. There has certainly been an assumption within parts of the French NGDO community that the old ways of working are best. This can be inferred from the fact that most developmental NGOs still refuse to encourage integration of developing countries into the global free market and from the way that some have even persisted with their advocacy of food self-sufficiency and 'self-directed development'. This unerring faith in past practices can also be discerned in the way that many NGDOs have continued to pursue the kind of traditional modes of recruitment, which have led to a preponderance of voluntary personnel and a high staff turnover. It is, moreover, apparent from the excessive attachment, which some NGDOs show towards the notion of *filières*, that is, the idea that particular vocations are reserved for people or organisations with specific qualifications. This latter phenomenon is perhaps most clearly illustrated by the reluctance of many *développementalistes* to branch out into the field of emergency relief work. Indeed, one senior figure in the CCFD even told the author that this type of activity, with its neglect of the underlying causes of the challenges facing the developing world, was something of a 'no-go area' for many *développementalistes* (Interview, 2003).

Falling short on resource stabilisation techniques

Given the presence of such constraints, it seems clear that French NGDOs have not been in a position to optimise their resource opportunities or to make full use of the resource stabilisation techniques outlined in Chapter 3. As can be seen from our RD model (Figure 3.1), these dependence-minimisation strategies include lobbying, control techniques and resource diversification (RDVN). Each of these will be examined in turn.

In the case of lobbying, French NGDOs have historically been slow, and often reluctant, to invest a great deal of their time and energy in advocacy work targeted at the one actor that can single-handedly shape their legal and fiscal context, namely the French state. They have, no doubt, had many reasons for this reticence. Some have been afraid that they might end up losing out in the distribution of official subsidies, particularly at times when the state is cutting back on aid to NGDOs (Boisgallais and Fardeau, 1994: 7). Others have simply not understood the nature of the lobbying process. Thus, as the economist, Philippe Hugon, has argued, French NGDOs have emerged out of a Latin culture and have tended to equate advocacy with 'a process of negating the suggestions of official actors' (Interview, 2004).

Whatever the reasons for the late development of NGDO advocacy work, the fact is that French NGOs did take a long time to join forces and engage in coherent lobbying of the French authorities. This is clear from the fact that the first fully-functional, overarching federation, *Coordination SUD*, was not created until 1994. And even then, this grouping did not enjoy the full support of the NGO movement or, indeed, include, within its membership, the largest French NGO of all, namely MSF.[4] This makeshift approach to lobbying has, in fact, remained a feature of French NGDOs, even after the establishment of *Coordination SUD*. This should be clear from the following observations. First, French NGDOs have continued to be far from systematic in their attempts to form links with government officials, MPs or senators with specific interests in overseas development (Interview with the CRID, 2003). Second, they have generally neglected to set up offices in Brussels, New York or Geneva, despite the potential influence that such missions could exert on international institutions, such as the World Bank, the UN and the main paymaster of these institutions, the American Congress. Third, many *développementalistes* have, perhaps because of taboos about money that are prevalent in French culture, traditionally been reticent about engaging in high-profile campaigns that call on the state to channel more aid specifically through French NGDOs. Fourth, most French developmental NGOs have built up alliances in an *ad hoc* manner. This has, in turn, led them to gravitate towards actors, such as pressure groups, trade unions and various members of the *altermondialiste* movement, who are generally quite radical and who, through a process of association, serve to detract from the image of moderation and professionalism, which many NGDOs have built up over recent years. Finally, French developmental NGOs have, notably since the 1994 Rwanda crisis, ratcheted up their criticism of the French state for its collusion with African dictators, its neo-colonial practices and its rent-seeking behaviour.[5] The problem with this approach is that, as Smillie (1999: 10) has pointed out,

> Where advocacy is concerned, there are two problems in NGO financial dependency on government, especially in a contractual arrangement. First, all governments are preternaturally wary of organisations with a penchant for advocacy and reform. Campaigns and crusades, even the most temperate, are not the stuff of government. In the abstract, advocacy has its place, but in the cold light of a contracting morning, it attracts little in the way of understanding and tolerance.

As to the second resource stabilisation strategy, this involves various control techniques that are designed to shape the way that NGDOs are perceived by the state and their wider environment. The first such approach involves efforts by NGOs to highlight their comparative advantages over other potential service providers. Some French NGDOs have baulked at this kind of self-promotional strategy (sometimes termed 'buffering') out of a reluctance to denigrate other NGOs, something which is 'just not done' (Fowler, 2000: 112) in non-governmental circles. Others have resisted this practice out of a refusal to engage in the form of mediatisation and sensationalisation that is usually associated with *urgenciers*; or indeed out of a reluctance to draw attention to their core advantage, their low cost, which is primarily a function of the fact that most of their staff are local employees and paid only a fraction of the French minimum wage. In a similar vein, most NGDOs have been reticent about seeking special treatment from the French state. They have, in particular, been wary of calling for the type of semi-exclusive partnerships enjoyed by large NGOs in countries, such as Britain, Sweden and Denmark. Equally, they have tended to be lukewarm about pragmatic but inegalitarian state-led proposals, which would accord a separate legal status to leading *urgenciers* and *développementalistes*, thereby distinguishing them from the many thousands of associations lumped together under the 1901 law.

A related technique, which has also been underemployed, involves the control by NGDOs of the information that they disseminate about themselves. French developmental NGOs have, of course, appreciated the need to portray their work in a positive light and suppress bad news stories about the misuse of funding, inappropriate activities or, indeed, failed development projects. However, as official reports by Blum (2005 and 2007) and the *Cour des Comptes* (2005) have amply demonstrated, French NGDOs have often, rather than putting a spin on the data at their disposal, simply failed to report back on their activities in a punctual, accurate or coherent fashion, thereby giving the impression that they are not in control of information about themselves. This impression has been compounded by the fact that they have extremely poor archival facilities, that they have gone to such great lengths to bury negative evaluations and that they have, more generally, remained impregnated by a culture of secrecy, which serves to impede any form of independent scrutiny, however benign (see Chapter 6).

A third technique, also under-used, involves a collaborative approach that is aimed at securing higher levels of resources from actors, such as the state. The problems of working collaboratively and forming federations with fellow NGDOs have already been highlighted above in relation to lobbying. But the same difficulties can also be discerned in other contexts. Thus, for example, many NGDOs, long accustomed to competing with each other for funds, have found it hard to develop partnerships and to submit joint bids for official funding under 'the new contractual arrangements'.[6] Furthermore, developmental NGOs have often found it difficult to work with each other in the field, particularly where the organisations concerned come from ideologically different backgrounds or employ different approaches to project delivery (see case study, Chapter 9). The bottom line is that many French NGDOs have become accustomed to their own autonomous ways of working and have been reluctant to change or to engage in any kind of permanent alliances with other non-governmental actors. With few exceptions, the most notable of which being the 2004 'merger' between *Vétérinaires Sans Frontières* and the *Centre International de Coopération pour le Développement Agricole* (CICDA), the French NGO sector has been marked by a near-total absence of formal 'joint ventures' or 'take-overs'.[7]

Turning to the final strategy, *resource diversification* (RDVN), this has also been underemployed, or even mis-used, by some French NGDOs. Some of these organisations could, in fact, be accused of being a little too hasty to turn down, or to impose a ceiling on, resources from central government. Large NGDOs, such as the CCFD and SC-CF, have placed a cap on state funding, which rarely exceeds 10 per cent of their overall resources. Other NGDOs, such as the *CIMADE* and *ATD Quart Monde*, have regularly accepted an even lower proportion of their revenue from the state

(2.9 per and 2.2 per cent, respectively) (CCD, 2008: 29 and 30). Others still have either accepted none at all from the French government (e.g. *Emmaüs International*) or they have refused monies for certain purposes (e.g. humanitarian work following the war in Iraq). In this latter context, a senior representative of *TDH-France*, has stressed that

> ... if we could have our own funds, ultimately if we could do without official finance, I think that we would.... We cannot and have to recognise this fact. But we do not want this funding to go beyond a certain threshold, as this might threaten our independence ... and if funding were to be subject to a clause that ran counter to our philosophy, we would renounce that funding. (Interview, 2003)

In following this rather moralistic approach, many NGDOs have, no doubt, missed out on opportunities for state funding, and some may even have lost out in instances where their objectives have been broadly consistent with those of the government. This observation is particularly true of small NGDOs, some of which fall into the category labelled by Bossuyt and Develtere (1995: 77) as stubborn organisations which 'keep their eyes shut' and seem determined to preserve their autonomy and 'stay small' at all costs. It does, however, also apply equally to a broad swathe of NGDOs which have refused to become involved in the more mediatised emergency relief work that attracts such substantial flows of aid from the state and international organisations. Their somewhat 'irrational' approach to this issue is summed up by a senior figure from the CCFD, who told the author: 'We do not get involved in emergency work. We are not humanitarian NGOs.... We cannot do everything ... we do not have the culture.... Indeed, the term "humanitarian" is not a concept espoused by the CCFD. It is in fact something, which really does not appeal to us' (Interview, 2003).

While there may be perfectly rational reasons for resisting the temptation of additional state funding, this approach does appear, *a priori*, to be counter-intuitive from a RD perspective, given that, as Fowler (2000: 106) claims,

> Few NGDOs ... have a luxury of choice to decline funding offers. There is also a moral pressure not to turn money away. The need is so enormous, and something useful can always be done for the poor. The best must be made out of a bad compromise. Such pragmatic reasoning is understandable.

The refusal to accept government monies, or to seek them out proactively, does seem to be at odds with RD theory, particularly when the advantages of French state funding are taken into account. These include its stability, its predictability and, in the case of larger programmes, its pluri-annual nature.

Other benefits of state assistance include the fact that it allows for a fairly high level of overheads (around 10 per cent of project costs), that it can cover 75 per cent of the price-tag of programmes co-funded under *la nouvelle contractualisa-tion* and that it can, albeit in breach of government regulations, finance an even higher percentage of the cost of some projects 'under convention' (*Cour des Comptes*, 2005). Another advantage of official subsidies is that they offer the prospect of an ongoing financial relationship with the state and the chance to become one of a number of French NGDOs to benefit from substantial and regular yearly funding, without having to jump through the many hoops associated with a truly competitive bidding process (*Cour des Comptes*, 2005).

Significantly too, this tendency for some NGDOs to impose limits on state funding brings with it two important disadvantages. First, it requires these organisations to engage in a more active RDVN strategy, which itself entails costs, as NGDOs are obliged to multiply the number of exchanges in which they are involved. RDVN can, in turn, create the need for management structures, which are more professional and sufficiently complex to deal with a wide range of actors, many of whom have different and, at times, conflicting demands. As Froelich (1999: 262) puts it,

> ... a greater variety of resource providers typically leads to a corresponding increase in funding criteria, and satisfying the criteria of one provider may preclude satisfying another. Resulting goal conflicts and organizational tensions can be difficult to manage.... Maintaining the increasingly complex dependency relationships is also expensive, as each income stream requires considerable management effort for ongoing success....

Froelich also astutely observes that

> Disparate types of resource providers tend to differ in their views of effectiveness, creating a melange of performance indicators and contributing to confusion about the extent of mission accomplishment.... Ultimately, the multiple roles and directions of nonprofit activity can result in 'mission vagueness'... and an unclear charitable purpose. (Ibid)

The second disadvantage of this approach is that the alternative resources, which French NGDOs end up pursuing, also have their own drawbacks. Some of the shortcomings associated with state and private funding have already been touched upon in our general discussion of this issue in Chapter 3. Details of the official and private resource flows available to French NGOs have also been set out in Chapter 4. Here the aim will be to offer a French NGDO perspective on the drawbacks and, later in this chapter, the advantages of each of these revenue flows. The focus will initially be on 'other official resources' (local government, bilateral and international donors) before turning to revenue from 'private sources' (private companies,

consumers of commercial services, foundations and civil society organisations, the donor public and core supporters).

Other official resources

To begin with revenue from French *local or territorial authorities*, here the
main disadvantage is that the overall amount of money available from this
source has been small, making it only really attractive to local and regional
NGDOs engaged in micro-level development projects (CCD, 1987: 84). Thus,
whilst some regional authorities, such as Rhônes-Alpes, have been very generous, the majority have not, with the result that local government sources
have consistently provided less than 5 per cent, and sometimes less than
2.5 per cent, of total French NGO income (see Table 4.3). Significantly too,
this situation looks unlikely to improve, since France's territorial authorities
have, ever since securing authorisation via the 1992 Act on the Territorial
Organisation of the Republic, preferred to engage in their own, quite distinct set of international development projects (sometimes referred to
collectively as 'decentralised cooperation').[8] They have done so through
their own channels (e.g. twinning arrangements and other international
partnerships) and have, in the process, become competitors for the comparatively small pot of central government money available to non-state actors
via the French Foreign Ministry co-funding unit, the MCNG. Most local
authorities have, nonetheless, continued to fund NGDOs. But many have
attached conditions to their support and required NGDOs to take on the
role of 'service agents' (Interview with Christian Feuillet, 2003). Some have
even imposed strict preconditions on their assistance, refusing funding to
faith-based NGDOs and to organisations based in regions other than their
own, particularly Paris-based NGDOs, which are assumed to be national
level actors that already have an 'unfair advantage' in terms of their proximity to the French central state (Interview with DCC, 2003).

Turning to the income provided by IOs and *other bilateral donors*, the principal drawbacks associated with this funding are that it is open to fierce
international competition, subject to bureaucratic delays and generally
geared towards costlier projects and, hence, towards larger NGOs.[9] Another
potential difficulty arises from the fact that these monies come, in the first
instance, from the French government or other central states and do, in
some respects, represent an alternative form of, rather than an alternative
to, central government support.

In the case of revenue from other donor agencies, such as the DFID (Britain),
SIDA (Sweden) and USAID (the United States), the main disadvantage of this
funding is that it is hard to obtain and only likely to be secured where
French NGOs can offer expertise that is not readily available in the donor
country concerned. A related drawback is that this assistance has tended to
favour a small number of actors (around two dozen in 1999), most of which
are medium-sized or large (CCD, 2001a: 12). A further problem relates to the

fact that the sums of money involved have, at least until recently, not justi-fied the sheer amount of work involved in seeking out this income from such a diverse range of donors, with such different application processes and evaluation criteria (Interviews in Paris, 2003).

As regards *international organisations*, the World Bank is, no doubt, the most problematic source of monies for French *développementalistes* and other NGOs. This institution was originally set up as an 'inter-governmental organ-isation' and given a remit to 'work first and foremost with governments' (Smillie *et al.*, 1999: 285). It was not, as such, seen as a mechanism to pro-vide support directly to NGOs; and it has never, in fact, provided more than around 5 per cent of official funding to French NGOs. The Bank has proven especially ill-suited to the needs of French *développementalistes* on a number of grounds. The first is that it produces all its documentation, including its tenders, in English and makes no systematic attempt to translate this material into French. The second is that it has demonstrated a propensity to favour direct collaboration with NGOs from the Southern rather than the Northern hemisphere. Indeed, the former secure almost three-quarters of all project funding and do so, at least partly, at the expense of French *développementalistes* and other NGOs which serve as intermediaries between governments in the North and NGOs in the South (World Bank, 2001). The third relates to the Bank's lengthy bureaucratic procedures, which can be cumbersome and financially expensive for the kind of small- and medium-sized NGDOs that are prevalent in France. The fourth is that the Bank tends to view NGDOs essentially as service delivery agents rather than as partners, who need to be consulted on what is happening on the ground.[10] The final reason is that the Bank is, at best, an unknown quantity for French devel-opmental NGOs and, at worst, an ideological 'enemy to be struck down' (Interviews in Paris, 2003). It may forever be associated, in the minds of NGDO practitioners, with the economic austerity measures of the 1980s and with continuing pressures for US-led neo-liberal market reforms in the global era. This latent resentment is recognised by the CRID, which notes how 'some in the French NGDO landscape refuse any co-funding from the World Bank' (Interview, 2003). Needless to say, those French *développemen-talistes*, which do seek monies from the Bank, have to find a way of justify-ing this to, or concealing it from, their own core supporters.

Some of the above drawbacks apply equally to the UN and its agencies. These international bodies are not only highly bureaucratic, but they are also very dependent on compulsory and voluntary contributions from a reluctant American Congress and other, increasingly cost-conscious lead-ing member states. As should be clear from Chapter 4 (Table 4.4), the bulk of French NGO funding from the UN (somewhere between 87 per cent in 1995 and 61 per cent in 2005) has come from only two agencies, namely the UN High Commission for Refugees and the World Food Programme. It follows that these monies have been primarily destined for French *urgenciers* rather than developmental NGOs. The latter have, moreover, due to language barriers and a lack of permanent representation in New York, found it hard to develop a close relationship with the UN. Indeed, only a few French NGDOs have even tried to secure accreditation from the UN, or more specifically its Economic and Social Committee or ECOSOC (Herlemont-Zoratchik, 2002: 113).[11]

Turning finally to the European Commission, this has been the most important source of international funding. It has, in fact, become 'a', if not 'the', critical resource for French NGOs *urgenciers*, such as *Première Urgence* and *Aide Médicale Internationale* (CCD, 2008: 29–31). Such high levels of funding are, however, less common in the case of French NGDOs, which are, in the words of one senior representative from the *Haut Conseil*, 'not among the most effective when it comes to securing funding from line B7-6000' (Interview, 2003).[12] A similar observation is made by the *Commissariat Général* (2002: 103), which points out that 'competition for European resources is ferocious' and that French NGDOs are less well placed to take advantage of this funding than, say, British applicants, who have for years enjoyed support from the UK permanent representation in Brussels.

European monies have also entailed a number of other disadvantages. The first is that they have failed to keep up with rising levels of demand from NGOs across Europe and to represent a guaranteed or stable source of revenue from one year to the next.[13] A case in point was the way in which European funding to *Équilibre* – a French *urgencier* which had expanded its operations dramatically in the early 1990s – simply dried up after the Bosnian crisis.[14] The second drawback is that European funding has a technocratic bias, which has made it a particularly problematic source for French volunteer agencies. With their emphasis on young, relatively inexperienced staff, these organisations have been under-valued by the Commission, which prefers to send experienced technicians and highly qualified experts to plug the skills gaps in specific sectors of developing economies (Interview with the DCC, 2003). The third, closely related problem is that European support has tended to 'discriminate against small NGOs' and to be oriented essentially towards large organisations, which, alone, have the capacity to submit complex bids, to promise the required levels of evaluation, and to muster together the 15 to 25 per cent stake, which must be provided by NGDOs before the Commission will co-finance their project (Ibid).[15] In this context, Blum (2005: 18) has noted that

> When the Commission issues a tender, it is very demanding in terms of the selection of NGOs which are eligible for its funding. To gain access, an NGO has to be sufficiently well known and must propose a strategic programme-based approach; line up a strategic partnership...; enjoy co-funding from its own national government... [and be part of] a

consortium of NGOs in which must always figure a beneficiary, that is, a Southern NGO.

The final drawback is that European funding is prone to bureaucratic delays and to strict independent management audits, notably on grants above €100,000. As Blum has observed, French NGDO 'complaints regarding the EU are close to those targeted at the national government: a failure to provide stop-gap funding in transitional years, ... a ceiling of 7 per cent on the funding of overheads, [and] very short deadlines for responding to tenders' (Ibid).

Private resources

Private resources present a different set of problems. The first of these is cost-related, as the CCD (2001: 22) has recognised, commenting that 'It is probably a lot cheaper to raise funds from official bodies than it is to secure them from private sources'.[16] The other main drawbacks are outlined succinctly by Froelich (1999: 259), who has remarked that

> A strategy relying on private contributions is associated with higher revenue volatility compared to the other funding strategies. Goal displacement effects are also greater, evidenced by donor facilitation of broadly acceptable traditional pursuits, and encouraging controversy avoidance and tempered innovation in recipient organizations.

No doubt the most problematic form of private funding comes from commercial companies. This source has never risen much above 5 per cent of total private revenue (Table 4.5), and, according to the CRID, some NGDOs would 'not even entertain the prospect of seeking monies or sponsorship' from these profit-making actors (Interview, 2003). Similarly, a senior figure from the CCFD has observed that this kind of commercial partnership has been 'difficult for militants and even some permanent staff to swallow' (Interview, 2003). Underpinned by an 'ideology which refuses profit', French NGDOs have undoubtedly harboured real reservations about commercial firms, which they see as harbingers of the free market.[17] They have remained sceptical of the pledges that commercial companies have made in relation to corporate social responsibility and they have worried that, by accepting private company support, they will see their effectiveness undermined, their legitimacy eroded and their critical resource jeopardised. Equally, they have been concerned that 'their expertise, contacts and local knowledge may be used to commercial ends', and that their association may end up 'being manipulated, becoming a promotional tool for companies, which merely claim to have an altruistic interest in the developing world'. In particular, they have been anxious not to 'sell their soul' by accepting monies from arms companies or other firms, such as Nestlé, which have faced criticism from NNGDOs in the past. In addition, they have been wary of other forms of support from companies. These include the offer of in-kind gifts and even of staff for overseas voluntary work. However, the former are frequently deemed 'unusable and dangerous because of the risks of corruption and the costs of transport', whilst the latter are accused of diluting the spirit of NGDO solidarity.[18]

Another potentially problematic source of revenue for French NGDOs has been their own commercial services and products. These income-generating activities are often hard to distinguish from fund-raising from the donor public itself (via, for instance, the sale of greeting cards and raffle tickets). A clearer distinction can, nonetheless, be drawn in the case of the plethora of ethical investment schemes, which now compete for the revenue of a relatively small number of 'socially responsible' savers. These savings products are designed to generate 'rent' or unearned income in the form of interest – a highly questionable source of funding from the standpoint of many Left-leaning NGDOs. Another example of the dangers associated with commercial activities has been the way in which the fair trade organisation, the *Fondation Max Havelaar*, has transformed itself into a company in all but name. This foundation has started to attend the Davos World Economic Forum for business leaders and politicians (against which the *altermondialiste* movement has mobilised its own 'counter-summits' in Porto Alegre and elsewhere). It has also used French supermarket chains as a major outlet for its products, even turning a blind eye to apparent abuses of its fair trade label by multinational companies in search of international respectability.[19] The success of the *Max Havelaar* approach, if it inspires others to follow suit, could mean that NGOs may become sucked into the logic of the market and indistinguishable from companies, thereby eroding their claims for fiscal and other benefits.

Another comparatively minor source of revenue totalling, between 1991 and 2005, only 5 to 14 per cent of private resources has been civil society organisations, such as other NGOs and private foundations (see Table 4.5). While less contentious, these largely philanthropic sources of income do, nonetheless, entail disadvantages. In the case of transfers from other NGOs, here the danger is that French NGDOs may find themselves accepting monies, which were originally accorded as subsidies to the donating NGO by states and other official actors (*Cour des Comptes*, 2005). There is also a risk that income provided by larger, foreign NGOs and affiliates of French NGOs based in other countries may result in a process of institutional isomorphism and push French developmental NGOs further down the road towards espousing the broad trends outlined in our introductory chapter. As regards support from private foundations, the main problem, in this instance, is the competitive nature of the bidding process for this funding in a country where such foundations are a comparatively rare phenomenon. Another concern is that these foundations tend to impose quality constraints, benchmarks for accountability and a host of 'conditionalities or at least broad guidelines', which are often just as onerous as anything demanded by the state (Blum, 2005: 20).

Turning finally to the critical resource, namely the donor public and the volunteer base, here too there are drawbacks. The first relates to the fact that the French public has never traditionally been, and is still not, particularly generous by comparison with the domestic public in many other OECD member countries. This fact is brought out by the CCD (1987: 14), which shows how the average French person, whose income stood at 83,518 francs in 1985, gave only 10.6 francs a year to NGOs, thereby placing the French public in fifteenth place out of the 18 OECD donor states. This point is echoed by Archambault (1997: 208), who has observed that, in 1990, only 43 per cent of French people made a sizeable donation compared to 75 per cent of Americans. The same author has calculated that the average American gave 9.5 times more to the non-profit sector than the average French citizen (Ibid).[20] She has also observed that the French public typically uses up only a fraction of its tax deductible allowance for donations. Echoing Tocqueville's observations about the weakness of French civic culture and its over-reliance on the state, Archambault (Ibid: 210) has noted that

> ...the lack of giving in France is not only a problem of tax-encouragement. It is more a very deep-rooted cultural problem. In France, the state is assumed to be responsible for every public interest concern and once the citizen has paid taxes...he or she is exempt from public matters. This mentality still exists though it is decreasing.

The second, closely related disadvantage of donations from the public relates to their volatility. The fickleness of this source has been commented upon by the CCD (1987: 52), which notes how 'the nature of these funds confers a relatively shaky quality upon the main source of funding of NGOs...that is to say the generosity of the donor public'. This volatility is an inescapable reality for a number of reasons. For a start, public donations tend to be seasonal in nature, with high points at Christmas and Lent. They are also, quite often, one-off payments – in cash, through the internet or via text messaging – rather than regular direct debits or legacies, the latter of which is in particularly short supply (see Table 4.5). In addition, these donations are, in the case of faith-based actors, no longer underpinned by high levels of support for the Church. Indeed, as Archambault (1997: 18) has noted, 'Nowadays France is the European country where religious observances are the lowest (13 per cent of the adult population) and stated atheism the highest (14 per cent)'. Furthermore, while public donations rise at times of natural or man-made disasters (e.g. Rwanda, Kosovo, the South Asian tsunami), they are generally much lower in non-crisis years, thereby making long-term planning difficult (Ibid). These monies also tend not to flow in the direction of developmental NGDOs, whose longer-term work appears less immediate and less morally gratifying. They are channelled instead towards *urgenciers*, who are aided in no small measure by their close links with the media, their emotive advertising campaigns highlighting the victims of catastrophes, and their widely recognised specialist expertise in emergency relief work. To illustrate, each of the main French *urgenciers* (MSF, MDM, ACF) secured, in the way of private donations for victims of the South Asian tsunami, four times more than the largest NGDO, the CCFD.[21]

Reliance on donations from the general public is, moreover, a risky business given how reluctant the latter is to finance anything other than NGO operational activities (CCD, 1987: 164). Indeed, as Blum (2005: 20) has pointed out, NGOs 'encounter some difficulty in obtaining funds aimed at financing their structures. The citizen, who is quite prepared to make a donation in support of children in refugee camps, is much less so when it comes to paying the salaries of NGO practitioners'. Furthermore, the public can easily become distracted by other good causes, not least issues such as poverty in France, which is consistently one of the main concerns identified in the 'Barometer of International Solidarity', the CCFD's annual survey of public attitudes towards overseas development issues.[22] The French public can also be prone to compassion fatigue, particularly when its confidence is rocked by NGO scandals. The most infamous incident involved the cancer charity ARC (see Chapter 6). But a stream of other scandals has also dented donations, not least the allegation in 2002 by Sylvie Brunel, a former President of ACF, to the effect that staff within this organisation led freewheeling life-styles. This attack alone was enough for ACF to declare a deficit of €1.4 million in 2002 (Blum, 2005: 24). It was followed by more serious accusations, in a 2002 UNHCR enquiry, that 67 local employees in around 40 French and other emergency NGOs had sexually abused minors in refugee camps in Sierra Leone, Liberia and Guinea and used food as a means of payment.[23] More recent revelations have centred on the French NGDO, *Arche de Zoé*. This organisation, which claimed to be helping orphans of the conflict in the Sudan, was found, in 2007, to be engaged in trafficking 103 children from neighbouring Chad to prospective adoptive parents in France.[24]

Turning finally to the volunteer base of French NGDOs, this can also present drawbacks. As noted in Chapter 4, French NGDOs are generally more reliant on volunteers than their European counterparts (Woods, 2000: 19), with small organisations finding themselves particularly dependent on these activists and on the fees of their members (CCD, 1987: 57). This over-reliance on volunteers can be problematic in a number of ways. To begin with, these grassroots supporters are often only available for short periods, which militates against learning, professionalisation and forward planning. Furthermore, this resource is not easy to capture or replicate since, as Brown and Korten (1991: 54) make clear, 'voluntary energies are not easily controlled, ... difficult if not impossible to buy and ... largely inaccessible to development planners, bureaucrats, and technicians'. Thus, even though volunteers and militants are still quite easy to recruit from within the ranks of the general public, there is no guarantee that these volunteers will always be available in sufficient numbers, given that some NGDOs (e.g. *TDH-France*) have struggled to attract younger supporters and given that all French NGDOs now face increasing competition for the time and energy of these actors from more radical organisations within the *altermondialiste* movement. Significantly too, the number of activist recruits can drop suddenly in the face of scandals in the non-profit sector.[25] Thus, whilst opinion polls typically reveal that young people have a strong desire to engage in NGO work, their 'confidence is nonetheless fragile whenever there is a hint of financial scandal'. Finally, and perhaps most importantly, these grassroots volunteers are generally more militant than permanent head office staff. They tend, as such, to tie the hands of managers and discourage them from engaging in certain types of strategic decision-making, from seeking monies from particular companies (*Handicap International* has its own blacklist) or, indeed, from submitting funding bids to official organisations, such as the World Bank. These militants can, moreover, lead French NGDOs to undertake more radical advocacy work than might be consistent with a resource-oriented strategy which is geared towards optimising levels of assistance from the state or other official bodies.

Enacting their environment

It follows, then, that French developmental NGOs have not maximised their resource opportunities vis-à-vis the state. It cannot, however, be assumed from the above analysis that French NGDOs have been acting out of line with RD theory. It will, in fact, be argued here that they have engaged in a broadly accurate reading of their wider resource environment. This assertion is based upon two main observations: first that French NGDOs have, over the global era, gone a long way towards overcoming the various constraints on their strategic decision-making; and, second, that they have been making ever more concerted efforts to pursue resource stabilisation strategies.

Overcoming strategic constraints

French NGDOs have, inevitably, found it difficult to overcome historico-cultural constraints on their decision-making. There are signs, nevertheless, that some of the old guard, notably the unreconstructed cold warriors and second-generation *soixante-huitards*, no longer hold sway over the NGDO movement. These actors would appear to be giving way to a new breed of managers, who are now more explicitly interested in results and professionalism (Haddad, 2002). There is also now, working its way through the ranks of the NGDO movement, a whole generation of highly qualified recruits, whose technocratic tendencies and careerist ambitions are often barely disguised (Dauvin *et al.*, 2002). Needless to say, this new generation has not been scarred by any of the ideological battles of the past, notably the colonial liberation struggle, the Cold War and the debate surrounding *tiersmondisme*.

There is, at the same time, evidence to suggest that French NGDOs are beginning to overcome their institutional constraints and lack of organisational capacity. They have done so in a number of ways. First, they have substantially increased their participation in federations (see Chapter 2). Second, they have demonstrated a growing readiness to adopt a specialist focus (e.g. the emergence of 'briefcase' NGDOs focusing exclusively on issues, such as AIDS or microcredit). Third, some NGDOs have become polyvalent (e.g. the *Guilde Européenne du Raid*) and a few have even dabbled in emergency-related work (e.g. *Secours Catholique-Caritas France*). Fourth, many NGDOs have pooled their expertise and submitted collaborative funding bids under *la nouvelle contractualisation*. Fifth, some larger, accredited volunteer agencies have provided technical support to smaller organisations through a process known as *portage*. This arrangement has allowed the latter to send volunteers under the more favourable terms offered by recent legislation on *le volontariat*.[26]

Learning to use resource stabilisation techniques

Given this lessening of the strategic constraints on decision-making, French NGDOs have been better placed to make greater, if by no means optimal, use of resource stabilisation strategies. The first of these strategies involves advocacy work designed to shape their relationship with the state. French developmental NGOs have, over the last decade or so, significantly enhanced their capacity to engage in such lobbying activities. Thus, they have formed a host of specialist coalitions, federations, networks, consortiums and informal alliances (see Chapter 2). Larger NGDOs have also begun, as from the mid-1990s, to establish their own advocacy departments and to develop closer working relations with environmental and other pressure groups. Armed with such an enhanced capacity for advocacy work, French NGDOs have, unsurprisingly, engaged in larger scale campaigns, some of the most sophisticated of which have been coordinated by the CRID and have targeted French politicians at election times.[27] While their lobbying has often been hard-hitting, French NGDOs have steered clear of the kind of court cases that have dogged pressure groups, such as *Agir Ici* and *Survie* over recent years.[28] They have also sidestepped the more extreme positions, and above all the violence, adopted by radical elements within the *altermondialiste* movement.[29] Instead, they have demonstrated a certain readiness to work within the parameters of the existing political system by lobbying primarily through joint NGO–state forums. To illustrate, French NGDOs have used the *Commission du Volontariat* and the CVCA, respectively, to call for a new legal status for volunteers and for a better fiscal environment. Equally, they have made representations within the CCD for higher levels of government aid and for improved co-financing terms.[30] They have, moreover, used their links with the French Foreign Ministry to appeal for financial support to help form specialist evaluation units like the F3E. In addition, they have made the most of their presence within officially subsidised NGO bodies, such as CONCORD, to push for French and wider international agreement on issues, such as debt cancellation, the international criminal court and the Ottawa Treaty banning the sale of landmines.[31]

The second strategy relates to *control techniques*. Here, French NGDOs have, for example, sought to control demands from the state by making themselves appear more attractive, even indispensable, to the French authorities. Whilst avoiding the kind of self-promotional strategies, which they associate with their Anglo-Saxon counterparts, French NGDOs have, nonetheless, engaged in greater efforts to convince the government that they are professional in their procedures, their codes of practice and their financial management. They have also regularly alluded, in their campaign literature, to what they perceive to be their comparative advantages or 'unique selling points'. These are deemed to include their high levels of flexibility and innovation, their developmental effectiveness, their proximity to, and special relationship with, indigenous populations and their knowledge on the ground. They are also said to involve their critical mass of expertise within federations (e.g. *Plateforme Dette et Développement*) and, in the case of larger NGDOs like the CCFD, their relative financial autonomy and their institutional capacity to coordinate complex multi-actor programmes (Interview with CCFD, 2003).

Developmental and emergency NGOs' techniques to control information have, indeed, remained poor but have, at least, been consistent and rational. Thus, developmental NGOs have persistently sought to portray themselves in a favourable light, suppressing bad news stories and under-reporting – on their websites and in their publications – the level of subsidies they receive from the French state (*Cour des Comptes*, 2005). In so doing, they have been behaving rationally and playing to the gallery of their militant activists by exaggerating their degree of autonomy and concealing the fact that they are unable to deliver on many of the unrealistic promises, which they make in relation to overseas development. They have, at the same time, been reassuring a relatively uninformed donor public, who want to believe not only that their donations are making a difference, but also that the organisation of their choice is operating effectively. This is, no doubt, particularly true in the case of individual donors contributing to faith-based bodies with which they have a religious affiliation.

The last technique, namely collaboration between NGDOs to control demands imposed on them, has become a major feature of French NGDO behaviour over the global era. This is clear from the fact that nearly all

NGDOs have joined some kind of network or federation (see Chapter 2). It can also be discerned in the way that NGDOs, such as the GRET, IRAM and DIAL, have begun working together in consortiums to tackle specific issues, such as PRSP consultation processes (World Bank, 2001).[32] This readiness to cooperate can also be detected on the ground, even in cases where NGDOs have very different working methods and ideological backgrounds (see case study, Chapter 9).

Turning lastly to RDVN strategies, here it is important to correct the impression created earlier in this chapter, namely that NGDOs have been picking and choosing when it comes to funding and other forms of support from the state. Whilst this may be true of leading *urgenciers*, such as MSF and MDM, which can rely on solid networks of private donors, and faith-based actors, such as the SC-CF and CCFD, which are guaranteed a steady flow of income at key moments in the religious year, it is not the case for the vast majority of French NGDOs. The bulk of these organisations have, for all their rhetoric on the value of autonomy, been very keen to secure higher levels of official support from the state. Some have sought recognition by the Council of State of their 'public utility status'. Others have looked to the Foreign Ministry to provide formal accreditation of their standing as volunteer agencies. Nearly all have endeavoured to secure more grant funding from the government. Indeed, in this latter context, *Coordination SUD* has openly asserted that 'contrary to conventional wisdom' NGOs would 'like to be a little more dependent' on the French state (CCD, 2003: 7). That this is no hollow statement is clear from the fact that the number of NGO bids for co-funding has consistently exceeded the amount of monies available from the Foreign Ministry. Thus, for example, in 2002, some 575 applications were submitted, yet only 454 or 79 per cent of these were actually financed (*Cour des Comptes*, 2005: 3). Another useful indicator is the total number of NGOs receiving state support: some 158 in 2006.[33] As will be recalled from the last chapter, a number of these organisations have benefited from particularly large sums under the 'new contractual arrangements' and a handful of French NGDOs, some 15 in total, have come to depend upon the state for two-thirds or more of their income.[34]

It follows, then, that most French NGDOs have not, in fact, been over-hasty in turning down offers of assistance from the state. Nor has their objective normally been to pare down support from the French authorities to the bare minimum. They have, rather, been engaged in a resource diversification strategy, which seeks to stabilise resource flows and to avoid over-dependence on central government. In so doing, French NGDOs have – it will be argued here – been acting in ways which are broadly consistent with the logic of RD theory. A number of points can be made in support of this assertion.

The first is that state funding is known to generate awkward dependencies, to expose NGDOs to co-optation and to lead to 'imbalanced compromise not in the NGDOs favour, with a negative impact on autonomy and ways of working' (Fowler, 2000: 121). It can mean that non-governmental actors lose the sense of their original mission, become more accountable to donor states than local beneficiaries (Hulme and Edwards, 1997) and become vulnerable to changes of government and delays in state funding cycles. Finally, it can require them to 'follow highly formalized and standardized procedures' and to adopt a bureaucratic structure that is 'cumbersome' (Fowler, 2000: 57) and 'similar to that of government agencies' (Froelich, 1999: 260).

The second reason for avoiding over-reliance on government funding is that the French state has a poor reputation in terms of its foreign and development policy towards the developing world, particularly its former colonies in Africa. The French authorities have, for example, been criticised by civil society actors for their involvement in the Elf scandal in the early 1990s, their role in events leading up to the 1994 Rwandan genocide, and their collusion with literally dozens of autocratic African leaders.[35] The French state has also been attacked for its squandering of official aid on 'white elephant' projects, its weak evaluative mechanisms and its overemphasis on the promotion of French culture, at the expense of developmental concerns.[36] Against such a backdrop, French NGDOs have, unsurprisingly, been anxious that their relationship with the government should not erode their legitimacy and jeopardise their critical resource. They have been all too aware that 'by opting openly for ... contractual strategies' with the state, they 'run the risk of gradually losing their status as virtuous actors engaged in a resistance movement' and, eventually, of being 'ousted by new social movements' (Pech and Padis, 2004: 88).

The third argument for a proactive RDVN strategy is that French government support has simply not been available in sufficient quantities, even to many NGDOs that are willing to become more heavily dependent upon this resource. Indeed, with only 38 per cent of their total revenue coming from the state and other official sources in the late 1990s, French NGOs have found themselves well behind their counterparts in Denmark (65 per cent), Sweden (58 per cent), Holland (46 per cent) and the United Kingdom (47 per cent) (Woods, 2000: 17; Ryfman, 2004: 41). They have received the lowest level of aid in Europe and their awareness-raising activities, in particular, have been chronically underfunded by the French authorities. Indeed, the French government has not even set aside a budget specifically for development education, which is a much lower state priority than in countries such as Holland and Canada (OECD, 2004: 25).[37]

All too conscious of this history of chronic neglect, French NGDOs have come to the view that the French state is not 'the' or even 'a' critical resource and is, perhaps, never likely to be. They have recognised that the government, contrary to its often affirmed rhetorical commitment to cooperate with NGDOs, is simply unwilling to offer enough incentives to persuade them to rethink their long-standing survival strategy based on self-reliance.

They have also correctly surmised that the French state does not, and may never, truly appreciate their comparative advantages and that it will probably always prefer to use its own agencies, local authorities or private companies, all of which are more prepared to 'fly the French flag' (Charasse, 2005: *passim*). Crucially, too, they have realised that too close a relationship with the French authorities could alienate their militant supporters, who are wary of instrumentalisation. It could even lead to NGDOs being 'squeezed out of their niche, unable to recruit volunteers and experiencing falling donations', as they find themselves 'rejected by a whole new generation of activists as irrelevant, co-opted, or a part of the system which they are fighting'.[38]

On top of all these concerns, French NGDOs have had to bear in mind one final argument for looking beyond state funding, namely the inherent advantages of the RDVN process itself. As suggested in previous chapters, these benefits include the fact that such an approach spreads the risk of over-reliance on the government or any other single source of income. It also encourages innovation, adaptation and, arguably, greater effectiveness, as NGDOs learn to compete for funding from a range of different resources. Relatedly, RDVN allows French NGDOs to tap into a range of alternative resources, each of which brings its own particular advantages, as will be demonstrated below.

Other official resources

To begin with assistance from local government, this has a number of advantages. First, it can represent a large share of the income generated by many local and regional NGDOs. Second, it is often complemented by non-monetary support in the form of training, technical feedback, manuals and even logistical back-up in the field (*Région Île de France*, undated: 4). Third, this type of aid from elected local authorities can confer a degree of legitimacy on the non-governmental actors selected for funding. Finally, it can even form the basis of wider alliances between local government and NGDOs within joint forums, such as the *Haut Conseil de la Coopération Internationale* and the various *Assises de la Coopération Décentralisée*.[39]

As regards revenue from bilateral donor states and international organisations, the key advantage of this assistance is its sheer size. As will be recalled from Chapter 4, bilateral donors now provide French NGOs with sizeable sums of money, none more so than USAID, which provided M€14 in 2005 alone (CCD, 2008: 28). Some of these donors (e.g. the DFID or SIDA) do, moreover, have a strong reputation for their work on poverty reduction, and their offer of funding to French NGDOs confers a seal of international approval on these organisations.

As for the World Bank, this has been stepping up its support to French NGDOs over recent years (see Table 4.4). It has also become a more respectable source of income, ever since it moved away, in the early 1990s, from market fundamentalism and adopted a strategy geared towards reducing poverty and building strong civil societies. Recognising this paradigmatic shift, 44 per cent of French NGOs now deem the overseas operations of the Bank to be 'positive', while 65 per cent view the recent evolution of its discourse in a favourable light (World Bank, 2001: 47).

As to the UN, this has continued to be viewed by French NGDOs as the most representative of all the international organisations. It is deemed to offer assistance, which is not oriented towards any kind of neo-liberal agenda and which is free from any restrictive forms of conditionality. While the UN does provide the bulk of its financial and logistical support to *urgenciers*, it is nonetheless beginning to supply NGDOs with substantial financial aid through its various subsidiary organisations (e.g. the UNDP, UNICEF) – so much so, in fact, that the majority of these UN organs have now written codes of conduct for their exchanges with NGOs.[40] The UN in New York has, moreover, continued steadily to increase the number of non-state members of ECOSOC, thereby allowing French NGDOs and many other actors the chance to feed their views into debates and resolutions being passed within the UN General Assembly.[41]

The European Commission offers the most tangible benefits, constituting the critical resource for a number of French *urgenciers* (e.g. *Solidarités*) and even for a handful of developmental NGOs (e.g. ACTED or *Agence d'Aide à la Coopération Technique et au Développement*) (CCD, 2008: 28–32). That the Commission is generally receptive to funding bids from French NGOs is clear from the fact that the latter are now the third largest recipient of European assistance, after British and German NGOs.[42] Crucially, too, the European Commission, with its strong focus on poverty eradication and civil society capacity-building, is widely held to be a relatively neutral donor and one which is unlikely to compromise the core poverty-reducing mission of French NGDOs. It is – despite being traditionally linked to questionable trade-related dumping practices and a deeply protectionist Common Agricultural Policy – generally regarded as one of the donors whose aid programme is least driven by narrow *realpolitik* concerns.[43] Finally, it is one of the few IOs over which French NGDOs can exert a direct and significant influence through advocacy networks, such as Eurostep, and European NGO forums, such as CONCORD.

Turning to *private support*, this is, as demonstrated in Chapter 4, available in greater quantities than assistance from the state or other official sources. Its key advantage is that it provides legitimacy and recognition for the efforts of non-governmental actors and, at the same time, affords them considerable autonomy in their actions and discourse. Just about all types of private resources bring potential benefits. This is true even in the case of support from commercial companies, whether this be in the form of sponsorships, technical expertise or longer-term partnerships. These latter contractual arrangements are particularly valuable, signalling a form of recognition of growing NGDO effectiveness and offering these NGOs stable, longer-term resource flows. Thus for example, WWF has entered into an agreement with the cement manufacturer Lafarge, which brings in €1.1 million a year for the WWF's Forest Reborn Project. CARE-France has also benefited from its partnership with the travel agency Havas to promote socially responsible tourism, while FIDH has used its contractual relationship with the French supermarket chain, *Carrefour*, to foreground issues, such as workers' rights in developing countries (Aoust *et al.*, 2004: 67–76). Significantly, each of these NGDOs has been able to claim that these partnership arrangements have increased their scope to exert reverse influence and to impress upon companies the importance of concepts, such as sustainable development and corporate social responsibility.

As regards revenue from 'commercial' sources, this has the distinct advantage that it can, in theory at least, be expanded exponentially. It is also largely free from the conditions associated with assistance from official actors or, for that matter, private companies and foundations. The commercial transactions involved – whether they involve the sale of craftwork through the outlets of *Artisans du Monde* or the fifty or so ethical investment schemes currently on the market – are generally based upon ethical codes, fair trade practices and a strong commitment to the 'social economy' or *économie solidaire*. These activities should not, as such, pose any major problems for most fair-minded activists within the NGDO movement. The same should, equally, be true of the recent actions undertaken by the fair trade foundation *Max Havelaar*. While this pioneering organisation has been criticised for over-commercialising its products, its overriding aim appears to have been the quest for financial autonomy, and the extra revenue it has earned has, in fact, been ploughed back into new commodities.

As for support from other Northern (including French) NGOs and private foundations, here the benefits have greatly outweighed any possible drawbacks. Most revenue from other NGOs can justifiably be viewed as a symbol of the generosity of spirit that binds together the French NGDO sector. This income is particularly welcome, as it is suggestive of a form of solidarity that would be unthinkable in a profit-driven sector anxious to reward shareholders above all else. As for grants from private foundations, these are especially prized for three main reasons: first, because they are so rare in the French context; second, because they are acquired through a rigorously competitive bidding process, which in no way discriminates in favour of larger organisations; and third, because they confer a degree of recognition on NGDOs, which can enable these actors to secure further subsidies from other sources, such as IOs and private companies (Froelich, 1999).[44]

Turning finally to the critical resource, namely donations from the public and support from volunteer activists, this is the most highly valued of all resources in French NGDO circles. As for donations, these have a number of key advantages. The first is that they bring moral legitimacy to NGOs, which is particularly important given that these actors are not elected bodies, and their criticism of the state would seem hollow without this wider public backing. As Henri Rouillé d'Orfeuil, President of *Coordination SUD*, put it, these hard-earned donations 'show the confidence of citizens in the work of associations' and are 'in some ways a sign that these French donors believe that "another world is possible" and that they trust those working for associations to devote themselves to its construction.' A second, closely related benefit is that these monies bring 'autonomy in terms of policy stances and action which is irreplaceable' (*Commissariat Général*, 2002: 125), something which NGDOs, such as the CCFD, with high levels of such donations, are keen to underline (Interview, 2003).[45] Needless to say, this independence gives some NGDOs the freedom to make their own policy choices and to engage in value-driven advocacy campaigns, which may be both critical of, and embarrassing for, the French authorities. The lobbying activities of French NGDOs within the CRID, *Plateforme Dette et Développement* and *Plateforme Contrôlez les Armes* are a case in point.[46]

A third major advantage of donations from the public is that they are free from any explicit conditions. Thus, while the public is extremely censorious wherever there is a whiff of scandal and can be quite demanding in terms of value for money, it remains nonetheless a disparate group of actors who are essentially uninformed about what NGDOs are doing in France (*ici*) and, above all, in the field (*là-bas*). It is simply not a cohesive unit with a single voice or set of quality demands. Rather, it is an ensemble of 30 million potential donors (Blum, 2007: 11), who do not have the time, energy or, in most cases, the interest to monitor NGDO operations. A final strength of these contributions is that they are – with the notable exception of legacies, which tend to favour domestic medical 'charities' – available in large quantities. Thus, overall donations from the donor public have held up well over recent years, consistently making up between 60 and 70 per cent of total private resources (CCD, 2008: 12).[47] These donations have even shown an ability to grow significantly at times of highly mediated crises, such as the December 2004 tsunami. This natural catastrophe brought with it a 35 per cent increase in private funding in 2005; not to mention a significant (58 per cent) rise in the number of donors, which grew from €3.6 million in 2004 to €5.8 million in 2005 (CCD, 2008: 12).[48] Significantly too, opinion polls taken by the CCFD, the *Fondation de France* and *the Institut Français d'Opinion Publique* (IFOP), consistently suggest that the French public still has confidence in NGOs, as well as a continuing readiness to fund them at much higher levels than other parts of the French non-profit sector.[49]

The militant base, the other component of the critical resource, also offers a number of major advantages to French NGDOs. The first is that this grouping of actors – which includes fee-paying members, activists based in France, volunteers working overseas and some expatriates on local contracts – provides its services either free of charge or at well below market rates. In so doing, it allows French NGDOs to claim a comparative advantage over government contractors in terms of cost effectiveness.

A second strength of this militant base is that it represents a major source of dynamism, autonomy and legitimacy, thereby helping French NGDOs to remain true to their original mission. The presence of a large numbers of volunteers at home and overseas does, moreover enable these developmental NGOs to keep in touch with the beneficiaries of their actions, notably the rural and urban populations of developing countries. Significantly too, this activist core often supplies the bulk of the staff hours involved in the running of French NGDOs. These grassroots supporters are the heart and soul of these organisations. They are, in many respects, an 'internal' resource rather than an externally sourced supply of voluntary energies. They are, in other words, an integral part, perhaps even the *sine qua non*, of most NGDOs. This fact has not gone unnoticed by organisations, such as the CCFD, which has clearly asserted its desire 'to maintain [its] militant side' and stressed that 'this is a question of values' (Interview, 2003). The same point has been made more forcefully by Pechs and Padis (2004: 71), who have argued that NGOs 'live to a large extent for civic forms of engagement... they exist only because they embody values and beliefs deemed worthy of defending. That is why they absolutely have to remain in tune with the aspirations of their supporters'.

The last obvious benefit of these voluntary resources is that they appear, much like public donations, to be available in large quantities. This is illustrated by the fact that French NGOs have traditionally had the highest proportion of voluntary staff in Europe and that so many returning French volunteers remain engaged in some kind of international solidarity work for the rest of their lives (Ponsignon, 2002). In this context, Brown and Korten (1991: 54) have noted how 'voluntary energies... exist in potentially inexhaustible quantities' and how they represent the 'lifeblood' of movements which 'do not have access to much financial capital or political power'. The same authors have argued that these 'energies may be subject to self-reinforcing escalation'. In effect, the presence of militants within an organisation is said to lead to the adoption of more radical postures, which in turn facilitates the recruitment of further waves of young volunteers disillusioned by the failure of conventional approaches to the challenges of the developing world.

It follows from the above that this critical resource has offered French NGDOs benefits they cannot ignore and which they cannot do without. It has also presented them with a dilemma, which is summed up by Pfeffer and Salncik (1978: 27) as follows:

> Faced with conflicting demands, the organization must decide which groups to attend to and which to ignore. When the criteria are compatible, the organization would find that satisfying one group would

also increase the satisfaction of others. The existence of incompatible demands raises the possibility that the organization may not be able to maintain the necessary coalition of support. Favoring one group offends another.

Confronted with this, at times, stark choice, French NGDOs have consistently felt the need to respect the wishes of their militant base and donor public and to give these priority over the exigencies of actors which are of secondary importance in resource terms, notably the French state. They have, in other words, oriented their strategies more with their critical resource than with the state in mind. That this is the case has been amply demonstrated by our findings in previous chapters. It is particularly evident in the way that French NGDOs have steered clear of pressures from the state for 'bureaucratic' forms of professionalisation, which conflict with demands from the donor public for more flexible and innovative responses to the challenges of developing countries (see Chapter 6).[50] It is also clear from the way that these NGDOs have espoused a more radical economic and political agenda than anything which the French authorities could possibly countenance (see Chapter 7). In so doing, they have sought both to tap into and to address the French public's particularly deep-seated reservations vis-à-vis globalisation.[51]

Conclusion

This chapter began by asking whether French NGDOs, in refusing to move squarely into line with the putative trends outlined in our introduction, have been acting out of line with RD theory. It has presented some limited evidence to suggest that NGDOs have allowed historico-cultural, ideological and institutional constraints to get in the way of strategic decision-making and of an 'optimal' reading of their resource environment. On balance, however, it has argued that French developmental NGOs have overcome most strategic constraints, actively pursued resource stabilisation strategies and engaged in a broadly accurate reading of their resource environment. In line with the logic of RD, they have avoided relying too heavily on, or linking themselves too closely to, a French state, which has been mired in controversy over its role in various African countries and which has chronically underfunded the NGO sector. Conversely, they have consistently focused their energies on their core supporters and given priority to their demands over the exigencies of the French authorities. French NGDOs have, in effect, been happy to take on the role of the 'piper'; but it has been their critical resource, and not the French state, which has been calling the tune.

Yet, while French NGDOs do appear to be behaving in ways that are consistent with the RD perspective, it is less clear that the actor, which controls the legal and fiscal climate in which they operate, namely the French central state, has been doing likewise. There, is of course, insufficient space here to explore whether the French authorities have been adhering to the tenets of RD theory. This is, in many ways, a separate question and one which cannot adequately be covered by our RD model in Chapter 3. Indeed, as Mowjee (2001: 210) has observed, 'resource dependence theory [only] focuses on the dependent organisation and its strategies to reduce dependence rather than on both sides of the relationship.' RD can, as such, shed light on the behaviour of French NGDOs, but is less well adapted to explaining the actions of the French government.

With these provisos, it should, nonetheless, be possible to make some tentative observations about the behaviour of the French authorities vis-à-vis NGDOs. The state's recent concessions to the non-profit sector are not difficult to explain from a resource dependence perspective and would appear to be a consequence of pressures from key players within its own resource environment. These pressures have come from the French electorate or taxpaying public, which has displayed more confidence in the moral authority of NGOs than it has in the French state, particularly since revelations regarding the latter's implication in events surrounding the Rwandan genocide.[52] They have also emanated from France's normally cautious quality press, which has recently become much more critical of the country's questionable practices in former African colonies.[53] They have, lastly, arisen from French NGDO federations, such as *Coordination SUD*, which have stepped up their pressure for higher levels of aid to be channelled through French civil society actors.[54]

Other pressures on the French government have emanated from international organisations, such as the EU, which has been proactive in promoting a common European development, foreign and security policy, whilst also pushing for a greater emphasis on human rights and civil society capacity-building in official overseas aid programmes.[55] Another set of demands has come from within the wider French political establishment. These have included initiatives by reformist prime ministers, such as Edouard Balladur, Alain Juppé and, above all, Lionel Jospin, who oversaw major aid reforms in the late 1990s. They have also involved pressures from the Ministry of Finance, which has been the driving force behind the LOLF, that is, the ongoing internal audit process, which requires the French state to find ways of operating more effectively and cheaply across the public sector. Equally, they have taken the form of recommendations by parliamentary *rapporteurs* (Blum, 2005 and 2007; Barrau, 2001; Penne *et al.*, 2002), who have called on the French authorities to make better use of NGDOs as partners, service providers and vectors for French influence.

Yet, despite the scale of these pressures, the French authorities have still managed to place clear limits on their support to NGDOs. Seen through the prism of RD theory, the state could, perhaps, be accused of misreading its environment and stubbornly refusing to appreciate the comparative advantages of French NGOs. It is certainly the case that the French authorities have faced constraints on their strategic decision-making. The first set of limitations has been historico-cultural and ideological and has revolved around the long-standing reservations of a Republic with regard to unelected intermediaries, such as NGDOs. These doubts have been voiced at the highest levels of the political establishment, not least by former French Foreign Minister Hubert Védrine, who claimed in *Le Monde Diplomatique* (December 2000) and in his book, *Les Cartes de la France à L'Heure de la Mondialisation*, that NGDOs are 'active minorities, self-designated powers', which lack transparency and are in no way democratically representative.

The other main constraints have been institutional and have been a function of France's hydra-headed overseas development administration. The complexity of this bureaucracy has made it easy for conservative elements within the French state to bury innovative suggestions for more effective use to be made of NGDOs (Devin, 1999). It has also enabled some elite officials (*énarques*) within aid-policy-making departments and overseas missions to ensure that the work of their units is not sub-contracted to NGDOs. It has, finally, allowed the aid administration to persist with ineffective working practices and to pursue a funding policy towards NGDOs, which does little to encourage greater professionalisation on the part of these actors (*Cour des Comptes*, 2005).

The above analysis represents a crude RD reading of the behaviour of the French authorities towards NGDOs. Yet this explanation would appear to miss the point, insofar as it is premised on the assumption that the state actually wishes to secure the products, services and comparative advantages which French NGDOs have to offer. This may well not be the case. Indeed the French government may not be primordially interested in these services, however efficiently, cheaply or professionally NGDOs may be able to provide them.[56] Instead, the state, for all its rhetoric on poverty reduction and democracy-building, may still be much more fundamentally concerned with the so-called 'national interest' and with the promotion of France's political influence, trading interests and cultural *rayonnement*. These are clearly not goals which interest French NGDOs or which open the door to closer NGDO-state collaboration. They are, however, objectives, which the French state is keen to pursue through its own extensive aid apparatus, through French local authorities and through private companies, all of which have proven more enthusiastic than French NGDOs when it comes to 'flying the flag' for France.

9
Working Together in the Field:
A Case Study from Cameroon

The previous chapter argued that French NGDOs have, in resisting too close a relationship with the French state, been 'enacting' their resource environment and acting broadly in line with RD theory. This finding was based upon a desktop survey of overarching trends in the policy discourse, procedures and priorities of French NGDOs. It was also premised upon the assumption that it was not the French authorities but a more militant donor public and activist base, which was the critical resource of these NGOs. While this assumption holds true in most cases, it is not always correct, as the French state can be the critical source of funding in relation to specific NGDO programmes. In such circumstances, have French non-governmental actors been willing to collaborate more fully with the state or have they continued to maintain a 'respectable' distance? This question will be central to this chapter, which will begin by setting out the criteria employed in choosing our case study, namely the *programme concerté pluri-acteurs* (henceforth the PCPA) in Cameroon. It will then briefly outline the origins and evolution of this French NGDO–state civil society building programme. It will show how the PCPA has involved a particularly supportive approach by the French authorities and will assess whether French NGDOs have responded positively to these overtures. Finally it will seek to explain French NGDO involvement in the PCPA in terms of RD theory.

Choosing a case study

So, why study the PCPA? There are a number of reasons for this choice of case study. The first is that it is one of the more ambitious programmes initiated under the 'new contractual arrangements'. It is, as such, a scheme in which the French state represents the critical resource and where, from a resource-dependence perspective, French NGDOs have substantial incentives to collaborate closely with the French authorities.

The second is that the PCPA offers insights into the workings and activities of a broad spectrum of old and new French NGDO actors. These include, for example, faith-based *développementalistes*, such as the CCFD and the *Secours Catholique-Caritas France*; secular 'briefcase' NGDOs, such as AIDES; private volunteer organisations, such as the *Service Protestant de Mission* or DEFAP; the state-financed volunteer agency, the *Association Française des Volontaires du Progrès*; and other groups with links to the *altermondialiste* movement, notably the French communist-leaning trade union, the *Confédération Générale du Travail* or CGT. As discussed below, most of these actors work through local partners. Others act as service delivery agents (the AFVP) or as consultants (the GRET and the CIEDEL are two technical NGOs which have participated in the planning and pre-evaluation of this programme).

The third reason is that the programme has the potential to serve as a model for a future partnership between the French state and NGDOs. From the point of view of the French authorities, the PCPA offers the chance to undertake large-scale development work at low cost and without having to micro-manage every detail. From the perspective of French NGDOs, it provides an opportunity to conceptualise and to help implement a programme in one of their own priority areas and with only limited risk of interference or, indeed, co-optation by the state.[1]

A number of methodological concerns are raised by this choice of case study. The first is that a solitary example of fieldwork is not enough to draw any firm conclusions about the recent evolution of the French NGDO sub-sector or, indeed, to test the validity of our theoretical framework. There is, of course, some truth in this observation. However, the fact is that an in-depth study of this kind can lay down the markers for future research and can provide unique insights into the complexities of NGDO–state collaboration on the ground. The single case study approach is especially valuable in this instance, as it allows the author to draw heavily upon authentic primary documentation; a lengthy field trip to Cameroon; extensive interviews with French NGDO practitioners and officials in Yaoundé and Mbalmayo as well as informal discussions with dozens of local Cameroonian NGOs.

A second possible concern is that the PCPA may simply not be appropriate for the purposes of this analysis. The fact is that this programme did not actually begin its first year of operation until 2006 and has still to undergo any formal process of evaluation. Furthermore, it currently includes actors, such as trade unions, whose agenda is not the same as that of NGDOs; and, in the future, it aspires to include an even wider array of civil society organisations, with yet more diverse priorities.[2] Significantly too, it is not a classic example of a project or programme in the field, given that it has, until recently, been largely piloted from Paris by officials based in the French Foreign Ministry and by NGDO staff located in the CCFD head office. Ultimately, however, these concerns over the appropriateness of the PCPA are misplaced. Thus, whilst the PCPA is new, it has been in the process of gestation since 2002 and it has built upon a whole series of earlier schemes developed under the 'new contractual arrangements', not least the *programmes prioritaires* in Palestine and Vietnam, the *Programme Concerté Maroc* (PCM), as well as the *Dotations au Partenariat* (DAP) in Tunisia, Cameroon and Madagascar.[3] Furthermore, even if this programme does include a diverse range of civil society actors, there is no escaping the fact that it is essentially a NGDO affair, coordinated by the CCFD, on the French side, and by its partner, the BASC, in Cameroon. Finally, while the PCPA was initially piloted largely from Paris, it has never been an experiment carried out via remote control.

A third, closely related objection is that this programme is atypical of French NGDO fieldwork as a whole. Thus, as will be seen later, the scheme clearly reflects new, indeed 'revolutionary' thinking in both NGDO and state circles (Cumming, 2007). For a start, it is the first ever PCPA and operates on an unusually large scale. It also involves particularly high levels of state co-funding, an exceptionally large number of French civil society actors and almost unprecedented levels of planning. Finally, it is underpinned by objectives which are more politically interventionist than those normally espoused by French NGDOs (Ibid). Yet, while the PCPA is certainly an 'innovative programme' (Interview with CCFD, 2005), it should not be seen as an unrepresentative or unique experiment. For a start, it is an example of fieldwork in Africa, which is the continent that has served as the main 'laboratory' for donor prescriptions for overseas development and that has taken up the greatest amount of French NGDO time, money and energy. The PCPA is, moreover, one of many programmes to have been undertaken under the 'new contractual arrangements'. Over a dozen of these macro-level schemes have been completed and subjected to evaluation by the NGDO evaluation unit, the F3E.[4] In theory at least, any one of these programmes could have formed the basis of a case study for this book. However, the PCPA has been selected, as it draws upon the author's own independent monitoring of NGDO–state programme activities in the field rather than relying upon the partial and, for the most part, uncritical syntheses of evaluation reports posted on the F3E website.

Origins and evolution of the PCPA

So what precisely is the PCPA and how did it come about? It is a multi-actor consultative programme, which involves the French state, French civil society and Cameroonian civil society.[5] It aims to 'strengthen the ability of Cameroonian civil society to negotiate, participate in and exert influence over the definition and implementation of public policy, particularly in the process of debt reduction and development, as well as in the process of democratising the social, economic and political life of the country'.[6]

The objectives of the PCPA reflect its origins in the international Jubilee 2000 campaign, which called on industrialised states to cancel Third World debt. In France, this campaign was fought by *Plateforme Dette et*

Développement, an unprecedented coalition of over 20 French NGOs and trade unions. In Cameroon, it was waged by a *Plateforme d'Information et d'Action sur la Dette*, which included members from local NGOs, churches and trade unions. These *plateformes* or thematic federations did not simply disband after securing substantial pledges of debt reduction, under the Highly Indebted Poor Countries Initiative or HIPC (the donor community scheme for multilateral debt reduction)[7] and the *Contrat de Désendettement et de Développement* or C2D (France's own programme for bilateral debt cancellation).[8] Instead, they sought to ensure that the debt-conversion monies released by these initiatives were used by the Cameroonian government in line with the country's PRSP, that is, the public expenditure plan drawn up by the Cameroonian state, in consultation with civil society and at the behest of the World Bank.

These same *plateformes* soon realised, however, that Cameroonian civil society actors, including those present on the HIPC steering committee on debt cancellation, were simply being ignored by the autocratic regime of Cameroonian President Paul Biya.[9] They attributed this partly to the intransigence of the highly centralised Cameroonian state and partly to their own lack of political and institutional capacity. With this in mind, these civil society coalitions communicated to the French Foreign Ministry, in June 2002, their interest in a development programme that would bolster the capacity of Cameroonian civil society.

The French Foreign Ministry, or more specifically the *Mission de Coopération Non-Gouvernementale* (MCNG), the unit in charge of co-financing development programmes, was well prepared to respond to this request, as it was already involved in talks with actors from the French *Plateforme Dette* over ways of ensuring the effectiveness of its own bilateral debt initiative, the C2D. In December 2002, therefore, the Foreign Ministry and French NGDOs formed a joint programme committee, which invited the CCFD, the DEFAP and the French trade union, the CGT, to undertake a mission to Cameroon in January 2003. Drawing upon the findings of that mission, this joint committee then constructed the basic framework for a multi-actor scheme. This programme outline was subsequently approved by the relevant committee of the *Commission Coopération Développement* and informed the call for tenders, which the Foreign Ministry issued in March 2003. It also formed the basis of the actual bid for funding, which was submitted by members of *Plateforme Dette*.

As soon as that application had been accepted in May 2003, it became imperative to decide who exactly should be involved in the PCPA and in what capacity. On the French side, a key role would be assigned to the Foreign Ministry and to those civil society actors who had helped draft the bid: the AFVP, the CGT, the DEFAP, the SC-CF and, above all, the CCFD, which was designated as the overall coordinator of this programme. On the Cameroonian side, the major players would be those organisations which had helped to prepare and disseminate information about the bid. These included religious organisations such as *BASC-Caritas* and the *Fédération des Églises et Missions Évangéliques du Cameroun* or FEMEC (the local partners of the CCFD/ SC-CF and DEFAP, respectively), the *Confédération du Secteur Public* (a trade union movement with links to the CGT), APDHAC (a human rights organisation) and the *Fédération des Organisations de la Société Civile Camerounaise* or FOSCAM (a collective body of Cameroonian NGOs). All of the above organisations came together, along with a handful of co-opted members, to form the original steering committee of the PCPA.[10]

With the key actors in place, it was possible to hone in on, and finesse, the priorities of the programme. While these had already been sketched out in the application for funding to the MCNG, the goals in question had neither been discussed nor 'owned' by large sections of Cameroonian civil society. To allow this to happen, an extensive process of consultation was launched across the country, with four workshops taking place in March and April 2003 and a 'general assembly' being convened in Mbalmayo in March–April 2004. A separate consultation exercise was also conducted by a designated French specialist and two Cameroonian experts. It sought to identify the needs of Cameroonian civil society and to set out those objectives, structures and activities around which some kind of consensus could be formed. This latter exercise gave rise to a feasibility report in June–July 2004. The finalisation of this study did not, however, trigger the start of the PCPA itself, which was delayed by a number of factors. These included the lengthy negotiations involved in constructing such a complex programme and the cyclical nature of French government funding (for budgetary reasons the French state could not finance the PCPA proper before the end of 2005) (CCFD, 2006: 8). They also revolved around the fact that Cameroon itself had yet to give the starting signal for the PCPA, having failed to reach 'completion point', that is, the moment at which it could fully access the huge sums of debt relief available under the HIPC and C2D programmes.[11]

Nevertheless, in October 2004, an interim pilot scheme was set up to maintain momentum and to avoid giving the impression that Cameroonian civil society was being abandoned before the PCPA had even got off the ground. This pilot phase allowed time to recruit staff in France and Cameroon and to draw up key documentation: the charter fixing the values and aims of the programme, an operational manual laying down the role of all those involved and their relationship with other actors, together with a guide setting out the procedures for the management of budgets. This stage also enabled participants to finalise the core priorities of the PCPA, namely citizens' control over government policy-making (especially spending linked to debt cancellation funds), reducing corruption, tackling AIDS and defending human rights. In addition, it allowed for some preliminary activities to be undertaken, not least a detailed assessment of the strengths and weaknesses of recent Cameroonian advocacy work (e.g. the campaign by ACAT Littoral for penal reform and lobbying by REDS against the testing of the drug Tenofovir on prostitutes in Douala) (CCFD, 2006: 19 and 28). Finally, the pilot phase enabled programme organisers to reach a consensus upon how the PCPA would be structured and how it would work in practice.

As can be seen from the organigramme in Figure 9.1, it was agreed that Franco–Cameroonian thematic groups should be established and that they should put forward a number of proposals. Equally, it was decided that these recommendations would then be discussed in a wider PCPA forum and submitted for the approval of the Joint Strategic Steering Committee or JSSC (made up of 11 Cameroonian and 4 French civil society organisations: the CCFD, SC-CF, AFVP and the CGT).[12] Furthermore, it was resolved that the decisions of this JSSC would be operationalised by a nine-strong Cameroonian steering group and that this latter grouping would be backed up by a technical team of six paid staff (CCFD, 2007b: 21) and by a range of indigenous watchdog bodies (see Figure 9.1).[13]

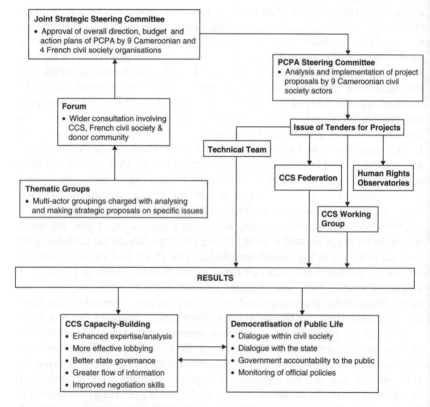

Figure 9.1 Organigramme of the key structures involved in the PCPA (as from 2006)

Source: Adapted from an unpublished report by the CCFD (2006: 26). Note that CCS stands for Cameroonian Civil Society.

This pilot phase ended in December 2005 with a strongly attended forum in Mbalmayo. This gathering signalled the start of the PCPA proper, a four-year programme for which a total of €2.5 million was set aside. It also laid out the broad priorities and activities of the scheme for 2006. These actions included the financing of a study on reform of the new penal code, as well as the creation of a national human rights observatory to collect and disseminate information, to build a database, and to draw up a 'white paper' on human rights. They also involved the hosting of a national anti-corruption day on 9 December, the organisation of nationwide advocacy campaigns to improve access to healthcare for AIDS victims (CCFD, 2006: 45), and the funding of a unit with recognised expertise on the theme of debt and poverty reduction.

The first year ended in February 2007 with a major forum in Bamenda. This latter gathering also launched the second year of the programme. This most recent phase has seen a renewed emphasis on training in the art of lobbying at the national level, with particular efforts being made to strengthen the work of the expert cell on debt and to enhance its capacity to track funds released under the C2D. The organisers of the PCPA have, at the same time, created two new regional observatories on human rights in Cameroon, set up a national network to fight corruption and provided support to a coalition of Cameroonian actors pushing for radical changes to the way that AIDS victims are treated. They have, in addition, reached agreement on the mechanisms by which the PCPA should be monitored and evaluated. In particular, they have decided that evaluation work should be overseen by a suitably qualified Cameroonian technical consultancy and by the GEMDEV, a highly regarded French grouping of development economists.[14]

Overtures by the French state

As can be inferred from the above summary, the French state, although not actually the inspiration behind the PCPA in Cameroon, has played a highly supportive role. It has done so for a number of reasons. First, the programme fits comfortably with France's recently adopted policy priorities on civil society building and poverty eradication (see Chapter 7). Second, it is a low-cost affair run essentially by Cameroonian and French civil society actors. This is a key consideration at a time when the French state is faced with spending restrictions imposed by the European Stability Pact and by its own auditors via the LOLF. Third, the PCPA appears to offer a tangible return on taxpayers' money by helping to ensure that the colossal 'conversion funds' freed up by the French government's bilateral 'Debt Reduction-Development Contract' (the C2D) are actually spent on alleviating Cameroonian poverty. Fourth, it should allow the French state to improve its image in the eyes of African peoples in general and Cameroonian civil society in particular. The

PCPA is, in fact, a way of demonstrating that France can rise above its earlier policy of dealing exclusively with African elites and propping up authoritarian leaders, such as President Biya.

Finally, the PCPA is a way of asserting France's leading nation status as a donor in Cameroon, by laying down a larger scale and more ambitious civil society building programme than any of the schemes currently being undertaken by other donors. The latter include programmes devised by the World Bank, the DFID (United Kingdom), the Centre for Rural Education and Development Action (Canada), the Friedrich Ebert Foundation (Germany) and the Dutch and German overseas development bodies, the SNV and the *Gesellschaft für Technische Zusammenarbeit* (GTZ).[15] Another, much larger European Commission civil society project has been under discussion since 2001 but this scheme has been beset by problems and has still to get off the ground. Needless to say, all of these competing programmes are designed to enhance the advocacy capacity of Cameroonian civil society organisations and some of them have even been informed by 'rival', liberal, 'Anglo-Saxon' thinking, which considers civil society as a substitute for the state, rather than simply as a guarantor of a more effective and accountable Cameroonian government.[16]

Against this backdrop, it is hardly surprising that the French government has given such strong backing to French NGDOs involved in the PCPA. It is also not astonishing that the state has tried to use these high levels of support to push NGDOs in the direction of the broad trends outlined in our introductory chapter. In this latter context, the French authorities have, for example, sought to develop a closer rapport with French NGDOs by offering them very favourable terms: 75 per cent of the cost of this programme is covered rather than adhering to the co-funding norm of 50 per cent from the state and 50 per cent from NGOs. The state has, moreover, promised a substantial amount of assistance (around €2 million); made this available on a pluri-annual basis; and taken exceptional measures to put together a package of stop-gap funding for the pilot phase of the PCPA. Significantly too, the French Foreign Ministry has not confined itself to its traditional role of mere 'cash dispenser' but has instead offered logistical support and technical advice, above all through the medium of a designated MCNG official, who took part in all the main preparatory discussions, from the time of the joint programme committee, set up in December 2002, through to the steering group charged with overseeing the pilot phase (CCFD, 2006: 10).[17] Finally, the Foreign Ministry, has labelled this programme 'a priority' and has been quick to establish forums in which French officials and NGDO representatives can collaborate more effectively (Interview with DEFAP, 2003).

At the same time, the French administration has urged the French NGDOs involved in the PCPA to undertake some 'bureaucratic' forms of professionalisation. To this end, it has set out a number of quality-related requirements in the original competitive tender for the programme. It has, more specifically, stipulated that the NGDO coordinator should commission a feasibility report by external consultants, that it should create adequate and appropriate structures for the running of this programme and that it should show strong commitment to strategic management techniques, such as logical framework analysis, independent evaluations and formal lesson-learning.

Finally, the state has also pressed the French *développementalistes* and volunteer organisations participating in the PCPA to take on more explicitly the role of service provider. The Foreign Ministry, in particular, has underlined the 'agency' status of these NGDOs by signing a detailed contract with the programme coordinator on the French civil society side, namely the CCFD. It has further encouraged the idea that these French developmental NGOs are acting as service deliverers by allowing some of them to make no contribution to the 25 per cent NGDO stake in this co-funded programme. The Foreign Ministry has, finally, added to the impression that NGDOs are, at best, subordinate partners by laying down the ground-rules for presenting the PCPA to the Cameroonian authorities. It has, in particular, advised French NGDOs not to over-politicise the PCPA or to encourage the view that it is aimed at creating a rival, 'democratic' force alongside the Cameroonian state.[18]

Relatedly, the French state has hoped to ensure that French NGDOs will, in the context of the PCPA, serve as a vector for the spread of France's influence, culture and ideas. It has made it easier for NGDOs to take on such a role by altering its own policy priorities in ways which make them more palatable to French and Cameroonian civil society actors. In this latter context, the French authorities have moved away from their earlier, some would say purely rhetorical, demands for neo-liberal reforms and begun to advocate poverty-reduction measures and civil society building programmes as the answers to the challenges facing Cameroon. The French administration has, moreover, even launched a number of initiatives aimed at embedding participatory forms of democracy and a strong civil society.[19] To illustrate, it created, in 1994, the *Fonds Social de Développement* (FSD), which has enabled civil society actors to initiate poverty-reduction projects in Cameroon and many other African countries. Then, in 1995, the French aid mission, the SCAC, introduced the DAP, which provided funding for French NGDOs wishing to strengthen the institutional backbone of Cameroonian civil society.[20] More recently, in 2003, the SCAC oversaw, jointly with other bilateral donors, a feasibility study for a multi-donor programme known as the *Facilité d'Actions Collectives pour les Initiatives Locales de Solidarité* (FACILS). This scheme was funded under the auspices of the HIPC initiative and sought to ensure that Cameroonian civil society actors were fully involved in local development and poverty-targeted projects.[21]

Embracing the state's advances or keeping a safe distance?

Unsurprisingly perhaps, French NGDOs have embraced the above overtures and shown themselves keen to be involved in a programme, which they, in many ways, initiated. Yet, even in the case of the PCPA where the French state has represented the 'critical resource', NGDOs have remained wary of going too far down the road of financial dependence, bureaucratic professionalisation or service delivery work. Each of these dimensions of the French NGDO approach will be discussed below.

A new partnership or just a brief flirtation?

French developmental NGOs have generally welcomed the introduction of the PCPA as evidence that the French government may, one day, be prepared to move towards the kind of balanced and properly funded partnership which they have long requested. A handful of NGDOs have gone further and agreed to invest their own time and money in the PCPA. In so doing, they have shown their readiness to take advantage of the state's favourable co-funding terms and the offers of technical support from the MCNG. In addition, they have demonstrated their willingness to liaise with the French authorities in all the consultative forums and decision-making committees associated with the PCPA.

At the same time, however, the French NGDOs engaged in the PCPA have realised that – even though the French government has made exceptional efforts by its own standards – the level of official support involved has simply not been high enough to lay the basis for a solid NGDO–state partnership. They have, in other words, recognised that the volume of state assistance for the PCPA is actually quite small (around M€2) and a veritable drop in the ocean compared to the amount of debt relief accorded by France to Cameroon (M€285 in 2007) under the HIPC and C2D (Carrez, 2006). Equally, French NGDOs have been all too aware of the danger that, due to the vagaries of state funding cycles, official assistance could just dry up, as nearly happened in the months following the completion of the feasibility report. They have, at the same time, been mindful of risks associated with non-monetary forms of government support. Thus, while French NGDOs have welcomed the involvement of French officials in preparatory forums, they have been anxious to ensure that the latter do not gain undue influence over a programme that is essentially the responsibility of Cameroonian civil society. In this latter context, they managed to block, in 2004, a state-led proposal which would have allowed the QUANGO-like volunteer agency, the AFVP, to act as a service agent in the delivery of a civil society building programme, which is supposed to be about the *autonomisation* of Cameroonian non-state actors.

Embracing professionalisation or just going through the motions?

French NGDOs involved in the PCPA have also been quite prepared to professionalise their working practices along the lines recommended by the state. On the financial accountability front, for example, they have taken a number of measures to gain the confidence of their Foreign Ministry backers. They have, for example, recruited the services of a chartered accountant to audit the PCPA accounts. The CCFD, specifically, has offered financial expertise to the BASC to help in the handling of substantial PCPA-related monies delegated to this small Cameroonian partner organisation. It has, in addition, provided the services of a suitably qualified CCFD volunteer and of two French interns to help the BASC produce key documentation, namely manuals on financial procedures, a study on advocacy techniques, and a directory of Cameroonian NGOs (CCFD, 2006: 31).

At the same time, the French NGDOs involved in the PCPA have taken account of the state's requirement that planning, evaluation and learning be built into the programme. In line with the government's wishes, they have appointed two Cameroonian consultants and one French specialist to help plan the PCPA and to draft a feasibility report. They have also agreed to use forward-planning tools, such as the logical framework, and to work towards the various target indicators designed by the French external consultant. Indeed, one French NGDO representative (Interview, 2004) even commented that the 'logframe' idea has proven to be a 'good way of working with people without directing them too much, but obliging them all the same to respect a certain logic...'. As regards evaluation, here, too, French NGDOs have been broadly receptive to the state's demands. They have, for example, carried out their own monitoring missions to assess project work and they have also begun putting in place formal mechanisms for evaluation. In this latter context, French NGDOs have established contact with the French research centre, the GEMDEV, and have helped set in motion the search for a suitable Cameroonian evaluator.

Finally, French NGDOs have been keen to draw and disseminate lessons throughout the PCPA process. Some have even viewed the PCPA itself as a product of learning, emerging as it did from constructive criticism by the consultancy-based French NGDO, the CIEDEL, of earlier *programmes prioritaires* in Vietnam and Palestine.[22] For some participants, it has been a case of 'learning-by-doing' and adapting policies and structures as they go along. This is amply illustrated by the way in which the charter on the workings of the annual PCPA forum was regularly modified to take account of the difficulties encountered during the pilot phase.[23] For other NGDOs, the emphasis has been on more formal, research-based learning. In pursuit of this latter goal, a synthesis report was prepared at the end of the second year of the PCPA and a methodological reference work should be compiled by the end of the third year. Also in this formal learning context, GEMDEV and a Cameroonian consultancy will each offer methodological support to one French and one Cameroonian PhD student undertaking research into the PCPA.[24] In parallel, a wider, cross-cutting process of lesson-learning from this type of programme will be carried out through the F3E, with the support of the CIEDEL.[25] The plan is that the lessons learned from the PCPA will eventually be disseminated by participants by way of a database, a formal report and an edited book.

Despite moving some considerable way towards the type of professionalisation advocated by the French administration, French NGDOs have been reluctant to 'standardise' their working practices (Wallace *et al.*, 1997). This can be inferred from the fact that they have fallen so far behind schedule on the formal evaluation and learning front. According to a CCFD report (2006: 38–9), 'The external evaluation, which had initially been planned for the pilot phase, was postponed to the end of the year, following a decision by the JSSC, in consultation with the Foreign Ministry. No formal evaluation of the pilot phase has, as such, been undertaken'. One knock-on effect of this has been that PCPA organisers have been able to make self-gratulatory statements under the guise of evaluation, with the CCFD (2006: 42) noting simply that 'The objectives of the pilot phase have been achieved'. A second consequence has been to give PCPA participants more scope to push forward their own conception of the evaluation process, which differs from the technocratic, top-down, accountable procedures advocated by the state, and involves more participatory, bottom-up, action-led forms of learning from experience. Needless to say, such an approach, which takes into account social processes and affective factors, can come to radically different conclusions, adjudging projects to have worked even where empirically measurable objectives have not been met.

There are two main reasons for French NGDO reservations regarding state-led forms of professionalisation. The first involves their frustration regarding the cumbersome nature of bureaucratic state procedures and planning cycles. Many French NGDOs participating in the PCPA have felt a deep-seated desire to return to traditional militant modes of action and get on with the business of doing rather than consulting, planning or evaluating. They have also found it difficult to deal with shortfalls in government aid and with French state demands for an immediate response as soon as official monies do eventually arrive. A recent CCFD report (2006: 29) has highlighted these concerns, pointing to 'the disparity between militant volunteer work and the technocracy needed in the set up and implementation of an important programme'. It has suggested that these bureaucratic procedures have 'discouraged certain organisations' – a reference no doubt to the DEFAP, which was a founder member, but which no longer takes part in any of the PCPA decision-making mechanisms.

The second reason relates to concerns over the capacity of Cameroonian civil society, as the actor which is ultimately responsible for the success of the PCPA, to carry out the programme. French NGDO misgivings are hardly surprising given that the component parts of Cameroonian civil society actually had to be identified at the start of the programme and given that most of these organisations are of recent origin, small, chronically underfunded, operational only at a local level, and devoid of any significant experience of political lobbying.[26] French NGDOs worries are also under-standable given that the Cameroonian non-state actors are, despite their obvious lack of any overarching institutional structures, being called upon to play a key role in coordinating a complex and highly 'professional' pro-gramme, which involves a multitude of actors with different personalities, priorities and working methods. As one delegate told the author at the 2004 Mbalmayo meeting, Cameroonian civil society is 'being asked to run before it can walk'.

Operating 'for' or 'on' the state?

Finally, French NGDOs have, in the context of the PCPA, shown themselves willing to take on elements of the role of service provider on behalf of the French state. They have moved away from their earlier localised, micro-project approach towards the kind of macro-level national programme delivery that the state prefers. They have also signed up to a contractual arrangement with the state and have failed, in some cases (e.g. the AFVP, AIDES), to make any financial contribution to the cost of the PCPA, thereby placing themselves squarely in the category of 'service agents'. Equally, they have gone along with a steer from the French authorities and ensured that their discourse regarding the policy objectives of the PCPA is not inflam-matory and that their documentation is 'written in softer tones' (Interview with French NGDO, 2004).

The French NGDOs taking part in this programme have also served, to some extent, as a vector for France's language, policies and ideas. For a start, they have conducted their operations almost entirely in French and failed to translate much of their documentation into English. In so doing, they have, quite unintentionally, helped to spread the use of the French language (one of France's core foreign policy objectives) and reinforced the marginalisa-tion of Cameroon's Anglophone minority (CCFD, 2006: 42). Second, they have built upon their own existing partnerships in Cameroon to develop a rapport with literally hundreds of Cameroonian civil society actors.[27] In so doing, they have again, quite unwittingly, allowed the French authorities an opportunity to establish direct contact with actors other than pro-gov-ernment elites and to repair the damage that has been done to its image by years of collusion with authoritarian African regimes. Third, French NGDOs have helped to disseminate ideas about civil society, democracy and citizen-ship, which are essentially Western and, in some cases, French in origin. They have, in the process, set aside their rigorous attachment to *autono-misation* (the view that African peoples should choose their own develop-ment models) and accepted the value of some forms of 'interference' in the internal affairs of a sovereign state. Fourth, French NGDOs have pragmat-ically accepted the underlying logic of a programme, which is designed to help Cameroonian civil society ensure that debt conversion funds are wisely spent. In so doing, they have had to overlook two awkward facts: first, that the original debts themselves were generated out of irresponsible lending, and second, that debt conversion funds only come on stream once countries have reached 'completion point', that is, the stage at which they have satisfied the World Bank and IMF of their track record on market reform and sound economic governance.

Ultimately, however, it would be wrong to label the French NGDOs participating in the PCPA as 'service agents'. Thus, most of these organisations have been anxious to preserve a degree of autonomy by contributing to the 25 per cent NGDO stake and by retaining discretion over important processes (e.g. staff recruitment). Furthermore, while French NGDOs have agreed not to over-politicise the programme, this should not be taken to imply that they have simply fallen in line with the French state's conception of the PCPA. In fact, they have actively sought to exert reverse influence on French officials in designated committees, such as COPIL, and in other forums, such as *Plateforme Dette*. At the same time, French NGDOs have remained quietly sceptical about their own government's quite limited conception of the PCPA (as a mechanism essentially for ensuring that French debt relief monies are spent in line with the country's PRSP and the expectations of French taxpayers) (Interview with SCAC, 2004). Privately, they and their Cameroonian partners have continued to harbour more ambitious objectives. They have, in particular, viewed the PCPA as a way of promoting participatory democracy from the bottom up, and ultimately, as a means of creating a dynamic civil society, which is capable of linking in to the wider construction of a 'global civil society'. A leading figure within Cameroonian civil society (Interview, 2004) has stressed that the PCPA is not just about ensuring the poverty orientation of French debt conversion funds but is

> something much larger...much more political...; people feel this sense of purpose which is strong...we are in the process of...anchoring a civil society which knows how to speak out, how to lobby...and that is highly political...it goes way beyond the little bit of money on offer.

The French NGDOs involved would echo this view and challenge any suggestion that they have been acting as a vehicle for the spread of the French culture and language. First, they would point out that they have invited Cameroonian English-speaking provinces to be a full part of the process and that they have even held one of their forums in the Anglophone province of Bamenda (CCFD, 2007b: 6). Second, while they have, indeed, facilitated contact between the French state and Cameroonian civil society, French NGDOs have only done so with a view to empowering the latter vis-à-vis the intransigent Biya regime. They have not, as one representative of Cameroonian civil society intimated to the author (Interview), 'become a vector for the French government...' or enabled the latter to 'use the PCPA to reinforce its domination' and 'exert more influence over Cameroon via French civil society'.[28]

Finally, French NGDOs have been anxious to avoid imposing a Western, liberal or even a French model on Cameroonians. To this end, they have ensured that Cameroonian civil society has had an input at every stage of the PCPA process. They have also stressed that the whole programme is underpinned by a pragmatic form of *autonomisation*, whereby Cameroonians are encouraged to think about a range of approaches and then decide for themselves how they wish to organise their civil societies and shape their future relations with the Cameroonian state. This thinking is broadly consistent with the underlying philosophy of partnership, which is the hallmark of most *développementalistes* and volunteer organisations. So too is the other concept on which French NGDOs have insisted, namely 'appropriation'. Here, Cameroonian civil society does not simply borrow Western concepts such as democracy, human rights and civil society. Instead, it is urged to adapt these ideas to its own local situation, to own them, and to participate in their realisation. In other words, Cameroonian organisations are placed at the heart of the programme, are encouraged to develop their own version of 'civil society' and exhorted to establish a collective dynamic, which will continue beyond the life of the PCPA. An example of appropriation, which emerged from a thematic group that the author attended in April 2004 in Mbalmayo, related to the need to give special attention to the human rights situation of refugees, albinos and AIDS sufferers.

Resource dependence

Overall, French NGDOs have clearly been prepared to get much closer to the French authorities in the case of the PCPA than they have in other circumstances, where state resources have been less critical and less readily available. They have, in effect, been quite ready to 'muck in' and collaborate pragmatically with the French government, even if they have stopped short of serving as mere service agents or vectors on its behalf. How does this approach fit with RD theory? Have French NGDOs been misreading or 'enacting' the resource opportunities available from their environment?

Misreading their environment?

There is, of course, some evidence to suggest that French NGDOs involved in the PCPA have not engaged in an optimal reading of their resource context. Needless to say, these developmental NGOs have been marked by many of the historico-cultural and ideological constraints outlined in Chapter 8. This is particularly true of faith-based organisations, such as the SC-CF, and left-leaning trade unions, such as the CGT, which have faced a long history of neglect from France's secular Republic and which have continued to harbour a good deal of suspicion towards the French government. The same applies, albeit to a lesser extent, to other French non-state actors involved in the PCPA and, before that, in *Plateforme Dette*. Indeed, the whole motivation of these organisations for joining forces in the first instance had been their disillusionment with the failure of the French state and the donor community to engage in a rapid debt cancellation process.

A second set of constraints has been institutional. Action-oriented French NGDOs have, for example, faced problems adapting to bureaucratic state procedures and lengthy funding cycles. They have also displayed traces of bureaucratic inertia, particularly when it comes to harmonising their quite distinct working practices with those of other French non-state actors. This institutional resistance to change is perhaps best illustrated by the reluctance of NGDOs, such as the AFVP and DEFAP, each of which expatriates its own volunteers to Cameroon, to adapt fully to the logic of *autonomisation* espoused by the CCFD and SC-CF.[29]

Faced with the above constraints, NGDOs have not always been able to engage effectively in the various resource stabilisation techniques at their disposal. They have undertaken lobbying work but have thrown all their eggs into one basket and concentrated their advocacy efforts in relation to this programme on one relatively junior actor, the MCNG. While this has borne fruit, it has, nonetheless, been a strategy that neglects more powerful actors, such as the AFD, the Finance Ministry, the wider Foreign Ministry and the *Elysée*, many of which are less than enthusiastic about this programme and could even bring about its undoing.[30]

Similar criticisms might be made of their use of 'control techniques'. French developmental NGOs have clearly found it hard to manipulate information about the PCPA, given that the French state has been so heavily involved at every stage of its conceptualisation. They have also found it difficult to present a united front in their dealings with the French authorities. They have been hampered in this respect by the fact that some NGDOs are more dependent on the state than others: the CCFD and SC-CF have a dependency ratio of not more than 10 per cent, whereas the AFVP relies on the government for around two-thirds of its income and has no private source of revenue whatsoever. Arguably too, they have been held back by inherent ideological differences between the non-state actors involved (e.g. the SC-CF, as an arm of the Catholic Church, and the formerly communist CGT), as well as by latent concerns about the 'hegemonic' role being adopted by the CCFD, as the coordinator of this programme and various other schemes under *la nouvelle contractualisation* (Interviews in Yaoundé, 2004).[31]

Significantly too, French NGDOs have not rigorously adhered to the logic of resource diversification in relation to this programme. Thus, despite the fact that the French authorities are clearly the critical resource in this context, French developmental NGOs have certainly not been falling over themselves to become involved in the PCPA. Indeed, only 5 of over

20 French non-state actors involved in *Plateforme Dette* actually signed up to this programme, with one founding member, DEFAP, later withdrawing from all of its core activities. Only a few others (e.g. *Agir Ici*, CIEDEL, Friends of the Earth, FIDH) have since been attracted to the PCPA and most of these have remained on the margins of a scheme, which seems unlikely ever to live up to its original objective of helping to create a wider partnership between French and Cameroonian civil societies (CCFD, 2006: 31). At the same time, French NGDOs have also refused to admit publicly how difficult it would be to replace the role of the French state in the case of the PCPA. One French delegate commented that the programme would be worth doing, even if it had to be financed entirely out of NGDO resources (Interview, 2004). Such a claim is, however, questionable given the price tag associated with the PCPA compared to, say, the average cost of a NGDO project in Cameroon.[32] Other French developmental NGOs have, similarly, taken the view that alternative funding could easily be secured from the likes of the European Commission and the World Bank. While this is no doubt true, the bottom line is that any change of funder would lead to significant delays, which would break the momentum of the PCPA and result in the programme taking on a quite different complexion.

On balance, however, the evidence is stacked against the above reading of French NGDO behaviour. The reality is that these non-governmental actors have been acting broadly in line with RD theory and enacting their resource environment. They have simply not allowed historico-cultural, ideological or institutional constraints to get in the way of their pragmatic and product-ive collaboration with the French state on the ground in Cameroon. They have set aside their fear of instrumentalisation by the state. Equally, they have shown flexibility on the ideological front by toning down their earlier dogmatic interpretation of *autonomisation* (see Chapter 7), which could have ruled out their involvement in a programme that helps to prescribe and lay down the bases of a future Cameroonian civil society. Furthermore, they have overcome institutional constraints and bureaucratic inertia by taking on board state-led strategic management techniques and creating their own best practice manuals and lesson-learning tools.

French developmental NGOs participating in the PCPA have also, for the most part, not allowed the above constraints to get in the way of their use of resource stabilisation strategies. Thus, whilst NGDOs have, indeed, con-centrated on lobbying the MCNG, they have also increasingly kept other actors, such as the AFD, the SCAC and the French embassy in Cameroon informed of key developments in the programme. French NGDOs have, moreover, engaged in various control techniques. Thus, they have sought to 'manipulate' information wherever they have had any degree of discre-tion. A case in point is the way they have taken advantage of the absence of any formal evaluation process to produce self-congratulatory statements, not only on their performance to date, but also on the extent to which the programme is appreciated by Cameroonian civil society as a true 'example of a dynamic partnership' (CCFD, 2006: 36). French developmental NGOs have also aimed to control the state's perception of them by highlighting their comparative advantages at every stage of the programme. Without sensationalising their strengths, they have, nonetheless, let it be known that they are the ones with the ability to reach the poorest, with an impressive range of expertise on debt issues and, above all, with the civil society contacts on the ground in Cameroon. French NGDOs have, moreover, sought to 'control' or limit the state's demands on them by pulling together at crucial times in the programme, notably at the moment of the original bid, at the end of the feasibility report (when an anxious request had to be submitted for the funding of a pilot phase) and at the close of this latter phase, when roles were allocated to civil society organisations in the final structures of the PCPA programme.

Finally, French NGDOs have also followed a RDVN strategy, which reflects a broadly accurate reading of their wider environment. Contrary to what their message to radical militant supporters might suggest, they have been quite happy to work together pragmatically with the French state in building what is, in some ways at least, a Western-style civil society in Cameroon. They have embraced the generous funding terms offered by the French authorities and they have welcomed the high daily rates available for the time and energy they have invested: AIDES, for example, claimed €300 a day for the three-and-a-half weeks that it allocated to the PCPA during the conceptualisation phase (CCFD, 2007b: 20).[33]

At the same time, however, French NGDOs have rightly recognised the need to avoid becoming over-reliant on French government funding. They have been well aware of the danger that too close an association with the French authorities – for years the single most important external backer of the autocratic Biya regime – could erode their legitimacy in the eyes of French and Cameroonian civil societies. Equally, they have appreciated the risks associated with state funding cycles, which nearly caused the programme to stall after submission of the feasibility report. They have, moreover, been aware of the more serious threat to the survival of the PCPA as a whole, which arises out of more conservative parts of the French political establishment (see below). Furthermore, they have realised that, while government funding has been adequate in relation to the PCPA, the sum involved has remained quite limited in absolute terms, amounting to around €2 million and destined to last only for four years. This is less than a third of the size of the €9 million civil society programme planned by the EU and is hardly enough to enable Cameroonian civil society to become a permanent force in Cameroonian political life.

Significantly too, French NGDOs have recognised that, while the French state is the critical resource in relation to this programme, it is not the critical resource for NGDO operations more generally. They have, as such, quite rightly pressed on with a RDVN strategy designed to avoid over-dependence on the French authorities. In line with this thinking, they have looked to the European Commission as a future donor and possible successor to the French Foreign Ministry once the PCPA reaches the end of its current cycle. Some French NGDOs have gone further and publicly mooted the possibility of taking up an offer from the Commission to stand in 'immediately' as the main funder of the programme.[34] Less contentiously, they have implicated the European Commission and the German development agency, the GTZ, in the co-funding of two important PCPA-related activities: the Ombé II meeting, which brought together a hundred or so Cameroonian civil society actors in the context of the HIPC; and the *Forum Syndical*, which assembled 200 trade unions in a meeting, which denounced the pro-Biya bias that has marked the Cameroonian trade union movement (CCFD, 2006: 11). In a similar vein, they have invited the Canadian International Development Agency to co-fund a programme on electoral legislation and have asked the Dutch state-subsidised NGO, SNV, to finance provincial seminars on budgetary issues (CCFD, 2007b: 9). Finally, they have taken steps to keep all donors with an interest in civil society building in Cameroon informed of their progress on the PCPA, thereby opening up future possible revenue streams.

Also in line with this RDVN strategy, French developmental NGOs have looked to their core supporters to make up the 25 per cent stake needed to take part in this co-funded programme. These NGDOs have not lost sight of the fact that it is the donor public and their militant activists who have provided the money, voluntary energies, cost effectiveness and moral legitimacy, which have made French NGDOs attractive to the French state in the first instance. In effect, French NGDOs have recognised that they cannot afford to jeopardise support from their critical resource – even for the sake of higher-than-average levels of state assistance in the context of the PCPA. They have realised that they have to continue catering for their grassroots supporters, who like to see action and specific achievements in exchange for their donations of money and time; and who are unlikely to be excited by a slow, painstaking and relatively expensive civil society-building programme, such as the PCPA. French NGDOs have, of course, been aware that they have some scope to control the information that their donor public receives, not least given that private donations are generally fungible and given that the programme in question is taking place out in the field. But they have also been deeply conscious of how porous the frontiers are between what goes on in Paris (*ici*) and operations in Africa (*là-bas*). This is particularly true in the case of the PCPA, which has to some extent been piloted by officials from the French Foreign Ministry and NGDO practitioners based in head offices in Paris.

Overall, French NGDOs have realised that they cannot be seen to be an agent of the French state doing its bidding on a programme, which might be misunderstood by their militant activist base. As such, they have not trumpeted their involvement in the PCPA and have glossed over two uncomfortable issues: first, the fact that this programme appears, on the face of it, to involve the North explaining to the South how to build its own civil society; and second, the distinct possibility that the PCPA will ultimately serve to integrate Cameroon more fully into the existing capitalist politico-economic system. Instead, they have played down the scale of the French state's contribution and talked up the extent to which they, and their Cameroonian partners, have discretion over the running of the PCPA. In so doing, French NGDOs have been playing to the gallery of their own core supporters and seeking to avoid the accusation that they are promoting a programme, which is about encouraging activism, without themselves enjoying a significant degree of autonomy.

Conclusion

Earlier chapters have shown how French NGDOs have resisted the temptation to move too close to the state or to the wider international trends set out in our introductory chapter. They have suggested that this behaviour has been broadly consistent with RD theory given that French NGDOs generally operate in a climate, which is less than favourable to closer collaboration with their own central government. This chapter has sought to test this finding against French NGDO practice in the field and has focused specifically on a case study where the French authorities have been providing large-scale support. It has asked whether French NGDOs have been more receptive to state overtures in this instance or whether they have stubbornly continued to remain aloof.

Honing in on the PCPA in Cameroon, this chapter has shown how French NGDOs have not engaged in an optimal reading of their resource opportunities but that they have, broadly speaking, enacted their environment, overcoming constraints on their strategic decision-making and actively pursuing the various resource stabilisation techniques at their disposal. It follows that French developmental NGOs have been acting in line with RD theory and giving priority to the demands of what is normally their 'critical resource', the donor public and activist volunteers, over and above the exigencies of the French state, whose level of support for the PCPA is unlikely to be replicated extensively in other NGO–state projects and programmes. They have also, understandably, shown concern about the possible reaction of their core supporters to any overly close NGDO cooperation with the French authorities.

In pursuing doggedly their core resource, French NGDOs would appear to be behaving rationally and in ways which are not that different from other NNGOs. Where the difference lies is, of course, in the fact that the critical resource in the case of many NNGOs is very often their own central state, which has been pushing them away from a militant grassroots agenda and towards the wider state-led international trends set out in the opening chapter.

Whether French NGDOs have, indeed, been reading their environment correctly must ultimately depend, at least partly, upon whether or not they have been correctly interpreting the French state's attitude towards them and its willingness to fund them. This is, in many ways, a separate question and one which can only be answered through a detailed study of the rationale of the French authorities and through the elaboration of a separate RD model for the state and its resource environment. While there is no space to provide such an analysis here, a few tentative observations can be made about the motives of the French authorities in relation to the PCPA. In this context, it should, above all, be stressed that the French political establishment has failed to give its wholehearted backing to this scheme. The exception to this rule is the MCNG, the mission which has taken the lead on, and co-funded, the PCPA. Other parts of the French Foreign Ministry have been more equivocal. Thus, the Foreign Ministry's representatives on the ground – its embassy in Yaoundé and its aid mission, the SCAC – have welcomed the PCPA as a way of promoting democratic accountability and guarding against misuse of the monies freed up by the C2D. Yet, they have also been wary given that they are in the firing line for any protests raised by the Cameroonian authorities or by the wider French political establishment (Interview, 2004). As for the AFD (the French aid agency specialised in 'hard', productive investment projects and charged with executing the C2D), this has seen the PCPA as a useful way of identifying representative and moderate institutions, which speak for the Cameroonian people. It has, however, remained sceptical of 'fads' that emerge from international development circles and has had particular doubts about the 'soft' training and consultative activities funded by the PCPA (Interview, 2004). Lastly, as regards the most important actor in the French political establishment, the *Elysée*, this has so far adopted a hands-off approach and allowed a junior government department, the MCNG, to take the lead. Given, however, that the Africa cell or 'service' of the *Elysée* has long been charged with nurturing close ties with Francophile African elites, and given that successive French Presidents have a history of backing autocratic African regimes, it is not impossible that the *Elysée* could become a serious obstacle to the PCPA. This could happen if the programme were to provoke vociferous protests from the Biya regime or if it opened up fault lines in Cameroonian society such as the urban–rural divide, the cleavages separating the Muslim North from the essentially Christian South or, most seriously of all, the rift between the French-speaking majority and English-speaking minority.[35]

From a crude RD perspective, it might be thought that the French state has been misreading its own resource environment and failing to appreciate the comparative advantages that French NGDOs have to offer in the Cameroonian context. Some more conservative elements within the French political establishment have no doubt continued to baulk at the idea of

NGDOs playing a role in the delivery of French foreign policy and they have held on to their deep ideological reservations about supporting unelected intermediaries operating between France's Republican state and its citizens. These doubts have, almost certainly, been intensified by the suspicion that some NGDOs may not be legitimate or representative of the interests of the people. This danger has been quite real in the case of the PCPA, where some of the Cameroonian organisations eligible for support from this pro-gramme could conceivably be associated with Cameroonian opposition par-ties or could even be 'sponsored by the ruling party and geared towards countering the activities of other associations fighting for empowerment and democracy'.[36]

On closer inspection, however, it can be observed that this ambivalence on the part of the French authorities towards the French NGDOs involved in the PCPA has less to do with ideology; and more to do with the state's pragmatic pursuit of the 'national interest'. In effect, the wider French pol-itical establishment does not have any overriding interest in what French NGDOs have to offer in terms of civil society building and poverty-reducing activities. It does, of course, want these non-governmental actors to encour-age stability and to ensure sound use of French taxpayers' money. But it is, above all, concerned to ensure that a highly political programme, such as the PCPA, should not jeopardise France's hard nosed *realpolitik* interests in this central African country. Cameroon is, after all, a reliable ally at Franco-African summits and at the UN, even if Cameroonian loyalty to France was questioned in 2003 at the time of voting over the war in Iraq.[37] On strategic grounds, Cameroon is also important as a source of oil and nat-ural gas[38] and a stable African country which plays host to a 6,000-strong French community.[39] Economically, it is of interest as a source of lucrative consultancy contracts and as the largest economy in the central belt of the Franc Zone.[40] It is also as a useful market for French exports (worth M€513 in 2003), the location for 160 French subsidiaries, and a magnet for M€367 in French foreign investment.[41] Cameroon is of value in cultural terms too. Home to the third highest number of French speakers in sub-Saharan Africa, it is a country which France – following its recent loss of influence in Francophone states such as Rwanda and the Democratic Republic of Congo (DRC) – is very anxious to keep firmly rooted in the French-speaking world.[42] This task is not made any easier by Cameroon's bilingual status or by its decision to join both the *Organisation Internationale de la Francophonie* and the essentially Anglophone Commonwealth in 1991 and 1995, respect-ively. Nor has it been facilitated by the emergence of the English-speaking Social Democratic Front and the secessionist Southern Cameroon's National Council (SCNC) as important political parties.[43]

10
Conclusion: A Distinctive Role in International Development

Northern NGOs have long faced a dilemma over whether to embrace closer cooperation with the state or to prioritise autonomy over dependency. This issue has come to the fore over the global era and is now a recurring theme in the NNGO literature. These writings point to the emergence of three broad trends: a general improvement in the terms of the NNGO–state relationship, a professionalisation of NNGOs and an alignment of their priorities with those of the state. These trends are often assumed to hold good across the Northern non-governmental sector and to be of particular relevance to Anglo-Saxon actors. But can they apply equally to NGOs operating in quite different social and political traditions? Can they, more specifically, be applicable to French NGOs? This latter question has been at the heart of this study, which began, after a short introduction, by honing in on a sub-sector of French NGOs, namely *les développementalistes* and *le volontariat*, and showing why these NGDOs are worthy of a study in their own right.

Chapter 3 then identified a suitable theoretical framework, RD, with which to explain the recent evolution of French NGDOs and their relations with the government. It set out a RD model and a crude working assumption that NGOs, be they Northern or French, might normally be expected to move closer to the state insofar as the latter is providing stable, predictable and, in many cases, critical resources. Chapter 4 followed this up by sketching out the resource landscape of French NGDOs and suggesting that the critical resource in the French context has not been the state, but the donor public and the NGDO volunteer base, whose demands may well conflict with those of official resource providers.

Chapters 5 to 7 looked for any empirical evidence to suggest that French NGDOs have moved closer to wider international trends. Chapter 5 demonstrated how the legal, financial and consultative relationship between French developmental NGOs and the government has improved, but not enough to form the basis of a genuine partnership. Chapter 6 showed how French NGDOs have accepted the need for some state-led forms of professionalisation, whilst at the same time holding on firmly to many of their

199

traditional, militant, even amateurish practices. In a similar vein, Chapter 7 argued that, while these non-governmental actors have displayed a greater readiness to deliver many of the policies and ideas of the French government, they have stopped short of serving as agents or vectors on its behalf.

Chapter 8 then explained this limited evolution on the part of French NGDOs towards wider Northern trends in terms of RD theory. It found that, in spite of constraints on their strategic decision-making, French NGDOs appear to have been acting broadly in line with our working assumption and with the RD perspective. They have been correctly reading the opportunities available to them in their resource environment and have, above all, recognised the need to give priority to the demands of their critical resource – the donor public and their activist supporters – over the exigencies of the French state, which is a comparatively minor source of revenue and which is, ultimately, less interested in tapping into the poverty-reducing expertise of French NGDOs than it is in pursuing its own *realpolitik*-type ambitions in the Southern hemisphere.

Chapter 9 then asked whether the same limited evolution of French NGDOs in the direction of wider international trends can also be discerned in instances where the French state constitutes the critical resource. The focus was on the PCPA, a joint NGDO-government programme to build civil society in Cameroon. This case study found that developmental NGOs have cooperated much more closely with the French authorities in the field (*là-bas*) than the rhetorical discourse of their head offices (*ici*) might otherwise suggest. In effect, French NGDOs have been playing to the gallery of their core supporters and talking up their distance from the government, whilst actually being quite willing to 'muck in' and get their hands dirty alongside the state – particularly where the latter is providing sufficient incentives and its priorities are broadly compatible. They have been able to 'reconcile' these two courses of action, thanks largely to the fact that collaboration in distant parts of the world can be more easily concealed from domestic NGDO activists.

Overall the findings of this book provide a fresh perspective on a little known, but important, set of actors, French NGDOs. They also offer insights into the place of these organisations in the wider NNGO context. Needless to say, the results of this study cannot serve to corroborate or invalidate the existence of any of the broad trends in NNGOs outlined in our introduction. They do, however, suggest that claims about developments in NNGOs, which draw exclusively on examples of Anglo-American NGOs, do need to be modified to take account of the specificities of non-governmental sectors in countries, such as France, which have quite different socio-political traditions. The distinctiveness of the French NGO sector and the extent to which it represents, in the words of Meckstroth (1975) 'a most different system' or case study should perhaps not be overstated; but nor should they be completely brushed aside. With reference to French NGOs as a whole, the World

Bank (2001: 17) has, in fact, contended that 'Compared to their European counterparts, French NGOs are, at one and the same time, more numerous, smaller...and less well-off'. This is most clearly illustrated by the fact that the top ten French NGOs, which collect 80 per cent of all resources, have an accumulated budget which is smaller than that of OXFAM UK (Rubio, 2004: 188). It is equally apparent from the fact that the French NGO sector has a total budget of around €700 million, which is less than that of the richest American NGO, World Vision USA (Zimet, 2006: 54).[1] The reasons for the small size of so many French NGOs are said by the Bank (2001: 17) to be

> historic (competition with the state which has its own organised aid machinery); cultural (in Germany and Holland, NGOs are closely linked to the Churches, which finance them generously); psychological (their quest for independence militates in favour of the creation of new structures); as well as legal and fiscal (French legislation governing donations and legacies provides fewer incentives to the donor public and to company sponsors).

All of the above factors have been particularly relevant in the case of French *développementalistes* and voluntary agencies. These NGDOs have, in fact, retained a number of distinctive features of their own. First of all, they have continued to emphasise acts of solidarity over technocratic professionalism. This is clear from the reluctance of most *développementalistes* to budget for any internal evaluations of their work. Equally, it is evident from the way that French volunteer agencies have persisted in sending inexperienced young volunteers overseas and ignored the European 'norm' of deploying specialist technicians and more mature volunteers (Interview with DCC, 2003). Second, French NGDOs have shown a continuing reluctance to move into the realm of humanitarian assistance. While work in this field is recognised as vital, it is still largely associated in the minds of NGDO practitioners, with sensationalism, mediatisation and shorttermism. Third, they have maintained particularly strong links with local NGDOs and other partners in the Southern hemisphere. While these ties have provided a deeper appreciation of the needs of indigenous peoples, they have also limited the opportunities of French NGDOs, particularly those operating solely through local actors, for expansion. They have, moreover, restricted the scope of French NGDOs to engage in emotive advertising, celebrity-led campaigns or shock fund-raising techniques, as well as imposing strict limits on their capacity to professionalise the delivery of projects co-funded by the state. Finally, French NGDOs have retained an extremely strong militant base, with exceptionally large numbers of French volunteers and local/regional associations. In so doing, they have been able to tap into a wider disquiet among the French public, which is significantly more troubled by the implications of globalisation than its counterparts in

Anglo-Saxon and Nordic countries (Fougier, 2006: 37–9). This unease has been most clearly reflected in a recent opinion poll, which suggested that 53 per cent of French people saw globalisation as having a negative effect on the domestic economy (compared to a European average of 37 per cent) and that 50 per cent of French citizens believed that the globalising process was not benefiting developing countries (compared to an EU average of 43 per cent).[2] These wider economic concerns have, in turn, enabled French developmental NGOs to secure their future by recruiting a whole new generation of young activists, eagerly looking for alternative solutions to the challenges of the developing world. They have also, arguably, allowed these NGDOs to maintain a more radical critique of the donor community's approach to overseas development than that adopted by NGOs in most other OECD countries.

At the same time, however, it would be wrong to overstate these specificities. This research has actually demonstrated that French NGDOs have generally been operating in ways which are not that different from other NNGOs and which are broadly consistent with RD theory. They have, as previous chapters have shown, sought closer partnership with, and more resources from, the state, wherever these have been available and broadly compatible with their own mission. French NGDOs have, moreover, set aside much of their scepticism and taken steps to professionalise their practices along the lines required by the government. Equally, they have modified their priorities in an effort to promote closer collaboration with, and to allay the suspicion of, a secular French Republic that has yet to shake off completely its ideological concerns about supporting these unelected intermediaries between state and citizen. Yet French NGDOs have not been altogether successful in this last task and have simply had to 'scrape by' in an environment, which is much less propitious to NGDO development than that of many other Northern countries.

The unfavourable nature of this climate can be gauged from a number of indicators. First, French NGOs as a whole have continued to benefit from less generous fiscal concessions than many of their Anglo-Saxon counterparts (*Commissariat Général*, 2002). Second, French NGOs still do not enjoy the kind of long-term partnership agreements with the state that are available to their counterparts in Denmark, Sweden and Britain.[3] Third, French NGOs are a long way from securing the type of privileged access to official policy-makers, which is offered to, say, Dutch, Nordic and British NGOs. Fourth, they continue to receive the lowest levels of official aid support in the EU, excluding, of course, NGOs based in the countries of Central, Eastern and Southern Europe. Finally, French *développementalistes* and volunteer associations, in particular, have continued to rank outside the top tier of European, let alone NNGOs.[4] Indeed, it might be added that the leading French developmental NGO, the CCFD, is actually a much smaller affair in France, a Catholic nation, than the largest Catholic NGOs (CAFOD in the United Kingdom and CRS in the United States) are in Protestant, Anglo-American countries.

The above findings are, of course, tentative and could usefully be corroborated or challenged by a range of future research. There would, for instance, be real value in deepening this survey by testing its findings against the following: case studies of French NGDO-government programmes in continents other than Africa; schemes not taking place under the rubric of 'the new contractual arrangements'; and projects where the French state is not 'the' or even 'a' critical resource. There would also be a strong argument for widening this project. Thus, for example, research could be undertaken to explore the evolution of other types of French NGOs (notably pressure groups and *urgenciers*) and to establish whether there is any solid empirical basis to the claims made in much of the non-profit literature regarding the emergence of broad trends in NNGO–state relations. Equally, there would be a case for studying, in detail, the recent evolution of NGOs from Northern countries other than France. These could be examined either individually or in line with the categories designated by Archambault (1999) via her 'Rhineland', Anglo-Saxon, Nordic and Mediterranean models of the non-profit sector (see Chapter 1). The focus would be on whether or not these NNGOs have, as was tentatively implied in Chapter 3, been acting broadly in line with RD theory. The emphasis of this and other research could, equally, be on ways of stretching the RD framework to enable it to shed more light on the NGDO–state relationship. As noted in earlier chapters, the RD model of NNGO behaviour is uni-directional and hones in almost exclusively on the resource environment of NGDOs and on the influence, which is exerted on these non-governmental actors by resource-rich organisations, such as the state. Needless to say, there is nothing to prevent future analysts from drawing up a RD model of one or more Northern states and their particular resource environments. Nor, for that matter, is there any reason why a set of interlocking RD models should not be devised for NNGOs and Northern states.

Whither French NGDO–state relations?

The quest for answers to the above wide-ranging questions must clearly be left to future scholars. For now, it is thought useful to work on the assumption that French NGDOs have indeed been acting rationally in their resource interests, but in a less than propitious context. If so, what does this suggest about the likely future evolution of French developmental NGOs and their relations with the state? Will they gradually move closer to the French authorities and to wider international trends? Are they simply behind other NNGOs and is it only a matter of time before French NGDOs and the state are working hand in glove? Are they, in effect, just temporarily lower down than, say, their Anglo-Saxon counterparts on a graph, which has, as its vertical axis, 'dependency-autonomy' and, as its horizontal axis, 'level of resources'?

It is, of course, difficult to generalise about future French NGDO relations with the state. These will inevitably differ from one developmental NGO to the next, in line with the demands of particular ministries (see Chapter 4) and the individual characteristics of the NGDOs themselves. The closeness of these ties will depend, to a large extent, upon the size of developmental NGOs, with medium-sized actors typically being the most receptive to state overtures (Cohen, 2004). It will also be a function of the institutional capacity of NGDOs, with some smaller organisations simply lacking the critical mass required to work closely with central government. Equally, these relations will vary according to the philosophical or ideological outlook of different NGDOs, with secular organisations often finding themselves more dependent on official funding than faith-based actors, which can fall back on church networks. Future NGDO–state relations will, moreover, depend upon whether or not the developmental NGO concerned has a track record of working with central government. The CCFD is particularly strong on this point and has taken on a coordinator role in numerous programmes co-funded under *la nouvelle contactrualisation*. Others, such as *ATD Quart Monde*, fare less well on this score. Finally, the proximity of their ties to the state is likely to vary according to the sector of activity in which NGDOs are involved. Clearly, NGDOs engaged explicitly in poverty-reducing and civil society building activities should anticipate the prospect of closer collaboration with the government, even if they may never attract the same level of official – essentially international – resources as leading *urgenciers*, such as MDM and ACF.

While all these variables will be important, the key determining factor from a RD perspective is likely to be the critical resource and whether this remains the donor public and militant volunteer base or shifts to become another actor, such as the French state.[5] Clearly, this latter scenario would change the whole incentive system for French NGDOs. It would mean that there would be an overriding resource-related interest in catering to the views of the government and less need to take on board the demands of militants. It would not, of course, mean that all French NGDOs would automatically fall in line with wider international trends or be lured into a service agency function or, for that matter, that they would stop criticising the French authorities. But many would do some or all of these things, and, as our case study has shown, most NGDOs are happy to follow the money as long as the aims of the programme are broadly compatible with their own.

At the moment, there are, in fact, ominous signs that the current critical resource might be weakening. The fact is that absolute levels of income from the donating public are not, despite a number of recent fiscal concessions, rising at the same rate as the demand from organisations competing for these monies. The reasons for the sluggish growth in these donations by members of the general public (compassion fatigue, falling church attendance, assumptions about the responsibilities of the state in development matters, and susceptibility to NGO scandals, such as the recent *Arche de Zoé* affair) have already been examined in Chapter 8 and need not be repeated here. As regards the increase in demand, this has come partly from French *urgenciers*, which have adopted sophisticated marketing techniques and which enjoy a media appeal that enables them to soak up the bulk of French public donations. It has also emanated partly from 'foreign' NGOs, such as *OXFAM France-Agir Ici*, the Islamic Popular Front and the American branch of World Vision, which have begun eating into the private revenue sources of French NGDOs.[6] Another source of demand has come from new social movements and pressure groups, such as ATTAC, which have risen to prominence in France and indeed globally over the last decade or so (Walters, 2003) and which now compete with French NGDOs for the hearts and souls of much-needed volunteers and activists.

There is, equally, some evidence to suggest that the French state might be prepared to move into more of a 'critical resource' type role or at least be 'less stingy' vis-à-vis French NGDOs.[7] Recent French governments have, in fact, made numerous overtures to NGDOs, notably the fiscal concessions offered to individuals and companies wishing to make donations, the introduction of 'the new contractual arrangements' and the rolling out of large-scale programmes, such as the PCPA to Guinea, Algeria and the Congo.[8] The government of French President Nicolas Sarkozy, elected in May 2007, is likely to try to build on these measures, not least since this administration incorporates within its fold a number of former NGO practitioners and others with links to social movements. These include one of the founders of MSF and MDM, Bernard Kouchner, who has been appointed Foreign Minister, and a former head of the ACF, Jean-Christopne Rufin, who has been nominated Ambassador to Senegal.[9] Sarkozy himself has firmed up the practice tentatively established by President Chirac of granting audiences to NGOs. He has consulted environmental pressure groups regularly on climate change and has met French developmental, human rights and emergency NGOs to discuss pandemic diseases (November 2007) and to explore issues on the agenda at the G8 summit in Heiligendamm (June 2007).[10] The president has, in fact, promised to receive French NGOs every three months and has explicitly reaffirmed France's pledge to double aid channelled through NGOs by 2009.[11]

Ultimately, however, the likelihood is that most French NGDOs will continue to muddle through with the help of their existing critical resource. The donor public in France, though not noted for its generosity, has stood the test of time as a revenue stream; and recent opinion polls continue to point to a higher level of public trust in NGOs than in any official agencies involved in overseas development. Significantly too, the threat of competition from other non-state actors should perhaps not be exaggerated. Thus, *urgenciers* would appear – partly because the rewards are not so great and partly because of a typically French tendency to demarcate the lines between different specialisms – reluctant to move wholeheartedly into long-term development work. They have also been unable to prevent developmental NGOs from taking a share of the extra private donations, which are generated at the time of crises, such as the South Asian tsunami of December 2004 (CCD, 2008) and Cyclone Nargis in Burma in May 2008. As regards 'foreign' NGOs, these do not always find it easy to implant themselves in France due to the historically poor fiscal climate and owing to cultural and linguistic factors. To illustrate, the UK pressure group, Amnesty International, and the British NGO, OXFAM, have both found it difficult to make rapid headway in France.[12] The threat from 'foreign' NGOs has also been attenuated by the fact that some French non-governmental actors are also seeking donations from private donors in other OECD countries. This trend is, moreover, likely to continue since France's ratification, in 1996, of Treaty 124, a convention, which allows French NGOs with branches in other parts of Europe to benefit from the same fiscal and legal advantages as are offered to the NGOs originally formed in those countries (*Commissariat Général*, 2002: 46). Finally, while it is true that social movements and *altermondialiste* pressure groups are in some ways competitors in the eyes of French NGDOs, they also represent a vector for recruitment for these non-governmental actors. This is particularly true of groupings, such as ATTAC, which has generated great enthusiasm within French society, but which appears to have lost much of its original momentum (Walters, 2006).

At the same time, it seems likely that support is always going to remain half-hearted from conservative elements within the French political establishment, which have continued to harbour ideological doubts about NGDOs and baulked at the 'intrusion' of these unelected intermediaries into the field of foreign policy (Devin, 1999: 75). As Cohen rightly observes, whilst French 'officials claim that the state needs to maintain a capacity for "state-to-state" international aid', there is no escaping the fact that 'France wants to continue to act directly without going systematically through NGOs.' The jury is out on whether the Sarkozy administration can really make a difference. There was, of course, little support in NGO circles for the Presidential candidacy of the 'neo-liberal' Nicolas Sarkozy. There remains, since his election, a feeling that even those ministers and ambassadors, who have their origins in the non-governmental movement, will do little of substance to help and will either be co-opted or find themselves constrained by France's slow-moving diplomatic machinery.[13] There is certainly a question mark over whether the Sarkozy administration can fulfil any of its wider pledges on aid and whether it will remain committed to poverty reduction and to large-scale NGDO programmes under 'the new contractual arrangements'.[14] The French government's stance may well shift, once, as widely predicted, the Millennium Development Goals of halving world poverty by 2015 are not met and the international donor community begins to look for another approach to the challenges of the developing world. The French authorities might seek to backtrack on their pledge of doubling aid to NGOs (Carrez, 2006) and give priority instead to other non-state organisations. State funding could go increasingly to low-cost Southern NGOs, which are already benefiting from the recent devolution of some the government's co-funding arrangements to French embassies in Senegal, Madagascar, Cambodia, Guinea and the Yemen.[15] Perhaps however, French official monies are more likely to be directed towards private companies, which are noted for their professionalism and flexibility, and, indeed, towards local authorities, which are elected bodies with extensive international networks and with a vested interest in 'flying the flag' for France (Devin, 1999: 76).

Without substantially greater state support, the likelihood is that French NGDOs will remain small, unable to rival leading French *urgenciers* (which could form a breakaway group) and ill-equipped to compete with their Anglo-Saxon counterparts in terms of their professionalism, critical mass, reflective capacity or even mass membership. They will also face strict limits on their ability to operate on a large-scale and do 'more good' for the peoples of the developing world. This seemingly bleak future is certainly not the one predicted by most official publications (DGCID, various years), parliamentary reports (Blum, 2005) or even independent analyses (Cohen, 2004), which tend to envisage ever closer collaboration between French NGDOs and the French state. Yet, such a scenario may actually serve French NGDOs well in the short to medium term by allowing them to retain their avant garde stance within the *altermondialiste* movement and by enabling them to hold on to a degree of international prominence, which is disproportionate to their small size. The continuing absence of any sustained support from the French authorities should also enable NGDOs to eschew some of the compromises associated with closer dealings with the state, maintain a respectable distance from the failures of official donors over the last few decades and avoid being labelled as 'unhappy agents of a foreign aid system in decline' (Pearce, 2000: 24). It should, equally, help them to preserve the militant attributes and core values, which they will need if they are to continue holding out for a 'better' world.

Annex A: List of Interviews

French and other officials

November 2003	*Délégation Humanitaire*, French Foreign Ministry, Paris
December 2003	*Mission Pour la Coopération Non-Gouvernementale*, French Foreign Ministry, Paris
March 2004	*Agence Française de Développement*, Yaoundé
April 2004	*Service de Coopération et d'Action Culturelle* (two officials), Yaoundé
April 2004	European Commission, Yaoundé
April 2004	GTZ (German Development Agency), Yaoundé
April 2004	MINEPAT (Cameroonian Government), Yaoundé

French humanitarian NGOs

November 2003	Michel Brugière, President of *Médecins du Monde*
November 2003	Benoît Miribel, Executive Director of *Action Contre la Faim*, Paris
December 2003	Jean-Hervé Bradol, President of *Médecins Sans Frontières*, Paris
December 2003	Board member, *Médecins Sans Frontières*, Paris
December 2003	Nathalie Herlemont-Zoratchik, *Handicap International*, Lyon

French developmental NGOs

October 2003	Henri Rouillé d'Orfeuil, President of *Coordination SUD*, Paris
October 2003	Pierre Castella, President of *Solagral*, Paris
November 2003	Christophe Courtin, CCFD, Paris
November 2003	Denis Brandt, DEFAP, Paris
November 2003	*Délégation Catholique pour la Coopération* (two representatives), Paris
November 2003	*Terre des Hommes-France* (two representatives), Paris
December 2003	Michel Joli, President of the AFVP, Paris
December 2003	CCFD (three representatives), Paris
December 2003	Michel Wagner, President of CLONG-V, Paris
December 2003	Bernard Pinaud, President of the CRID, Paris
December 2003	Hélène Rossert, President of AIDES, Paris
March 2004	Elisabeth Paquot, GRET, Yaoundé
March 2004	Jean-Paul Everard, *Secours Catholique-Caritas France*, Mbalmayo
July 2005	CCFD (one representative), Paris
July 2005	Marie Youakim, RITIMO, Montpellier

Other French and Cameroonian 'civil society' actors

November 2003	François Mabille, Catholic University, Paris
November 2003	Senior representative, *Haut Conseil de la Coopération Internationale*, Paris

December 2003	Christian Feuillet, *Conseil Régional*, Île-de-France, Paris
December 2003	François-Xavier Verschave, *Survie*, Paris
December 2003	Sarah Pellet, CNCDH, Paris
January 2004	Philippe Hugon, Nanterre University/ ex-HCCI member, Paris
March 2004	BASC-Caritas (two representatives), Yaoundé

This list does not include several extended discussions with Cameroonian civil society organisations other than the BASC (e.g. the FEMEC, REDS, APDHAC). Confidentiality has been respected wherever it has been requested.

Annex B: List of Main French NGO Federations

Federation (date formed)	Core function	Members and partner organisations of federation (& web address)
Coordination SUD (1994)	Overarching federation	129 members (www.coordinationsud.org). See this federation's website for a full list.
CRID- *Centre de Recherche & d'Information pour le Développement* (1976)	Represents interests of NGDOs with local partners in the South & the ex-communist bloc	49 members (www.crid.asso.fr): 4D (*Dossiers & Débats pour le Développement Durable*), *Accueil Paysan*, ADER (*Association pour le Développement Économique Régional*), AFED (*Association Femmes & Développement*), *Agir Ici, Aide & Action, Aide Odontologique Internationale, Architecture & Développement*, ASFODEVH (*Association pour la Formation en Développement Humain*), ASPAL (*Association de Solidarité avec les Peuples d'Amérique Latine*), AUI (*Action d'Urgence Internationale*), CARI (*Centre d'Actions & de Réalisations Internationales*), CCFD (*Comité Catholique contre la Faim & pour le Développement*), *Chambre des Beaux-Arts de Méditerranée, CIMADE-Département Solidarité Internationale, Eau Vive, Éléctriciens Sans Frontières, Emmaüs International, ENDA Europe, Enfants du Monde-Droits de l'Homme, Étudiants & Développement, Féderation Artisans du Monde, Fonds Mondial de Solidarité contre la Faim, Forum de Delphes, France-Amérique Latine* (FAL), *France Libertés, Frères des Hommes*, GRDR (*Groupe de Recherche & de Réalisations pour le Développement Rural dans le Tiers Monde*), IDD (*Immigration Développement Démocratie*), IFAID Aquitaine (*Institut de Formation & d'Appui aux Initiatives de Développement*), IPAM (*Initiatives Pour un Autre Monde*), IRFED (*Institut International de Recherche & de Formation Éducation & Développement*), ISF (*Ingénieurs Sans Frontières*), *Juristes Solidarités*, MADERA (*Missions d'Aide au Développement des Économies Rurales en Afghanistan*), *Maisons Familiales Rurales, Max Havelaar France*, OFCI (*Observatoire Français de la Coopération Internationale*), *Les Pénélopes, Les Petits Débrouillards, Peuples Solidaires*, RITIMO (*Réseau des Centres de Documentation pour le Développement & la Solidarité Internationale*), *Secours Catholique-Caritas France, Secours Populaire Français, Sherpa, Survie, Terre des Hommes-France, Tourisme & Développement Solidaires, Traditions pour Demain, Yamana*

Federation (date formed)	Core function	Members and partner organisations of federation (& web address)
CLONG-Volontariat (1979)	Represents interests of volunteer agencies	14 members (www.clong-volontariat.org): ACF (*Action Contre la Faim*), AFVP (*Association Française des Volontaires du Progrès*), ASMAE (*Association Soeur Emmanuelle*), *ATD Quart-Monde*, BIOFORCE, CEFODE (*Coopération & Formation au Développement*), DCC (*Délégation Catholique pour la Coopération*), DEFAP (*Service Protestant de Mission*), ERM (*Enfants Réfugiés du Monde*), FIDESCO, GREF (*Groupement des Retraités Éducateurs Sans Frontières*), HI (*Handicap International*), MDM (*Médecins du Monde*), SCD (*Service de Coopération au Développement*)
Groupe Initiatives (1993)	Consultancy NGOs offering technical advice	7 members (www.groupe-initiatives.org): AVSF (*Agronomes & Vétérinaires Sans Frontières*) CIEDEL (*Centre International d'Études pour le Développement Local*), ESSOR, GRDR (*Groupe de Recherches & de Réalisations pour le Développement Rural*), GRET (*Groupe de Recherche & d'Échanges Technologiques*), HSF (*Hydraulique Sans Frontières*), IRAM (*Institut de Recherches & d'Applications des Méthodes de Développement*)
Coordination d'Agen (1983)	Initially represented interests of *urgenciers*	12 members (no website): *Aide Médicale & Développement, Auteuil International, Biologie Sans Frontières, Enfants du Mékong*, FERT, *Fondation Raoul Follereau, Groupe Développement, Guilde Européenne du Raid*, IECD, *Kinésithérapeutes du Monde*, PlaNet finance, SIPAR
CNAJEP- *Comité National des Associations de Jeunesse & d'Education Populaire* (1968)	Represents youth & popular education movements	71 members (www.cnajep.asso.fr). See CCD (2007: 12) for a detailed list
FORIM- *Forum des OSI issues des Migrations* (2002)	Develops immigrants' home towns	29 members (www.forim.net). See CCD (2007: 14) for a full list.

Source: www.coordinationsud.org and CCD (2007: 9–16).

Annex C: Key French Members of the *Altermondialiste* Movement

Field of activity	Organisations
Development	*Agir Ici pour un Monde Solidaire, Association Internationale de Techniciens, Experts et Chercheurs*, CCFD, *Centre d'Études et d'Initiatives de Solidarité Internationale*, CRID, *Frères des Hommes*, GRET, *Ingénieurs Sans Frontières, Peuples Solidaires, Réseau-Afrique-Europe, Foi et Justice*, RITIMO, *Secours Catholique, Solagral, Survie, Terre des Hommes*
Environment	*Amis de la Terre, Ecoropa, Greenpeace*
Solidarity	*ATD Quart Monde, Emmaüs France*
Fair trade	*Fédération Artisans du Monde, Max Havelaar France*
Human rights	CIMADE, *France Libertés, Ligue des Droits de l'Homme, Mouvement contre le Racisme et pour l'Amitié entre les Peuples*
Feminism	*Coordination des Associations pour le Droit à l'Avortement et à la Contraception, Marche Mondiale des Femmes, Les Pénélopes*
Minorities	*Act Up-Paris*

Source: Allait (2007: 103).

Notes

1 Introduction: French NGOs in a global context

1. Original citations in Ryfman (2004: 22–4). Translations here and throughout this study by the author.
2. Some NGOs, even in these early years, came to rely heavily on their own governments; this was true particularly of CARE (originally known as the Cooperative for American Remittances to Europe) in the United States, which became dependent on US government food aid surpluses as from the mid-1950s (Campbell, 1990).
3. Note that the *Nederlandse Organisatie voor Internationale Bijstand* or NOVIB has been known as OXFAM-NOVIB since 1996. Stichting Nederlandse Vrijwilligers or SNV translates into English as the Foundation of Netherlands Volunteers.
4. Germany was the first donor to establish co-funding arrangements (Smillie, 1999: 9).
5. BMZ is an abbreviation of *Bundesministerium für wirtschaftliche Zusammenarbeit und Entwicklung*, which is the full name of the Federal Ministry for Economic Cooperation and Development. The German NGO federation, *Verband Entwicklungspolitik deutscher Nichtregierungsorganisationen* or VENRO, was established in 1995.
6. Similarly, in Norway, some NGOs rely on the state for over 90 per cent of their funding, whereas in Sweden, there is considerable interchange of personnel between the government and non-government sectors (Randel and German, 1999: 183 and 211).
7. Note that the comments in the Preface are made by Jean Bonvin, President of the OECD Development Centre.
8. Britain's Joint Funding Scheme (1975–99) was replaced by the Civil Society Challenge Fund, which places emphasis on working with a wider range of civil society organisations and stresses capacity-building of NGOs in the Southern hemisphere, rather than direct implementation of poverty-related programmes by UK-based NGOs.
9. The term *anti-mondialisation*, common in the 1990s, has, since around 2002, been replaced in France and Latin countries by *altermondialisme*, which suggests that solidarity-based globalisation can be a good thing. See www.hcci.gouv.fr/lecture/note/altermondialisme-antimondialisation.html.
10. These are said to include CARE, CRS, MSF, OXFAM, SCF and World Vision.
11. See, for example, E. Godin and T. Chafer, *The End of the French Exception*, Berghahn Books, Oxford, 2005.
12. The same author admits, nonetheless, that France 'borrows from the various models', sharing its links to a 'Bismarckian' social security system with the Rhineland model, its emphasis on the welfare state with the Scandinavian approach, its stress on decentralisation and partnerships between NGOs and local authorities with the Anglo-Saxon approach, and its recent and troubled history with the Mediteranean model (Ibid).
13. Note that the Union of International Associations includes within its directory multinational companies and other transnational organisations.

14. This recommendation has, equally, been put forward by Carrez (2003) and Penne *et al.* (2002).
15. For the concept of 'most different' and 'most similar' systems, see Meckstroth (1975).
16. The exception to this rule will be the local partner organisations of French NGDOs, whenever the role of these SNGOs is vital to the success of a programme (as in our case study in Chapter 9).

2 Zooming in on French NGOs

1. Hitherto, they had been referred to by the League of Nations as 'transnational organisations' or 'international associations (Blum, 2005: 4).
2. Cited in Ryfman (2004: 34).
3. This Convention is often referred to as Treaty 124.
4. NGOs are assumed to form a 'third' sector, distinct from the 'first' (the government) sector and the 'second' (the commercial) sector.
5. The OECD questionnaire is sent out every five years or so.
6. Confusingly, some French associations use the term *organisation non-gouvernementale* to refer to Anglo-Saxon NGOs (Blum, 2005: 4).
7. ASI is more popular, as it refers to the legal form ('association') and to positive solidarity work rather than the negative 'non-governmental' label. OSI is more inclusive, allowing account to be taken of foundations and private organisations other than associations (*Commissariat Général*, 2002: 16).
8. Into this latter category might fall private diplomatic mediator organisations which, despite their NGO status, often serve the state in an official capacity. These include the Carter Foundation and International Crisis Group (Rubio, 2002: 67–8).
9. Exceptions include *ENDA Tiers Monde*, which was established in Senegal in 1972 before going on to form branches (e.g. *ENDA Europe*) in OECD member countries, such as France.
10. See Dauvin *et al.* (2002: 391–4) for details.
11. In other ways, however, leading French *urgenciers*, such as MSF and MDM, have acted in line with Korten's generational strategy and taken on a major role in developing the health sectors of developing countries. Similarly, the CCFD has moved away from a purely operational concern with projects and adopted more of a capacity-building function designed to develop links between civil societies in the South and global financial institutions.
12. The CCFD claims to spend only 1.4 per cent of its budget on religious and ethical activities; see CCFD, 'Faits et Chiffres de l'Année', *Supplément à La Lettre du CCFD*, no. 26, 2005, p. 4.
13. The CFSI was previously known as the *Comité Français Contre la Faim* and, before that, as the *Comité Français pour la Campagne Mondiale Contre la Faim*.
14. Note that much of the non-profit literature in English and, hence, some of the quotations in this book, use the term 'NGDOs' to refer both to NGOs active in long-term development work and to those engaged in emergency relief activities.
15. Greenpeace was founded in Canada in 1971, with the French branch emerging in 1977. WWF was established in the United Kingdom in 1961, with an affiliate in France in 1973.
16. FIDH now includes 155 human rights organisations from across the world; see www.fidh.org.

17. See www.doctorswithoutborders.org/aboutus/org.cfm.
18. This right has been enshrined in various UN Resolutions, including 43/131 of 1988, 45/100 of 1990 and Security Council Resolution 688 of 5 April 1991; see Beigbeder (1992: 85).
19. MSF was expelled from Ethiopia, in 1986, for publicly protesting against the forced population transfers organised by the Ethiopian government and its use of international aid as an instrument of war. MSF withdrew from Rwanda, in 1994, when donor states refused to supply the UN with the troops needed to disarm Hutu *genocidiaires*, who were wreaking havoc in refugee camps in the Democratic Republic of the Congo.
20. Figures given by Emmanuel Fagnou, Executive Director of *Coordination SUD*, *communiqué* of 3 September 2004, www.coordinationsud.org/article.php3?id_article=770.
21. MDM took the view that MSF was becoming too bureaucratic, too reluctant to allow individual doctors to denounce human rights abuses, and too focused on classic projects at the expense of more sensational operations.
22. Note that the *Comité Français pour l'UNICEF* often appears in the top five French NGOs. However, its NGO status is questionable, given that it is really a fund-raising collection agency on behalf of an international organisation, namely the United Nation's Children's Fund.
23. Relatedly, Hatton (2002) also refers to grey areas, such as the establishment of teaching structures in refugee camps; the distribution of seed for crops in emergency situations; or support for social systems in conflict-ridden countries (Ibid).
24. Similarly, the CCD (1999: 31) notes that NGDOs do not intervene exclusively in stable conditions. It points to the work of the CCFD and SC-CF during times of crisis under the Pinochet regime in Chile.
25. According to Blum (2005: 13), *Handicap International* now engages in long-term projects focused on sustainability and sends out expatriate staff on low-paid, local contracts.
26. This distinction is likely to have some resonance for a number of years, given the difficulties which most emergency-related NGOs have in recruiting highly qualified medical and other staff in Northern countries, let alone in parts of the developing world, where their salaries are unlikely to compete favourably with those of international organisations.
27. The MCNG did, nonetheless, set aside M€2.3 between 2000 and 2002 for immediate post-emergency activities; see www.diplomatie.gouv.fr [accessed 18 April 2003].
28. In the 1960s, many *développementalistes* sent out expatriates, who took on tasks better left to the indigenous population of developing countries. By the 1970s, they had become wary of the danger of substitution and had begun to work primarily through local partners (Rubio, 2002: 47).
29. See CCFD, *Faits et Chiffres 2006*; CCFD, Paris, 2006, pp. 2–3; and CCFD, *Rapport d'Activité 2002*, CCFD, Paris, 2002, p. 43.
30. In 1999, the total income of the SC-CF actually exceeded that of MSF (M€70.1) by rising to M€150. However, only M€ 33.8 of this was for international solidarity work (Potevin, 2000).
31. According to Michel Wagner of the CLONG-V 'It is understood that, with only very rare exceptions, volunteers will not be replaced...which means that they have two years to train the person from the country concern who will take over the role' (Interview, 2003).

32. Note that these percentage figures are based upon a total which excludes AFVP volunteers.

33. This is well over four times the amount secured by the DCC (CCD, 2008: 53).

34. www.afvp.org/-Nos-ressources-financieres-.html.

35. See C. Daum (ed.), 'Typologie des Organisations de Solidarité Internationale issues de l'Immigration', January 2000, www.hcci.gouv.fr. This mistrust may lessen with the decision by French President Nicolas Sarkozy to set up, in 2007, a Ministry for Immigration, Integration, National Identity and Solidarity-Based Development.

36. See OECD, 'Philanthropic Foundations and Development Cooperation', *DAC Journal*, vol. 4, no. 3, 2003, p. 33.

37. See Centre de Documentation Tiers Monde, *Répertoire des Acteurs de la Coopération et de la Solidarité Internationale en Languedoc-Roussillon*, First Edition, October 2001.

38. See communiqué by the Executive Director of *Coordination SUD*, Emmanuel Fagnou, 3 September 2004, www.coordinationsud.org/spip.php?article770. Note that lower estimates by official bodies are cited in Chapters 4 and 8.

39. Cited in CCD (2001: 3).

40. Only 1.3 per cent of NGOs focused solely on emergency work, 1.9 per cent exclusively on volunteering and 7.6 per cent entirely on development education activities (Ibid).

41. See E. Fagnou, *communiqué* of 3 September 2004, www.coordinationsud.org/article.php3?id_. Note that, in 2004–05, some M€596.6 were collected by these actors (CCD, 2008: 10).

42. See CCFD, *Rapport d'Activité 2002*, CCFD, Paris, *passim*; and Godfrain (2004).

43. APRODEV is also known as the Association of World Council of Churches related Development Organisations in Europe.

44. www.concordeurope.org/Public/Page.php?ID=8.

45. The abbreviation 'SUD' stands for *Solidarité, Urgence, Développement*.

46. The *Guilde Européenne du Raid* is a multi-skilled NGO, which engages in development projects, sends out volunteers and provides technical support to other NGOs.

47. For further details of this *Forum des Organisations de Solidarité Internationale issues des Migrations*, see www.coordinationsud.org/spip.php?article664.

3 The quest for a theoretical framework

1. For a short review of IR theories on which this paragraph draws, see Yujun Mei, *The Changing Discourse of International Humanitarian Charitable-Relief NGOs*, PhD, Arizona State University, 2003.

2. According to Pfeffer and Salancik (1978: 11): 'Organizational effectiveness is an external standard of how well an organization is meeting the demands of the various groups and organizations that are concerned with its activities [...]. Organizational efficiency is an internal standard of performance. The question whether what is being done should be done is not posed, but only how well is it being done'.

3. See M. Langley, 'Mr. Rose gives away millions in donations, not a cent of control', *Wall Street Journal*, 26 March 1988, pp. A1, A10.

4. Note that ministerial positions have tended to go only to leading figures within humanitarian NGOs. Thus, Claude Malhuret, a founder and former President

of MSF, served as France's Minister for Human Rights (1986–88), whilst Bernard Kouchner (founder of MSF and MDM) has been Health Minister (1992–93; 1997), Social Affairs Minister (1998) and Foreign Secretary, since 2007.

4 French NGDOs and their resource landscape

1. These figures do not include the 'accession states' of Central and Eastern Europe.
2. *Le Monde*, 4–5 February 2001.
3. See comments by Jean-Louis Sabatié, Head of the MCNG, in CCD (2001: 15).
4. This fund was established to help French overseas aid missions alleviate the negative social impact of the devaluation of the African (CFA) franc in 1994. It represented 261 million francs over a three year period in the mid- to late 1990s (OECD, 2000:70).
5. This Ministry increased its allocation to these *académies* from €23,000 in 1994 to some €50,300 in 1999 (*Commissariat Général*, 2002).
6. This annual subsidy works out at the equivalent of 2000 tonnes of cereal.
7. Seventeen of the NGOs funded by the AFD in 2005 had a budget of more than €1 million (CCD, 2008: 23).
8. This official estimate includes monies provided by the AFD, an aid agency for which the Foreign Ministry now shares responsibility with the Ministry of Finance.
9. According to one MCNG official: 'I have colleagues here who believe that local authorities form part of civil society. I'm not saying that it is the official policy of the Foreign Ministry' (Interview, 2003).
10. According to the CCD (2001: 16), NGO income from these sources rose by an average of 11 per cent a year between 1991 and 2000–01.
11. The first category included *Aide et Action* and IRAM; the second included the AFVP and the *Centre International de Développement et de Recherche* (CIDR); and the third involved the GRET and *Programme-Solidarité Eau* (Ibid).
12. The UN as a whole increased its number of French NGO recipients from 22 in 1999 to 40 in 2005 (World Bank, 2001: 17; CCD, 2008: 26).
13. This budgetary line (B7-6000) concerned 55 French NGOs and involved an average of M€1.1 in 2005 (CCD, 2008: 26).
14. EuropeAid is the Directorate-General responsible for implementing external EU aid programmes and projects. It takes account of strategies designed by the DG Development for the African Caribbean and Pacific regions and the DG External Relations for the rest of the world.
15. The decree of 6 January 1989 draws a legal distinction between *mécénat*, where the sponsor acts in the general interest and receives nothing in return, and *parainnage*, where the sponsor offers support and expects to benefit directly from his or her action.
16. *Magasins U* gave ACF €315,000 in 1999 and €540,000 in 2004; see wwo.fr/ong-146-ACTION-CONTRE-LA-FAIM.php. For details of the WWF partnership, see Aoust *et al.* (2004).
17. *Faim et Développement* was set up by the CCFD in 1983. *Épargne Solidaire* has involved 14 NGOs including ACF, AMI, *Handicap International* and MDM. The number of such products accredited by FINANSOL rose from 12 in 1997 to 53 in 2008; see *Les Échos*, 12 April 2008.
18. Membership fees can be significant for smaller NGDOs and for pressure groups, whose members engage with the organisation mainly at the intellectual level.

They are not a major resource for leading *urgenciers* (MSF and MDM each has less than 5000 members), perhaps because the cost of consulting the membership may outweigh the financial value of the subscriptions (Rubio, 2004: 184–5).

19. Exceptions include *Handicap International*, Amnesty International and the *Comité Français pour l'UNICEF* (Rubio, 2004: 184).

20. See OXFAM, *Accounts and Reports 06–07*, OXFAM, Oxford, 2007, p. 17.

21. Total French foundation funding, all causes included, rarely exceeds 0.09 per cent of French GNP, whereas American foundations, all told, are reckoned to dispense around US$26 billion a year. The latter include the Bill and Melinda Gates Foundation, which is the largest private source of funding in the fight against AIDS (Rubio, 2004: 280).

22. For the problems with in-kind donations, see RITIMO (2006). In the case of medicines, there is now illicit trafficking of donated drugs in France (Blum, 2005: 19).

23. The annual telethon by the Muscular Dystrophy Association raised M€102 in 2007 for medical research; see www.afm-france.org/afm-english_version.

24. These figures do not include the 5000 organisations which also count as NGO 'members' (CCD, 2008:7). Seventeen of the 159 NGOs surveyed by the CCD had more than a hundred members, whilst 18 had over a thousand. Fifty-four organisations had between one and 99 *adhérents* (Ibid).

25. Official figures greatly understate these numbers. Thus, the CCD (1995: 49) records only 13,000 such *bénévoles*, noting simply that they make up three-fifths of the French NGO workforce and equate to only 7597 full-time jobs. *Bénévoles* differ from *volontaires* in that they are completely unremunerated, have no separate legal status and normally offer their services for shorter periods, sometimes outside their normal hours of employment (Halba, 2003).

26. See www.coordinationsud.org/spip.php?article666.

5   French NGDOs and the state: paving the way for a new partnership?

1. See www.diplomatie.gouv.fr/fr/actions-france_830/ong-organisations-non-gouvernementales_1052.

2. See *Coordination SUD*, 'Les Associations de Solidarité Internationale et l'État', cited in *Commissariat Général* (2002: 179).

3. According to the CCD (2008: 3), the 18 largest French NGOs have a budget of over M€10, whilst the 46 smallest have less than €200,000 to spend.

4. Resources from the French state amounted to 21 per cent of total French NGO revenue in 2005 (excluding the tsunami factor). They represented 15 per cent of official funding available to large NGOs, compared to 34 per cent and 49 per cent, respectively, for medium-sized and small NGOs (CCD, 2008: 22).

5. For a legal history of the French non-profit sector, see *Conseil d'État*, 'Rapport Public 2000: Jurisprudence et Avis de 1999', *Études et Documents*, no. 51, Documentation Française, Paris, 2000.

6. In his famous study, *De la Démocratie en Amérique* (1835 and 1840), Alexis de Tocqueville noted that there was a much stronger civic culture in America than in France, where the rise of a powerful centralised state, legitimised by Republican ideals, militated against the emergence of a dynamic 'associative' life within French society.

7. For the text of this law, see http://www.legifrance.gouv.fr/.

8. Public utility status was typically only granted by the Council of State to large, well-known and privately funded NGOs, with at least 200 members (Rubio, 2004: 41).

9. The French state offered co-funding of NGO projects on a 50/50 basis. This compared unfavourably with Finland (60 per cent), Belgium, Germany and Ireland (75 per cent), Norway and Sweden (80 per cent) and Denmark and Holland (up to 100 per cent) (OECD, 1988: 97).

10. The BLONG took over from an earlier *Bureau des Œuvres Privées*, which provided subsidies to religious missions engaged in educational work as well as to faith-based volunteer agencies. It had only five members of staff and was chronically underfunded (Devin, 1999: 69–72).

11. As long as they are non-profit making, French associations are exempt from paying VAT and various corporation taxes; see www.legislationline.org/.

12. Commercial activities are allowed, as long as they contribute to a philanthropic social goal and never enter into competition with the services of companies operating in the same sector (*Commissariat Général*, 2002: 41).

13. This level of relief was allowed on up to 5 per cent of a company's annual turnover. See F. Fiard, 'Redynamiser le mécénat et la générosité', *Aventure*, no. 98, autumn 2003, www.la-guilde.org/article.php3?id_article=322.

14. These associations include the *Restos du Coeur*, the SC-CF, the *Secours Populaire*, the Salvation Army and the Red Cross.

15. A variation on these programmes are *Dotations au Partenariat*, whereby a cluster of French NGOs develop management and other training programmes for non-state actors in the Southern hemisphere (Ibid).

16. In 2005, the French state allotted some M€1.7 to help NGOs employ staff through this scheme (CCD, 2008: 23).

17. This requirement is written into the labour codes via a law passed on 4 February 1995 (Rubio, 2004: 49).

18. The French Foreign Ministry has, moreover, agreed with the World Bank that France's 'Fiduciary Trust for Consultants', which funds World Bank-coordinated consultancies of up to 60 days and technical studies lasting around 190 days, should now be open to bids from French NGOs (World Bank, 2001: 34–5).

19. Previously, these commissions, which review France's development assistance programmes to specific countries, had excluded NGOs and invited only politicians and officials from France and the beneficiary country. Since 1994, a technical secretariat has been in place to help organise the participation of French NGOs and local authorities in these commissions; see www.resacoop.org/fiches/fic_pg42.htm.

20. The HCCI has, nonetheless, piloted a project in Senegal in 2001 (*Commissariat Général*, 2002: 94).

21. Since 1999, the CICID itself has met every two months and involved the dozen or so ministries involved in French foreign aid policy.

22. http://www.diplomatie.gouv.fr/fr/actions-france_830/

23. The CNVA was formed in 1983 and examines wide-ranging issues affecting all French associations. The working group behind the 2002 *Commissariat Général* report included representatives from NGOs such as *Handicap International*, the CIDR, *Écoliers du Monde*, the CCFD, the ACF and the CIRAD.

24. *Le Figaro Magazine*, 18 November 2006, p. 23.

25. These NGOs are the *Agence d'Aide à la Coopération Technique et au Développement* (ACTED), the AFVP, the GRET, *Handicap International*, *Partage*, *Première Urgence* and *Solidarités* (Ibid).

26. Donations to NGOs benefiting from the higher rate of tax relief rose by 291 per cent between 1995 and 1999 and the number of households donating increased by 70,000. Those on the lower rate saw only an increase in donations of 11 per cent and a fall in the number of donor households of 62,000 (CCD, 2001a: 7).

27. *Agence France Presse*, 7 September 2006.

28. The original thinking behind these new arrangements can be traced back to a report by Bernard Husson, Director of the NGO, CIEDEL; see B. Husson (ed.), *Recherche pour la Diversification et la Contractualisation des Rapports entre les ONG et les Institutions Publiques*, CCD, Paris, 1991.

29. Note that large volumes of official co-funding were secured in the late 1990s by NGDOs such as the CIDR (M€0.7), *Eau Vive* (M€2.1) and *Environnement et Développement du Tiers Monde* or ENDA (M€1.1); see Potevin (2000: 11).

30. Note that the CCD is assisted greatly in the preparation of these financial overviews by RITIMO.

31. Created, in 2000, by the *Guilde Européenne du Raid*, this NGDO agency specialises in micro-credit.

32. Blum's statistics are drawn mainly from the CCD report (2003: 6). The percentage figure for the United States is given in Carrez (2003: 54).

33. Comments to the French Senate by Alain Pichon of the *Cour des Comptes* on 25 October 2005; see www.senat.fr/rap/r05-046/r05-0467.html.

34. Procedural details given in Potevin (2000: 17).

35. NGDOs can only benefit from this form of funding where, for example, the size of the development programme does not exceed 35 per cent of their annual budget over the last three years (*Cour des Comptes*, 2005).

36. Classic micro projects attracted far more MCNG funding, and volunteer agencies received half of all co-funding in the same year (Ibid).

37. These opinions have related to issues ranging from sustainable development through to good governance, health, higher education and research. Two-thirds of them were at the request of the French government or the National Assembly's Finance Committee (OECD, 2004: 25).

38. Comments to the French Foreign Affairs Committee, 'Report of Meeting no. 33', Wednesday 16 May 2001, www.assemblée-nationale.fr.

39. The NGO representative is, nonetheless, often consulted either ahead or after meetings of the CICID.

40. Comments by *Coordination SUD* President, Henri Rouillé d'Orfeuil, in CCD (2001a: 13).

6 Towards professionalisation?

1. Note that *développementalistes* also have to manage the more difficult task of filtering down state-led demands for greater professionalism to local partner organisations, charged with delivering development programmes.

2. New Public Management is a philosophy used by governments since the 1980s. It seeks to modernise the public sector and orient it more towards the market and greater efficiency, whilst at the same time minimising any negative social side effects; see, in this context, Boston *et al.* (1996).

3. Facing competition from American faith-based NGOs, the *Secours Catholique* has, nonetheless, moved from three to six collections per year (Interview with François Mabille, 2003).

4. The most infamous advertisement was probably the *Action Contre la Faim* poster showing two images of the Somalian girl, Leila: one of her emaciated during the famine and one of a well-fed girl after the supply of food aid. NGDOs, such as *Secours Catholique* and *ATD Quart Monde*, have been among the most reluctant to engage in such techniques or, indeed, any other marketing strategies (Condamines, 1989: 45).
5. The RITIMO (2006) guide explains, for example, how donations in the form of food, clothes, medicines and books are often ill-adapted to local needs and can disrupt local producers.
6. See the annual survey by the CCFD (*Baromètre de la Solidarité*). See also Fondation de France, *La Générosité des Français, Étude sur les Dons Déclarés (1990–1994)*, *Fondation de France*, Paris, 1996.
7. For studies of these management issues, see Dauvin *et al.* (2002) and Deler *et al.*, 1998.
8. See www.crid.asso.fr for the campaign by the CRID ahead of the 2001 French local elections (*Ma Commune, C'est la Planète*).
9. See A. Hudson, 'Making the Connections' in Lewis and Wallace (2000: 94).
10. These federations were the CRID (1976) and CLONG-V (1978).
11. For the genesis of this federation and the role of the 'Group of 21' (NGO and other leaders who engaged in close negotiations with President François Mitterrand's first socialist government), see J.-C. Dubarry, *Analyse de l'Enquête de l'Intercollectif*, PhD, Grenobles, 1984.
12. www.hcci.gouv.fr/lecture/synthese/histoire-osi-ong.htm#a.
13. Paradoxically, in 1980, some NGOs refused to take part in an awareness-raising initiative by the government-led *Association pour la Recherche et l'Information sur l'Aide au Développement* (ARIADE). They argued that the state would be securing too great an influence over public opinion on overseas development matters. ARIADE was disbanded in 1983 after organising a Third World day for schools in October 1981, a poster campaign and several television programmes; see J.-M. Hatton, *Les OSI et le Développement du CRID*, report to the FNDVA, CRID, Paris, 1998.
14. See comments by J.-M Hatton, former President of the CRID (1986–90) in the Preface to Maradeix (1991).
15. For a detailed account, see Hatton *et al.* (2006).
16. This committee was launched by French President Charles De Gaulle in response to a famine appeal by the Food and Agriculture Organisation. It included leading French trade unions, the Red Cross, the SC-CF and the CCFD. In 1994, it became the CFSI; see Hatton (2006).
17. A precursor to the CLOSI, the *Intercollectif des Associations de Solidarité Internationale et de Développement*, was formed in 1982. This brought together 72 associations and carried out, with Development Ministry support, the first substantial survey of the NGO sector. See Intercollectif, *Les Associations Nationales de Développement (ONG): Enquête Realisée auprès de 61 ONG*, Intercollectif, Paris, 1982.
18. Among the French NGOs which benefit from this status are MSF, MDM, ACF, the CCFD, SC-CF and the DCC.
19. This latter scheme, which came into force in 2006, is supposed to move the entire administration from 'management by means' to 'management by objectives' as well as ensuring accountability 'right up to the last euro' OECD (2004: 62).

20. Note that 41.1 per cent of French central state resources go to the top 55 French NGOs (CCD, 2008: 19).

21. Government funding has enabled this federation to increase its staff from around three in the early 1990s to 12 in 2003 (Interview with *Coordination SUD*, 2003)

22. The French Education Ministry, in consultation with the CCD, adapted the French education system to take account of the need for awareness-raising work (CCD, 1987: 158). Organisations such as the *Réseau Éducation au Développement* in Montpellier now provide bulletins for teachers on themes, such as sustainable development. For more detail on the evolution of teacher training in this field, see E. Servonnat, *Les Enseignants face à l'Éducation au Développement*, Mémoire, Toulouse, Université le Mirail, September 1996.

23. Furthermore, all NGO bids for projects in Senegal and for health projects in Mali are now referred to France's local aid mission in these countries. They are then subjected to examination by representatives of the French and Senegalese/Malian states and civil societies. See Foreign Ministry, *Vade-Mecum: le Cofinancement des Projets des OSI*, vol. 1, 2002, p. 104.

24. The F3E was formed out of a merger of two smaller units set up a few years earlier, namely the *Fonds d'Études Préalables* (FEP) and the *Fonds pour les Évaluations et les Études transversales* (FEE). Its evaluation work is now mainly carried out by consultancy-type NGDOs, such as the GRET, IRAM and CIRAD.

25. This network was formed in 1995 and is specialised in rural development in the South. It has a 5000-strong membership, two-thirds of which are located in Africa. Financed by the French Foreign Ministry, it serves as a forum for the exchange of expertise (*Commissariat Général*, 2002: 169).

26. For a summary of this survey, see S. Gouraud, 'Le Volontariat de Solidarité Internationale', *Aventure*, no. 98, autumn 2003, www.la-guilde.org/article. php3?id_article=286.

27. In 1979, half of all volunteers were *coopérants* undertaking an alternative to national service, whereas this proportion had fallen to under 20 per cent in 1998 (CCD, 2001b: 70).

28. For newsletters, see, for example, the bi-monthly *Messages du Secours Catholique* and two-monthly *Causes Communes* (CIMADE). For guides, see RITIMO, *Partir pour être Solidaire*, RITIMO, Paris, 2002; and V. Hordan-Pinaud, *Les Métiers de la Solidarité Internationale*, L'Harmattan, Paris, 1997. Some RITIMO centres also have starter kits for volunteers.

29. The GEMDEV was created in 1983 and is a scientific interest group attached to the French Ministry for Higher Education and Research.

30. One such dispute involved federations geared towards overseas operations and those oriented towards work in France. The latter, which included youth movements, believed that the CRID, CLONG-V and *Coordination d'Agen* should pay more towards the cost of the running of *Coordination SUD*; see Hatton *et al.* (2006).

31. According to the CCD (2008: 7), 112 of the NGOs it surveyed belong to a network, with only 47 organisations (over half of which were very small) operating completely outside of such a framework.

32. Such qualifications include France's 'Higher National Diploma' in prosthetics, much needed by organisations like *Handicap International*.

33. Cited in *Le Point*, 7 May 2002.

34. Cited in *Le Point*, 7 May 2002.

35. In 2005, French NGOs employed 29,477 overseas local staff and 4,462 expatriates (including 2204 volunteers), together with 4,659 volunteers and 366 internees active in France (CCD, 2008, 35).
36. *Coordination SUD* (2004: 64), for example, puts the figure at 150,000 *bénévoles*.
37. Official funding from this scheme dried up in 2007 to the dismay of some NGDOs, which had used it to take on young employees without incurring the heavy social security costs associated with recruitment; see comments by Senator Michel Destot to French Foreign Affairs Committee following the submission of the Blum (2005) report on 13 April 2005.
38. According to the CCD (2008: 41), only 41 of the organisations surveyed did not subject their accounts to any specific checks. Some 108 employed auditors and 10 bookkeepers, whilst 14 NGOs had their accounts checked by the *Comité de la Charte* and 16 saw their books scrutinised by the *Cour des Comptes* in 2005.
39. The Salvation Army, ARC and the *Association Française contre les Myopathies* (AFM) have all undergone such audits; see *Le Point*, 22 November 2007.
40. http://stephanie.dupont3.free.fr/derives.htm. The fall-out from these cases was extremely damaging and prompted the French press to publish inflammatory articles, asking 'Where are the billions donated to charity all going?', 'What is your money being used for?' and 'What are they doing with your donations?' Cited in Haddad (2002: 49).
41. Note also that checks are only effected on NGOs which collect more than €500,000 a year in donations (Blum 2005: 28).
42. This report focused on *Coordination SUD* and three NGDOs: the GRET, AFDI and *Eau Vive*.
43. See www.coordinationsud.org/article.php3?id_article=770.
44. See CRID, 'Dire la solidarité', *Les Cahiers de la Solidarité*, May 1998.
45. See www.coordinationsud.org.
46. Since 2000, RITIMO is accredited by the Education Ministry as a complementary teaching establishment. In this capacity, it has the right to engage in teacher training and other activities in the school and university sectors.
47. CCFD, *Terre d'Avenir: Rapport d'Évaluation*, CCFD, Paris, June 1992.
48. This event had its origins in the *Assises de la Coopération et de la Solidarité Internationale*. It first took place in October 1997 and is now a regular nation-wide gathering of all French state and non-state actors involved in international development.
49. See C. Cyrot and A. Saou, *Évaluation de la Semaine de la Solidarité* (no. 174, synthesis report), 2004, www.f3e.asso.fr/spip.php?rubrique222&var_recherche=semaine%20solidarite.
50. This federation is coordinated by the CFSI in France, SOS Hunger in Belgium and SOS Hunger in Luxembourg.
51. www.comitecharte.org/ewb_pages/p/presentation_historique.php. Around 20 of the 80 members are local authorities; see www.f3e.asso.fr/spip.php?rubrique6.
52. See www.f3e.asso.fr. These preparatory costs are usually 8 per cent of the total budget for the study and were originally somewhere between 3000 and 20,000 francs.
53. For details of the *Comité d'Échanges, de Réflexion et d'Informations sur les Systèmes Épargne-crédit*, see www.cerise-microfinance.org/publication/pdf/cerise-RA2003.pdf.
54. For F3E guides on methodology, evaluation, impact, monitoring and the logical framework, see http://f3e.asso.fr/spip.php?rubrique291.

55. See, for example, C. Cyrot and E. Paquot, *CRID- Évaluation du Programme Acteurs Solidaires 1996–2000*, (135 Ev.), March 2003.
56. Some evaluations have already thrown up issues, such as the importance of more diverse and effective partnerships with companies; see E. Paquot *et al.*, *Artisans du Monde- Évaluation du Collectif "De l'Éthique sur l'Étiquette"*, (115 Ev.), July 2003.
57. This group was created in 1993 and it set up, around ten years later, an expert panel within *Coordination SUD* known as the 'Synergy Quality Project'. Its aim was to identify best practice in humanitarian operations.
58. Other such attempts to define and measure quality include the *People in Aid Code* and a European code of practice known as the *Déclaration de Madrid*.
59. The FIDH is one exception, allocating 10 to 20 per cent of the cost of its programmes to evaluation (Ibid).
60. This type of professionalism gives preference to rich over poor, blueprints over adaptation, things over people, quantity over quality and the powerful over the weak.
61. Following the ARC scandal, the share of total French NGO revenue from private sources fell from 61 per cent in 1991 to 58 per cent in 1994 (Devin, 1999: 72).

7 Working for or working on the state?

1. Citing a CCFD publication (*Fêtes et Saisons*, no. 391, 1981), Joly (1985: 31) notes how 'For one lot, the abuse of human rights is synonymous with dictatorships, torture, imprisonment, psychiatric clinics; for the others, it is hunger, shanty towns, illiteracy, unemployment, the absence of healthcare.'
2. Note, however, that the more militant *urgencier*, MDM, has participated in the *Agir Ici* campaign against the privatisation of basic services; taken part in social forums in Europe and Porto Alegre; and even chaired workshops at these *altermondialiste* gatherings; see S. Cohen 'ONG: Une Implication à Géometrie Variable' in Fougier (2004: 39).
3. This 'Campaign for Access to Essential Medicines' was launched in 1999 to protest against the prohibitive price of life-saving drugs, encourage research into much-needed but less lucrative medicines, and secure an 'exemption' from free trade rules on medical products. See www2.paris.msf.org/site/site.nsf/.
4. According to Algrin (1988), the CCFD used donations to fund Marxist-leaning organisations involved in social agitation in Latin America and Africa.
5. The French administration did actually carry out a very large number of micro-level projects, but did so through its own official missions rather than through NGOs.
6. See W.W. Rostow, *The Stages of Economic Growth*, Cambridge University Press, Cambridge, 1960.
7. For the full definition by the CIMADE, see Joly (1985: 32).
8. For a review of these arguments, see www.hcci.gouv.fr/lecture/synthese/sy001.htm.
9. Micro-credit schemes began in earnest in the 1980s. They involve small loans over a short period to individuals or groups of individuals, often women, who do not have access to classic banking services. Ethical investments began in France in the 1980s, whilst fair trade has been propounded by French NGDOs since the 1960s.
10. For example, in October 1990, *Frères des Hommes* asked its members to send postcards to the French President calling on him to do more to promote democracy

in Zaire. This country and Togo were also the focus of a highly critical 'counter-summit' organised by *Agir Ici, Survie* and French NGDOs in 1994; see Agir Ici and Survie, *L'Afrique à Biarritz*, Karthala, Paris, 1995.

11. MSF withdrew its humanitarian operation from Rwandan refugee camps in Zaire in November 1994, claiming that Hutu militiamen were using the camps to prepare attacks on Rwanda's Tutsis.
12. FDH, *Une Seule Terre*, September–October 1991, p. 3.
13. *TDH-France* and *Peuples Solidaires* have called for an additional protocol, which would be added to the 1966 Pact on Economic and Social Rights and would give peoples legal recourse at the national and international level. A working group on this issue was formed within the CRID in 2002.
14. The value of NGDOs in this context has been enhanced by the fact that the French authorities have drastically reduced the number of overseas technical assistants from 23,000 in the early 1980s to around 2000 at the turn of the millennium (Penne, 2002: 63).
15. Although *urgenciers* predominated, the CCFD was also present in Rwanda at this time, helping a consortium of Belgian associations to reconstruct the judicial system (CCD, 1999: 40).
16. M. Doucin, 'Société Civile Internationale et Diplomatie: l'Exception Française', in Samy Cohen *Les Diplomates, Négocier dans un Monde Chaotique*, Autrement, Paris, 2002, pp. 90–1.
17. France effectively doubled its contribution from M€150 in 2004 to M€300 in 2006; it is now the world's largest donor to this fund; see www.ambafrance-ca.org/.
18. www.diplomatie.gouv.fr/fr/pays-zones-geo_833/.
19. According to the OECD (2004: 34), the proportion of French bilateral assistance rose from 62 to 76 per cent (compared to an OECD average of 36 per cent) between 1999 and 2002.
20. Official figures suggest that 46 per cent of this assistance has been directed to sub-Saharan Africa, with 9 per cent going to the Maghreb and Middle East. The actual share of co-funding to the African continent is, however, nearer to two-thirds of the total when Foreign Ministry allocations of aid to projects in France (15 per cent of total) are removed from its statistics; see DGCID, *Rapport d'Activité*, DGCID, Paris, 2002.
21. The funding for projects in Africa in 2002 included M€878 for *Eau Vive* in the Sahel; M€872 for the CCFD in Morocco, M€480 for a Senegal river project by the *Groupe de Recherche et de Réalisations pour le Développement Rural* (GRDR), M€395 for the CCFD in Central Africa and M€281 for a food security project by *Afrique Verte* in the Sahel; see *Cour des Comptes* (2005: 47).
22. In 2002, the share of co-funding amounted to 13 per cent for Latin America and the Caribbean and 11 per cent for Asia; see DGCID, *Rapport d'Activité*, DGCID, Paris, 2002.
23. Comments by Philippe Étienne to the French Senate; cited in Charasse (2005: 17).
24. This post was given, in 1991, to Michel Faucon, former President of the CRID (1986–90).
25. According to the French Foreign Ministry (Potevin, 2000: 9), France devoted 60 per cent of its co-funding monies to volunteer agencies, which was far more than the European average of between 10 and 30 per cent.
26. France has marked her distinctiveness from Anglo-Saxon donors and most of the G8, by sending Ministers to attend all the World Social Forums and contributing

to the funding of the G8 counter-summit in Évian and the European Social Forum in 2003 Fougier (2006: 7).

27. President Chirac mooted the idea of a Tobin tax at the 2002 Johannesburg summit. France actually introduced a scheme for 'taxing' airline tickets in 2006. The latter will bring in M€200 a year, 90 per cent of which will be for UNITAID (an international facility to purchase medicines) and 10 per cent will help reimburse monies borrowed under the International Financial Facility (a fund for purchasing life-saving vaccines); see Carrez (2006).

28. Speech by President Jacques Chirac at the 2002 Johannesburg summit; see *Xinhua*, 3 September 2002.

29. The Franco–Swedish working party dismissed any idea of a 'global government'. Similarly, in 2006, the French inter-ministerial forum the CIDIC, adopted a policy on global public goods but restricted this issue to efforts to prevent the spread of pandemic diseases, the protection of biodiversity and global warming; see DGCID, *Les Notes du Jeudi,* no. 61, 21 September 2006, DGCID, Paris.2006

30. In 1996, the French government terminated its contract with FONJEP, in response to protests from the *Cour des Comptes* (2005) and the European Commission over the way the state-FONJEP relationship breached European competition laws.

31. Note that the FONJEP and AFVP enjoy a significantly greater share of total official funding than second tier NGO beneficiaries: the *Secours Catholique* (3.4 per cent), the GRET (3.3 per cent) and the CCFD (2.0 per cent). Figures relate to 2003; see http://www.diplomatie.gouv.fr.

32. According to Godfrain (2004: 11), a majority of the 1811 volunteers in 2003 were active in the education, training and health sectors. They were, moreover, qualified primarily in the fields of health (19 per cent), education (13 per cent), management and accounting (10 per cent), agronomy (6 per cent) and business and economics (6 per cent).

33. Cited in *Commissariat Général* (2002: 179).

34. Private funding made up 86, 72 and 69.5 per cent of the budgets of MSF, MDM and *Handicap International*, respectively, in 2003; see www.hcci.gouv.fr/lecture/synthese/histoire-osi-ong.htm#a.

35. Around 80 per cent of state assistance to NGOs has come in a relatively untied form, with only 20 per cent falling under the rubric of funding placed 'under convention'; comments by Philippe Etienne in Charasse (2005: 32).

36. Whilst a quarter of France's official bilateral aid programme is devoted to education, this assistance is focused less on primary education and more on secondary schools for French expatriates, sponsorship of African elites and subsidies for higher education; see DGCID, *Rapport d'Activité*, DGCID, Paris, 2005.

37. In his concluding statement, President Chirac thanked NGOs involved in the counter-summit to the G8 meeting in Évian and asserted that their views on many issues were 'of a nature to influence the thinking and decision-making processes of the summit; see Jacques Chirac, Press Conference, 3 June 2003, Évian, www.g8.fr/evian/english/navigation/news/news_update.

38. Note that French NGOs at the 1992 Rio Earth summit prepared two documents: *Construire la Démocratie Internationale* (to be annexed to the French government's own report) and a *White Paper* prepared by the CRID and other federations (CCD, 1999: 44).

39. CRID, 'Solidarité internationale: nouveaux enjeux, nouveaux acteurs', *Cahiers de la Solidarité*, no. 12, CRID, Paris, October 2002, p. 5.

40. See, for example, the CCFD campaign, launched in March 2001 and entitled 'Mets la Pression', which called for better coordination and higher volumes of development aid (www.ccfd.asso.fr).
41. Mgr André Lacrampe (Bishop of Ajaccio), 'Carême et solidarité: Dette des pays pauvres et aide au développement', 5 February, 2002, www.cef.fr/catho/actus/archives/2002.
42. See Agir Ici, *Assez de Promesses: Annulons la Dette*, campaign no. 70, March–July 2005.
43. The CRID (2002: 9) has, in fact, subscribed to the Millennium Development Goals 'as long as they are deemed a minimum'.
44. For a French NGDO critique of PRSPs, see www.hcci.gouv.fr/lecture/synthese/sy001.htm.
45. OXFAM was dubbed by many French NGDOs as 'ultra-liberal' (Fougier, 2004: 81–4) following its publication of a paper calling for greater integration of developing countries into the free market system; see Kevin Watkins and Penny Fowler, *Rigged Rules and Double Standards: Trade, Globalisation, and the Fight against Poverty*, OXFAM, Oxford, 2002.
46. Among the most prominent French NGDOs within this movement are the CCFD, the CRID, *Peuples Solidaires* and *TDH-France*. See Allait (2007: 103) and Annex C.
47. See, for example, Agir Ici, *Le Dumping Commercial: l'Europe Casse la Barbuque en Afrique*, campaign no. 20, October–November 1993; *Favorisons un Commerce Nord/Sud*, October–November 1993, campaign no. 20 bis; and *FMI: Sortir de l'ImPAS*, April–September 2000, campaign no. 50.
48. See CRID, 'Position du CRID: L'Aide Publique au Développement', Paris, 26 June 2002, p. 6. *Peuples Solidaires* has held on to this doctrine, whilst widening it to insist that the self-directed development should also involve regional economic integration; see www.peuples-solidaires.org.
49. Mugabe was invited to the 2003 Franco–African summit despite his regime's pariah status (http://news.bbc.co.uk/2/low/africa/2782433.stm). Éyadema received staunch support from France for almost 40 years (http://news.bbc.co.uk/2/hi/africa/830774.stm), while Biya continues to benefit from French indulgence (see Chapter 9).
50. These include the 1948 Universal Declaration of Human Rights and the 1966 Protocol on Economic and Social Rights.
51. See L. Levi, 'Globalization and a World Parliament', *The Federalist Debate*, no. 2, 2001, pp. 4–6. See also Agir Ici, *Halte à l'OMC: Campagne pour un Accès Universel aux Services Fondamentaux*, campaign no. 62. This called for basic services to be exempt from the drive towards privatisation spearheaded by the WTO.
52. For a list of self-funded CCFD projects, see CCFD, *Commission Diocèses-National Projets*, CCFD, Paris 18–19 October.

8 A resource dependence perspective

1. Note that the terms 'misreading' and 'correctly interpreting' are not normative statements but should be taken to imply consistency or inconsistency with the logic of RD theory.
2. For a study of the profile and social background of those recruited by leading French *urgenciers*, see Dauvin *et al.* (2002).
3. Archambault (1997: 48) estimates that the 1901 law has facilitated the creation every year of around 70,000 associations.

4. MSF considers itself an international rather than a French player, but does attend all important meetings involving French NGOs (Interview with *Solagral*, 2003).

5. See, in this context, the 15 or so *Dossiers Noirs* produced by *Agir Ici/ Survie*; and the annual report on French overseas development policy, compiled by the *Observatoire Permanent de la Coopération Française* (OPCF).

6. Between 1996 and 2002, only about ten French NGOs benefited from the early schemes (the *conventions programmes*) funded under the new contractual arrangements; see F. Fiard, *communiqué* in *Aventure*, no. 96, autumn 2002, www.la-guilde.org.

7. Other examples include the absorption of Band Aid (created in 1984 by Sir Bob Geldof) into *MDM-France* in 1991; and the more recent partnership between OXFAM and its closest ally in France, *Agir Ici* (Ryfman, 2004: 78).

8. Seventeen of the 23 French regions included overseas development activities in their work schedule for 2000–06; see CRID, *Les Cahiers de la Solidarité*, February 2004. Three thousand territorial authorities are thought to be active in 115 countries with an estimated budget of M€200 (OECD, 2004: 34).

9. According to the CCD (2008: 19), 77.8 per cent of international resources go to the top 18 French NGOs.

10. See L. F. Salmen an A. P. Eaves, 'Interactions between NGOs, Governments and the World Bank', in Paul and Israel (1991: 94–133).

11. Membership of ECOSOC imposes an obligation on NGOs to 'behave themselves' or risk losing this accreditative status under the provisions of UN Resolution 1996/31 (Herlemont, 2002: 112).

12. Exceptions to the rule include NGDOs such as *Mission d'Aide au Développement des Économies Rurales* (MADERA), the GRET and IRAM, which received 82.5, 58.8, 43.3 per cent, respectively, of their resources from international (mainly European) sources in 2004–05 (CCD, 2008: 30–2).

13. At least one in five perfectly good applications are rejected by the Commission; see D. Haslam, 'Untying Aid and the NGO Co-financing Budget Line', BOND, October 2004, www.globalpolicy.org/ngos/fund/2004/1004untying.htm. In 2000, moreover, the European Commissioner Poul Nielson curbed funding to the liaison committee for NGOs vis-à-vis the EU (then called the CLONGD-EU), precipitating its demise and the emergence of CONCORD.

14. For details of the subsequent bankruptcy of this organisation in 1998, see M. Deprost, *ÉquiLibre, une Faillite Humanitaire*, Éditions Golias, Paris, 2003.

15. The European Commission has moved beyond its previous 50/50 co-financing arrangements but now insists that NGOs provide financial contributions rather than offers of staff time (*Cour des Comptes*, 2005).

16. According to the CCD (2001: 20), administrative costs associated with raising funds from the general public eat up 19.5 per cent of the revenue secured.

17. Comment by E. Barrau, 'ONG: Entre exigence d'indépendance et recherche de financement', *Aventure*, no. 93, autumn 2001, www.la-guilde.org/article.php3?id_article=348.

18. Comment by E. Barrau, 'ONG: Entre exigence...', *Aventure*, no. 93, autumn 2001. Such employees are thought by some NGDOs to be engaging in 'humanitarian tourism'.

19. See C. Jacquiau, *Les Coulisses du Commerce Équitable*, Mille et Une Nuits, Paris, 2006.

20. The figures for France improved following the 2004 tsunami, when between 65 and 67 per cent of French adults claimed to have made a donation; see *La Nouvelle République du Centre Ouest*, 7 December 2005.

21. On average, leading *urgenciers* received between M€9 and M€10 compared to M€2.4 for the CCFD. These figures exclude the *Croix Rouge Française* which, as the main campaign coordinator received M€113 and the SC-CF, which as an arm of the Church straddling the *urgencier*-NGDO divide, collected M€34 (Blum, 2007: 48).
22. In 1996, this 'barometer' found domestic poverty to be the top priority for 63 per cent of French people, with overseas development coming in sixth place with only 6 per cent.
23. http://stephanie.dupont3.free.fr/derives.htm.
24. See Chrisian Troube, *Les Forcénés de l'Humanitaire: Les Leçons de l'Arche de Zoé*, Autrement, Paris, 2008.
25. In 1999, only 42.5 per cent of French people expressed confidence in NGOs; see CCFD, *Baromètre de la Solidarité Internationale des Français*, CCFD, Paris, 10th survey, 1999.
26. The *Guilde Européenne du Raid* has engaged in a policy of *portage* towards associations such as *Enfants du Mékong* and *Enfance Espoir*; see S. Gouraud, 'Un parcours de citoyenneté', *Aventure*, no. 98, autumn 2003, www.la-guilde.org/article. php3?id_article=286.
27. See www.crid.asso.fr for the campaign ahead of the 2007 Presidential elections (*L'État d'Urgence Planétaire: Votons pour une France Solidaire*).
28. The most infamous law-suit was taken out, in 2001, against *Survie* by three African heads of state, namely Omar Bongo (Gabon), Idriss Déby (Tchad) and Dénis Sassou-Nguesso (Congo). They claimed that the book, written by this organisation and entitled *Noir Silence*, constituted a defamation of foreign heads of state.
29. See I. Sommier, *Les Nouveaux Mouveaux Contestaires*, Flammarion, Paris, 2003, pp. 176–89.
30. To illustrate, the CCFD called, in the late 1980s, for 10 per cent of French aid to be reserved specifically for French NGO project work; see C. Le Proux, *Les Relations Extérieures du CCFD*, CCFD, Paris, p. 52.
31. For a list of CRID, *Agir ici* and Eurostep campaigns, see, respectively, www.crid. asso.fr, www.oxfamfrance.org/ and www.eurostep.org/.
32. DIAL or *Développement, Institutions et Analyses de Long terme* is a research unit, which brings together the expertise of the AFD and the IRD.
33. www.diplomatie.gouv.fr/fr/actions-france_830/ong-organisations-non-gouvernementales_1052/.
34. According to the French Foreign Ministry, some of the larger subsidies have gone to the CICDA (M€2.44), JISF (M€4.57) and the CCFD (M€ 2.29) (Potevin, 2000: 11).
35. See F. Verschave, *Noir Chirac*, Arènes, Paris, 2002; F. Verschave, *Complicité de génocide? La Politique de la France au Rwanda*, La Découverte, Paris, 2004; and Agir Ici and Survie, *France-Zaire-Congo 1960–1997*, Harmattan, Paris, 1997.
36, See respectively, S. Brunel, Le *Gaspillage de l'Aide Publique*, Seuil, Paris, 1994; Lancaster (1999); and (OECD, 2004).
37. In the mid-1990s, Archambault (1997: 210) observed not only that there was 'no education in philanthropy' in state-run (as opposed to private Catholic) schools in France, but also that there was a decline in 'the traditional civic education which taught children about public concerns'.
38. Cited in T. Allen, 'The Future of International NGO Programme', Summary Paper for BOND, June 2004, www.bond.org.uk/pubs/futures/launch_writeup.pdf.

39. For the report of the first of these *Assises* or periodic gatherings of local author-ities, mayors and civil society actors interested in international development, see French Foreign Ministry, *L'Action Internationale des Collectivités Locales*, Foreign Ministry, Paris, 2003.
40. See, for example, UNESCO, *Directives concernant les Relations de l'UNESCO avec les Organisations Non-Gouvernementales*, UNESCO, New York, 1995.
41. The UN is also opening its doors increasingly to consultation with French and other NGDOs. Thus, the UN Non-Governmental Liaison Service (NGLS), established in New York in 1975 and Geneva the year after, is now proactive in facilitating NGO participation in UN events and processes. See www.un-ngls.org/documents/publications.en/develop.dossier/dd.04/05.htm#05.
42. In 2001, French NGDOs received 17 per cent of their total resources from the European Commission; and over recent years, they have secured over 8 per cent of the total assistance available from the Commission (Blum, 2005: 18).
43. See, for example, the *Agir Ici* campaign *Exportations de Poulets: l'Europe Plume l'Afrique*, no. 68, October 2004 to February 2005.
44. According to the CCD (2008: 16), some 25 medium-sized and 11 small NGOs received a share of the M€8 disbursed by foundations in 2005. The top 18 NGOs, which secured 79.4 per cent of all private NGO resources only enjoyed 45.9 per cent of the income from foundations.
45. Thus, as one senior CCFD representative made clear to the author: 'In France, we are...the largest NGO in terms of private resources...and the fact that we work with our own resources gives us great autonomy' (Interview, 2003).
46. French members of this last *plateforme* include the CCFD, *Amnesty International-Section Française* and *OXFAM International-Agir Ici*; see http://fra.controlarms.org/pages/080314-news-fra. Their action has helped to generate the EU Code of Conduct on Arms Exports (May 1998), which 'rules out' the sale of arms to coun-tries where they risk being used for internal repression or external aggression. See www.fas.org/asmp/campaigns/code/eucode.html.
47. This is all the more remarkable since private contributions represented, in 1990, only 7.1 per cent of total revenue for the French non-profit sector as a whole (Archambault, 1997: 130).
48. In 2005, an additional M€88 were collected, which were not directly related to the tsunami (Ibid).
49. According to a survey by BVA-CCFD-*La Croix-France Info*, published on 14 October 2004, 59 per cent of French people expressed confidence in NGOs to combat world poverty, compared to only 52 per cent for the French state; see www.coordinationsud.org/article.php3?id_article=770.
50. NGOs 'compete to keep down their declared overheads, as though spending on management were synonymous with inefficiency. Low overheads are thus still a criterion against which public opinion measures an NGO's effectiveness'; see T. Wallace, 'New Development Agendas: Changes in UK NGO Policies and Procedures', *Review of African Political Economy*, vol. 24, no. 71, 1997, pp. 35–55.
51. The CCFD found, in its January 1997 'Baromètère de la Solidarité Internationale', that 49.9 per cent of French people wanted donor states to pay more attention to the social impact of their policies on developing countries, while some 35 per cent thought it 'urgent to consider alternative development models'.
52. See, for instance, G. Prunier, *The Rwanda Crisis*, Hurst, London, 1995.
53. See, for example, Patrick de Saint-Exupéry's articles in *Le Figaro*.

54. The President of *Coordination SUD*, Henri Rouillé d'Orfeuil, recently called for a 'contractual mandate', whereby the state should, in line with the European average, channel 5.1 per cent of total assistance through NGOs; see www.coordinationsud.org/spip.php?article683.
55. The June 2000 Cotonou Agreement requires that European development aid should seek to strengthen civil society in developing countries. The EU also introduced, in 2002, the European Initiative for Democracy and Human Rights, which has helped to reorient European efforts away from electoral assistance and towards a more participatory approach. See Richard Youngs, 'European Approaches to Democracy Assistance', *Third World Quarterly*, vol. 24, 1, 2003, pp. 127–38.
56. For the distinction drawn by Pfeffer and Salancik (1978) between 'efficiency' and 'effectiveness', see the endnotes to Chapter 3.

9 Working together in the field: a case study from Cameroon

1. In 1922, France was given a League of Nations mandate to run four-fifths of this former German protectorate (the other fifth falling under British responsibility). In 1946, Paris was accorded trustee status by the UN but did little to prepare this territory for self-government.
2. Trade unions are included in the standard UN definition, which encompasses 'church-related groups, trade unions, cooperatives, service organizations, community groups and youth organizations, as well as academic institutions'; see United Nations Development Programme, *UNDP and Civil Society*, New York: UNDP, 1993, p. 1. For details of the French government interpretation of the term 'civil society', see Chapter 2.
3. The PCM, in particular, was devoid of any collective strategy and simply provided monies for projects by 15 French civil society actors and around 40 Moroccan partners.
4. See www.f3e.asso.fr. See *Commissariat Général* (2002: 143–5) for a list of the 36 evaluations commissioned by the MCNG up to 2002.
5. Reference is also made in the primary literature to the role of the Cameroonian state as a fourth protagonist. Although the latter is now regularly informed of developments, it was originally out of the loop and remains the main target of most PCPA advocacy work.
6. CCFD, *Demande de cofinancement présentée au Ministère des Affaires Étrangères*, MAE, July 2004.
7. Launched in 1996, then enhanced in 1999, the HIPC was the first comprehensive international effort at debt reduction. It freed up monies for local development and poverty-reduction programmes and broke new ground by allowing the cancellation of debts owed to the World Bank and IMF.
8. The C2D is France's bilateral debt reduction initiative. It complements the multilateral debt relief accorded under the HIPC and is worth M€300 over the first three years and more than a billion euros over its 15-year life span. Cameroon will continue to repay its bilateral debts, but these will be converted into grants and used for poverty-reducing programmes. See www.ambafrance-cm.org/html/camfra/debt.htm.
9. This committee is unique to Cameroon and was formed, at donors' insistence, in December 2000. It is chaired by Cameroon's Finance Minister and has

19 members: 7 from the Cameroonian government, 5 from the donor community and 7 from Cameroonian civil society.

10. The other (Cameroonian) members included *CGT-Liberté, Réseau Éthique, Droits et SIDA, AFISAF, UNAPHAC* and CRAC.
11. This point is reached when a state has implemented its PRSP for one year and adhered to an IMF poverty reduction and growth programme for six months. It had originally been scheduled for 2004 and would have released 90 per cent of Cameroonian debts owed to the World Bank and IMF as well as affording access to bilateral relief under the C2D. It was not reached until mid-1996, at which point the C2D was signed by France and Cameroon.
12. The thematic groups on AIDS and debt include, respectively, AIDES and SC-CF.
13. These bodies include a working group, a federation and several observatories engaged in monitoring the economic and human rights record of the Cameroonian state.
14. The competitive tender for an independent French evaluator was posted on the F3E website, with a closing date of April 2008.
15. The concentration of donors on Cameroon is, at least partly, due to the fact that it experienced colonial rule by Germany, Britain and France.
16. These federations include *Forum Cameroun, Plateforme d'Action et de Développement,* FOSCAM and the *Groupe des 22.*
17. The SCAC, France's aid mission, has barely been involved but is technically responsible for liaising with the Cameroonian government on the programme.
18. French officials have sought to portray this programme as a mechanism which will enable the Cameroonian government to enhance its legitimacy vis-à-vis the electorate and the donor community. They have, in this context, spoken of 'democracy' as a 'long term goal' rather than an immediate objective. See CCFD, *'Demande de Co-financement présentée au MAE'*, July 2004 (unpublished), section 3.1.1.
19. For some experts, civil society has several key functions in shaping democracy, whilst, for others, the causative links are by no means clear. See, respectively, L. Diamond (ed.), *The Democratic Revolution*, New York: Freedom House, 1992; and A.M. Simone and E. Pieterse, 'Civil Societies in an Internationalized Africa', *Social Dynamics*, vol. 19, no. 2, 1993, pp. 41–69.
20. See E. Beaudoux and A. Lambert, *Évaluation Rétrospective des Dotations au Partenariat*, 2004, www.f3e.asso.fr.
21. MCNG, *'Appel à Proposition'*, MCNG, Paris, 2003; see www.diplomatie.gouv.fr.
22. See R.-M. di Donato *et al.*, *Évaluation des Programmes Prioritaires Palestine et Vietnam*, MAE, Paris, 2001.
23. These included the problems involved in agreeing the role of thematic groups; the responsibilities of the PCPA coordinator; and the mechanisms for designating members of steering groups (CCFD, 2006: 38–9).
24. Supervision will be undertaken by the CCFD, the BASC, the JSSC and the French Foreign Ministry.
25. A steering committee comprising the Foreign Ministry, the CCFD, the BASC and the F3E has piloted the lesson-learning process with help from an external consultant from the CIEDEL. The latter organisation has organised a seminar on lessons learned and is preparing a report on this subject. A cross-cutting evaluation has, moreover, been undertaken on the PCPA mechanism as a whole; see CCFD, CFSI, Solidarité Laïque, MAE, *Capitalisation Transversale des Programmes Concertés Pluri-Acteurs*, www.f3e.asso.fr.

26. Notable exceptions include trade union movements, like the *Confédération du Secteur Public*, and church-led organisations, such as *BASC-Caritas* and FEMEC, which operate nationally through local networks.
27. According to the CCFD (2007b: 9): 'Over 100 Cameroonian civil society actors took part in the Bamenda forum, 225 have participated in PCPA training sessions and 160 have been supported by actions financed by this programme'.
28. The French state is not, in fact, interested in multiplying its contacts with either French or Cameroonian civil society. Rather, it seeks to deal with a single contractual partner, who can coordinate the views of all the NGDOs involved in any particular programme. This, indeed, was one of the main reasons why it introduced the 'new contractual arrangements.'
29. There is, nonetheless, a sound RD-related reason for not wishing to see all the project work devolved to local Cameroonian NGOs. Thus, more funding would be accessible to the DEFAP and, above all, the AFVP if they were to act as service providers.
30. They have, nonetheless, updated the SCAC and AFD on progress at meetings with the JSSC in November 2004, January 2005 and November 2005 (CCFD, 2006: 38).
31. The CCFD has, for example, also coordinated the PCM in Morocco (Phase I); and it remains the coordinator of the PCPA in Guinea.
32. In 2003, the CCFD's stake averaged less than €18,000 in the three other projects it was undertaking in Cameroon; see CCFD, *Comission Diocèses- National Projets*, CCFD, Paris, 18–19 October 2003.
33. Other organisations did bid for PCPA monies, and the French NGO known as the Panos Institute is involved in a small MCNG-funded media programme that runs in parallel to the PCPA.
34. For details, see C. Brodin, *'Le Renforcement des Capacités de la Société Civile'*, HCCI report, April 2005, www.hcci.gouv.fr/lecture/etude/renforcement-societe-civile-sud-lutte-pauvrete.html.
35. Eighty per cent of the population speak French and the other 20 per cent speak English. The Anglophone minority has been marginalised since 1972, when the federal system of government, adopted at the time of independence, was replaced by a unitary and Francophone-dominated state. Anglophone Cameroonians have been discriminated against on language grounds and denied equal access to education and to senior civil service jobs. Concentrated in the North and South Western provinces, they have been an easy target for repression. See S. Dicklitch, 'Failed Democratic Transition in Cameroon: A Human Rights Explanation', *Human Rights Quarterly*, vol. 24, 2002, p. 160.
36. Francis Nyamnjoh, 'Cameroon: A Country United by Ethnic Ambition and Difference', *African Affairs*, vol. 98, 1999, p. 115.
37. Despite backing, at the March 2003 Franco–African summit, a joint declaration on Iraq opposing the war, Cameroon was more circumspect later that year as a temporary member of the UN Security Council. See *Agence France Presse*, 8 March 2003.
38. Cameroon is both an oil-producer and a *conduit* to the Atlantic for landlocked countries such as Chad and the Central African Republic (CAR). It has estimated gas reserves of 110.3 billion cubic metres; see *Africa Review World of Information*, 23 September 2003.
39. www.ambafrance-cm.org/html/fracam/consul/comfranc.htm.

40. The French groups to benefit from Cameroonian privatisations include *Bolloré* (Camrail) and *Somdiaa* (Sosucam). Cameroon's economy makes up half the total wealth of the *Communauté Économique et Monétaire d'Afrique Centrale*, which includes Gabon, Chad, Congo Brazzaville, the CAR and Equatorial Guinea; see www.ambafrance-cm.org/html/fracam/agendas/agen2003.htm.
41. www.ambafrance-cm.org/html/camfra/econo/fracem.htm.
42. Côte d'Ivoire has the most and the DRC the second most regular speakers and occasional users of French; see *Haut Conseil de la Francophonie, La Francophonie dans le Monde 2004–2005*, Larousse, Paris, 2005.
43. The SDF is perceived by many Cameroonians as an Anglophone party, supported by Nigeria. The SCNC formed a breakaway 'government' in July 2001 and subsequently applied for membership of the Commonwealth on behalf of the proposed independent Republic of Southern Cameroon.

10 Conclusion: a distinctive role in international development

1. World Vision collects nearly $2 billion (US) across the world every year; 900 million of this is secured by its American branch (Zimet, 2006: 48).
2. See European Commission, *Flash Eurobarometer 151b: Globalisation*, realised by EOS Gallup Europe, November 2003, p. 72 and p. 92. By contrast, only 22 per cent of respondents from Ireland and Sweden shared the first concern; and only 31 and 33 per cent, respectively, harboured the second set of reservations.
3. The first tentative 'partnership framework' was signed, in 2001, between the AFD and *Écoliers du Monde-Aide et Action* (see Chapter 4).
4. Potevin (2000) lists the five largest NGOs in Europe, in 1999, as all being British, German or Dutch: OXFAM (M€196.4), *Misereor* (M€156.7), SCF (M€153.7), *NOVIB* (M€150.2) and another Dutch organisation, *CORDAID* (M€136).
5. Statistical trends suggest that IOs are a more likely candidate to become the critical resource (see Chapter 4). But the support of these actors has been less evenly spread than aid from the state and it has been directed primarily towards large *urgenciers* (CCD, 2008).
6. *OXFAM France-Agir Ici* opened its first shop in Lille, Northern France in 2007; see *Agence France Presse*, 18 April 2007.
7. Comments by Stéphane Hessel to the French Foreign Affairs Committee, *Compte Rendu* no. 33, 16 May 2001, p. 2.
8. www.diplomatie.gouv.fr/fr/actions-france_830/ong-organisations-non-gouvernementales.
9. *La Lettre du Continent*, 5 July 2007.
10. See, respectively, *Les Échos*, 5 June 2007 and *Agence France Presse* 30 November 2007 and 4 June 2007.
11. *Agence France Presse*, 6 June 2007.
12. In 2006, OXFAM France still only had an annual budget of M€1.2, a drop in the ocean compared to the M€650 in resources garnered by OXFAM International. OXFAM France has avoided competing with *Emmaüs International* or *Fédération Artisans du Monde* in the sale of second-hand clothes and fair trade articles; see *Acteurs Publics*, 13 December 2006.
13. *Le Monde*, 18 December 2007.
14. French government pledges relate to the doubling of development assistance to Africa by 2010 and the attainment of the UN target for aid of 0.7 per cent of GNP

by 2012 (promised, but never achieved, by successive French administrations since 1981).

15. The threat of such a diversion of official aid should not be overstated, as these SNGOs are often organically tied in to partnership arrangements with French NGOs, which enable the latter to hold on to the bulk of the funding. According to the World Bank (2001: 44–5), most French non-governmental organisations work with local partners in the South, but, in over half their projects, the French association remains in charge of the operation. Support for local associations amounted to only 10 per cent of NGO expenditure in 2000–01 (CCD, 2005: 25).

Bibliography

Agir Ici (1993), *Les Décideurs Politiques et leurs Relations N/S, Répertoire du Citoyen Solidaire*, Agir Ici, Paris

Algrin, M. (1988), *La Subversion Humanitaire: les Bonnes Œuvres du CCFD*, Jean Picollec, Paris

Allait, E. (2007), *L'Altermondialisme: Mouvance ou Mouvement?*, Ellipses, Paris

Aoust, J.-M. *et al.* (2004), *Quand ONG et PDG Osent*, Eyrolles, Paris

Archambault, E. (1997), *The Non-Profit Sector in France*, Manchester University Press, Manchester

Archambault, E. (1998), 'European System of Accounts: The French Case', *Voluntas*, vol. 9, no. 4, pp. 375–83

Archambault, E. (1999), *Le Secteur sans But Lucratif en France et dans le Monde*, Laboratoire d'Économie Sociale, Paris

Auger, P. and Ferrante, J.-L. (2004), *Greenpeace: Controverses autour d'une ONG*, La Plage, Paris

Barrau, A. (2001), *Rapport d'Information no. 3283*, The Committee on Finance, the Economy and Planning, National Assembly, 26 September

Beaudoux, E. (1996), *Guide Méthodologique: L'Évaluation: Un Outil au Service de l'Action*, IRAM, Paris

Beigbeder, Y. (1992), *Le Role International des Organisations Non Gouvernementales*, Librairie Générale de Droit, Brussels

Bettati, M. and Dupuy, P.-B. (eds) (1986), *Les ONG et le Droit International*, Economica, Paris

Blair, T. (1999), 'The Blair Doctrine', speech to the Chicago Club, 22 April 1999, www.pbs.org/newshour/bb/international/jan-june99/blair_doctrine4-23.html

Blum, R. (2005), *Rapport d'Information sur les ONG Françaises no. 2250*, French Foreign Affairs Committee, National Assembly, 13 April

Blum, R. (2007), *Rapport d'Information no 3743*, French Foreign Affairs Committee, Assemblée Nationale, 20 February

Boisgallais, A.-S. and Fardeau, J.-M. (1994), *La Mouche du Coche, Groupes de Pression et Changement Social, l'Expérience d'Agir Ici*, Fondation pour le Progrès de l'Homme, Paris

BOND (2007), *Freedom of Information Act Consultation: BOND Submission*, March, www.cfoi.org.uk/pdf/BOND.pdf

Bossuyt, J. and Develtere, P. (1995), 'The Financing Dilemma of NGOs', *The Courier ACP-EU*, no. 152, pp. 76–8

Boston, J., Martin, J., Pallot, J. and Walsh, P. (1996), *Public Management: The New Zealand Model*, Oxford University Press, Auckland

Bratton, M. (1989), 'The Politics of Government–NGO Relations in Africa', *World Development*, vol. 17, no. 4, pp. 569–77

Brown, D. and Korten, D. C. (1991), 'Working More Effectively with NGOs', in S. Paul and A. Israel (eds), *Non-governmental Organizations and the World Bank*, World Bank, Washington D.C, pp. 44–93

Brown, S. L. and Eisenhardt, K. M. (1998), 'Competing on the Edge: Strategy as Structured Chaos', Harvard Business Review Press, Boston

Cameron, J. and Mackenzie, R. (1995), *State Sovereignty, Non-Governmental Organisations and Multilateral Institutions*, Foundation for International Environmental Law and Development, London

Campbell, W. J. (1990), *The History of CARE: A Personal Account*, Praeger, New York

Carrez, G. (2003), *Rapport no. 1110*, The Committee on Finance, the Economy and Planning, National Assembly, 9 October

Carrez, G. (2006), *Rapport no. 3363*, The Committee on Finance, the Economy and Planning, National Assembly, 12 October

Cassen, B. (2003), *Tout a Commencé à Porto Alègre...*, Mille Forums Sociaux, Mille et une Nuits, Paris

CCFD (2006), *PCPA Cameroun, Phase Pilote: Compte Rendu Technique Final*, Unpublished Report, CCFD, Paris

CCFD (2007a), *PCPA-Orientations Stratégiques, Année 2*, Unpublished Report, CCFD, Paris, July

CCFD (2007b), *Rapport Final-PCPA Année 1*, Unpublished Report, CCFD, Paris, September

Centre Tricontinental (1997), 'Les ONG: Instruments du Néo-libéralisme ou Alternatives Populaires', *Alternatives Sud*, vol. 5 (special issue)

Cernea, M. (1988), *Nongovernmental Organizations and Local Development*, World Bank Discussion Paper no. 40, Washington, D.C

Chambers, R. (1994), *Challenging the Professions*, Intermediate Technology Publications, London

Chandler, A. (1977), *The Visible Hand*, Harvard University Press, Massachusetts

Charasse, M. (2005), *Rapport no. 46*, Senate session on 'Cour des Comptes Communication: les Fonds Octroyés aux Organisations Non-gouvernementales', 25 October

Clark, A. M. (1995), 'Non-Governmental Organisations and their Influence on International Society', *Journal of International Affairs*, vol. 48, no. 2, pp. 507–25

Clark, J. (1991), *Democratizing Development: The Role of Voluntary Organizations*, Earthscan, London

Cohen, S. (2004), *A Model of its Own? State–NGO Relations in France*, US–France Analysis Series, The Brookings Institution, Washington D.C

Collard, D. (1978), *Altruism and Economy*, Martin Robertson, Oxford

Commissariat Général du Plan (2002), *L'État et les ONG: pour un Partenariat Efficace*, Documentation Française, Paris

CCD (1987), *Argent, Associations, Tiers Monde*, Documentation Française, Paris

CCD (1988, 1995, 2004, 2007), *Solidarité Internationale: Répertoire des Acteurs*, CCD, Paris

CCD (1992, 2001a, 2003, 2005), *Argent et Organisations de Solidarité Internationale*, CCD, Paris

CCD (1999), *Coopération et Solidarité Internationale, une Décennie de Changements*, CCD, Paris

CCD (2001b), *Pour un Volontariat d'Avenir: Regards Croisés sur le Volontariat de Solidarité Internationale*, Documentation Française, Paris

CCD (2008), *Enquête Argent ASI 2004–2005*, Final Provisional Draft (Version 5b), 31 January

Condamines, C. (1989), *L'Aide Humanitaire, entre la Politique et les Affaires*, L'Harmattan, Paris

Conseil Économique et Social (1994), *La Situation et le Devenir des Associations à But Humanitaire*, Direction des Journaux Officiels, Paris

Coordination SUD (2004), *Les ONG dans la Tempête Mondiale*, Éditions Charles Léopold Mayer, Paris

Cour des Comptes (2005), *Les Fonds Octroyés aux Organisations Non-Gouvernementales par le Ministère des Affaires Étrangères*, Communication to the Finance Commission, National Assembly, 15 June

CRID (2002), *Position du CRID: le Financement du Développement Durable*, CRID, Paris, 10 April 2002

Cumming, G. (2007), 'Promoting Democracy in Cameroon: A Revolutionary French Approach?', *International Journal of Francophone Studies*, vol. 10, no. 1, pp. 105–20

Dardelet, B. (1995), *Donner, Ça Coule de Source: Favoriser le Don, Réflexions et Propositions*, Les Presses du Management, Paris

Dauvin, P., Simeant J. and CAHIER (2002), *Le Travail Humanitaire: les Acteurs des ONG, du Siège au Terrain*, Presses de Sciences Po, Paris

Deler, J.-P., Fauré Y.-A., Piveteau A. and Roca J.-P. (1998), *ONG et Développement: Société, Économie, Politique*, Karthala, Paris

Devin, G. (1999), 'Les ONG et les Pouvoirs Publics: le Cas de la Coopération et du Développement', *Pouvoirs*, vol. 88, pp. 65–78

DGCID (2002), *La Coopération Internationale du MAE: DGCID: Bilan et Perspectives*, DGCID, Paris

Dimaggio, P. and Powell, W. W. (1983), 'The Iron Cage', *American Sociological Review*, vol. 48, pp. 147–60

Douglas, J. (1987), 'Political Theories of Non-profit Organisations' in W. W. Powell (ed.), *The Non-Profit Sector: A Research Handbook*, Yale University Press, New Haven

Edwards, M. (1997), 'Organisational Learning in NGOs: What Have We Learned?', *Public Administration and Development*, vol. 17, no. 2, pp. 235–50

Edwards, M. and Hulme, D. (1995), *Performance and Accountability: Beyond the Magic Bullet*, Save the Children/Earthscan, London

Edwards, M. and Fowler, A. (eds) (2002), *The Earthscan Reader in NGO Management*, Earthscan, London

Fowler, A. (1993), 'NGOs as agents of democratisation: an African perspective', *Journal of International Development*, vol. 5, no. 3, pp. 325–339

Fowler, A. (2000), *The Virtuous Spiral: A Guide to Sustainability for Non-Governmental Organisations in Development*, Earthscan, London.

Fowler, A. (2002), 'Options, Strategies and Trade-Offs in Resource Mobilisation', in M. Edwards and A. Fowler (eds), *The Earthscan Reader on NGO Management*, Earthcan, London, pp. 366–85

Fougier, E. (2004), 'Le Mouvement Altermondialiste', *Problèmes Politiques et Sociaux*, no. 897

Fougier, E. (2006), 'La France Face à la Mondialisation', *Problèmes Politiques et Sociaux*, no. 920

French Foreign Ministry (2001), *Organisations de Solidarité Internationale et Pouvoirs Publics en Europe: Étude Comparative*, DGCID, Paris

Froelich, K. A. (1999), 'Diversification of Revenue Strategies: Evolving Resource Dependence in Nonprofit Organizations', *Nonprofit and Voluntary Sector Quarterly*, vol. 28, pp. 246–68

Gloaguen, P. (2002), *Le Guide du Routard de l'Humanitaire*, Hachette, Paris

Godfrain, J. (2004), *Rapport (no. 1556) sur le Projet de Loi relatif au Contrat de Volontariat de Solidarité Internationale*, the French Senate Foreign Affairs Committee, 28 April

Weiss, T. G. and Gordenker, L. (eds) (1996), *NGOs, the UN, and Global Governance*, Lynne Riener, Boulder

Gronbjerg, K. A. (1991), 'Managing Grants and Contracts', *Nonprofit and Voluntary Sector Quarterly*, vol. 20, pp. 5–24

Gronbjerg, K. A. (1992), 'Nonprofit Human Service Organizations', in Y. Hasenfeld (ed.), *Human Services as Complex Organizations*, Sage, Newbury Park, pp. 73–97

Gronbjerg, K. A. (1993), *Understanding Nonprofit Funding*, Jossey-Bass, San Francisco

Haddad, L. (2002), 'La Mue des Associations Françaises de Solidarité', *Économie et Humanisme*, no. 256, pp. 45–64

Hailey, J. (1999), 'Ladybirds, Missionaries and NGOs', *Public Administration and Development*, vol. 19, pp. 467–85

Halba, B. (1997), *Bénévolat et Volontariat dans le Monde*, Documentation Française, Paris

Hansmann, H. (1981), 'Consumer Perception of Nonprofit Enterprise', *Yale Law Journal* , vol. 90, pp. 1633–8

Hatton, J.-M (1988), *Les Organisations de Solidarité Internationale et du Développement du CRID*, IBISCUS- CHEAM, Paris

Hatton, J.-M. (2002), 'Panorama des Associations Françaises de Solidarité Internationale', in Commissariat Général, *L'État et les ONG*, Documentation Française, Paris, pp. 153–70

Hatton, J.-M. *et al.* (2006), 'Les OSI: Repères Historiques et Structuration dans leurs Relations avec les Pouvoirs Publics', www.hcci.gouv.fr/lecture/synthese/histoire-osi-ong.htm

Hayward, J. (2003), 'Reinventing the French State', in S. Milner and N. Parsons (eds), *Reinventing France*, Palgrave, London, pp. 48–62

Hazareesingh, S. (1994), *Poltical Traditions in Modern France*, Oxford University Press, Oxford

Herlemont-Zoritchak, N. (2002), *Illusions et Réalités de l'Idéologie Humanitaire: Les ONG 'Sans Frontières' sont-elles devenues des Acteurs de Paix?*, PhD Thesis, accessed via www.coordinationsud.org

Hodgkinson, V. A. (1989), 'Key Challenges Facing the Nonprofit Sector', in V. Hodgkinson and R. Lyman (eds), *The Future of the Nonprofit Sector*, Jossey-Bass, San Francisco, pp. 3–19

Holzer, B. (1994), *Les Leçons de la Solidarité, Vingt Ans au Service du CCFD*, Centurion, Paris

Hours, B. (1998), 'ONG et Idéologies de la Solidarité', in J. R. Deler *et al.*(eds), *ONG et Développement*, Karthala, Paris, pp. 34–43

Hudock, A. (1999), *NGOs and Civil Society: Democracy by Proxy?*, Polity, Cambridge

Hudson, A. (2001), 'NGOs' Transnational Advocacy Networks: from "Legitimacy" to "Political Responsibility"?', *Global Networks*, vol. 1, no. 4, pp. 331–52

Hulme, D. and Edwards, M. (eds) (1997), *NGOs, States and Donors: Too Close for Comfort?* Macmillan/ SCF, London

Husson, B. and Pirotte C. (eds) (1997), *Entre Urgence et Développement, Pratiques Humanitaires en Questions*, Karthala, Paris

Joly, C. (1985), *Les Organisations Non-gouvernementales Françaises de Développement: Présentation du Discours*, Economica, Paris

Keck, M. and Sikkink, K. (1998), *Activists Beyond Borders: Trans-national Advocacy Networks in International Politics*, Cornell University Press, Ithaca

Kenmogne, B. (2003), *Les Organisations Non Gouvernementales et le Développement Participatif: l'Engagement des Volontaires du Progrès au Cameroun*, L'Harmattan, Paris

Keohane R. O. and Nye J.-S. (eds) (1972), *Transnational Relations and World Politics*, Harvard University Press, Cambridge Massachusetts

Kilalo, C. and Johnson, D. (1999), '"Mission Impossible?" Creating Participation among NGOs, Governments and Donors', *Development in Practice*, vol. 9, no. 4, pp. 456–61

Korten, D. (1987), 'Third Generation NGO Strategies: A Key to People-Centered Development', *World Development*, vol. 15, pp. 145–59

Korten, D. (1991), 'The Role of Non-Governmental Organizations in Development', in S. Paul and A. Israel, *Nongovernmental Organizations and the World Bank*, World Bank, Washington D.C, pp. 24–43

Kuhnle, S. and Selle, P. (eds) (1992), *Governmental Understanding of Voluntary Organizations: A Rational Perspective*, Avebury, Aldershot

Lador-Lederer, J. J. (1963), *International Non-Governmental Organizations and Economic Entities*, Sythoff, Leyden

Lancaster, C. (1999), *Aid to Africa: So Much to Do ... So Little Done*, Chicago University Press, Chicago

Le Net, M. and Werquin, J. (1985), *Le Volontariat: Aspects Sociaux, Économiques et Politiques en France et dans le Monde, Notes et Études Documentaires*, Documentation Française, Paris

Lechervy, C. and Ryfman, P. (1993), *Action Humanitaire et Solidarité Internationale: les ONG*, Hatier, Paris

Lewis, D. (2001), *The Management of NGDOs: An Introduction*, Routledge, London

Lewis, D. and Wallace, T. (eds) (2000), *New Roles and Relevance: Development NGOs and the Challenge of Change*, Kumarian Press, Bloomfield

Liebschutz, S. F. (1992), 'Coping by Nonprofit Organizations during the Reagan Years', *Nonprofit Management and Leadership*, vol. 2, pp. 363–80

Mabille, F. (1999), *Le CCFD, de 1959 à 1969. Génèse et Institutionnalisation d'une ONG*, Éditions CCFD, Paris

Mabille, F. (2001), *Approches de l'Internationalisme Catholique*, L'Harmattan, Paris

Manji, F. and O'Coill, C. (2002), 'The Missionary Position: NGOs and Development in Africa', *International Affairs*, vol. 78, no. 3, pp. 567–83

Maradeix, M.-S. (1991), *Les ONG Americaines en Afrique: Activités et Perspectives de 30 ONG Non-Gouvernementales*, Syros, Paris

Marcussen, H. (1996), 'Comparative Advantages of NGOs: Myths and Realities', in O. Stokke (ed.), *Foreign Aid Towards the Year 2000*, Frank Cass, London

Martens, K. (2002), 'Mission Impossible? Defining Nongovernmental Organizations', *Voluntas: International Journal of Voluntary and Nonprofit Organizations*, vol. 13, no. 3, pp. 271–85

Meckstroth, T. W. (1975), '"Most Different Systems" and "Most Similar Systems": A Study in the Logic of Comparative Inquiry', *Comparative Political Studies*, vol. 8, pp. 133–77

Mercer, C. (2002), 'NGOs, Civil Society and Democratization: A Critical Review of the Literature', *Progress in Development Studies*, vol. 2, no. 1, pp. 5–22

Milner, S. and Parsons, N. (eds) (2003), *Reinventing France*, Palgrave, London

Minear, L. (1987), 'The Other Missions of NGOs: Education and Advocacy', *World Development*, vol. 15 (supplement), pp. 201–11

Mowjee, T. (2001), *NGO–Donor Funding Relationships: UK Government and European Community*, PhD Thesis, London School of Economics, London

MSF (2006), *Rapport Financier: Comptes 2006*, MSF, Paris

Murphy, B. K. (2000), 'International NGOs and the Challenge of Modernity', *Development in Practice*, vol. 10, nos 3 and 4, pp. 330–47

Najam, A. (1996), 'Understanding the Third Sector', *Non Profit Management and Leadership*, vol. 7, no. 2, pp. 203–19
ODI (1995), *NGOs and Official Donors*, Briefing Paper no. 4, Overseas Development Institute, London
OECD (various years), *Directory of Non-Governmental Organisations*, OECD, Paris
OECD (1988), Les *Partenaires dans l'Action pour le Développement: les Organisations Non Gouvernementales*, OECD, Paris
OECD (2000), *Coopération pour le Développement: France*, OECD, Paris
OECD (2004), 'DAC Peer Review of France', OECD, Paris, 2004
Pearce, J. (2000), 'Introduction' in J. Pearce and D. Eade (eds), *Development, NGOs and Civil Society: Selected Essays from Development in Practice*, OXFAM, Oxford, pp. 15–43
Pech, T. and Padis, M.-O. (2004), *Les Multinationales du Coeur: Les ONG, la Politique et le Marché*, Seuil, Paris
Penne G., Dulait, A. and Brisepierre, P. (2002), 'La Réforme de la Coopération à l'Épreuve des Réalités: un Premier Bilan 1998–2001', *Les Rapports du Sénat*, no. 46, Paris
Perrot, M.-D. (ed.) (1994), *Dérives Humanitaires: Etats d'Urgence et Droit d'Ingérence*, PUF, Paris
Perrotin, C. (2003), *Qu'est-ce que la Ligue des Droits de l'Homme?*, l'Archipel, Paris
Pfeffer, J. and Salancik, G.-R. (1974), 'Organisation Decision-Making as a Political Process: The Case of a University Budget', *Administrative Science Quarterly*, vol. 19, pp. 135–51
Pfeffer, J. and Salancik, G.-R. (1978), *The External Control of Organizations: A Resource Dependence Perspective*, Harper and Row, New York
Pirotte, C. and Husson, B. (1997), *Entre Urgence et Développement: Pratiques Humanitaires en Questions*, Karthala, Paris
Piveteau, A. (2004), *Évaluer les ONG*, Karthala, Paris
Ponsignon, J. (2002), 'Le volontariat et le bénévolat de solidarité internationale', *Aventure*, 96, www.la-guilde.org/spip.php?article287 [Accessed 21 January 2008]
Potevin, N. (2000), *Étude Comparative du Soutien des Gouvernements Européens et de la Commission Européenne aux ONG*, Commission Coopération Développement, Paris
Powell, W. W. (1987) *The Non-profit Sector: A Research Handbook*, Yale University Press, New Haven
Powell, W. W. and Owen-Smith, J. (1998), 'Universities and the Market for Intellectual Property in the Life Sciences', *Journal of Policy Analysis and Management*, no. 17, pp. 253–77
Powell, W. W. and Friedkin, R. (1986), 'Politics and Programs: Organizational Factors in Public Television Decision-Making', in P. DiMaggio (ed.), *Nonprofit Enterprise in the Arts*, Oxford University Press, New York, pp. 245–78
Powell, W. W. and Friedkin, R. (1987), 'Organisational Change in Nonprofit Organisations', in W. W. Powell (ed.), *The Non-Profit Sector*, Yale University Press, New Haven, pp. 180–92
Putnam, R. (1988), 'Diplomacy and Domestic Politics: The Logic of Two Level Games', *International Organization*, vol. 42, no. 3, pp. 427–60
Putnam, R. D. (2002), *Democracies in Flux: The Evolution of Social Capital in Contemporary Society*, Oxford University Press, Oxford
Randel, T. and German, J. (1999), 'Germany', 'Norway' and 'Sweden', in I. Smillie, H. Helmich, T. German, and J. Randel (eds), *Stakeholders: Government–NGO*

Partnerships for International Development, Earthscan, London, pp. 114–28, 183–94 and 210–21

Region Île-de-France (n.d.), *Solidarité Nord Sud- pour une Solidarité plus Réfléchie et Efficace (Guide Pratique)*, Région Île-de-France, Paris

Reille, X. (1990), *Étude sur les Relations CCFD/Entreprises*, CCFD, Paris, 15 March

Risse-Kappen, T. (1995), *Bringing Transnational Relations Back in: Non-State Actors, Domestic Structures and International Institutions*, Cambridge University Press, Cambridge

RITIMO (2002), *Partir pour être Solidaire?*, RITIMO, Paris

RITIMO (2006), *Le Don: une Solution?*, RITIMO, Paris

Robinson, M. (1997), 'Privatising the Voluntary Sector: NGOs as Public Sector Contractors', in D. Hulme and M. Edwards (eds), *Too Close for Comfort*, Macmillan/SCF, London, pp. 59–78

Roche, J.-J. (1999), *Relations Internationales*, LDJD, Paris

Rouillé d'Orfeuil, H. (1984), *Coopérer Autrement: l'Engagement des Organisations Non-gouvernementales Aujourd'hui*, L'Harmattan, Paris

Rouillé d'Orfeuil, H. (2006), *La Diplomatie Non-Gouvernementale*, Enjeux Planète, Paris

Rassemblement Pour la République or RPR (1994), *Les Relations entre les Pouvoirs Publics et les ONG Nationales et Locales*, RPR, Paris

Rubio, F. (2004), *Dictionnaire Pratique des Organisations Non-Gouvernementales*, Ellipses, Paris

Rubio, F. (ed.) (2002), 'Les ONG, Acteurs de la Mondialisation', *Problèmes Politiques et Sociaux*, no. 877–78

Rufin, J.-C. (1994), *Le Piège Humanitaire*, Pluriel, Paris

Ruttan, V. W. (1996), *United States Development Assistance Policy: The Domestic Politics of Foreign Economic Aid*, John Hopkins University Press, Baltimore

Ryfman, P. (1998), 'Urgence et Développement: Spécificité Française et Origine d'une Communauté d'ONG', in J.-P. Deler and B. Hours (eds), *L'Idéologie Humanitaire*, l'Harmattan, Paris

Ryfman, P. (1999), *La Question Humanitaire: Histoire, Problématiques, Acteurs et Enjeux de l'Aide Humanitaire*, Ellipses, Paris

Ryfman, P. (2004), *Les ONG*, La Découverte, Paris

Salamon, L. and Anheier, H. K. (1996), *Defining the Non-Profit Sector: A CrossNational Analysis*, Manchester University Press, Manchester

Salamon, L. and Anheier, H. (1997), *The Nonprofit Sector in the Developing World*, MUP, Manchester

Seibel, W. (1990) 'Organizational Behaviour and Organizational Function' in H. K. Anheier and W. Seibel (eds), *The Third Sector: Comparative Studies*, Walter de Gruyter, New York, pp. 107–23

Selznick, P. (1957), *Leadership and Administration*, Harper and Row, New York

Senarclens, P. de (2000), *La Mondialisation*, Armand Colin, Paris

Shalev, A. (1980), 'Industrial Relations Theory and the Comparative Study of Industrial Relations and Industrial Conflict', *British Journal of Industrial Relations*, vol. 18, pp. 26–43

Smillie, I. (1995), *The Alms Bazaar: Altruism Under Fire*, Intermediate Technology Publication, London

Smillie, I. (1999), 'At Sea in a Sieve?', in I. Smillie, H. Helmich, T. German and J. Randel (eds), *Stakeholders: Government–NGO Partnerships for International Development*, Earthscan, London, pp. 7–35

Smillie, I. and Helmich H. (1993), *Non-Governmental Organizations and Governments: Stakeholders for Development*, Development Centre, OECD, Paris

Smillie, I., Helmich, H., German, T. and Randel, J. (1999), *Stakeholders: Government–NGO Partnerships for International Development*, Earthscan, London

Smith, B. (1990), *More than Altruism*, Princeton University Press, Princeton

Smouts, M.-C., Battistella, D. and Vennesson, P. (2003), *Dictionnaire des Relations Internationales*, Dalloz, Paris

Sommier, I. (2003), *Le Renouveau des Mouvements Contestataires à l'Heure de la Mondialisation*, Flammarion, Paris

Stoddard, A. (2003), 'Humanitarian NGOs: Challenges and Trends', *Humanitarian Policy Group Briefing Paper no. 12*, July

Szarka, J. (2002), *The Shaping of Environment Policy in France*, Berghahn, Oxford

Tavernier, Y. (1999), *La Coopération Française au Développement*, Documentation Française, Paris

Temple, D. (1997), 'NGOs: a Trojan Horse', in M. Rahnema with V. Bawtree (eds), *The Post-Development Reader*, Zed Books, London

Tendler, J. (1982), 'Turning Private Voluntary Organizations into Development Agencies: Questions for Evaluation', *AID Program Evaluation Discussion Paper no. 12*, USAID, Washington

Terre des Hommes France (1998), *Halte à la Mondialisation de la Pauvreté: Reconnaître les Droits Economiques, Sociaux, Culturels pour Tous*, Karthala, Paris

Themudo, N. (2002), 'Managing the Paradox: NGOs, Resource Dependence and Political Independence', Conference Abstract, ISTR 5th Annual Conference, Cape Town, 7–10 July, www.istr.org/conferences/capetown/confprogram.htm. [Accessed 24 February 2008]

Théry, J.-F. (1996), 'Les Associations Reconnues d'Utilité Publique', *Regards sur l'Actualité*, no. 333, 2007, pp. 51–8

Tsikounas, M. (ed.) (1996), *Les Ambiguïtés de l'Humanitaire: de Saint Vincent de Paul aux French Doctors*, Arléa, Paris

Tuckman, H. P. (1998), 'Competition, Commercialization, and the Evolution of Nonprofit Organizational Structures', *Journal of Policy Analysis and Management*, no. 17, pp. 175–94

Tvedt, T. (1998), *Angels of Mercy or Development Diplomats: NGOs and Foreign Aid*, James Currey, Oxford

Useem, M. (1987), 'Corporate Philanthropy', in W. Powell (ed.), *The Nonprofit Sector: A Research Handbook*, Yale University Press, New Haven, pp. 340–59

Vakil, A. C. (1997), 'Confronting the Classification Problem: Toward a Taxonomy of NGOs', *World Development*, vol. 25, no. 12, pp. 2057–70

Védrine, H. (2000), *Les Cartes de la France à l'Heure de la Mondialisation*, Fayard, Paris

Verschave, F. X. and Boisgallais, A.-S. (1994), *L'Aide Publique au Développement*, Syros, Paris

Wallace, T., Crowther, C. and Shepherd, A. (1997), *Standardising Development: Influences on UK NGO Policies and Procedures*, Worldview Press, Oxford

Wallace, T., Bornstein, L. and Chapman, J. (2006), *The Aid Chain*, ITDG Publishing, London

Walters, S. (2003), *Social Movements in France*, Palgrave, London

Walters, S. (2006), 'À l'ATTAC: Globalisation and Ideological Renewal on the French Left', *Modern and Contemporary France*, vol. 14, no. 2, pp. 141–56

Warkentin, C. (2001), *Reshaping World Politics, NGOs, the Internet and Global Civil Society*, Rowman and Littlefield, Lanham

Weber, O. (1995), *French Doctors*, Robert Laffont, Paris

Weisbrod, B. (1974), 'Toward a Theory of the Voluntary Non-Profit Sector', in E. S. Phelps (ed.), *Altruism, Morality and Economic Theory*, Russel Sage, New York

Weisbrod, B. A. (1988), *The Nonprofit Economy*, Harvard University Press, Cambridge, Massachusetts

Weisbrod, B. A. (1998), 'The Nonprofit Mission and its Financing', *Journal of Policy Analysis and Management*, vol. 17, pp. 165–74

Weiss, T.-G. and Gordenker, L. (eds) (1996), *NGOs, the UN and Global Governance*, Boulder, Lynne Rienner

Weissman, F. (ed.) (2003), *A l'Ombre des Guerres Justes*, Flammarion, Paris

Wenar, L. (2006), 'Accountability in International Development Aid', *Ethics and International Affairs*, vol. 20, no. 1, pp. 1–23

Whaites, A. (ed.) (2002), *Development Dilemmas: NGO Challenges and Ambiguities*, World Vision, Monrovia

Wieviorka, M. (2003), *Un Autre Monde: Contestations, Dérives et Surprises dans l'Antimondialisation*, Balland, Paris

Willetts, P. (ed.) (1982), *Pressure Groups in the Global System*, Pinter, London

Willetts, P. (ed.) (1996), *The Conscience of the World: The Influence of Non-Governmental Organizations in the UN System*, Hurst, London

Willetts, P. (2002), 'What is a Non-Governmental Organization?', in *Encyclopedia of Life Support Systems*, EOLSS, Oxford (www.staff.city.ac.uk/p.willetts/CS-NTWKS/NGO-ART.HTM) [Accessed 20 January 2008]

Wood, A., Apthorpe, R. and Borton J. (eds) (2002), *Évaluer l'Action Humanitaire: Points de Vue de Practiciens*, Karthala, Paris

Woods, A. (2000), *OECD Facts about EU NGOs Active in International Development*, OECD, Documentation Française, Paris

World Bank (1990), *World Development Report*, Oxford University Press, Oxford

World Bank (2000–2001), *Attacking Poverty*, Oxford University Press, Oxford

World Bank (2001), *Enquête sur la Collaboration entre la Banque Mondiale et les Organisations Non Gouvernementales (ONG) Françaises*, World Bank, Paris

Youngs, R. (2003), 'European Approaches to Democracy Assistance: Learning the Right Lesson', *Third World Quarterly*, vol. 24, no. 1, pp. 127–38

Zimet, J. (2006), *Les ONG: De Nouveaux Acteurs pour Changer un Monde*, Autrement, Paris

Index

Note: Page numbers are given in **bold** only where the index entry concerned is subject to substantive and, often, extended treatment.

Action Contre la Faim (ACF), 15, 57, 64, 68, 102–3, 163, 204–5, 211, 217, 219, 221
Action des Chrétiens pour l'Abolition de la Torture (ACAT), 24, 181
Adjani, Isabel, 68
advocacy, 6, 13–14, **26–8**, 30, 33, 36–9, 44, **91–5**, 101, 104, 112, 129, 131, 137, 144, 148, **151–3**, 164–5, 170, 172, 181, 183–4, 187, 192, 231
    campaigning, 30, 68, **91–2**
    campaigns, 14, 27, 33, 39, 44, 68, 79, 92, 94, 98, 108, 110, 112, 129–31, 146, 153, 163, 165, 172, 183, 201, 229–30
    see also lobbying
Afghanistan, 29, 126, 210
Africa cell, 79, 197
Agence Française de Développement (AFD), 15, 57, 80, 87, 119, 192–3, 197, 229, 233–4
Agir Ici, 27–8, 92, 100, 130, 165, 193, 205, 210, 212, 224–5, 227–30, 234, 236
agriculture, 7, 123, 134, 142, 144
    food aid, 78, 213, 221
    food relief, 1, 29, 57
    food security, 29, 129, 146, 148, 225
    food self-sufficiency, 110, 151
    food surpluses, 4
aid missions, 57–8, 96, 121, 126, 132, 217
Aide Médicale Internationale (AMI), 29, 159
AIDES, 15, 120, 178, 189, 194, 208, 232
AIDS, 30
Amnesty International, 27–8, 34, 130, 206, 218, 230
anti-personnel mines, 3, *see also* landmines; Ottawa Treaty
apartheid, 2–3
ARC, 94, 96, 105, 163, 223–4
Arche de Zoé, 163, 205, 229

Asia, 37, 39, 61, 121, 124, 126–7, 134–5, 140, 225
Assises de la Coopération et de la Solidarité Internationale, 223
Association Française contre les Myopathies (AFM), 68, 94, 223
Association Française des Volontaires du Progrès (AFVP), 15, 24–5, 34, 36, 72, 74, 85, 95, 124, **137–9**, 178, 180, 182, 186, 189, 192, 208, 211, 216–17, 219, 226, 233
associations
    associations de 1901, 81
    associations de bienfaisance, 76
    Associations de Jeunesse et d'Education Populaire, 38
    Associations de Solidarité Internationale, 21, 218
    public utility associations, 73, 76, 94
    sporting associations, 64
    student associations, 109
    see also développementalistes; urgenciers
ATD Quart Monde, 25, 141, 154, 212, 221
ATTAC, 14, **27–8**, 36, 101, 151, 205–6, 243
autonomisation, 33, 129–30, 186, 191–3
autonomy, 5–6, 8, 17, 22, 25–6, 34, 49–50, 52, 141, 155, 166–7, 170–3, 190, 196, 199, 203, 230
awareness-raising, 27, 38, 55, 94, 96, 98, **107–10**, **112–13**, 221–2, *see also* development education

Band Aid, 228
Bangladesh Rural Advancement Committee (BRAC), 25
BASC, 179, 181, 187, 209, 232–3
Belgium, 4, 10, 19, 74, 85, 219, 223
bénévolat, 21, 241
bénévoles, 36, 69, 79, 95, 97, 103–4, 116, 218, 223

bilateral donors, 61, 157, 169, 185
   BMZ, 4, 213
   Canadian International Development
      Agency, 195
   GTZ, 184, 195, 208
   NORAD, 4
   SIDA, 4, 157, 169, 232
   USAID, 157, 169, 243
BIOFORCE, 95, 97, 101, 211
Biya, Paul, 147, 180, 184, 190, 194–5,
   197, 227
Blair, Tony, 2, 236
Bono, 68
Brunel, Sylvie, 103, 163, 229

Cameroon, 15–17, 36, 113, 147, **177–81**,
   183–6, 189, **191–6**, 198, 200,
   231–4, 238
Canada, 4, 10, 20, 38, 61, 74, 168, 184, 214
capacity-building, 32, 87, 130, 139, 170,
   175, 213–14
CARE, 2, 4, 19, 23, 25, 171, 213, 237
Caribbean, the, 37, 127, 135, 140, 217, 225
Catholic Relief Services (CRS), 1, 19, 25,
   203, 213
Central Africa, 39, 225
*Centre de Recherche et d'Information sur
   le Développement* (CRID), 27, 30–1,
   33, 38, 69, 79, 83–4, 86, 95–6, 101,
   104, 108–9, 112, 145–7, 152, 158,
   160, 165, 172, 208, 210, 212, 221–9,
   238–9
Chad, 163, 233–4
charities, 21, 76, 82–3, 172
charity, 7, 33, 68, 76, 82, 163, 223
charters, 104, 108
   Charter, UN, 18
   Comité de la Charte, **105–7**
church, 10, 14, 24, 33, 68, 127, 204, 231,
   233
citizenship, 37, 131
civil societies, 9, 13, 15, 20, 23, 37, 50,
   60, 63, 67, 75, 80, 84, 86–8, 96,
   101, 111, 114, 122, 131, 133, 136,
   139, 147, 157, 170, 175, **177–86**,
   188–91, **193–6**, 198, 200, 208, 217,
   230–3
civil society, *see* civil societies
civil war, 2, 5
Club des OSI, 80, 87

co-financing, *see* co-funding
co-funding, 2, 58, 60–1, 74, 78, **84–6**,
   110, 121, 123, 132–4, 139, 141,
   157–9, 166–7, 179–80, 184, 186, 195,
   207, 213, 219–20, 225, 228
Coluche, 14, 77, 83
*Comité Catholique Contre la Faim et pour
   le Développement* (CCFD), 2, 12,
   14–15, 24, **30–3**, 37–8, 64, 68–9, 78,
   90, 93–4, 100–1, 103, 107, 109, 112,
   115, 120, 130, 139, 152, 154–5, 160,
   163, 166–7, 172–3, **178–85**, **187–90**,
   192–5, 202, 204, 208, 210, 212,
   214–17, 219, 221, 223–7, 229–33,
   236–7, 239–40, 242
Comité Français Contre la Faim (CFCF),
   *see Comité Français de Solidarité
   Internationale*
*Comité Français de Solidarité
   Internationale* (CFSI), 24, 32, 57, 96,
   214, 221, 223, 232
*Comité Inter-Mouvements Auprès Des
   Evacués* (CIMADE), 25, 32–3, 38, 64,
   130, 154, 210, 212, 222, 224
*Comité pour les Relations Nationales et
   Internationales des Associations de
   Jeunesse et d'Éducation Populaire*
   (CNAJEP), 38, 96, 211
Commission Coopération Développement,
   11, 180, 241
communism, 120, 131
companies, 12, 19, 21, 39, 45–6, 50,
   63–4, 73, 77, 79, 82–3, 87, 102,
   108, 117, 121, 150, 156, 160–1, 164,
   169–71, 176, 205, 207, 213,
   219, 224
CONCORD, 9, 38, 92, 111, 166,
   170, 228
conditionalities, 145, 162, 170
Confédération Générale des Travailleurs
   (CGT), 178, 180, 181–2, 191–2, 232
consultancies
   CICDA, 33, 82, 139, 154, 229
   CIEDEL, 114, 178, 187–8, 193, 211,
      220, 232
   GRET, 25, 33, 78, 84, 90, 101, 114–15,
      138–9, 167, 178, 208, 211–12, 217,
      219, 222–3, 226, 228
   IRAM, 33, 114–15, 167, 211, 217, 222,
      228, 236

consultants, 15, 32, 90, 110, 115, 141, 178, 185, 187

contractual arrangements, new, 9, 58, **78–80**, 97–8, 102, 110, 141, 154, 167, **177–9**, 203, 205, 233, *see also la nouvelle contractualisation*

coopérants, 34, 74, 222

cooperatives, 21, 28, 231

Coordination d'Agen, 31, 38, 211, 222

Coordination SUD, 15, 38, 67, 80–1, 83–5, 87, 97–8, 100, 102, 109, 137, 141, 143, 152, 167, 172, 175, 208, 210, 215–16, 218, 222–4, 231

corporate social responsibility, 160, 171

corruption, 94, 117, 161, 181, 183

Cour des Comptes, 34, 55, 67, 78–9, 84, 98, 137–8, 161, 166–7, 220, 228

Croix Rouge, see Red Cross

Cyclone Nargis, 206

Darfur, 29

Davos World Economic Forum, 161

debt cancellation, 37, 39, 79, 87, 133, 136, 145, 166, 180–1, 192
  C2D, 136, 180–1, 183, 186, 197, 231–2
  HIPC, 180–1, 185–6, 195, 231
  Jubilee, 145
  Plateforme Dette et Développement, 39, 111, 166, 172, 179–80, 190, 192–3

decentralised cooperation, 157

decentralised credits, 58, 60

decolonisation, 1–2, 32, 71

Délégation Catholique pour la Coopération (DCC), 14–15, 34, 36, 74, 101, 157, 159, 201, 211, 216, 221

democracy, 123–4, 130–1, 136, 146–7, 176, 185, 189–91, 198, 224, 232
  grassroots democracy, 25
  participatory democracy, 124, 144
  see also democratisation

Democratic Republic of the Congo (DRC), 130, 215

democratisation, 129, 238

Denmark, 4, 10, 55, 84–5, 153, 168, 202, 219

Département Évangélique Français d'Action Apostolique (DEFAP), 14–15, 21, 34, 112, 178, 180–1, 184, 188, 192–3, 208, 211, 233

development assistance, 7, 80, 119, 134, 219, 234, *see also* foreign aid

development education, 15, 28, 33, 37, 39, 51, 58, 94, 96, 98, 104, **107–10**, **112–13**, 123, 131, 134, 168, 216
  Semaine de la Solidarité, 98, 223
  Student Solidarity Programme, 109
  see also awareness-raising

Development Ministry, French, 24, 57, **74–6**, 96, 123, 221

développementalistes, **30–4**, 36, 39, 89–90, 99, 113, 139, 144–5, 152–3, 158, 178, 185, 191, 199, 201–2, 215, 220

développeurs, see développementalistes

directors, 93, 96–7, 103
  directors' salaries, 151

donations, 32, 35, 46, 50–1, 64, 68, 73, 76–7, 91, **105–7**, 117, 137, **162–3**, 166, 169, **171–3**, 195, **204–6**, 216, 218, 220–1, 223–4

donor public, 16, 50, **63–4**, 68–9, 77, 90, 96, 98, 105, 116–17, 157, **162**, 166, **172**, 174, 195–6, 199, 200–1, 204–5, *see also* general public

droit d'ingérence, 2

dumping, 146, 170

Eastern Europe, 14, 37, 39, 140
  eastern bloc, 127, 140

Eau Vive, 107, 138–9, 210, 220, 223, 225

Écoliers du Monde, 38, 57, 219, 234

education, 6, 21, 32, 38, 55, 57, 83, 94, 96, 98, 100, **108–10**, 112, 121, 125, 130, 133–4, 136, 139, 142, 147, 211, 220, 222, 226, 229, 233
  School Days, 109
  school syllabus, 98, 109
  schools, 57, 100, 221, 226, 229

embassies, 55, 57–8, 96, 121, 126, 207

emergency NGOs, *see urgenciers*

emergency relief, 23, 36, 152, 155, 163, 214

ENDA, 137, 139, 210, 214, 220

environment, the, 3, 27, 45, 109, 120
  climate change, 205
  environmental protection, 23
  global warming, 226
  sustainable development, 39, 79, 109, 171
  see also summits

ÉquiLibre, 159
ethical investment products, 67
ethical savings schemes, 64
Ethiopia, 29, 215
EuropeAid, 32, 63, 217
European Commission, 15, **63**, 79, 84,
    159, **170**, 193, 195, 208, 226, 228,
    230, 234
European Commission Humanitarian
    Office (ECHO), 32, 63
European Convention on the
    Recognition of International NGOs,
    19, *see also* Treaty 124
European Stability Pact, 97, 183
European Union (EU), 63, 135, 160, 175,
    194, 202, 217, 228, 230–1, 236, 244
Eurostep, 38, 170, 229
evaluation, 6, 12, 16, 85, 90, **95–6**, 98,
    110–15, 158–9, 166, 178–9, 183,
    187–8, 193, 222–4
exceptionalism, 9

F3E, 90, **98–100**, **110–12**, 114–15, 139,
    166, 179, 187, 222–3, 232
fair trade, 33, 39, 64, 67, 83, 108–9, 129,
    161, 171, 224, 234
faith-based actors, 9, 21, 34, 162, 204
faith-based NGOs, 14, 24, 131, 220
Fédération Artisans du Monde, 33, 64, 212
*Fédération Internationale (des Ligues) des
    Droits de l'Homme* (FIDH), 27–8,
    130, 171, 193, 214, 224
federations, 15, 26, 28, 31, 33, **38**, 67,
    83, 94, 96–8, 101–2, 104, 108, 111,
    137, 151, 154, 165–6, 175, 180,
    210–11, 221–2, 226, 232
    CLOSI, 94, 96, 221
    Intercollectif, 94, 221
    see also under individual names
Finance Ministry, French, 79, 88, 145,
    192
financial accountability, 91, 94, 104, 187
    audits, 105–6, 160, 223
    see also professionalisation
financial management, 12, 116
*Fonds de Coopération de la Jeunesse et de
    l'Éducation Populaire* (FONJEP), 14,
    84–5, 124, 137, 226
food, *see* agriculture
foreign aid, 11, 84, 119, 207, 219, *see also*
    development assistance

Foreign Ministry, French, 4, 15, 25, 32,
    34, 71, 74, 79, 86, 97, 132, 134, 143,
    157, 166, 178, 180, 184, 195, 197,
    208, 219, 222, 225, 229–30, 238
foundations, development or political,
    8, 10, 14, 20, 35, 50, **67–8**, 73, 77,
    157, 161, 171, 214, 218, 230
    Bill and Melinda Gates Foundation,
        218
    Carter Foundation, 214
    Fondation de France, 67, 172, 221
    Fondation Max Havelaar, 35, 67, 161
    Fondation MSF, 120
    Fondation Raoul Follereau, 67–8, 105,
        211
    Friedrich Ebert Foundation, 184
Francophonie, 37, 83, 198, 234
French presidents, 79, 134, 205, 216,
    221, 224
    Chirac, Jacques, 134, 143, 205, 226,
        229
    De Gaulle, Charles, 221
    Mitterrand, François, 123, 221
    Sarkozy, Nicolas, 205–6, 216
French prime ministers
    Balladur, Edouard, 131, 175
    Jospin, Lionel, 58, 80, 135, 175
    Juppé, Alain, 175
    Raffarin, Jean-Pierre, 88
Frères des Hommes (FDH), 14, 24, 38, 64,
    69, 93, 225
Friends of the Earth, 193
fund-raising, 11–12, 15, 51, 68, 73, **81–3**,
    90–2, 109, 161, 201
    direct debit, 64
    legacies, 68, 73, 76, 162, 201
    telethons, 68

G8, Group of Eight, 79, 143–4, 205,
    225–6
Geldoff, Sir Bob, 68
general public, 49–50, 81, 95–6, 137,
    163–4, 204, 228, *see also* donor
    public
Germany, 2, 4, 8, 10, 14, 20, 38, 61, 68,
    74, 85, 97, 184, 201, 213, 219, 232,
    241
globalisation, 3, 8, 101, 120, 146, 151,
    174, 201–2, 213
governance, 7, 44–5, 129, 147, 182, 190,
    220

Greenpeace, 27–8, 212, 214, 236
Groupe Initiatives, 31, 33, 38, 111, 114, 211, *see also* consultancies
Guilde Européenne du Raid, 38, 112, 165, 216, 220, 229
Guinea, 163, 205, 207, 233–4

Haiti, 58, 132
Handicap International, 15, 29, 139, 143, 164, 208, 211, 215, 217–19, 222, 226
Haut Conseil de la Coopération Internationale (HCCI), 60, **79–80**, 86–8, 92, 112, 116, 209, 219, 233
health, 21, 57, 80, 87, 98, 109, 133, 139, 214, 220, 222, 226
  Alma-Ata Conference, 125
  healthcare, 121, 125, 133, 136, 142, 147, 183, 224
  medical research, 35, 76, 218
  medicines, 68, 121, 125, 221, 224, 226
Holland, 2, 4, 10, 55, 61, 74, 84–5, 97, 168, 201, 219
human rights, 3, 23, 27, 29–30, 43, 74, 79, 101, 120, 130–1, 136, 142, 147, 181, 183, 191, 205, 214–15, 224
  civil and political liberties, 120, 123, 129, 136
  economic, social and cultural rights, 30, 131, 147
  economic and social rights, 124, 129
humanitarian NGOs, *see urgenciers*

International Criminal Court, 3
International Monetary Fund (IMF), 44, 123, 144, 146–7, 190, 231–2
international organisations, 61, 102, 144, 158, 169–70, 215, *see also under individual names*
Iraq, 3, 155, 198, 233
Ireland, 219, 234
Italy, 10, 14, 61, 85

Japan, 13, 20, 61
Jospin, Lionel, *see* French prime ministers

Karembeu, Adriana, 68
Korten, David, 1, **22–3**, 42, 89, 99, 163, 173, 214, 236, 240
Kosovo, 3, 63, 162
Kouchner, Bernard, 28–9, 205, 217

landmines, 29, 143, 166
Latin America, 37, 94, 121, 124, 126–7, 130, 134–5, 140, 224–5
laws, 30, 42, 83, 226
  1901 Charity Law, 19, 21, 27, 35, 73
  1901 Law, 82, 95, 154, 227
  2002 Finance Law, 97
  Allarde Decree, 72
  Chapelier Act, 72
  LOLF, 97, 175, 183
League of Nations, 214, 231
Least Developed Countries (LDCs), 133, 140
Lebret, Father, 97
liberation struggles, 127, 150
Ligue des Droits de l'Homme (LDH), 27–8, 212, 241, *see also Fédération Internationale (des Ligues) des Droits de l'Homme*
lobbying, 9, 25, 27, 190, *see also* advocacy
local authorities, 15, 19, 60, 80, 86, 88, 134, 169, 176, 207, 213, 219, 223
  communes, 58, 60
  départements, 58, 60
  local governments, 57, 130
  regional authorities, 14, 58, 157
  territorial authorities, 58, 60, 157, 228
Luxembourg, 84, 85, 223

Madagascar, 39, 57, 179, 207
Maghreb, the, 25, 225
Malhuret, Claude, 28, 216
May 1968, 150
  soixante-huitards, 95, 150, 164
  see also militancy
media, the, 94, 113, 163, 205, 233
micro-credit, 57, 101, 111, 129, 220
militancy, 93, 99, 104, 107, 160, 164, 173, 204
  grassroots activists, 16, 69, 117
  militant base, 82, 88, 117, 150, 166, 169, **172–4**, 194–5, 201
  militantisme, 110
military service, *see* national service
minimum wage, 77, 153
Misereor, 2, 38, 234
Mission pour la Coopération Non Gouvernementale (MCNG), 58, 60, 78, 87, 90, 97–8, 119, 157, 180–1, 184, 186, 192–3, 197, 215, 217, 220, 231–3

missionary, 7, 34, 99
movement
  altermondialiste, 8, 14, 146
  ecological, 27
  feminist, 14, 27
  new social, 2, 168, 205
Mugabe, Robert, 147, 227
multinationals, 64

national service, 34, 74, 77, 100, 222
new contractual arrangements
  Dotations au Partenariat, 179
  PCPA, **177–98**, 200, 205, **231–3**, 237
  Programme Concerté Maroc, 179
  programmes prioritaires, 87, 179
  see also la nouvelle contractualisation
new public management, 90
Nielson, Poul, 228
Nobel Peace Prize, 29
North Africa, 34, 121, 124, 126–7, 135,
  140
Norway, 10, 43, 213, 219, 241
nouvelle contractualisation, la, 78, 84,
  86, 121, 165, 192, *see also* new
  contractual arrangements
NOVIB, 2, 213, 234, *see also* Oxford
  Committee for Famine Relief

oil, 121, 128, 198, 233
Organisation for Economic Cooperation
  and Development (OECD), 1–2,
  4, 11, 13, 15, 20–1, 38, 55, 74, 87,
  96, 119, 122, 124, 133, 135, 142,
  162, 168, 202, 206, 213–14, 216–17,
  219–21, 225, 228–9, 241, 243–4
*Organisations de Solidarité Internationale
  issues des Migrations* (OSIM),
  25, 34
Ottawa Treaty, 3, 166, *see also*
  landmines
Oxford Committee for Famine Relief
  (OXFAM), 1, 23, 67, 120, 146, 201,
  205–6, 213, 218, 227–8, 230, 234

Palestine, 39, 113, 137, 179, 187, 232
Peuples Solidaires, 131, 210, 212, 225, 227
philanthropists, 50
poverty reduction, 3, 136, 145, 169, 176,
  183, 206, 232
  PRSPs, 136, 146, 167, 180, 190, 227, 232

pressure groups, 10, 13–15, 18, **26–8**, 36,
  39, 54, 130, 153, 165, 205–6, 217
Princess Diana, 68
Private Voluntary Organizations (PVOs),
  4, 6
professionalisation, **5–6**, 8, **12–13**, 17,
  78, **89–92**, **96–7**, 99, 104, **116–17**,
  132, 163, 174, 176, 184, 186, 188,
  199, 220
  internet, 2, 15, 91–2, 109, 112, 115, 162
  learning, 90, **95–6**, **98–9**, 111, 114–15,
    125, 163, 185, 187–8, 193, 232
  logical framework, 6, 98, 110,
    185, 187
  marketing, 20, 51, 90, 205, 221
  quality benchmarks, 108, 112
  training, 12, 33, 67, 76, 78, 95,
    97–101, 108–9, 111–12, 123, 134,
    139, 142, 169, 183, 197, 219,
    222–3, 226, 233
  see also professionalism
professionalism, 6, 32, **89–90**, **94–5**,
  107, 117, 153, 207, 220, 224, *see also*
  professionalisation

realpolitik, 2, 120, 170, 198, 200
recruitment, 12, 32, 78, 100, 152, 173,
  190, 206, 223
Red Cross, 1, 28, 68, 219, 221, 229
refugee, 1, 163, 215, 225
rehabilitation, 31, 63
RESACOOP, 35
resource dependence (RD), 16–17, 41,
  45–7, **49–54**, **69–72**, 88–9, 116, 118,
  147, 149, 152, 155, 164, 167, **174–7**,
  191, 193, **196–7**, **199–200**, **202–4**,
  227, 233
resource diversification (RDVN), 47, 49,
  52, 152, 154, 156, **167–9**, 194–5
Restos du Coeur, 14, 83, 219, *see also*
  Coluche
revenue diversification, *see* resource
  diversification
RITIMO, 15, 19, 33, 36, 94–6, 108–9,
  112, 208, 210, 212, 218, 220–3, 242
Rouillé d'Orfeuil, Henri, 172, 208, 231,
  242
Rufin, Jean-Christophe, 32, 205, 242
rural development, 32, 125, 139, 222,
  see also agriculture

Rwanda, 3, 29, 132, 153, 162, 198, 215, 225, 229–30
Rwandan genocide, 63, 168, 175

Salvation Army, 219, 223
Sarkozy, Nicolas, *see* French presidents
Save the Children Fund (SCF), 1, 213, 234, 239, 242
scandals, 50, 94, 96, 105, 117, 163–4, 205
Secours Catholique-Caritas France (SC-CF), 14–15, 21, **24–5**, 30, 32–3, 64, 66, 93, 107, 120, 130, 137, 139, 154, 167, **180–2**, 191–2, 215, 219, 221, 229, 232
Secours Populaire Français, 24, 34–5, 96, 107, 138, 172, 210, 214–15, 218, 221, 229
Senegal, 78, 121, 205, 207, 214, 219, 222, 225
service delivery, **6–7**, 13, 23, 26, 53, 57, 90, 118, 132, 134, 136, 141, 148, 158, 178, 186
  service agents, 17, 85, 121, 157, **189–91**
  service provider, 9, 34, 84, 117–18, 120, 137, 139, 147, 185, 189
SNV, 2, 184, 195, 213
social capital, 10, 37
social development, 32, 113
social economy, 21, 39, 171
social forums, European or world, 9, 27, 224
  Porto Alegre, 161, 224
social justice, 6, 120, 150
Solagral, 24, 129, 208, 212, 228
Solidarité Laïque, 24, 69, 232
Solidarités, 109, 130, 170, 210, 219
solidarity, 112, 117, 145, 161, 171, 173, 201, 213–14
South Africa, 2, 39, 129
Southern NGOs (SNGOs), 14, 21, 128, 214, 235
Soviet Union, 29
sponsorship, 64, 217
structural adjustment, 2, 123, 129
  Doctrine Balladur, 123
  Doctrine d'Abidjan, 122
Sudan, 163
summits, 144, 198
  Conference on Women, 143

counter-summits, 146, 161
  Évian, 226
  Johannesburg, 226
  international conferences, 28, 79, 143
  Population and Development, 143
  Rio, 27, 135, 226
  Social Development, 55, 143
  WTO, 79, 144, 227
Survie, 27, 130, 165, 209–10, 212, 225, 228–9
Sweden, 10, 61, 69, 85, 136, 153, 157, 168, 202, 213, 219, 234, 241
Switzerland, 10, 61, 74, 85, 97

tax, 5, 14, 20, 27, 37, 76, 81, 83, 98, 145–6, 162, 175, 220, 226
  corporation tax, 73
  fiscal concessions, 3, 11, 50, 77, 83, 202, 204–5
  income tax, 73
  inheritance tax, 76
  Tobin tax, 27, 136, 146–7, 226
Terre des Hommes, 2, 12, 24, 36, 208, 212, 243
Third World, 2, 95, 109, 120–1, 126, 128–9, 150, 221, 231, 244
tiersmondistes, 24, 129
Togo, 130, 147, 225
Treaty 124, 206, 214, *see also* European Convention
tsunami, South Asian, 30, 32, 63, 68, 107, 162–3, 172, 206, 218, 228, 230

unemployment, 97, 100, 224
United Kingdom, 2, 10, 21, 61, 67–8, 85, 168, 184, 203, 214
United Nations (UN), 2, 18–19, 30, 61, 128, **133–6**, 143, 147, 153, 158–9, 170, 198, 215, 217, 228, 230–4, 238, 244
  ECOSOC, 19, 147, 159, 170, 228
  General Assembly, 147, 170
  Non-Governmental Liaison Service, 230
  Resolutions, 215
  UNDP, 61, 170, 231
  UNESCO, 230
  UNHCR, 61, 163
  UNICEF, 61, 112, 170, 215, 218
  UNITAID, 226

United States, 10, 21, 61, 68, 74, 84, 157,
    203, 213, 220, 242
universities, 20, 101, 111, 116
    GEMDEV, 101, 183, 187, 222
urgenciers, 15, 18, **28–32**, 36–8, 54, 57–8,
    61, 64, 78, 86, 90–1, 93, 107, 112,
    114, 120, 126, 129–30, 140–1, 143,
    153, 159, 163, 166–7, 170, 203–5,
    207, 211, 214, 218, 225, 227, 229,
    234, *see also under individual names*

Vatican, the, 24, 106
VENRO, 4, 213
volontariat, 30, 32, 36, 76, 81, 165, 199,
    211, 241
    CIVI, 79, 84
    CLONG-V, 31, 34, 38, 81, 100, 102,
        112, 151, 208, 215, 221, 222
    Commission du Volontariat, 76, 81, 165
    volontariat civil, 77

voluntary organisations, 14, 26
voluntary sector, 9, 17, 20, 41
volunteer agencies, 30, 32, 38–9, 76–7,
    83, 89, 95, 100, 104, 113, 143, 165,
    201, 219, 220, 225
volunteers, 31, 33–4, 36–7, 49, 50–1, 64,
    69, 74, 76–7, 79, 83, 93, 95, 99–100,
    102, 106, 111–12, 140, 163–6, 169,
    172–3, 192, 196, 201, 205, 215–16,
    222–3, 226

World Bank, 2–3, 38, 44, **61**, 80, 104,
    122–3, 136, 142, 146–7, 153, **158**,
    164, 167, **169–70**, 180, 184, 190,
    193, 217, 219, 228, 231–2, 235–7,
    240, 244
World Food Programme, 61, 158
World Vision, 22–3, 201, 205, 213, 244
Worldwide Fund for Nature (WWF), 27,
    34, 64, 171, 214, 217